Internment, Escape and Repatriation:

Graf Spee and Tacoma Seamen in Argentina and Uruguay during the Second World War

VOLUME ONE: 1939 - 1942

Bernard O'Connor

Copyright © 2022 Bernard O'Connor
All rights reserved.

Attempts have been made to locate, contact and acknowledge copyright holders of quotes and illustrations used in my work. They have all been credited within the text and/or in the bibliography. Much appreciation is given to those who have agreed that I include their work. Any copyright owners who are not properly identified and acknowledged, get in touch so that I may make any necessary corrections.

Small parts of this book may be reproduced in similar academic works providing due acknowledgement is given in the introduction and within the text. Any errors or suggested additions can be forwarded to me for future editions.

Bernard O'Connor
ISBN: 978-1-4583-4544-8

Contents

Foreword
Abbreviations used by the British Admiralty, Foreign Office and diplomatic personnel in their correspondence with Uruguay and Argentina
Chapter One: Background
Chapter Two: Developments in 1939
Chapter Three: Developments in 1940
Chapter Four: Developments in 1941
Chapter Five: Developments in 1942
Conclusion
Bibliography

Foreword

Many readers who pick up this book will have heard of the Battle of the River Plate, seen the 1956 film of the same title or read accounts of one of the most important maritime conflicts in the South Atlantic at the beginning of the Second World War. Those who know nothing or only little of this story, ships belonging to the British Royal Navy engaged *Admiral Graf Spee*, what they called a German 'pocket battleship,' off the coast of Uruguay on 13 December 1939. Heavily damaged by British shells, the ship's captain ordered a retreat into the mouth of the River Plate, and moored close to Montevideo, Uruguay. Unable to get repairs or more ammunition, the ship set sail on 17 December but instead of engaging the waiting British ships, the captain disembarked the officers and crew and ordered the *Graf Spee* to be scuttled, sunk, to prevent it from being captured by the British. Most of the men were transferred to shore by the German ship *Tacoma*. Others were taken ashore by tugs and lighters, flat-bottomed barges used to transfer goods and passengers to and from moored ships.

Accounts of the battle can be read in other books or found on British, German and South American websites. What follows is a documentary history of the events immediately preceding and following the internment of the German crews in Argentina and Uruguay, their escape attempts and, for most, their eventual repatriation. Based largely on correspondence between officers serving in the British Admiralty, officials in the British Foreign Office and personnel in the British Embassy in Argentina, the British Legation in Uruguay and British and American officials based in Washington, it is seen mostly through a British filter. There are also previously unseen documents from Argentine and Uruguayan government officials and interrogation reports of captured German officers.

Internment, Escape and Repatriation includes contemporary notes, memoranda of meetings and telephone conversations, reports, letters and telegrams, interrogation reports of captured Nazi agents who operated in South America as well as contemporary newspaper reports from Britain, Argentina, Uruguay, Australia, the United States and Japan. Extracts from more recent histories and websites focus on the experiences of some of the German internees. It sheds light on the previously untold human story of international and national diplomacy, grandiloquence, inter-department politics, legal issues and everyday administration with evidence of the tension, frustration, irritation, satisfaction and pleasure interspersed with elements of nationalist, racist and sexist prejudices.

Using predominantly primary sources, British Admiralty, Foreign Office and the Intelligence Services' files deposited in the National Archives in Kew, there are many cases where a document is mentioned but not included in the files. While the majority of the documents are dated and names provided, some are anonymous or have illegible signatures. As there were several postal deliveries each day, some documents may have been filed in the wrong order, especially where earlier telegrams had to be checked and then replaced. Hence, there may be some chronological inconsistencies.

Most communication, telegraphic cables, between the Admiralty and Foreign Office and the British Embassies and Consulates overseas was encoded before transmission. Most of the messages have the word cypher at the top and the initials O.T.P. at the bottom. Britain's Signals Section used a One Time Pad, a code only used for one message which the recipient, using the same One Time Pad was able to use to decode the message. That code was discarded and the next code used for the next message. The wireless telegraphists who copied the coded message had to decode, copy and pass the message to the relevant person or department. If it was in another building, this was done by a despatch rider. Many of the messages contain in brackets 'grp. und', 'grp. mut' or 'grp. omtd' meaning that a group of letters in the message was undecipherable, mutilated or omitted and therefore unable to be decoded. From the context, what was thought to be the missing word or words were added.

There is a degree of repetition when different people correspond giving details of the same event. There are missing accents on many of the Spanish words. Spanish-speaking officials included them in their correspondence but the non-Spanish speakers did not. Transcribing the text, for ease of typing, most are omitted. Text in square brackets is the author's explanation but on occasions the original writer used them. Question marks in square brackets mean the name or definition is not known. Anyone who does know or who can add any new details, particularly on the escapes, please contact the author so that an improved edition can be published.

I need to acknowledge the research facility provided by the staff of Australia's Trove website, the University of California Riverside's California Digital Newspaper Collection, Newspaper.com and the British Newspaper Archive for providing access to contemporary newspapers. The staff at the National Archives in Kew, London, have been enormously helpful in generating an online catalogue of their documents which facilitated the location of relevant files. We particularly appreciate the assistance given by Steven Kippax, the Special Operation Executive (SOE) historian and founder of the online SOE group. He and Fred Judge, the Chief Archivist at Chicksands Military Intelligence Museum, have compiled lists of SOE files and personnel and answered almost all of our queries. Angie Watkins at Ludlow Library was particularly helpful in accessing the British Newspaper Archive to locate *Graf Spee* articles. The Hyperwar website provided valuable detail of the movements of the *Graf Spee* prior to her scuttling and the *Tacoma,* one of the ships carrying her escaped officers and crew. Michael Pocock's Maritimequest website contains crew members and their relatives' reminiscences, newspaper articles and photographs related to the *Graf Spee*. Carlos Benemann generously shared his knowledge of the officers and crew and provided additional details which enhanced my understanding of Uruguay's and Argentina's history. I must also congratulate Leandro Bustamento whose *Los Rostros del Graf Spee* has used recently released Uruguayan Ministry of Foreign Affairs documents to publish details of the 1,055 crew and their photographs. Malcolm Collis of the HMS Ajax and River Plate Veterans and Peter Hore helped with some of the abbreviations.

As *Internment, Escape and Repatriation* is a documentary history, the reader, especially the aspiring diplomat or intelligence officer, will enjoy the intellectual challenge of making deductions, presumptions and assumptions, drawing their own conclusions and recognising allusions, inferences and innuendos. Having used predominantly British primary sources, there is very much a British filter and the reader will be able to identify evidence of nationalism, class, racism, sexism and humour.

For anyone employed by, who worked for or who is planning to join the Navy, other armed forces, national government, the diplomatic service or the intelligence services, *Internment, Escape and Repatriation* does not provide accounts of the exciting and glamorous life often portrayed in old books and films but provides insight into the everyday realities of life administering an unusual aspect of the Second World War.

Bernard O'Connor © 2022

Abbreviations used by the British Admiralty, Foreign Office and Diplomatic personnel in their correspondence with Uruguay and Argentina

ACNS: Acting Chief Naval Staff
ADC: Assistant Director of Communications
ADM: Admiralty
ADNI: Acting Director Naval Intelligence
AM: Admiralty Message
ASE: Admiralty Signal Establishment
AWI: America and West Indies
BAD: British Admiralty Delegation (Washington)
BERCOMB:
BNA: British Naval Attaché
BNSO: British Naval Security Office
BAOR: British Army of the Rhine
BSC: British Security Coordination (New York)
BT:
CA: ?Civil Attaché/Civil Affairs/Chief Adviser
CA/DP: ?Chief Adviser/Displaced Persons
CAO:
CCLB:
CCSO: Chief Consular Security Officer
CD: Corps Diplomatique
CGRM: ?Controller-General Royal Marines
CIB:
CIC: Commander in Chief
CISO: Chief Information Security Officer
CNI: ?Co-ordinator of Naval Intelligence/Commander Naval Installations
CONCOMB: ?Control Commission Berlin
COS: Chiefs of Staff
CPO: Chief Petty Officer
CS: ?Chief of Staff/Consular Security
CSDIC: Combined Service Detailed Interrogation Centre
CSO: Chief Security Officer
CW:

DA/SW: ?Deputy Adjutant South West
DAQMG: Deputy Assistant Quartermaster General
DAS:
DC: ? Director of Communications
DCD: ?Director Communication Development
DCNS: Deputy Chief Naval Staff
DDIC: Deputy Director Intelligence Corps
DDNI: Deputy Director of Naval Intelligence
DDOD: Deputy Director of Operations Division
DEE: ?Director of Electrical Engineering
DEWD: Director Economic Warfare Division
DMI: Director of Military Intelligence
DMS: ?Director of Medical Services
DNC: Director of Naval Construction
DNI: Director of Naval Intelligence
DNO: Director of Naval Ordnance
DOD: Director of Operations Division
DOM: Director of Movements
DOP: Director of Plans
DOT: ? Department of Transport/Director of Operational Training
DPD: ?District Port Director
DRW:
DSD: Director of Signals Division
DSO:
DSR: ?Director of Scientific Research
DST: Department of Sea Transport
DTASW:
DTD:
DTM:
E. in C: Engineer in Chief
E.I. East Indies
ETA: Estimated Time of Arrival
FBI: Federal Bureau of Investigation
FIDS:
FNLO: ?French Naval Liaison Officer
FO: Foreign Office
FOCNA: ?Flag Officer Commanding the North Atlantic
FOGMA: ?Flag Officer Governing Mediterranean Area

FOLEM: Flag Officer Levant & Eastern Mediterranean
FOSH: ?Foreign Office Schleswig Holstein
FOWG: Foreign Office West Germany
GFR: Gefreiter – Lance Corporal in German military
Grp. Mut: Group of coded letters mutilated - illegible
Grp. Undec: Group of coded letters undecipherable
GSI (B):
HBM: His Britannic Majesty
HE: His Excellency
HM: His Majesty
HMG: His Majesty's Government
HMS: His Majesty's Ship
HMT: His Majesty's Transport
INF: Information Section/Service
IP: Intelligence Procurement
Int: Intelligence
JSM:
LSI (L): Landing Ship Infantry (Large)
M: Military Branch of the Admiralty
MA: Military attaché
MEW: Ministry of Economic Warfare
MFA: Minister of Foreign Affairs
MFc: ?Ministry of Finance
MI: Ministry of Information
MOI: Ministry of Information
MOVLO:
MSy: ?Ministry of Supply
MWT: Ministry of War Transport
NA: Naval Attaché
NABA: Naval Attaché Buenos Aires
Nav. Sec: Naval secretary
NCO: Non-Commissioned Officer
NDCO:
NID: Naval Intelligence Division
NIF: Naval Information Staff
NL:
NO i/c: Naval Officer in Charge
NS: Naval Secretary
OD: ?Officer of the Day

OIC: Officer in Charge
Ops: Operations
OR: Other ranks
OTP: One Time Pad
PAS: Principal Assistant Secretary
PET:
PIR: Prisoner Interrogation Report Record
PL: ?Private Letter
POW: Prisoner of War
PSTO: Principal Sea Transport Officer
RASAD: Rear Admiral South American Division
RDF: Radar Direction Finding
RFA:
RM: Royal Marines
RNFIU: ?Royal Naval Forward Interpretation Unit
RNVR: Royal Navy Volunteer Reserve
RO: ?Radio Officer
RS: Radio Signal
SBNOL Senior British Naval Officer Latin America
SBNOW.At.: Senior British Naval Officer Western Atlantic
SD: Sicherheitdienst (Nazi Party and SS's intelligence agency)
SKL: Seekriegsleitung. (German Naval Command, Operations Division)
SL: Sea Lord
SNORSCA: Senior Naval Officer Red Sea and Canal Area
SO(I): Staff Officer (Intelligence)
SOND: Secretary's Office Naval Department
SS: Sailing Ship
TOO:
Tsy: ?Transport Secretary
UFSET: United States Forces European Theater
UKSR:
USN: United States Navy
VAM: Vice Admiral Mediterranean
VCNS: Vice Chief Naval Staff
WCO:

WD: War Department
WO: War Office
WR: War Room
WRH:
WSA: War Shipping Administration
YE: Your Excellency

Chapter One: Background

German colonists in South America date back to the early 16th century when the Holy Roman Emperor Charles V gave land in Venezuela to the German Wesler Bank in exchange for the money he had borrowed. Klein Venedig (Little Venice), developed as a sugar cane plantation worked by 4,000 black African slaves while German explorers searched for 'El Dorado'. The colony failed when many settlers died of tropical diseases and the Spanish governor executed their leaders. During the 17th and 18th centuries, German Jesuit priests were active in Paraguay and the Rio de la Plata.

The American Revolution between 1765 and 1791 and the French Revolution in 1789 encouraged similar revolutions in South America with people wanting to remove Spanish and Portuguese control. During the Wars of Independence, Hansa [German] traders provided South American rebels with arms and shipping.

Alexander von Humboldt's publications following his exploration of the coast of South America between 1799 and 1804 encouraged German merchants to settle in Latin American port cities. Some married local women became landowners, and joined local oligarchies. German mercenary soldiers served in Brazil and fought in South American civil wars. (https://www.encyclopedia.com/humanities/ encyclopedias-almanacs-transcripts-and-maps/germans-latin-america)

There was a major influx of Germans into South America during the 19th century following the end of the Napoleonic Wars which had brought a period of peace and economic stability to Europe.

In the 1830s the Brazilian government brought German peasants to colonize the southern frontier in Santa Catarina, Rio Grande do Sul, and, later, Paraná. Ascending the rivers, Germans formed rural and small-town communities that retained a Germanic imprint for more than a century. Chile brought Hessian colonists to the southern frontier in the 1850s and 1860s. There, isolated from centers of Chilean population, they created a similar Germanic zone. Bernhard Forster (Friedrich Nietzsche's brother-in-law) headed a utopian colony in Paraguay in the 1880s. Well into the twentieth century, Germans continued to found or join agricultural colonies, particularly in southern Brazil, Chile, Argentina, Uruguay, and Paraguay. They played a major role, for example, in the opening of Argentina's Misiones Territory between the two world wars. In Guatemala they were prominent in the coffee industry. [...]

As Germany rose to world power after 1871, German communities in Latin America remained small and typically comprised of well-to-do merchants; bankers; managers and technicians of German electrical, chemical, metallurgical, and pharmaceutical firms; and educators and public service professionals under contract to Latin American governments. German military advisers were influential in Chile, Argentina, and Bolivia. Germans proved adaptable to Latin American business and social conditions, and—sheltered by insular, status-conscious, and largely Protestant communities—slow to assimilate. (https://www. encyclopedia.com/humanities/encyclopedias-almanacs-transcripts-and-maps/germans-latin-america)

Germany's colonial expansion in the Pacific during the second half of the 19th century included the island of Samoa, northeast New Guinea and the ports of Tianjin and Qingdao on the northeast coast of China, the latter becoming the base for Imperial Germany's Far East Squadron. Consequently, German merchants developed import and export businesses in most South American ports, exploiting the economic development of the Argentine Pampas, particularly wheat and cattle.

According to a map published in a 1942 report entitled 'Action in Latin America' by the Special Operations Executive, Britain's clandestine warfare organisation, for the British Cabinet Office, Uruguay had meat whereas Argentina had meat, hides, casein (a milk protein), fats, glycerine, linseed, tanning, wool, oil and wolfram. 'German control in States of Misiones, Corrientes and Entre Rios. 150,000 in Buenos Province. 500,000 Italians in Buenos Aires and many more in States of B.A. and Rosario [largest city in Santa Fe province]. Strong in Montevideo. Very strong German colonies in Rio Negro.' (TNA CAB 122/1587)

The meat processing plant in Fray Bentos which exported canned beef to Europe, North America and Asia was constructed by Germans and funded by British money. Britain's interest in South America was also linked to trade, not just with the countries on the continent, but also with its colonies in Australia, New Zealand, the Pacific islands, Shanghai, Hongkong, Singapore and 'Imperial India'. Until the construction of the Panama Canal in 1914, the route between the Atlantic and Pacific Oceans was round the Cape of Good Hope. Although an early British colony developed in Belize, Central America, Britain's major interests were the Falkland Islands and South George Islands where the British Royal Navy and its merchant ships could find shelter, food and water.

Like Germany, Britain had commercial and financial interests in South America and embassies and consulates in the major cities. British investment led to the development of most of South America's railways and coal found an increasing market not just for trains but also for industry and the domestic market.

Whilst there had been a friendly commercial rivalry between the two countries, the outbreak of the First World War in 1914 dramatically increased tensions. In particular, military targets were their merchant navies and colonies defended by the German Kriegsmarine and the British Royal Navy. Three months after the start of the war, there was a naval battle between the German and British ships off the southwest coast of South America. Vice-Admiral Graf Maximilian von Spee of the East Asia Squadron (Ostasiengeschwader or Kreuzeergeschwader) of the Kaiserliche Marine, the German Imperial Navy, met a squadron of British ships commandeered by Rear-Admiral Sir Christopher Cradock off the coast of central Chile near the port city of Coronel. When British intelligence learned from intercepted radio German wireless messages that the East Asia Squadron had left their base in the German colony of Qingdao (Tsingdao) on the northeast coast of China to attack the British merchant fleet operating the trade route along on the west coast of South America, the British Admiralty ordered Cradock to locate and destroy the squadron.

On 1 November, Spee's superior force of three light cruisers, SMS *Dresden, Leipzig and Nurnberg* and armoured cruisers SMS *Scharnhorst* and *Gneisenau,* encountered Cradock's two armoured cruisers, the flagship, HMS *Good Hope* and HMS *Monmouth*, the light cruiser HMS *Glasgow* and armoured merchantman HMS *Oranto*. Spee's ships sank HMS *Good Hope* with the loss of 1,600 lives and damaged HMS *Monmouth*. Although only three German crew were injured, von Spee lost half his ammunition which was irreplaceable. Cradock retreated to the British supply base in Stanley on the Falkland Islands. Spee was given a hero's welcome by the Germans living in Valparaiso, Chile. (Battle of Coronel, World War 1 at Sea - Naval Battles in outline with Casualties etc. naval-history.net. 30 October 2013; https://en.wikipedia.org/wiki/Battle_of_Coronel)

The British Admiralty responded by sending two modern battlecruisers, HMS *Invincible* and HMS *Inflexible*, to engage von Spee's squadron. They docked in Stanley on 7 December alongside armoured cruisers HMS *Carnarvon, Cornwall* and *Kent*, the armed merchant cruiser HMS *Macedonia* and light cruisers HMS *Bristol* and *Glasgow.*

Spee assembled his squadron off the Falkland Islands assisted by colliers SS *Baden*, SS *Santa Isabel* and SS *Seydlitz*. The following day, 8 December, the British spotted the German ships and their British battlecruisers and cruisers hunted them down and sank all the

German fleet except *Dresden* and *Seydlitz*. How many Germans were lost is unknown but Admiral Spee and his two sons were amongst the dead and 215 were rescued. The British claimed light damage to their ships and a few injuries. (https://en.wikipedia.org/wiki/Battle_of_the_Falkland_Islands)

Allied blockades of South American ports brought economic hardship. According to encyclopedia website,

> ...in Argentina and more notably Brazil (which declared war on Germany in 1917) nationalist riots destroyed property and terrorized individuals. German immigration resumed after 1918, now including war veterans and political irreconcilables, young people without prospects, businessmen ruined by inflation, and ethnic Germans driven from Russia and eastern Europe by war and Slavic nationalism. In the 1930s the Nazi government proselytized in German collectivities overseas, stimulating pan-German nationalism and creating the illusion of a resurgent worldwide German cultural community. Nazi publicists reckoned "racial" Germans to number 900,000 in Brazil, 240,000 in Argentina, and 50,000 to 80,000 in Chile. As war approached in Europe, Nazi activities provoked fear that German communities represented potential "fifth columns" (a pro-German population]. Armed uprisings in Brazil and Chile in 1938 that appeared to implicate Nazis, and rumored plots in Argentina and Uruguay, caused Latin American governments, particularly Getúlio Vargas's dictatorship in Brazil, to restrict sharply the autonomy of German (and other ethnic) schools, churches, newspapers, and social institutions.
> (https://www.encyclopedia.com/humanities/encyclopedias-almanacs-transcripts-and-maps/germans-latin-america)

In 1936, in recognition of von Spee, the Germans named the Deutschland-class "Panzerschiff (armored ship) built in Wilhelmshaven the *"Admiral Graf Spee."* Although nominally less than the 10,000 tons maximum imposed on German ships following the Treaty of Versailles, once her armaments were added, her full load displaced 16,000 tons. The British nicknamed it a "pocket battleship."

Hans Eubel, the last surviving *Graf Spee* sailor, died in Uruguay in 2017 aged 101. Amongst his possessions were photographs of his ship which led to an article into *El Pais,* a Uruguayan newspaper. Its translation reads:

> It was Thursday, August 31, 1939 when the Graf Spee was a little north of the Equator. She had been traveling for ten days since she had left the port of Wilhelmshaven in Germany. And at that

point, the crew only thought of meeting the Altmark tanker, which would happen the next day, to get the diesel consumed by the modern engines of the battleship. All crew aft! It was the order that the sailors received. The commander read them a message that had just arrived by radio: the German troops would cross the border into Poland at 4:45 a.m. from Germany. Nobody knew what decision England and France would make after the invasion (they say that not even Hitler himself knew), but they sensed it. With a glass of wine and accordion music, sitting on the deck under a tropical sky dotted with stars, those young people received the news of the beginning of the war. Thousands of kilometers from their homeland and their families. Far from knowing the atrocities that Nazism would later commit, under whose banner they would have to fight.

But also, that announcement was the end of the romance between man and machine. The twilight of those days when the Graf Spee, which had been launched in early 1936, sailed across the seas, landing in several cities without firing a single shot. It was time to send the English merchants to the bottom of the ocean. And the winding road to the tomb of Montevideo began.

Much has been written about the so-called Battle of the Río de la Plata (which actually occurred in the Atlantic), although not so much is known about the intimacy of the German tank crew, some of whom ended up living and raising families in Uruguay. and Argentina. The Graf Spee was the most powerful naval device of its time, but it was also home to more than 1,000 souls who lived within its walls, stories about which, thanks to a fortuitous find, a small window is opened today through which you can throw a look.

On Thursday, September 14, 2017, the German sailor Hans Eubel, the last survivor of the "pocket" battleship, died in Punta del Este. He came to live 101 years and was based in Uruguay since 1981 when he arrived with his Argentine wife of German parents. At just 22 years old, Eubel was a shortstop and the one in charge of launching the reconnaissance plane carrying the Graf Spee. But also, he was a skilled draftsman. He was a lover of photography, with a sensitivity such as capturing images of dolphins or seagulls on the side of the warship.

More than 80 years after he took a series of photographs of his trips aboard the Graf Spee, these ended up in the hands of businessman Alfredo Etchegaray, the last owner of the extraction rights of the ship, from which pieces such as its rangefinder and the famous eagle or figurehead were removed. After a long process of digitizing negatives and analysis (there are 245 images), the existence of the material is revealed today for the first time in Revista Domingo.

"History is fundamental because it is part of our roots and our culture. But in this case, through exhibition and analysis, it allows us to reflect, which helps us to grow and live with ourselves and with others, "says Etchegaray. And he adds: "These images are an invaluable contribution to memory, in times when many families get rid of their memories without giving them their due value."

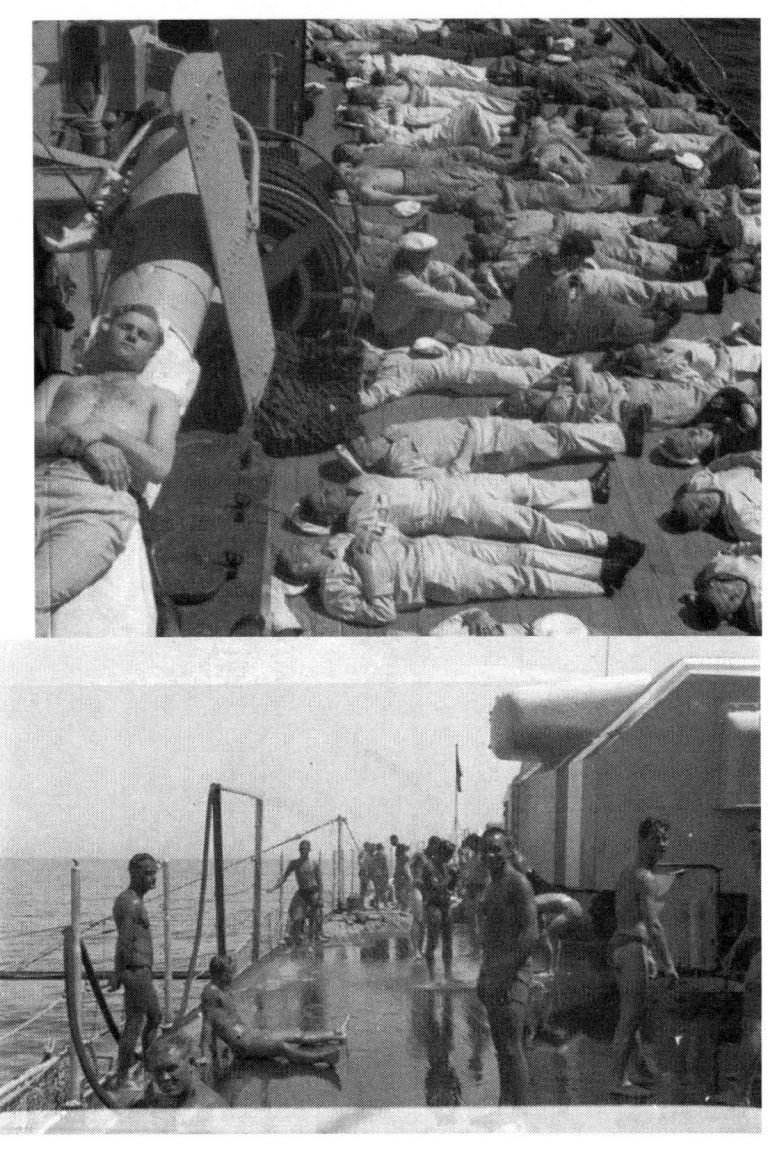

Hans Eubel's photographs of life on board the Graf Spee (El Pais, (Montevideo), 5 December 2021)

Scarcity and rats on board

Every encounter with the supply ship Altmark was a source of joy for the crew of the Graf Spee, who for a few days could indulge in some gastronomic luxuries and get out of the routine in which rice had long since replaced potatoes. According to NCO Herbert Klemm in his personal diary, "the shortage of products that could be purchased in the canteen was increasing; there were no buttons for pants or cigarettes missing, but shampoo and soap, as well as shaving supplies or toothpaste, were all but gone. Beer was rationed at 200 liters a day. In the hairdresser the situation was even worse, the combs were toothless remains. The state of the hair clippers was such that they did not cut but plucked, the military haircut was no longer possible. But the worst of the situations was the rationing of toilet paper: only 1/3 of a roll per man per month ".

As explained to Revista Domingo by researcher and writer Daniel Acosta y Lara, Captain Walter Kay, the ship's first officer, was in charge of discipline on board. Considered a very tough character, he was not particularly appreciated by most of the crew.

"Among the activities carried out by the crew when the ship was in port was hunting rodents", comments the author (together with Federico Leicht) of the book Graf Spee: 1939-2014 from Wilhelmshaven to the River of the Silver.

Since the days of sailing and wooden hulls, rats have been one of the endemic pests on board any ship. "Captain Kay paid for the capture of each specimen with money from the on-board canteen. The crew were summoned in front of Kay's office door to present the tails of the captured rodents. The first officer counted them, paid the corresponding sum, and disposed of them by throwing them through the porthole (window). Several crew members noted that this routine was repeated each time. And for the next opportunity, they arranged one of the boats under the porthole, managing to collect most of the tails that the officer discarded, presenting them again at the next appointment," adds the historian.

Peace (musical) notes

In the summer of 1936, after the start of the civil war in Spain, the Graf Spee was deployed in Spanish waters to participate in non-intervention patrols off the coasts controlled by the Republican side. On May 20 of the following year he was in Spithead, in the south of the United Kingdom, to represent Germany in the coronation ceremonies of King George VI, and then returned to Spain for a new patrol, which was followed by trips to Sweden and other destinations very far from the Río de la Plata. Most of the photographs taken by the last survivor of the Graf Spee correspond to these courses, in which one can see, for example, the stable band that the battleship had.

"It was a wind orchestra made up of 25 musicians and as many instruments. They performed songs during the visit of diplomatic, civil and military personalities, when dances were organized on board", says Acosta and Lara.

Due to the need to use the available spaces for the storage of food, the place where the Spee's library was available was converted into a flour warehouse, so one of the only distractions on board were the concerts provided by the orchestra.

During the Battle of the Río de la Plata, the musicians were transformed into combatants. Some of them, who were in exposed positions, suffered injuries and even lost their lives.

The orchestra's instruments, some damaged during the war, were on board the Graf Spee when it was blown up off the Punta Yeguas area. Upon arriving in Buenos Aires, the musicians were able to acquire second-hand instruments and organize again.

Life on the high seas

The crew of the Graf Spee lived isolated from the world. Only a few knew what was going on beyond the ship's rail: those with the thunderbolt insignia on their left sleeve, the radio operators. Aware of their privilege, they used to "sell" the information they had.

"Beer, cigarettes and delicacies from the canteen were used to find out how the last Schalke 04 game had turned out or what the political situation was at the time. Although the ship had a loudspeaker system, information was not communicated on a regular basis. This role was fulfilled by the on-board diary, a mimeographed sheet that broadcast the news of the moment ", recalls Acosta and Lara.

From drinking water, tea, coffee or a plate of hot food, everything had to be available to ensure the health, performance, and morale of the 1,188 men aboard the battleship. For this it was necessary to have a kitchen and a bakery that could satisfy so many needs. "From the administrative staff to the kitchen assistants, some 20 people with the necessary training operated these sections of the ship. In the German navy the galley was called Kombüse and in the Spee it was located in the middle of the ship. It occupied a fairly limited space taking into account the importance of the role it performed ". (*El País*, Montevideo, 5 December 2021)

Chapter Two: Events in 1939

The Hyperwar website, the official chronology of the US Navy in the Second World War, provided a detailed but somewhat repetitious account of the movements of the *Admiral Graf Spee*. It stated that on 1 September 1939, the ship, which had left Wilhelmshaven, Germany, on 21 August for the South Atlantic, rendezvoused with the German tanker *Altmark* southwest of the Canary Islands. The fuel oil carried in *Altmark*'s bunkers had been obtained in August at Port Arthur, Texas. *Admiral Graf Spee's* sistership, the *Deutschland*, which had departed Wilhelmshaven on 24 August, was deployed to raid commerce in the North Atlantic. At that time, the United States Government's isolationist policy meant that she had not entered the war.

On the same day, 1 September, German troops invaded Poland. Britain's response was to declare war on Germany two days later. On 11 September, the *Graf Spee* rendezvoused again with the *Altmark* to get more provisions. 'Security measure of launching the warship's AR 196 pays dividends, as British heavy cruiser HMS *Cumberland* is spotted closing the area. *Admiral Graf Spee* and her consort alter course and are thus not sighted.' A fortnight later, '*Graf Spee* and *Deutschland,* poised in the South and North Atlantic, respectively, received their orders to begin commerce raiding operations. On 30 September it was reported that 'European war again comes to the Americas: German armored ship *Admiral Graf Spee* stops and sinks British steamship *Clement* 75 miles southeast of Pernambuco, Brazil, 09°05'S, 34°05'W.' The same day, 'Word of German armored ship *Admiral Graf Spee*'s sinking of British freighter *Clement* reaches British Admiralty, which begins disposition of ships to meet the threat posed by the surface raider in the South Atlantic.'

Four days later, 'British Admiralty and French Ministry of Marine form eight "hunting groups" in the Atlantic and Indian Oceans to counter the threat posed by German armored ship *Admiral Graf Spee*. That same day, the object of that attention, *Admiral Graf Spee*, captures British freighter *Newton Beech* in the South Atlantic at 09°35'S, 06°30'W.'

On 7 October, she 'stops and boards British freighter *Ashlea* in the South Atlantic at 09°00'S, 03°00'W, and after transferring her crew to *Newton Beech*, sinks *Ashlea* with demolition charges.' The following day, she 'takes on board crews of British freighters *Ashlea* and *Newton Beech* in the South Atlantic and sinks the latter with demolition charges.'

On 10 October, she 'stops and puts prize crew on board British freighter *Huntsman* in the South Atlantic at 08°30'S, 05°15'W.' On 15 October, she 'meets tanker *Altmark* and refuels.' Two days later, she 'transfers crew of British freighter Huntsman to tanker Altmark; Huntsman is then sunk with demolition charges at 16°00'S, 17°00'W.' The following day, 18 October, she 'transfers crews of British freighters Newton Beech and Ashlea to tanker Altmark. The two German ships then part company for a time.'

On 22 October, 'German armored ship Admiral Graf Spee stops British freighter Trevanion, embarks her crew, and sinks the ship at 19°40'S, 04°02'W.' Almost a week later, she 'makes rendezvous with tanker Altmark near Tristan de Cunha. The warship refuels from the auxiliary, and transfers British freighter Trevanion's crew to her.'

On 15 November, she 'makes rendezvous with tanker Altmark near Tristan de Cunha. The warship refuels from the auxiliary, and transfers British freighter Trevanion's crew to her.' The following day, she 'stops Dutch freighter Mapia in Indian Ocean but, since the latter is a neutral ship, permits her to proceed unharmed.'

The two ships rendezvoused in the South Atlantic on 26 and 27 November 27 and the Graf Spee refuelled. Two days later, she 're-embarks from accompanying tanker Altmark all British merchant marine officers from the six ships that the "pocket battleship" has sunk up to that point. The officers are to be taken back to Germany; the crewmen remain imprisoned on board Altmark '

On 2 December, she 'stops British freighter Doric Star; the warship then torpedoes, shells, and sinks the merchantman at 19°15'S, 05°05'E.' The following day, she 'stops British freighter Tairoa; the warship then sinks the merchantman at 21°30'S, 03°00'E. Ironically, the same day Commodore Commanding South Atlantic Station, Commodore Henry H. Harwood, orders his three cruisers to concentrate off the River Plate estuary on 12 December.'

On 6 December, German armored ship Admiral Graf Spee refuels from tanker *Altmark* in South Atlantic, roughly 1,700 miles from Montevideo, Uruguay.' The following day, she 'stops and sinks British freighter *Streonshalh* at 25°01'S, 27°50'W.' (https://www.ibiblio.org/hyperwar/USN/ USN-Chron/USN-Chron-1939.html)

Sir Eugen Millington-Drake, the British Naval Attaché in Uruguay, confirmed that the British were listening to, deciphering and translating German naval messages transmitted between the Graf Spee and German High Command.

On 9 December ACHILLES was reported at Montevideo. The departure of the British merchant vessels HIGHLAND MONARCH (14,000 tons) from the Plate about 5th December and ANDALUSIA STAR from Buenos Aires on 8th December (estimated by Langsdorff [Hans Langsdorff was Captain of the Graf Spee] was likely to be in SPEE's vicinity on 10th December if bound northeast) and the report that RENOWN and ARK ROYAL were to operate from Ca[e Town were among the almost daily items of Intelligence received from Germany about this time. (Millington Drake, E. *The Drama of Graf Spee and the Battle of the Plate: A Documentary Anthology 1914 – 1964,* Peter Davies, 1964, p.161)

On 13 December, 'British heavy cruiser HMS *Exeter,* light cruiser HMS *Ajax,* and New Zealand light cruiser HMNZS *Achilles* (Commodore Henry H. Harwood, RN, flag in *Ajax*), which had rendezvoused the previous day, engage German armored ship *Admiral Graf Spee* in the Battle of the River Plate. The "pocket battleship" knocks *Exeter* out of action and damages her consorts, but is compelled by the damage inflicted by her lesser-gunned adversaries (which are fought, as First Lord of the Admiralty Winston S. Churchill writes, "with the utmost resolution and skill") to retire toward Montevideo, Uruguay. *Exeter,* badly damaged, withdraws to the Falkland Islands (see 14 December.). The U.S. Navy studies the Battle of the River Plate from a perspective of drilling gunners to maintain fire by local (rather than a centralized director) control. To this end, a scenario similar to the River Plate engagement is included in an exercise in 1940. In addition, the Director of Fleet Training considers the "proper use of smoke either as a defense measure or as a means of covering movements of an attacking force" extremely important, and points out the demonstrable effectiveness of a smoke screen "as a means of protection for light forces" employed by Commodore Harwood in the battle with *Admiral Graf Spee.*'

The following day, she 'puts in to Montevideo, Uruguay, for repairs. British light cruiser HMS Ajax and New Zealand light cruiser HMNZS *Achilles* maintain patrol off the 120-mile wide River Plate estuary. British heavy cruiser HMS *Cumberland* reinforces *Ajax* and *Achilles* that night.' (https://www.ibiblio. org/hyperwar/USN/USN-Chron/USN-Chron-1939.html)

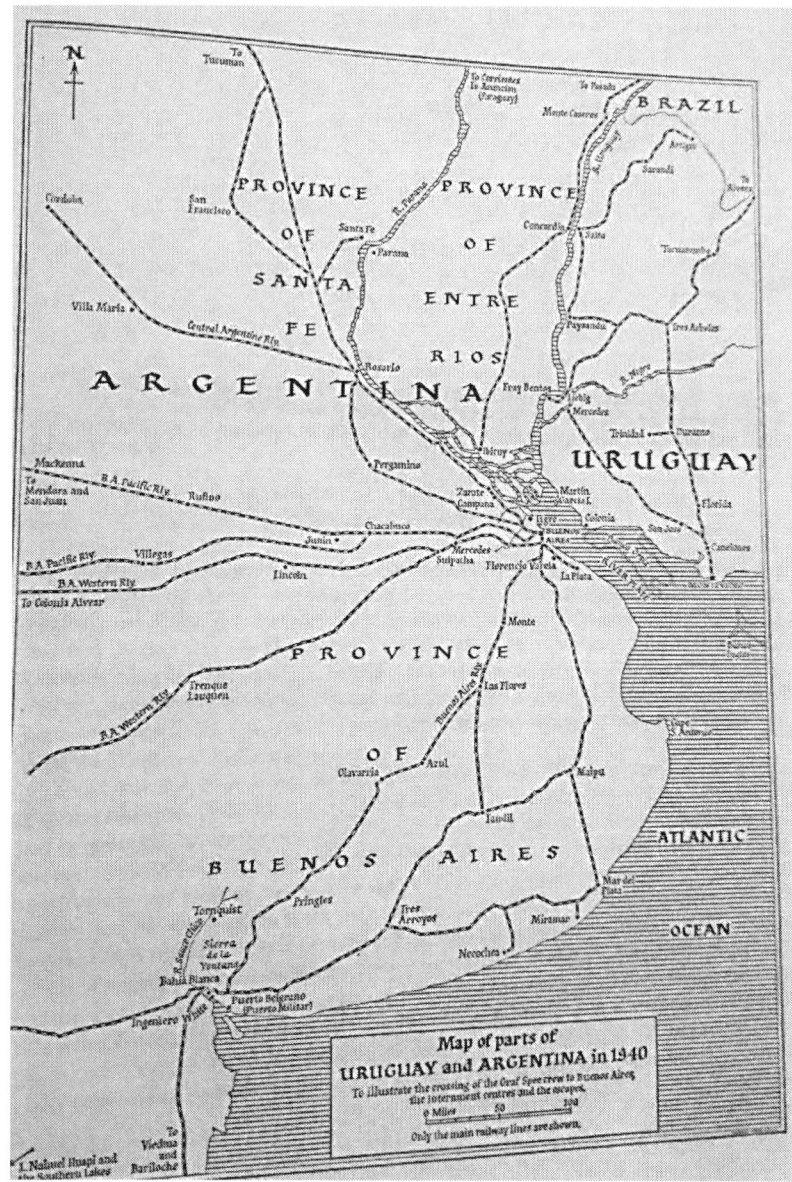

(Millington Drake, Eugen, *The Drama of Graf Spee and the Battle of the Plate: A Documentary Anthology 1914 – 1964,* Peter Davies, 1964)

On 14 December, The *Madera Tribune* was one of the first newspapers to report on what became known as the Battle of the River Plate.

POCKET SHIP SPEE IS TRAPPED
GERMAN SEA RAIDER SEEKS REFUGE MONTEVIDEO
AFTER SPECTACULAR NIGHT FIGHT

Desperate Break to Escape or Interment to Be Fate of Small Battleship Badly Damaged in Long Sea Battle Off South America

MONTEVIDEO, Uruguay, Dec. 14— Sources close to the German Legation said today that the German pocket battleship Admiral Graf Spee, here to bury her dead and make repairs after a running naval battle yesterday with three British cruisers, "probably will leave within a week.' Guarding against the possibility that the German war vessel would attempt to put out to sea, the British cruiser Achilles kept a death watch on the Graf Spee, determined that it should not again escape to raid allied commerce on the high seas.

SEA DASH

The first move to settle the status of the Graf Spee was made when German Minister Otto Langmann sent a note to Foreign Minister Alberto Guani of Uruguay reportedly asking permission to disembark the crew of the Graf Spee. The German legation, after predicting that the Graf Spee would not remain to be interned in Uruguayan waters, said that the vessel's machinery had not been damaged in yesterday's battle and that she had not been hit below the water line. The German minister visited the foreign office after Millington Drake, British minister, had conferred with Guani. Its crew at battle stations, gun crews manning its eight six-inch guns, the Achilles steamed slowly back and forth in the River Plate, just outside territorial waters, as the Graf Spee lay within the inner harbor.

PLAN FOR DASH

From Montevideo to nearby Punta Gorda, back and forth, the gray British cruiser maintained its watch. Its fellow cruisers Exeter and Ajax—the Exeter herself damaged in a long running fight with the formidable German raider —were believed nearby. It was evident that the British ships had foreseen the possibility of a desperate break for the open sea by the Admiral Graf Spee. The Achilles alone was to be seen from the docks here—aside from the Graf Spee, damaged, 36 of its men killed and 60 wounded, in the biggest and most dramatic naval battle of the war. It was up to the Germans to decide whether their crack ship should make a desperate dash for the Atlantic after repairs, or be interned for the duration of the war.

IS BADLY DAMAGED

A United Press correspondent who boarded the Graf Spee was able to survey exterior damage. Two shells had pierced its thick fighting tower, entering on the port side and emerging on the starboard side. Two sections of its thick armored plate had been smashed in the fore part of the ship on the starboard side. Five impacts, apparently from small shells, were noted on the water line on the port side. One of the two airplanes on the ship's deck had had its tail shot off; part of its fuselage was gone. Extent of interior damage could not be ascertained as nobody was allowed inside the ship. Indications were that a dramatic climax, in a sudden dash by the Graf Spee for the sea, or an anti-climax-internment—was Imminent.

HEAVY CASUALTIES

Despite the death watch of the British cruisers, it was believed that German authorities, with the German legation in constant contact with Berlin, were considering whether to order a break for liberty despite the damage to the Graf Spee and the loss in casualties of nearly 100 of its normal complement of 926 officers and men. Official sources reported that the Admiral Graf Spee had been hit on the captain's bridge, in a clothes room and in the officers' mess, and in front of a powder [explosives] room. Her captain was reported to be a casualty, with an arm wound. It was reported that the Exeter, flagship of the British South American squadron, suffered one direct hit.

SPECTACULAR SHOW

Pursued relentlessly by the British cruisers, the Admiral Graf Spee had sought vainly to escape to the open sea. The British ships, miles speedier, forced her toward the Uruguayan coast, and in the early summer night, as thousands of tense Uruguayans watched from shore, she steamed slowly along the south coast, her searchlights. playing on the resort beaches and anchored. The three British cruisers steamed behind her and dropped anchor at Punta Caretas, 10 miles southeast of Montevideo where a point of land just out at the junction of the river plate Estuary and the Atlantic. Germany's ship, which for weeks had been raiding allied shipping in the South Atlantic, moved into the inner harbor and the most seriously wounded of her crew were brought ashore and taken to a military hospital at Maciel, outside Montevideo.

CAPTIVES ABOARD

Aboard the Admiral Graf Spee were the captains of six British merchantmen which the pocket battleship had sunk, A spokesman for Otto Langmann, German minister, announced that they would be landed today. News of the fight had spread along the coast, and was the signal for German merchantmen to start for home in the belief that the British navy watchodgs had been concentrated off the River Plate, Surveyors were expected to board the Admiral Graf Spee today to ascertain the extent of its damage It was entitled under international law to seek the safety of a neutral port and effect repairs. How long it would be permitted to stay, without being interned for the duration of the war, was up to Uruguay.

BATTLE STARTED YESTERDAY

Hugo Ricaldone, secretary to President Alfredo Baldomir, said that the German ship would be permitted to remain in port 30 days. It was indicated that the long fight between the Graf Spee and the British ships started some time yesterday. There had been persistent reports of firing off the coast, and there was strong evidence that British sources here had reason to believe that the British cruisers, main part of the South American division of the British America and West Indies squadron, were closing in on formidable German raider. From officials who boarded the Admiral Graf Spee as soon as it entered Uruguayan waters, the United Press obtained a first hand German account of the battle.

FRENCH SHIP DECOY

Flushed with its triumphs in weeks of raiding, the German ship sighted the French passenger liner Formose. 9975 tons, of Havre, hundreds of miles off the coast, and made for her. The Germans suspected today that she was a decoy, for it was not long, according to the accounts, that the 6985 ton cruiser Ajax, using every ounce of her power, raced over the horizon.

SPEED AIDS BRITISH

The 10.000 ton German ship had six 11-inch guns against the eight 6-inch guns of the Ajax. But the Ajax had 32.5 knots speed to the Spec's 25. As the Ajax closed in, she began calling by radio to the Exeter and Achilles for support. Her guns opened. There was a race in toward the coast. At 8:30 yesterday morning, according to the German reports, the real fight started at the mouth of the River Plate, between the Ajax and the Spee. Early yesterday afternoon, it was related, the Exeter appeared, then the Achilles. The Achilles remained a short distance away, protecting the Formose which had steamed for the coast. The ships moved slowly in toward the Uruguayan coast, their guns roaring.

LONG RANGE DUEL

The ships were miles apart, firing at long range, as they neared the coast. They were sighted from the Uruguayan and Argentine coast about 6 p. m. yesterday, the Admiral Graf Spee far in advance. Heavy firing started again at Bp. m. It ceased and restarted at 9 p. m. The Ajax closed in and the German ship was forced up the coast to port. The Formose made for Buenos Aires, across the Plate estuary. German

Minister Langmann, after his visit to the Admiral Graf Spee, alleged that most of the German wounded had been victims of "mustard gas bombs"—presumably meaning shells, as bombs are normally thrown by hand. Use of gas shells in naval warfare, it was believed, would be a new departure, Langmann, however, attributed the "eye injuries" of several German seamen to the "bombs." (Madera Tribune, Vol. LXXV, No. 36, 14 December 1939)

Henry McCall, later promoted to Admiral, British Naval Attaché in Argentina (Millington-Drake, op.cit.)

Captain Henry McCall, the Naval Attaché at the British Embassy in Buenos Aires, compiled the following report for the Admiralty.

ACTION OFF THE RIVER PLATE
DESPATCH No. 4 NAVAL ATTACHE   SECRET
BRITISH EMBASSY, BUENOS AIRES, 21st December, 1939

1. On Thursday, 14th December having heard that a German armoured ship had sought refuge in Montevideo Harbour, after action with our forces I proceeded by aeroplane to Montevideo arriving there about 18.00.

2. The Admiral Graf Spee was anchored in the middle of the Ante-port showing little damage after her engagement of the day before, apart from a large hole just abaft the port hawsepipe, a hole that appeared to go clean through the control tower, and. her aeroplane-wrecked. Closer examination revealed the damage as telegraphed in my 1800/14, i.e.:

Main armament: no direct signs of damage

Secondary armament: Starboard pair anti-aircraft guns probably out of action

One Searchlight damaged.

Rangefinders on fore superstructure probably out of action

Control tower: four hits, probably efficiency seriously impaired.

Aeroplane wrecked.

Torpedo tubes no damage.

Engines: no evidence of damage.

Hull: large hole on port side; fore mess-deck other minor holes.

A2 source reports two holes below waterline.

In all about 50/60 hits, but difficult to assess damage without getting on board

Unconfirmed report; shell burst in sickbay killing twenty-five men

Port midship 6 gun also disabled.

It was subsequently suspected that one, if not two, of the 11 guns in her foremost turret were out of action. There were a number of pock-marks on the ship's side, probably caused by bursts-short.

3. I found that the Staff Officer, Intelligence Lieutenant-Commander Johnston, in conjunction with Captain Hamond and the other Officers of the Naval Control were taking all possible steps to ensure that movements on board the Admiral Graf Spee were being closely watched, and arrangements had been made to communicate by W/T. with HMS Ajax in as short a time as possible.

4. I would like here to emphasise the initiative and capability that has always been shown by Lieutenant-Commander Johnston. The organisation, he had set up, in his capacity as Intelligence Officer worked efficiently and smoothly throughout an exceedingly strenuous and trying time. He and those employed on ciphering duties were practically continuously on duty from the time the Admiral Graf Spee was originally encountered until her final destruction. This applies equally to Officers of the Naval Control Staff who were responsible for watching her movements, patrolling in tugs and the like.

5. I would also like to bring to your special notice the work of Mr. H. John Garland who was alone responsible for wireless communications. The establishment of W/T communications with HM Ships from a neutral country is handicapped by neutrality laws, which forbid the use of transmitters ashore though there is no objection to having receivers. As reported in my War

Despatches Nos. 1, 2 and 5, arrangements had been made for the official Uruguayan W/T Station to transmit to the Falkland Islands at certain routine hours with the object of enabling HM Ships to intercept. A most efficient receiving set had been installed in the Consulate, which has been paid for by Mr. Millington-Drake, the British Minister. This receiving set has now well proved its worth and I recommend that the Admiralty should reimburse its cost to Mr Millington-Drake. It was Mr Garland who succeeded in arranging that the Uruguayan official W/T Station let go routine work to a large extent during the time Graf Spee was in harbour in order that we could transmit every two hours and, on occasions, even more frequently than this. As there was only one person in Uruguay, other than Mr Garland who was capable of receiving morse at speedy arrangements were made for Mr Fitch, the Manager of the Marconi Company, and for Mr Martin to fly over from Argentina to assist in watchkeeping. Mr. Garland is making out a separate report on communications which will be rendered as soon as received.

6. Our immediate concern was to let the Commodore know the instant the Admiral Graf Spee showed any signs of departure, and to ensure this the following steps were taken:

i) Watchers were placed on nearby ships

ii) Tugs and motorboats were hired for patrol and communication.

iii) (Though this could not be put into effect until the second day) A yacht was sailed out from Buenos Aires with the intention of stationing herself at the outer end of the channel, in order to indicate by a pre-arranged system of firing rockets which way the Admiral Graf Spee proceeded. (It was Paymaster-Commander Lloyd Hirst, my assistant in Buenos Aires, who organised this on his own initiative as well as taking other steps to watch possible anchorages in the River Plate should the Admiral Graf Spee bolt up the river).

iv) I gave authority to hoist the aerials and break the seals in the wireless cabinet of a merchant ship in harbour whose dynamo was kept running.

7. On the night of my arrival, I accompanied the British Minister, Mr. Millington-Drake, to the Minister for Foreign Affairs, to whom a note was handed requesting the Uruguayan Authorities to intern the Admiral Graf Spee should her stay in harbour exceed twenty-four hours, on the grounds that, having steamed into harbour at a high speed, she was in a seaworthy condition. The Minister for Foreign Affairs informed the British Minister that technical experts were on board examining the

damage and would report to him in due course as to her seaworthiness.

8. On Friday, 15th December, the British ship Ashworth was sailed at 17.00 and a note was handed in and accepted to the effect that the Admiral Graf Spee should not be allowed to sail for twenty-four hours after her departure.

9. During that day, for the first time, I understood, through receiving signals concerning oil fuel for HMS Repulse and Ark Royal at Rio de Janeiro, that the Commodore could expect no support for some days. I had previously hoped that such support was closer at hand.

10. Late that night, I again accompanied the British Minister to the Minister for Foreign Affairs with a note protesting that the Admiral Graf Spee was receiving assistance in skilled labour and material from the shore to make good her damage. I took the opportunity to protest to the Minister for Foreign Affairs that the measures adopted by the Uruguayan Government to hold her were in no way adequate, should she decide to break out in spite of our merchant ship having sailed. I suggested to him that, as there was no Uruguayan warship nor shore defence that could ensure that she did not sail, he should place an armed guard on board. He thereupon telephoned to the Minister for Defence, who informed him that he could not put an armed guard on board, but that he would put a tug with an armed party alongside and that this would be done forthwith. The tug was provided; later in the night, however, I discovered that she did not proceed alongside but remained at anchor close to her quarters - the sole armament I could see being one Naval Petty Officer with a pistol.

11. The following day, Saturday 16th December, I tried to get an interview with the Minister for Defence, General Campos, who is very pro-ally and whom I personally know quite well. My suspicions were that the Inspector General of Marine, Rear-Admiral Schroeder, who would advise him on such matters, was either pro-Nazi or in the pay of the Germans, and that he had probably told him that it was beyond the power of his forces to intern the Admiral Graf Spee. I wished to point out to General Campos that the presence of an armed guard on board would make it practically impossible for the Admiral Graf Spee to sail and that by the removal of certain parts of her main armaments she could be rendered helpless; or that he could make it difficult for her to proceed without a tug by mooring merchant ships between her and the entrance to the harbour. He however, very courteously, told me that he regretted that I could only see him through the Minister for Foreign Affairs.

12. Meanwhile an extension up to seventy-two hours in. all for making good seagoing defects had been granted, from the time of the completion of the inspection by the Uruguayan Authorities. She would, therefore, have to sail not later than 20.00 on Sunday, 17th December, or be interned.

13. Up till this time, I had the strong impression that the Uruguayan Government were conniving with the Germans to break the laws of neutrality by the following actions:

1) Allowing the Admiral Graf Spee to enter and use the harbour of Montevideo as a port of refuge after action for more than twenty-four hours.

2) Allowing her to stay more than twenty-four hours, having arrived in a seaworthy condition.

3) Allowing her to make good damage caused by battle.

4) Allowing her to obtain labour and material from outside sources to make good action defects, even after evidence of this had been submitted to the Authorities.

Although the first three of these points may in argument be considered doubtful breaches, there can be no question about the fourth: large oxygen cylinders, steel plates and other materials for repair, as well as workmen from the shore - all of which and whom probably came from Buenos Aires - were openly seen to be taken on board. Moreover, the Minister for Foreign Affairs was apparently difficult to approach and was not in a mood to receive any suggestions as to the steps that might be taken to prevent Admiral Graf Spee sailing.

14. On Friday, 15th December, at 17.00 another British merchant ship was sailed and a note again handed in and accepted to the effect that the Admiral Graf Spee should not proceed until twenty-four hours after her departure.

15. On Saturday, 16th December, every effort was apparently being made by the Germans to complete her repairs as soon as possible. She had provisioned but not oiled, but it was improbable that she required much oil as she had completed from the Altmark only a week previously, and it looked to me as if she might try to get away that night. I therefore advised the British Minister that I thought it would be well to tell the Minister for Foreign Affairs entirely unofficially and as a friend, that it would, be to our interests if she were delayed in going out of harbour. The Minister afterwards informed me that the Minister for Foreign Affairs was relieved to know this as up till then he had been in doubt as to what were our real desires. This understandable, as we had been pressing hard for her internment on the grounds that she had not left after twenty-four hours in harbour.

16. I am not attempting to include in this report full details of all the communications between the British Minister and the Minister for Foreign Affairs during this period. They have already been rendered in clear detail in the telegram from Mr. Millington-Drake to the Foreign Office; and I was only present at a part of some of his interviews.

17. On Sunday, 17th December, during the forenoon, all repair materials were taken ashore. The Uruguayan Authorities had issued a note prohibiting the sailing of any British ship after 20.00 the previous day as the Admiral Graf Spee was due to sail at 20.00 that evening. Everything looked as if she were going. Late in the forenoon, however, some extra boat traffic was observed and then the wounded were brought ashore. Shortly after 14.00, boat-loads of men and personal effects were seen to be transferring to the Tacoma lying a short distance away across the harbour. At first, endeavours were made to preserve secrecy. Canvas screens were rigged up over the gangway so that observers from outboard could not see what was being put into the boats, and the men going onboard the Tacoma were at once sent below. Later in the afternoon, however, all efforts to preserve secrecy were abandoned and boats full of men were openly ferried across the harbour. By 17.00 over seven hundred men had been counted leaving.

18. A note was handed in pressing for the internment of Tacoma on the grounds that she was a naval transport now.

19. It was not then clear what was her intention, but my suspicions were aroused because they had lowered, fuelled and re-hoisted a big motor-launch, leaving her ready to be lowered again. The rest of the story is open history.

20. At 18.17 o'clock the Admiral Graf Spee hoisted a large ensign on the foremast as well as at the main and left harbour, shortly afterwards followed by the Tacoma. Having left the harbour, the Admiral Graf Spee steamed to the south-westward and stopped about five miles from the entrance. The Tacoma anchored about two miles to the north-east of her. Several boats then left the Admiral Graf Spee for the Tacoma and two tugs and a lighter arrived from Buenos Aires. Her destruction was made as dramatic as possible. The first explosion took place exactly as the sun set, while all her crew were lined-up on the deck of the Tacoma making the Nazi salute. The whole procedure was watched by vast crowds from the shore.

21. Just before she blew up, I had sent Lieutenant Cassels of the Naval Control Service out in a tug to investigate what the tugs with the barge were doing, and he has rendered me an account

of the subsequent proceedings outside the harbour, of which the following is an extract:

On arrival at the dockside we heard the explosion in the Admiral Graf Spee and immediately boarded our tug. We had barely cast off when we were hailed by one of the Port Officials and instructed by him to take him on board. As we proceeded at full speed towards the wreck, it was evident that the Port Official knew absolutely nothing of what was taking place, and in fact he thought that some of the German crew was still aboard when the explosion occurred. We arrived alongside the Tacoma within twenty minutes of the explosion and found that the crew of the Admiral Graf Spee had already boarded two tugs and one barge belonging to Delfino Company of Argentina. The Port Official hailed the tugs and asked them under what instructions they were acting. He was informed that they were bound for Argentina in accordance with instructions from their Company. The senior Port Official, Senor Riquero, then appeared in another tug and orders were received from him that the Delfino boats were not to move away. However, one of these tugs proceeded away to the westward at full speed and was pursued. In addition to the tugs, there were four of the Admiral Graf Spee's boats under their own power, in one of which was Captain Langsdorff. As difficulty was being experienced in giving instructions to the German crew, Captain Langsdorff came on board our (Lieutenant Cassels') tug to act as interpreter. The Port Official informed Captain Langsdorff that as he had no knowledge that the tugs and barge had orders to leave Uruguayan waters, it was imperative for them to return to Montevideo. The Captain at first thought that he had been stopped because he was being accused of blowing up his ship in Uruguayan waters, and hastened to explain that he had been led to a pre-arranged spot, three miles off the coast, by a Uruguayan official tug and then gone on one mile further on his own initiative in order to avoid future argument. In this connection the Captain remarked: The English do not recognise a neutral territorial zone of more than three miles: that is why I sank my ship one mile further out than this limit so that I was free to act as I chose with the Argentine tugs and barge and the crew in them. The Port Official then pointed out that it was not a question of the sinking of the Admiral Graf Spee, but of the behaviour of the Argentine tugs and barge with which he was concerned. He insisted on an explanation of their apparently unauthorised transport of men and baggage and of their movements generally. Captain Langsdorff retorted that he had received full permission from the Uruguayan authorities to proceed to Argentina. As the Port Official had no knowledge of this, he was not prepared to accept the Captain's statement, and it was therefore decided to hail the Uruguayan Naval gunboat which had just arrived on the scene. The Commander of the gunboat had also received no instructions and he therefore sent a wireless message for orders. The reply was that the Germans were to be allowed to proceed without further hindrance.

22. On board the Admiral Graf Spee were sixty-one British prisoners from the ships Newton Beech, Ashlea, Huntsman, Trevanion, Africa Shell, Doric Star, Tairoa, Streonshalh

The Masters or chief officers of all these ships were amongst the sixty-one prisoners and those of the first four of them had previously been prisoners on board the Altmark. They were all landed the afternoon following the Admiral Graf Spee's arrival in harbour. From what they told me the following facts are established:

23. Details concerning their Altmark

a) The Altmark had filled up with oil fuel in Texas towards the end of August. She last topped up the ADMIRAL GRAFF SPEE on December 6th in approximate position 023 S. 026° W. It was then estimated she had about 3,000 tons of oil left.

b) Normally she cruised between the positions 10° and 20° South and 10° and 39° West, a 'super doldrum' where small boats were able to ply backwards and forwards without the least difficulty. She once remained stopped there for four days. The only time when she is thought to have left that area was during the twenty-eight-day period when the Admiral Graf Spee was operating in the Indian Ocean, when it is thought that she went south and east of the Cape, though this is not certain.

c) The Altmark had received orders to proceed to Bahia or Pernambuco should she fail to rendezvous the raider after a stated time.

d) The Altmark is a ship of some 20,000 tons and is supposed to be capable of carrying 14,000 tons of oil. She has fine lines and it was rumoured she could do over 25 knots. She has ammunition magazines, large storerooms for provisions, refrigeration, sixteen derricks and extremely up-to-date installation for loading. Two large guns are hidden behind flaps on which at present NORGE is written; two 3-centimetre pom-poms are on the after part of the bridge. It is considered possible that she will change her name and paint USSR instead of NORGE on her side. It is thought that it would be difficult to alter the appearance of the ship greatly.

e) The method of oiling was to tow the ship being oiled astern; the oil-pipe was supported by stirrups from the towing hawser and wrapped round the whole pipe at frequent intervals were cork floats.

f) On no occasion whilst the prisoners were on board Altmark was any submarine oiled, nor did they hear any talk, either on board the Altmark or Admiral Graf Spee of any submarines in the vicinity.

g) Captain Dahl of the Altmark was a reserve officer of the old school, who had been a prisoner of the last war in England, and bore us a grudge. He was a stern disciplinarian, feared, respected and disliked. The crew were merchant service; a hard-bitten, discontented lot. On board the Altmark the Admiral Graf Spee maintained a Naval guard, between the ship's crew there was constant friction amounting sometimes to free fights.

h) The treatment of the prisoners on board the Altmark was harsh in the extreme, more reminiscent of the days of slave-trading than of the present time.

i) The treatment received by the Indian prisoners on board was very much more lenient than that meted out to the remainder. This was for political reasons, and the Indians were told that when they eventually reached Germany, they would be allowed to proceed home via Italy.

j) The Officers were loud in their complaint of their treatment. Their flats were so over-crowded that they had no room between mattresses, which were covered with lice and vermin. They could only bath on the upper deck in a water ration of one quart of brackish water a day, which then had to be reserved for washing clothes. To wash in were only twenty bowls for the common use of Masters, Officers, and white and Lascar crews. There was little soap.

k) Eating utensils were improvised out of condensed milk tins and the bottoms of large tins for plates. The food was insufficient and very poor in quality.

l) The lavatories were open oil drums in the trunk ways leading to the flats, which always polluted the atmosphere. The Masters were humiliated by being made to empty the lavatories in the presence of British and Lascar crews. They only got exercise if the weather was perfect, and then for an hour and a quarter per day. Smoking was prohibited in the first two weeks, and afterwards limited. The punishment for breaking this rule was three days' confinement on bread and water.

m) There are now over three hundred prisoners on board the Altmark and the Captain has announced his intention that rather than give up his ship he will, if attacked, blow it up with all the prisoners on board.

n) Our Officers had little opportunity of acquiring information on board Altmark, but a rough sketch of her is enclosed.

24. Details concerning the Admiral Graf Spee

a) The conditions on board Admiral Graf Spee were very different. The prisoners were treated with consideration, were given the same food as the ship's company, allowed every opportunity for exercise on the deck and no restrictions were placed upon them in talking with the Officers or men. Captain Langsdorff was described as a very courteous, charming gentleman. A man of high though socialistic ideals. He told the British Captains that as they were going to be interned in Germany there was no reason why he should not talk freely with them.

b) It had been the intention of the Admiral Graf Spee to return to Germany by Christmas, but their plans had been upset by the Deutschland's encounter with the Rawalpindi. Captain Langsdorff said that after this encounter, he was aware that our patrols had been very much tightened up. I am not sure if he entirely based this on news from Germany, for he also stated that he was able to hear the call-signs of many British warships in the North Atlantic; further, that apparently W/T communications seemed to become more frequent when French warships joined in the Atlantic patrols.

c) Captain Langsdorff said that his ship would not proceed to any of the North Sea Ports in Germany, but to some port in East Prussia, where they would be more immune from air attack.

d) When the Admiral Graf Spee left Germany, the Captain told the ship's Company that their role was to sink merchant ships and to avoid encounter with any but inferior Naval forces. There were to be no Falkland Islands nor Coronels for them. On this account it was not his intention to close large convoys, but only the smaller ones which would be less heavily escorted.

e) When asked why he had proceeded to the South American coast, Captain Langsdorff stated that he thought things would become too hot for him near the African Trade Routes and that he was going to show himself off the River Plate before doubling back home to Germany. He had his eye particularly on the Highland Princess. When asked how he knew she was likely to be in that vicinity at a certain time, he said he had seen a copy of a daily paper on board the last ship he had sunk, which gave him the necessary information.

f) Captain Langsdorff made a point of never sinking passenger ships, as female passengers would have been an embarrassment. When told that the Highland Princess was a passenger ship, he said: Ah! They have but few passengers on board this time. In this he was correct.

g) He was under the illusion we had only one cruiser off the mouth of the River Plate and that in this area we convoyed a certain number of ships out with two destroyers, a force with which he considered he could easily cope.

h) It was Captain Langdorff's practice when approaching a ship to approach end-on flying a French ensign. When he came close to, he displayed a large notice board saying: Do not use your wireless or you will be fired, upon. In this connection all the prisoner-captains are unanimous that it is most desirable that the Allied warships should be able to indicate by some method to Merchant Ships they are approaching that they are Allied warships. They say they were always in doubt when a warship came up whose identity they could not discover, whether to send a wireless signal or not.

i) Some of the tales that the Masters have to tell of the courage of their Wireless Operators, into which one can read their own initiative and bravery, certainly merits investigation and probably recognition on their arrival in England. They are due to sail in the Highland Chieftain this week.

j) Discipline on board the Admiral Graf Spee was of a very socialistic order. Though the ship was clean and well-kept, Naval discipline as we know it was lax. Food was lacking in quantity and quality; Officers and men had the same. On the other hand, much attention was paid to physical drill, even to the extent of all Officers having to undergo it under the supervision of the executor Officer every day. The Officers and crew were mainly very young and inexperienced and the Captain frequently complained of this fact. Nevertheless their morale was high for they had been told most exaggerated stories about the speed of their ship and were under the impression that there were only three ships of the British Navy they had to fear for they could run from or out-gun all the rest. The prisoners formed the opinion that though the Captain was pro-Nazi, he was not rabidly so, and was disgusted with the rapprochement between Germany and Russia. The younger Officers were strongly pro-Nazi.

k) During the action, the prisoners, who were locked up below, had an opportunity of observing a between-deck action party working the other side of the bulkhead in which were some empty screw holes. They were unanimous that it was an extraordinary thing to see how the morale faded away in that party as the action progressed and they realised their ship was being hit. On arrival in harbour, when the prisoners were able to mingle with the ship's company again, they said morale no longer existed.

However, on the next day, when the dead were landed for Burial, a large funeral party of many hundreds was paraded and the appearance of the men was good: I should judge that the shock of the action had somewhat faded away. The men one could see on the deck of the Admiral Graf Spee appeared cheerful and happy; the drill of the boats-crews rivalled our own; and when they finally left the ship for the Tacoma the great majority seemed to be carrying out their orders smartly and contentedly.

l) I could see, however, a small number of both Officers and men who appeared to be resenting the operation of abandoning the ship. Montevideo rumour has it that the second-in-command entirely disapproved. I reported by cable, I consider that if the Captain had given orders for the ship to go to sea, he would have had little trouble, if any, with his ship's company. I give this as my opinion, but there is nothing more to go on so far but observation of the ship's company at work from close outside the ship.

m) Captain Langsdorff was under the firm impression during the action that Barham was in the offing. I imagine this was most probably wrong intelligence passed out by the British Legation in Montevideo and if so is a very good lesson to intelligence centres ashore. He also thought that we had a submarine off Montevideo and on that account, when he entered the harbour, he did so at high speed without stopping to embark a pilot.

n) His chief concern after being worsted in the action was that one of our cruisers should not arrive in Montevideo first and so deprive him of the right to enter.

o) After the action, talking to one of the British Captains, he said that when he sighted the cruiser and then the masts of two other ships, he was convinced that they would be the two escorting destroyers. He was amazed at the speed and manoeuvrability of our cruisers, and paid high tribute to the accuracy of the British gunnery.

p) He maintained that it was essential to enter harbour in order to render the ship seaworthy and to repair the ship's galley and bakery which had been completely destroyed, together with a large quantity of provisions which would have to be replaced.

q) The Admiral Graf Spee carried a specialist 'Professor', expert in codes. This man always accompanied the boarding parties in search of papers. He was reputed to be brilliant in everything connected with the handling of intercepted messages. He was suspected as being the Gestapo agent on board as he always kept himself to himself and was never seen conversing with anyone.

r) The boarding Officers were specialists, being Merchant Marine Officers, some of them with knowledge of the African coast and trade.

s) The prisoners asserted that the Admiral Graf Spee was magnificently equipped for many emergencies, and the following is a small - indication:

1) The crew were very considerably 'double- banked' being said to number 1,200.

2) She had a special supply of bombs for sinking merchant ships; they were bottle-shaped and kept, in a rack.

3) She is reported to have had an especially fine condensing system.

4) A peculiar fact is the rangefinder on the top of the superstructure, which was continually in use at sea and kept revolving all the time by motor.

t) Since starting to draft this letter, the news has been received of the suicide of Captain Langsdorff. I attribute his preferring to shoot himself after the event rather than being blown up with his ship to his principle that it was his duty to be with his ship's company until every possible provision had been made for them in the Argentine. This fits in with all the Merchant Captains tell me of him. He was obviously a man of very high character and he was proud of the fact that he had not been the cause of a single death as the result of any of his various captures.

25. All the above information has necessarily been gleaned in a very short space of time with a multitude of other affairs of immediate importance requiring attention. I recommend that more prolonged questioning of the British prisoners on their arrival in England will be well repaid.

26. I have not included in this despatch any account of the events subsequent upon the embarkation of the crew of the Admiral Graf Spee into the tugs and lighters, as I have only just arrived back in Buenos Aires and there are still a good many tangles to be unravelled before this part of the story is clear.

27. It was the greatest pity that for political reasons, Rear-Admiral Harwood's request for Ajax to visit Montevideo and Achilles to come to Buenos Aires could not be granted. The reason that the last-named could not come here was plain in view of the fact that the German crew had just landed and their disposal had not yet been decided upon. It would therefore, have been most unpolitic to have given the impression that we were backing our claims by a display of force. As His Majesty's Ambassador has reported to the Foreign Office, his action, in not even requesting the Minister for Foreign Affairs that she should enter harbour, has been fully justified in the subsequent attitude

of that Minister. On the other hand, if Ajax had been able to proceed into Montevideo and anchor in the same berth, so recently occupied by the Admiral Graf Spee, with her damage visible to all the populace, she would have had an amazing reception. It was fear that such a demonstration would get completely out of hand that probably led Dr. Guani, Minister for Foreign Affairs, to request she should not enter Montevideo for at least ten days, nor Punta del Este for two or three days -fear, that the Uruguayan Authorities could not control the crowds and possibly that the populace would make demands in allied favour that would embarrass the Government in its line-up with Pan-American solidarity.

28. It is interesting to note that whereas before the action, it would, probably be no exaggeration to say that over 99% of the Uruguayan population was strongly pro-ally, after the ceremonial funeral of the Admiral Graf Spee's dead, sympathy and compassion swung round to such an extent that opinion was almost equally divided. This sympathy was entirely dispelled when the German warship steamed out to her self-destruction, and more especially when the people learned that the Captain had not gone up with his ship. Many influential and knowledgeable people in Uruguay affirm that popular opinion is such that they might demand their Government to give us the benevolence of their neutrality; and if Ajax with Rear-Admiral Harwood, flying his Flag, had been able to enter harbour immediately after the action, the Government might have had to give way to popular feeling to maintain their position.

29. As it is, both Argentines and Uruguayans probably do not fall far behind the British Colonies in their regret that they have not been able to give an immediate welcome to our victorious squadron. Under these circumstances, I gave an interview to the local press, of which the following is the substance:

Captain H. W. U. McCall, Royal Navy, Naval Attaché at the British Embassy, Buenos Aires, in response to an invitation from La Nacion to give his views regarding the recent Naval action off the mouth of the River Plate, expressed, his regrets that, until the official account of the engagement is published, he could give no details, as his knowledge of what occurred was still only fragmentary.

The readers of La Nacion would already know, he said of the vast superiority in weight of fire of the Admiral Graf Spee over all the three opposing Cruisers put together, and that general surprise had been caused by the fact that an armoured ship of the power of the Admiral Graf Spee could be put to flight by three unarmoured Cruisers.

Nevertheless, it would be a mistake to reach the conclusion that the accuracy of fire of the German ship was poor; on the contrary, when the Admiral Graf Spee opened fire at a range of twenty-one kilometres, her very first salvo burst only three hundred metres from her target, and it could only have been by consummate skill that the Captains of the British Cruisers avoided being destroyed. This made it all the more wonderful that the British ships were able to close in to such a range that their smaller guns had the effect they did.

It is a great pity, added Captain McCall, that the people of the Argentine Republic have not been able to have an immediate opportunity of hearing a first-hand account from the British side of the action, but it is, of course, common knowledge that none of the British ships engaged in the action have yet put into any harbour on the Argentine or Uruguayan Coast, in spite of the damage they must have received, in fact, HM Ships are continuing at sea on their ceaseless but recently interrupted patrol, guarding the trade routes to South America.

30. Recommendations

I) That Masters of the ships who were prisoners on board should be interviewed on their arrival in England with the object of possible recognition of the services of themselves and their W/T Operators and to obtain further details concerning Altmark and Graf Spee.

2) That the Admiralty should reimburse Mr. Millington-Drake for the cost of the wireless reception set in Montevideo.

3) That consideration be given to some procedure whereby Allied men-of-war can make themselves known on their near approach to merchant vessels.

Otto Langmann, German Ambassador to Uruguay 1937 – 1942
(https://en.wikipedia.org/wiki/Otto_Langmann)

Alfredo Baldomir Ferrari, Uruguayan President 1938 - 1943
(https://upload.wikimedia.org/wikipedia/commons/c/c6/AlfredoBaldomir.jpg)

Juan José de Amézaga, Uruguayan President from 1943 to 1947
(http://mareometro.blogspot.com/2018/04/un-indiano-portugalujo-en-uruguay-juan.html)

Dr Alberto Guani, Uruguayan Minister for Foreign Affairs March 1938 -1943, then Vice President.
(https://www.biografiasyvidas.com/biografia/g/guani.htm)

Appendix IV of McCall's report was the German account of the Battle of the River Plate.

GERMAN OFFICIAL PRESS COMMUNIQUE on the BATTLE, as published in "LA PRENSA" 27th DECEMBER, 1939.

1. The GRAF SPEE was steering towards these coasts, not in order to make war on commerce, but to re-fuel, since her arrangements for supply by merchant ships recently had failed owing to the British persecution. Her intention was to enter Montevideo, Buenos Aires or Mar del Plata, and her meeting with the English Cruisers was entirely accidental.

2. She had no intentions as regards the FORMOSE (French s.s.) On the day of the fight she was on a course of 240° (W.S.W.) when she saw due West, that is between her and the coast, the three British cruisers in line ahead, led by EXETER.

3. She immediately engaged the most powerful, which was the EXETER, on a course practically parallel, and opened fire on her with both turrets. This was the principal action of the day. The distance apart was never less than nineteen thousand metres. EXETER manoeuvred skilfully, describing continuous zig-zags which made firing difficult, but nevertheless EXETER received many impacts which almost entirely put her out of action and which reduced her speed. The SPEE, for her part, received two impacts of 20 cms. (8") which destroyed her galley, bakery, forepeak etc., but which did not reduce her fighting capacity. Contrary to what has been stated, the fire control was not seriously damaged, in spite of a shot which had passed through the fire control tower; on the other hand, the destruction of the galley and bakery in a ship carrying a crew of one thousand is a serious injury from the practical point of view. The other two Cruisers, meanwhile, immediately manoeuvred to surround the SPEE, approaching her on either hand to within a minimum distance of eight thousand metres. At certain times this action obliged the SPEE to train her turrets off the EXETER in order to fire on one or the other cruiser, which, as is obvious, reduces greatly the efficacy of fire of the principal armament which is obliged to change its target frequently. Moreover, SPEE had to make violent changes of course to avoid may torpedoes. The British Cruisers, like the EXETER, were zig-zagging at high speed, thus throwing off the German fire; these tactics favoured the British ships

owing to their guns being of less calibre and consequently firing quicker (four or five salvoes a second).
4. The use of aircraft was confined to bombardment (of the SPEE) by one single British seaplane; the SPEE did not use her aeroplane.
5. The rest of the day, that is to say, all the afternoon, there were only sporadic exchanges of shots with AJAX and ACHILLES, who always manoeuvred at great range on either side of the Spee. It is not true that they closed to within a mile; nor that they made smoke screens. The smoke which was seen from Punta del Este was due to the British Cruisers.
6. SPEE continued without serious difficulty her course for Montevideo in search of supplies; to the need of these there was now added the lack of ammunition on account of the prolonged firing and the urgency or repairing the kitchen and bakery, not to mention defects of lesser importance.
7. The lack of ammunition was the reason why the GRAF SPEE could not leave Montevideo to renew the fight. According to the Authorities of the ship, the insufficiency of the period granted for the repairs of the ship implied, equally, the placing of the ship out of action. (Ibid.)

A second report was published in the *Madera Tribune* two days later.

NAZI WARSHIP FACES DEADLINE
GRAF SPEE COMMANDER IS ON SPOT
British Squadrons Await Decision of German Ship Master
FRENCH WILL ASSIST
Battleship Barham Is Said to Be Near Uruguayan Capital's Port

MONTEVIDEO, Uruguay. Dec. 16.—Nine hundred men aboard German pocket battleship Admiral Graf Spee faced today the alternatives of a suicide dash to set into the guns of an allied fleet or the interment of their proud ship for the duration of the European war. Sunday night —3 p. m. (EST) according to authoritative reports—was the deadline. It was reported that the British cruiser squadrons which had kept the death watch on the Graf Spee, steaming back and forth just outside Uruguayan territorial waters, had now become an allied fleet. It was reported though not confirmed that the French battleship Dunkerque, faster, larger, more powerful in every way that the Graf Spee, had arrived and was "standing by."

AIRCRAFT CARRIER

The British battleship Barham was reported in the vicinity. British reports indicated that the battle cruiser Reknown and the aircraft carrier Ark Royal—with 60 fighting planes aboard—were steaming at forced draft to be in at the kill if the Graf Spee made its dash. According to all reports, Britain or Britain and France combined now had off the mouth of the River Plate a fleet which should blow the Graf Spee to bits if it made the desperate choice of trying to break for safety. The Uruguayan government had made its decision yesterday, at a cabinet meeting, that the Graf Spee must go.

PLANS ARE RUMORED

High German and Italian diplomatic and naval officials conferred here today on what was persistently rumored as a plan for the German battleship to attempt to dash to sea while German reinforcements engaged British forces laying in wait for her. While the officials met at the German legation to draft plans for the Graf Spee, which is under orders to leave Montevideo before 8 p. m. Sunday night (6 p. m. EST) or be interned for the duration of the war, the United Press was informed reliably but unofficially that the commander of the refugee ship has been assured that aid is on the way to him. Reports, while not officially confirmed, indicated that the Graf Spee would not submit to internment and that it would make a run for the high seas, possibly under the screen of a naval battle between German and allied men o'war off the river Plate estuary.

SECRETLY DRAFTED

While British Minister Eugen Millington-Drake conferred with Uruguayan Foreign Minister Alberto Guani plans for the Graf Spee were drafted secretly at the German legation. It was not clear here as to where Germanys expected to obtain reinforcements in event they decide to run the British blockade off Montevideo. But it was pointed out that German submarines have been at sea since the start of the war and that the British admiralty had admitted that the pocket battleships Admiral Scheer and Deutschland, sister ships of the Graf Spee, are ranging the seas. In addition to reports of an impending naval battle to aid the Graf Spee to escape it also was reported here that Germany would attempt to transfer ownership of the Graf Spee to Italy. That report, too, was without confirmation although it was pointed out that Ballardi Ricci, Italian minister to Uruguay, participated in the conference at the German legation.

MORE REINFORCEMENTS

Three British destroyers., the Hardy. Hero and Hostile, arrived at Recife, Brazil, today and then steamed southward in the direction of Uruguay after a brief stay. The British battle cruiser Renown, 32,000 tons and aimed with six 15-inch guns, has requested permission to enter Rio De Janeiro harbor, it was announced officially today. Earlier reports that the British cruiser Achilles also had asked to enter Rio De Janeiro were described as erroneous. The Chilean government today granted the British embassy's request that the German merchant ship Dusseldorff, 4930 tons, captured by British warships off the Chilean coast yesterday, be allowed to put into a Chilean port as a prize of war.

TWO HOUR INSPECTION

It was understood that a 72 hour period for the Graf Spee departure dated from the hour, 2 p.m. (EST) Thursday, that an official Uruguayan naval commission, after a two-hour inspection of the Graf, reported to the government on its seaworthiness. The government communicated its decision to the German legation, and it was understood also to the British legation, yesterday afternoon. Britain had protested against the shelter given the Graf Spee, asserting that it was not unseaworthy in any sense and hence that it should have been ordered to go within 24 hours of its arrival at 11:55 p. m. Wednesday. The Germans had said that the ship's kitchen had been wrecked, it was understood, and that there was other damage rendering the ship unseaworthy.

INADEQUATE KITCHEN

British Minister Eugen Millington-Drake was reported to have said that though the lack of an adequate kitchen might make things inconvenient for the Germans, it did not make the Graf unseaworthy. Information had been received by the United Press that the Graf's 11-inch gun control tower had been wrecked during the battle with the British Exeter, Ajax and Achilles. The Graf Spee would not be entitled to have this control tower repaired. There was an atmosphere of increasing tension here as the hours ticked off toward the Graf Spee deadline. The German ship had landed eight gravely wounded in addition to its 36 dead; it was believed to have roughly 900 men left, possibly more.

NOT LOADING FUEL

It had been reported abroad that the Graf was taking aboard fuel. This was as she was lying alone at anchor, 60 yards from a Uruguayan official tug, the nearest craft to her. Navy men, noting that she lay low in the water, expressed belief that she had plenty of fuel aboard already. Without any basis, belief grew among the people of Montevideo that the Graf would make a run for it, despite the apparently hopeless odds against her. The cruisers Ajax and Achilles, which with the damaged Exeter drove the Graf Spee into port; the 10,000 ton, eight-inch gun, 31.5 knot cruiser Cumberland and the battleship Barham, 31,100 tons with eight 15-inch guns were believed already in the British watch.

FOUR ALTERNATIVES

There was believed to be a strong possibility that the battle cruiser Renown, 32,000 tons, with six 15-inch guns and 29 knots speed, and the aircraft carrier Ark Royal with its 60 planes, were here or hereabouts. There were four things for the Graf Spee to do if it elected to run into what was regarded generally as a death trap. There is a narrow five-mile channel, buoyed and flanked by sandbanks, between Montevideo and open water.

The Graf Spee could: 1— Turn right at it entered open water and seek to make a dash across a 17-mile expanse of estuary, a sort of no man's land, to a narrow 100-mile channel leading to Buenos Aires and a new shelter. 2 Leave as it entered, by turning left and hugging the Uruguay Atlantic coast. 3 Turn partly right and seek to gain the shelter of the Argentine coast, hoping afterward to get to the sea. 4 Make the break directly for sea. The belief was strong that if the Graf did try to make a break it would select the last course. Lieutenant Edgar Grigat, 25, of the Graf Spee, was directing his men during the battle of Montevideo when a shell struck and severed both his legs, it was reported today. His men tried to take him to the ship's infirmary. He knew he was dying and refused to go, ordering the men to tend others first. As he lay on the deck, he had his men tell him how the fight was going. They kept up the story until he died. (Madera *Tribune,* Vol. LXXV, No. 38, 16 December 1939)

According to British reports, the Graf Spee was hit more than 30 times by shells fired from Royal Navy vessels, rendering it practically unable to function. 37 German sailors were killed in the confrontation and Captain Langsdorff was wounded, along with 57 other of the Graf Spee's men.

The Hyperwar website reported that on 17 December, 'German armored ship Admiral Graf Spee, her allotted time in neutral Uruguayan waters for repair of damage received in the Battle of the River Plate having expired, and her crew transferred to freighter *Tacoma,* puts to sea from Montevideo, Uruguay, and is scuttled about five miles west-southwest of the entrance of Montevideo harbor, 35°11'S, 56°26'W. The destruction of *Admiral Graf Spee* comes, as First Lord of the Admiralty Winston S. Churchill later declares "like a flash of light and colour on the scene, carrying with it an encouragement to all who are fighting, to ourselves, and to our Allies" (see 30 December 1939 and 1 January 1940). *Admiral Graf Spee* had sunk nine British merchantmen during her cruise, totalling

50,089 tons of shipping. Not a single life had been lost in the process.'
https://www.ibiblio.org/hyperwar/USN/USN-Chron/USN-Chron-1939.html

Having been informed that the *Graf Spee* had sought refuge in Montevideo, Anthony Eden, the British Secretary of State for Dominion (Commonwealth) Affairs, sent the following telegram to Sir Esmond Ovey, the British Ambassador in Argentina, a position he had held since 1937.

> It is possible that GRAF SPEE, after leaving Uruguayan waters, may seek further refuge in Argentine waters. If this happens, you should press for her internment unless she leaves within twenty-four hours. Should the Argentine Government refuse to intern, you should be guided by the wishes of Commodore Commanding, South America Division, as regards decision whether or not to press for a short time limit on her stay in Argentine waters.
>
> Particular vigilance should be exercised to ensure that she does not embark ammunition, or in any other way increase her fighting strength. We suspect that German merchantmen, lying in Plate, may be carrying armament supplies and may attempt to tranship them to GRAF SPEE under the guise of innocent stores.
>
> In any case, there would be no excuse for her being allowed to effect further repairs is she can make passage from Montevideo to Argentine waters, unless she has sustained additional damage on the way affecting her seaworthiness. (TNA ADM 1/10803, 17 December 1939)

A search for Graf Spee on the Axis History Forum revealed a post by Tigre who included an extract from the diary of one of the German Artillery Officers, Frederick Rasenack, who recognised the gravity of the situation in his entry for 17 December.

> "I woke up around 04:50 AM and received the order to destroy the artillery system. I went to the commander to confirm the order. He had just arrived, and neither could fix anything in this endeavor. He looked very overworked and bleary-eyed. In low voice he confirmed this crucial order."
>
> With charges of hand grenades and hammers began the work of destruction inside the ship. The most precious central chronometers were saved - may still be necessary. During the evening meeting at the embassy it was discussed the situation of the crew. Under all circumstances should avoid being interned in Uruguay. For a transfer to Argentina they were considered the German freighter "Tacoma" and "Lahn" present in Montevideo.

The "Tacoma" was ordered to be ready to sail on 17 December and follow the warship. However, since large freighters, due to their draft, cannot run the direct route from Montevideo to Buenos Aires an alternative was envisaged and with the help of the naval attache, the Inspector of Hamburg-Süd in Buenos Aires, Captain Rudolf Hepe was commissioned to get three barges and make them sail for Montevideo on the night of December 17. Soon after, over the phone, encrypted confirmation came from Buenos Aires: "Everything in order .... provided two tugs and one light." This logistical support, which works to the last minute, remained hidden in almost all the stories about the end the Graf Spee. The essential action was to evacuate the entire crew to a German-friendly Argentina, where the sailors could have a benevolent regime of internment.

On the evening of December 17 the ship was scuttled by its own crew, which was totally rescued. In focus remained the borderline situation of a naval officer who breaking with tradition, followed his conscience and saved the lives of 1103 men. This was clearly reflected in the diary of the NCO (Maschinen-Obermaaten) Hans Götz that quoted the commander on December 17: "I will not let go out to the sea together to fight against a superior enemy force. I will prefer rather 1000 young alive than 1000 dead heroes."
(Führungsentscheidung in einer Grenzsituation:Kapitän zur See Hans Langsdorff vor und in Montevideo 1939.Vortrag für Klaus-Jürgen Müller zum 80 Geburtstag in der Helmut-Schmidt-Universität am 11. März 2010; https://forum.axishistory.com/viewtopic.php?f= 61&t=869&p=1965704&hilit=Tacoma #p1965704)

The British Foreign Office, Whitehall, London, S.W.1
(https://memoirsofametrogirl.files.wordpress.com/2021/01/fco-durbar-court-f.jpg?w=604)

The following day, 18 December, the *Boston Globe* reported,

    MONTEVIDEO, Dec.17 (AP) The german legation tonight made public Capt. Hans Langsdorff's protest over the time limit granted raider Admiral Graf Spee to stay in port to make herself seaworthy. Addressed to the German Minister to Montevideo, Otton Langmann, and dated abord the Graf Spee today, it read: "Mr. Minister, Before lifting anchor, I would not wish to leave unsaid through you my deepest gratitude for the innumerable demonstrations of sympathy and the chivalrous sentiment of the Uruguayan people towards my valiant dead and wounded.
    I shall never forget this sentiment of the Uruguayan people. In the same way, I should not like to omit, especially in regard to the

grave situation which now presents itself, an expression of my deepest gratitude to the Uruguayan authorities both for their swift measures of assistance upon the unexpected arrival and the very efficacious first aid dispensed to my injured and honours to my dead." (*Boson Globe*, Monday 18 December 1839)

On the same day, an unsigned note from the British Foreign Office to the British Embassy in Buenos Aires stated,

> The mere fact that provision is made for freedom of movement within the neutral jurisdiction upon the giving of parole [freedom for prisoners with certain conditions, like a promise not to leave the country], clearly implies that where parole is not or cannot be given, the officer or men must be confined within a strictly limited area such as a camp.
> As regards our own wounded, we had naturally expected that Argentina, in view of her clear obligations, would intern them. But even supposing she were entitled to drive a bargain with use on this question, the disparity of numbers involved on either side is so great that H.M.G. [His Majesty's Government] could not contemplate acceptance of such an arrangement.
> We attach the greatest importance to the adequate supervision of these men, and you should leave the Argentine Government in no doubt as to our feelings on this subject. They may have given evidence of their benevolence towards us in other directions, but we for our part have treated them handsomely in the matter of war time purchases, and you may, if it would help, make all possible use of this fact. [...] (TNA ADM 116/4180, 18 December 1939)

Ovey responded by sending telegram 332 the same day. Copies were sent to Montevideo, the Commander-in-Chief South Atlantic and the Rear Admiral South American Division.

> Having learnt that the majority of officers and crew of the Graf Spee had before the ship was scuttled been transferred to German oiler Tacoma and to Argentine tug and lighter (see my telegram No.350) sent for this purpose from Buenos Aires by Hamburg-American agents here, Assistant Naval Attache requested the police and Ministry of Marine about midnight yesterday to prevent their clandestine landing of which he had heard rumours to avoid internment.

This morning Counsellor enquired on my instructions as to the views of the Argentine Government regarding internment of these men.

Under Secretary of State for Foreign Affairs indicated that under Argentine law implementing article 10 The Hague Convention 1899 (on which Argentine Government are basing their action since they have never actually ratified the 1907 Convention) they were clearly due for internment by Argentine Government law; that local officials concerned had received their orders; and that instructions had been given to tugs regarding the port they were to make for. He also enquired as to the whereabouts of the Captain of the Graf Spee.

I learn that the tugs and barge crowded with German sailors are now lying in the ante-port at Buenos Aires. (Ibid.)

The Foreign Office's response, also sent to Montevideo on 18 December, stated,

My telegram 220 [of December 17th GRAF V. SPEE].

According to our information ships company of GRAF SPEE who have been removed to Tacoma at Montevideo have now been transferred to lighter and tugs belonging to Argentine shipping firm Delfino with object of effecting clandestine landing in Argentina.

If they arrive in Argentina you should represent strongly that crew should be interned. It is clear that Uruguayan Government would have been bound to intern them if they had been landed at Montevideo, and the action taken is an obvious desire for escaping internment by landing in another neutral country. The transfer to a German ship and thence to tugs owned by a pro-German firm (if Delfino is such) is obvious all one transaction organised by the German authorities, and the position is really the same as if the crew had been landed in the Argentine direct from the VON SPEE. Incidentally the employment of the lighter and tugs for the purpose of conveying the crew constituted unneutral service and British forces would be justified in capturing the vessels with a view to condemnation in the Prize Court. [Naval court that adjudicates the legality of ships and their goods captured in warfare.]

As the transfer from the VON SPEE took place at Montevideo before her departure and as she sank herself the crew cannot be regarded as in the position of shipwrecked crew picked up by neutral vessels after an engagement.

The crew are an organised body of combatants and if they are not interned are liable to be employed on German raiders, which may well be the object of their removal to Argentina.

Finally, it is possible in the circumstances to draw distinction between the position of this crew and the wounded landed from EXETER, and a deplorable impression would be created of the Argentine Government, who will]presumably intern in the latter case, were to fail to do so in the former. (Ibid, 18 December 1939)

The Barrier Miner, an Australian newspaper, reported the same day on the *Graf Spee* incident.

GRAF SPEE CREW TO BE INTERNED
SCUTTLED RAIDER'S MEN AT BUENOS AIRES
(Special to "The Miner")
NEW YORK, December 18.
WHEN part of the crew of the scuttled German raider Graf Spee, arrived at Buenos Aires in tug boats and barges today, maritime police surrounded the vessels and isolated the men. A high Argentine official said later that the men would be interned, says the American Press Association correspondent.

The arrivals included the raider's (commander Captain Hans Langsdorff). One message says that 600 of the crew arrived at Buenos Aires, but a member of the German Legation announced that the arrivals numbered 1000, including those from the German liner Tacoma.

The *Graf Spee* scuttled off the coast of Montevideo in December 1939 whose crew were interned in Argentina and Uruguay until 1946 (https://en.wikipedia.org/wiki/File:Graf_Spee_scuttled.png)

Australian newspaper cutting of *Graf Spee* (Courtesy of Anne and Robert Owen https://www.maritimequest.com/warship_directory/germany/pages/cruisers/admiral_graf_spee_australian_cuttings.htm)

German ship 'Tacoma' whose crew were interned in Montevideo between 1939 and 1946
(https://www.shipsnostalgia.com/media/tacoma.114689/)

The German press proclaims that Graf Spee's end will mark the beginning of new blows against England and the "blackmailer" Churchill. "He has done a dis-service to England by putting pressure on Uruguay to send out Graf Spee before she was navigable," say the newspapers. "Uruguay's action was an unfriendly one. She crassly broke international law under intimidation from Britain."

HITLER'S ORDERS

Hitler ordered that the pocket battleship, which cost £3,750,000, be scuttled, only after many hours ' of argument with his naval chief and technical experts, reports Reuter's Amsterdam correspondent.

Experts insisted that Graf Spee must not fall into British hands because the pocket battleship had an unusually high proportion of specially designed instruments and apparatus and a number of new secrets added only this summer.

A Berlin broadcast announces that Germany has handed to Uruguay a sharp protest against what is termed "a flagrant breach of international law" in falling to allow Graf Spee adequate time for repairs.

A Paris message says that highly placed officials declare that Germany knows she will lose the war, otherwise she would have allowed the Graf Spee to be interned, claiming her after the war. The slight damage which the raider inflicted and her inglorious end absolutely endorse the Anglo-French decision not to build similar vessels.

Another article the same day was headed,

COMMANDER IS SATISFIED
(Special to "The Miner")
NEW YORK, December 18.

Twenty hours after the German raider Graf Spee had been scuttled the torn und twisted wreckage was still burning today and occasionally explosions were heard, says a message from Montevideo.

Meanwhile, the weary officers and crew who left Uruguay after the vessel was sunk, have arrived at Buenos Aires, it is reported from the Argentine capital.

Questioned by the United Press correspondent, Captain Langsdorff, commander of 'the pocket battleship,' said: "I am satisfied I saved all my men."

Asked for a statement he said. "I have nothing else to say, old man. I have not rested since 8 o'clock last night, please, be nice and lay off."

Captain Langsdorff plainly showed signs of his ordeal. The crew, mostly youngsters of 18 to 21, were unshaven and were in soiled uniforms. They too, showed signs of fatigue. (*The Barrier Miner*

(Broken Hill), New South Wales, Tuesday 19 December 1939, p.3)

The Madera reported a similar story.

SPEE'S CREW NOT WORRIED OVER FUTURE
They Enjoy Meals Leaving Worries of World War to Countrymen
CAPTAIN IS PLEASED
Nazi Government Hoping Argentina Government to Free Men
BUENOS AIRES, Argentina, Dec. 19. Officers and men of the scuttled German pocket battleship Admiral Graf Spee ate heartily today, and seemed unworried about the war, as the Foreign Office made plans to intern them. Captain Hans Langsdorff, the Graf Spee's commander, had brought 1038 officers and men with him across the river Plate estuary from Montevideo where he had blown up his ship rather than face the British cruiser death watch which awaited it.
CAPTAIN SATISFIED
"I am satisfied I have saved all my men," was all he would say after his arrival here. Berlin dispatches had made it plain that the German government hoped that the Graf Spee men would be treated as "shipwrecked" mariners and released, to get home if they could. The Foreign Office made it plain, however, that the government intended to intern them all, probably on the small island of Martin Garcia, out in the river. The island is used for detention of Argentine political prisoners. Officers of the Graf Spee may be allowed to take up residence in Buenos Aires if they pledge themselves not to try to escape.
COMBINED FRONT
It was disclosed, regarding German protests against the refusal of Uruguay to give further shelter to the Graf Spee, that it was a combined front of 11 American republics, including the United States, which had forced the ship to go. German authorities, backed by Italian ones, had refused to order the ship to leave Montevideo. Uruguay consulted envoys of other American republics. The result was the firm statement that if she did not leave Montevideo Sunday night she would be interned for the duration of the war. It had been reported that 350 men of the Graf Spee were taken back to Montevideo in the German supply ship Tacoma, to be interned there. This proved incorrect.
FOUR ARRESTED
Apparently only four of the Graf Spee men stayed with the Tacoma and they were arrested yesterday and taken ashore at Montevideo on the accusation that they were implicated in blowing up the Admiral Graf Spee. The Uruguayan viewpoint

seemed to be that though the' Admiral Graf Spee was blown up just outside territorial waters, a launch from which the charge was detonated was just inside. Reports had circulated at Montevideo that the Admiral Graf Spee's crew had threatened to mutiny when the decision was made to scuttle the ship. But there was not the slightest sign of dissension or disaffection among the crew here. Then men, all youthful, were in good spirits though they were unkempt after a voyage across the estuary in tugs, a barge and a launch.

REJECT PROTEST

Foreign Office sources indicated that the government was prepared to reject any German protest against internment of the Admiral Graf Spee's men. It was held that the arrival of the Germans in ships for which they had evidently contracted eliminated I any possibility that they should I be considered "shipwrecked mariners" and not be interned under the Hague conventions. Crowds of friendly, sympathetic Argentinians gathered before the temporary internment bases to cheer and talk to the German seamen. The crowd became so great at one time last night that police had to close the street in front of the immigrant hostel. The Germans waded into the generous meals provided them, big bowls of soup, dishes of Argentine beef and fruits particularly. (*Madera Tribune*, Vol. LXXV, No. 40, 19 December 1939)

Cuartel Paso del Rey in Sarandi del Yi, Durazno, Uruguay, where the crew of the Tacoma were interned.
(http://www.uruguaydocumental.com)

The Germans on board the *Tacoma* were transferred to the Cuartel Paso del Rey (Barracks Quarter of the Passage of the King) in Sarandi del Yi, Durazno, where they were guarded by the Military District II infantry. (https://forum.axishistory.com/viewtopic.php?f=13&t=242942)

It is worth noting that no mention was found in the Foreign Office or Admiralty papers examined that it was standard operating procedure for all captured members of the British Armed forces to attempt escape. This order ensured that the Axis forces had to employ men, time and money not only in imprisoning Allied personnel and putting in place measures to prevent escapes but also in investigating, locating, arresting, interrogating and then re-imprisoning those that did. Those who managed to escape and return to Britain would have returned to their unit after a brief period of leave to continue the fight against the enemy. One has to imagine that it was standard operating procedure for all captured German officers and crew to escape. It is also important to note that Millington-Drake reported that German Naval Command forbade its officers from promising parole if captured. He also reported that Admiral Wilhelm Canaris, the head of the Abwehr, Germany's military intelligence organisation, issued instructions ordering the Graf Spee officers to escape using different routes to return to Germany and rejoin the Kriegsmarine. (Millington-Drake, op.cit. pp. 390,472)

Hans Langsdorff, Captain of Graf Spee (Millington-Drake, op.cit.)

Captain Hans Langsdorff and First Officer Kapitan zue See Walter Kay, later internment officer of Graf Spee internees (Das Panzerschiff ADMIRAL GRAF SPEE Verlag Ferdinand Schöningh, 2020 | doi:10.30965/9783657702626_011)

The American *Calexico Chronicle* reported the same day.
Awaiting Internment, Graf Spee Crew Grins
BUENOS AIRES. Dec. 19. (U.R)—Nearly 1000 officers and men of the scuttled German pocket battleship Admiral Graf Spee ate heartily today, and seemed unworried about the war as the foreign office made plans to intern them.
It was believed the crew members would be lodged until the end of the European war on the small island of Martin Garcia in the river Plate. The officers were expected to be allowed to live in Buenos Aires on their word not to attempt to escape. The foreign office indicated it would not allow any renewal of the diplomatic struggle between Great Britain and Germany over status of the Graf Spee and its crew. The fact Capt. Hans Langsdorff, his officers and crew were brought here aboard two Argentine tugs, a barge and a launch, the first three vessels evidently contracted for the trip by German diplomats here, preclude any argument

that the men are not liable to internment under The Hague convention, the foreign office said.

7000 Cheer Germans . . . The men arrived here after a 20-hour trip from the mouth of the river Plate, where the Graf Spee was blown up and sunk at dusk Sunday. Two hundred and fifty, including Capt. Langsdorff, were lodged temporarily at the naval arsenal. Visibly weary, Capt. Langsdorff personally supervised the landing of the crew members, barking orders as 7000 persons who jammed the small dock space loudly cheered the German sailors. (*Calexico Chronicle*, Vol. XXXVI, No. 90, 19 December 1939)

Ovey sent Eden telegram 355 with a copy to Millington-Drake on 19 December.

My telegram No. 352.

Having ascertained from my French colleague, who made enquiries adumbrated [outlined] in penultimate paragraph of my telegram No. 353, that good intentions of Argentine Government regarding internment did not go beyond leaving officers at liberty on parole and 1,000 off men "under police surveillance" and that a decree to this effect would be published within 48 hours, I immediately interviewed Under-Secretary of State for Foreign Affairs and subsequently telephones to the Minister of Foreign Affairs by arrangement in the sense of instructions contained in your telegram No. 221 most immediate. Ambassador had been given as excuse "material difficult of guarding and feeding 1,000 men for whole war."

Having first ascertained that intentions of Argentine Government were as reported by my French colleague (who has immediately sent a strong telegram to his Government about obviously insufficient measures proposed) I used all the eloquence at my command in the sense of your instructions, finally reading your telegram in full. I also pointed out the deplorable effect, which would be produced if, just as we had cleared the South Atlantic of one warship sent out to raid vital Argentine commerce, [grp. undec.] here of 1,000 trained German sailors acted as a reserve for manning raiders. I added that there had been a precedent in the case of Cap Trafalgar in 1914, whose crew were interned on an island in the River Plate. I pointed out as you had said that the whole thing was probably a German plot designed for the purpose of providing above crews with this opportunity; deplorable complications might result when these men were drafted as surely would be on such German raiders.

All I could get from His Excellency was an assurance that every precaution would be taken to prevent such a state of affairs. I told him privately of my refusal to approve of the visit of H.M.S. Achilles to Buenos Aires immediately after victory, in order to permit the Argentine Government to act, as I felt confident they would do, without any semblance of pressure from us. All I could extract from the Minister for Foreign Affairs was that I could [grp.undec.] in the event of [grp.undec] every precaution would be taken to prevent what I feared.

Argument in last sentence of your telegram No. 221 was of no effect as Exeter's wounded would have been treated as Argentine Government proposed to treat Germans. I finally begged Minister for Foreign Affairs earnestly to avoid any hasty act such as publication of decree and although this caused some annoyance on the grounds of interference with the sovereign rights the interview ended on a note of friendly agreement [gr.omit] [coded letters missing] that I could certainly inform you that I had made this request but could not say that His Excellency had made any definite promise.

Whole argument of course turned on the interpretation of the word internment in your instructions which I took throughout to mean keeping men permanently under guard. In view of very obvious [gr.undec.] at a proposed [?time limit for] statement regarding organised body of combatants in the last sentence of penultimate paragraph of your telegram I insisted throughout on this interpretation assuring Minister for Foreign Affairs that of course if I were wrong you would tell me so. Please make your requirements on this point abundantly clear in any further instructions both as regards officers and men. (TNA ADM 116/4180, 19 December 1939)

The file contained what looked like Ovey's draft communication written the same day.

Your telegrams Nos. 352 and 355 of December 18th.

I approve your action. Article 10 of Hague Convention No.X of 1899, under which Argentine Government are acting, provides that the internees must be guarded by the neutral state so as to prevent them from again taking part in the operations of the war. While in principle it is for the neutral Government concerned to decide on the precise nature of the steps to be taken, those steps must clearly be sufficient to ensure the fulfilment of the above obligation, and in view of the size and organised nature of the body of men to be interned, the extent of Argentine territory and the obvious possibilities of the men getting on board German ships, raiders or submarines, it is plain that a very considerable amount of strict surveillance will be necessary. The Argentine Government cannot evade their responsibility on the ground of the material difficulty of guarding and feeding the men, since this is precisely what they are explicitly bound to do, (though they are entitled to recover the expense from Germany). I am surprised that a ? of Argentine strength ? should consider it ? her capacity effectively supervise 1000 internees. Switzerland, not possessing any internment camps, is keeping interned German airmen in prison, and while we do not suggest such unpleasant measures in this case, it seems clear that nothing short of internment in camps under adequate supervision would ensure the fulfilment of Argentine obligations.

As the corresponding Article of the Convention on neutrality in land warfare (Article 11 of Convention No. V) allows the neutral to leave officers at liberty on giving parole not to leave the neutral territory without permission, it would be difficult for us to object to this, but the officers might well be confined to certain specified areas remote from the seaboard from which escape would be difficult.

I may have given evidence of their benevolence towards us in other directions, but we for our part have treated them handsomely on the matter of wartime purchases and you may if it would help make all possible use of this fact. (Ibid.)

A couple of days late, Ovey sent telegram 355 to Eden and Millington-Drake.

My telegram No. 355. Internment question.

Minister for Foreign Affairs asked me last night what was my impression of the Argentine decree. I replied that I personally felt hopeful that it would in its execution provide us with satisfactory safeguards but I was awaiting your further instructions.

His Excellency then volunteered (see paragraph 4 of my above mentioned telegram) no less than three times that the ACHILLES could come here whenever she wanted.
Rear-Admiral Harwood has been informed of this. (Ibid, 21 December 1939)

The Japanese *New World Sun* reported the death of Captain Langsdorff on 22 December.

Admiral Graf Spee. Most of our elders praised the captain for committing suicide because it was the tradition that a Japanese naval officer would have followed. The only difference was that a hara kiri may have been more dramatic and required greater courage. There are those who claim that the captain would have created a greater sensation by going down with his ship. Later developments may show that Captain Langsdorff made a tactical error in running into Montevideo. According to the British accounts, the Exeter which had eight-inch guns was put out of action with about the fifth salvo from the Graf Spee. Such being the case, by fighting it out with the smaller crafts, Ajax and Achilles, the pocket battleship may have won out. No one will know for a long time on what basis of the action of the German ship was determined. No matter what may be said otherwise, Captain Langsdorff died a hero's death. The world admires him for fulfilling his duty and for living up to the code of his profession. To have lived after a defeat would have been an inglorious thing. Now all is forgotten, excepting the manner which he carried out his duties and obligations during the final moments. (*New World Sun*, 22 December 1939)

On the same day, 22 December, Millington-Drake sent Edward Wood, Viscount Halifax, the British Foreign Secretary, a collection of correspondence relating to an earlier diplomatic incident between Germany and Uruguay. Although they were not filed in chronological order, they shed light on the tense political situation at the end of 1939.

My Lord,
I have the honour to refer to my telegram No. 150 of December 18th, paragraphs 3, 4 and 5, regarding an allegedly strong Note of protest addressed by the German Minister to the Minister for Foreign Affairs against a spectacular anti-Nazi poster, and stating that both the Senate and the Camber had requested the Minister for Foreign Affairs for an explanation (the Chamber by an interpellation [when a government minister is asked a formal question in parliament] and the Senate by a call for papers. I added that the morning press had reported the receipt of an explanatory Note from the German Minister putting an unobjectionable interpretation on the words complained of.
2. I have the honour to transmit herewith translation of the text of the German Minister's original Note and of his explanatory Note as published in the press on the 12th instant.
3. The interpellation in question took place in a secret session on the 10th instant, when it appears that the Minister for Foreign Affairs took the line that any possible objection to the original Note had been removed by the German Minister's explanatory Note, and that he had not as yet replied to the German Minister, as he had not yet received a report from the Municipality who had authorised the publication of the poster.

4. The poster and leaflet in question were described in my Memorandum of December 9th for the Minister of Information, copy of which is enclosed for facility of reference.

5. To comment briefly on the significance of this incident in connection with the naval battle and the visit of the "ADMIRAL GRAF SPEE" which followed immediately, I would say that until the Minister for Foreign Affairs published the German Minister's explanatory Note it looked as if public opinion, already incensed by the invasion of Finland as an aggravation of the invasion of Poland, might regard this incident as the "last straw", though it certainly did not deserve the importance given to it, any more than did the photograph of the quite legitimate German community meeting with Nazi trappings with which the poster made such play. Thus, when the prudent Minister for Foreign Affairs had of his own accord informed the League of Nations that Uruguay could not remain in the League unless it expelled the Soviet Government (with which Uruguay had broken of diplomatic relations in December 1935), it looked as if public opinion would insist on breaking off relations with Germany. Then, just in time, the German Minister's apologetic explanation pricked the bubble. Since then the naval battle and the "ADMIRAL GRAF SPEE" incident have seemingly such reinforced the view of the Minister for Foreign Affairs and of the President of the Republic that Uruguay must strictly adhere to the forms of neutrality within the Pan-American fold.

6. It remains to be seen whether they can persuade public opinion which, while appreciative of Pan-American support in the affair of the "ADMIRAL GRAF SPEE", has for its part paid little attention to the possibly incidental violation of territorial waters and even less to that of the security zone, but is enthusiastic about the exploit of the British cruisers and regards it as a stout blow struck for democracy.

7. On the other hand, the Minister of Finance, who has so far been perhaps the coolest in the Cabinet towards Great Britain, has in apparent recognition of the probable effects of the naval victory, just put forward a proposal for a quota of £1,000,000 here in order to give the fullest scope to the operation of the Trade agreement against credits in current account by British banks or by His Majesty's Government. This would bring about the closest economic cooperation between the two Governments which I have long advocated as the best means of securing the substance of benevolent neutrality, even though we may not secure its outward forms (see my telegrams No. 186 and No, 187).

8. Further, it is worth recording that in the course of a very long and friendly conversation yesterday, the Minister for Foreign Affairs told me that while he had so far received patiently the German Minister's protests at the allegedly excessive popular expression of anti-Nazi feeling, he would if these protests continued simply refer the German Minister to the Uruguayan Constitution and other laws which ensure complete liberty of speech and thought. It is possible that he gave the Chamber of Deputies an assurance in this sense in the secret session on the subject, and the mere fact of his request for a secret session suggests the existence of a certain tension in relations with the German Government.

9. Lastly, the Minister for Foreign Affairs finally agreed in principle to the proposed visit of H.M.S. "AJAX" to Montevideo in the first days of January, whereas he had previously shown anxiety to postpone it as long as possible. It is likely, therefore, that popular opinion will have a remarkable opportunity to manifest itself, and that such manifestation may not be without effect on the President of the Republic, the Minister for Foreign Affairs and the Cabinet. That is the most that can be said at a moment when if the super tension of the four days stay of the "ADMIRAL GRAF SPEE" in Montevideo harbour snapped at the moment of her self-destruction, yet there remains a state of tension quite as high as that which prevailed as a result of the invasion of Finland and the German Minister's above-mentioned Note of protest against the excessive expression of anti-Nazi popular feeling – a Note which may yet prove to be a Zinovieff letter [Fake letter published by the British Daily Mail newspaper four days before the General Election of 1924 pretending to be instructions from the Head of the Soviet Communist Party to the Head of the British Communist Party encouraging anti-British activities] in Uruguay's internal politics of neutrality. (TNA ADM/116/4180, 22 December 1939)

TRANSLATION ("EL PLATA" – 12th December, 1939)
INCIDENT BETWEEN THE NAZI LEGATION AND THE URUGUAYAN MINISTRY OF FOREIGN AFFAIRS

Text of the two Notes exchanged.

For some days past certain Argentine and Uruguayan newspapers have been dealing with a Note presented by the German Legation to our Chancellery protesting in objectionable terms against certain anti-Nazi methods of propaganda which were considered by that Legation to be damaging to its Government and even to its country.

In view of the seriousness of the matter we did not wish to accept those versions and endeavoured to obtain concrete information form the Chancellery; owing to the Minister's absence from Montevideo we were, however, unable to obtain it. The authentic text of the Note in question has now been given, and reads as follows: -

First Note

German Legation, A 460/39
Montevideo, November 22nd 1939

Monsieur le Ministre,

    I have the honour to refer to my Note of November 18th, No. A 455/39, in which I furnished [provided] Your Excellency with information regarding certain posters that have appeared on the walls of this city. I am now in possession of some pamphlets, of which I venture to attach a copy, for your further information, which have been distributed in the streets of Montevideo and also sent through the post. These pamphlets bear the usual stamp of the competent National authorities. In this respect I take the liberty of calling your Excellency's attention to the fact that in spite of having been authorised by the corresponding authorities these pamphlets do not bear the printer's name, which, so I am given to understand, is contrary to the provisions of the National decrees or laws governing the distribution of pamphlets.

    The text of these pamphlets reasserts that there exists in Uruguay a secret German police, this is expressed in offensive and odious terms.

    I call your Excellency's attention to this principally because in this pamphlet, authorised, as it were by an official Uruguayan distributor, speaks of me, in my official capacity as representative of the great German Reich, in a disrespectful manner and accuses me personally, as also the German colony here, of pursuing base ends in the country. The pamphlet is offensive to all Germans, as well as to the Reich itself.

    As regards what is "suspected" in the pamphlet, I shall not go into greater detail in view of the absurdity of such an accusation.

    I find myself, Monsieur le Ministre, to call your attention to the fact that the authorisation granted to these pamphlets and their distribution by a Department of the State, not only violates the declared neutrality of the Government of the Oriental Republic of Uruguay, but that, apart from the obligations imposed by that neutrality, they will adversely affect the existing relations between Germany and Uruguay.

I am also under the necessity of reminding Your Excellency that on numerous occasions I drew your attention to the fact that owing to the unlimited attacks against the system of government in Germany, and against my government itself, the day will inevitably come when a situation will have arisen in which the Uruguayan Government may find itself deprived of the necessary liberty of action.

Your Excellency will no doubt remember that I have also expressed to his Excellency the President of the Republic quite recently my concern in this connexion.

I have always received, verbally, an answer that such commentaries by the masses should not be taken, in this country, as being fundamental and that for this reason there could not exist any fear of the good relations between our two countries being endangered.

Nevertheless, these attacks against Germany are continually increasing, both in the press as well as by radio, pamphlets, etc., in spite of the fact that the German Reich had a commercial treaty with Uruguay and has also maintained cultural relations of great benefit to both countries, and in spite, moreover, of the fact that neither the German Government nor the German people,, nor the German colony here have given any motive to the people of this Republic to protest – these attacks, as I say, continue and increase.

In view of this state of affairs and having regard to the declarations of neutrality made by the Uruguayan Government, I find myself under the necessity of asking your Excellency to safeguard the German colony in regard to its honour, its institutions, and the respect which I merits.

I also ask your Excellency to take, through the medium of the corresponding National authorities, the necessary measures and precautions to stop immediately attacks and offences against the German diplomatic representation in Uruguay.

In view of the unusual importance of these matters, I earnestly and respectfully beg Your Excellency to take the necessary steps in the matter of my protests with the urgency which the case requires and to inform me what measures have been adopted in this respect.

In the meantime, I have, etc.
(Signed) LANGMANN.

"*El Plata*" continues: -

At the same time, however, it has been officially announced that, in view of the press comments on the matter, the Reich Minister personally handed to the Minister for Foreign Affairs another communication, referred to in the following declaration to the Chancellery.

Second Note

In view of the comments which have been made regarding a communication from the German Legation to the Ministry of Foreign Affairs, we feel it necessary to state that yesterday morning the Minister, Herr Otto Langmann, paid a visit to Dr. Guani for the purpose of delivering a letter which states that "At no time did he proffer any threatening word regarding the propagation of anti-Nazi manifestations, of which complaint was made, and that he wishes to sate, as he does in writing, the actual scope of that Note. With respect to those manifestations, this letter adds that, in accordance with previous conversations held, with the utmost reciprocal cordiality, with the Minister of Foreign Affairs, the fear was expressed that the Government of the Republic might perhaps some day find its liberty of action restricted, in accordance with the terms of its Constitution, for the purpose of maintaining strict neutrality, owing to the excited feelings among the masses – although at the same time sincerely recognising the evident impartiality of the Foreign Minister – which had been provoked by foreign propaganda, even though this propaganda obviously came from interested parties".

The communication ends with this paragraph: - "From this it will be seen that, as far as my Government is concerned, no word was spoke, of any action in this respect, nor was any threat uttered, thus showing that there was never any doubt about this matter."

Brief commentary by "El Plata": -

The incongruous nature of this second Note is obvious. If the German Minister is afraid that our Government lacks the constitutional means to curb anti-Nazi propaganda, when this propaganda assumes extreme proportions, he should understand that they are less likely to have those means so long as he adopts such an attitude. The excessive officiousness of the Nazi diplomatist is also obvious when he presumes by such means to maintain the neutrality of Uruguay against hypothetical contingencies; but there is no doubt that his Note does remove the offensive interpretation, as far as our Government is concerned, arising from the confused sense of a paragraph in the first Note.

If such an intention existed, it has now been rectified.

There still exists, nevertheless, the abusive pretention of the Nazi Legation, with respect to propaganda which, by reason of liberty of though guaranteed by our Constitution, is being carried out in the country against the International Politics of Nazism which is against all reason and justice, but to which we do not doubt the Chancellery will give the proper answer.

In the Chamber of Deputies.

At yesterday's Session approval was given to a motion by Dr. Frugoni calling for the Minister for Foreign Affairs to appear before the Chamber for the purpose of informing it regarding the action taken by his Department.

At the same time, the Chamber voted a communication to the Minister calling for information regarding the proposed withdrawal of Uruguay from the League of Nations. (Ibid.)

His Majesty's Minister at Montevideo presents his compliments to the Minister of Information, and has the honour to present herewith the under-mentioned documents.

BRITISH LEGATION,
MONTEVIDEO.
8th December 1939

MEMORANDUM REGARDING PUBLICITY AND PROPAGANDA.

Some little sensation was caused in Montevideo about the 20th November by the issue of an anti-Nazi poster – the first of its kind here – issued by a <u>Comité de Lucha contra el Nazismo</u> and reproducing a photograph of a meeting of Nazis in Montevideo in a well-known beer restaurant known as the <u>"Palacio de la Cerveza"</u>, to welcome the German Minister on his return from leave. The hall is shown decorated with two large Nazi flags but alongside of two Uruguayan flags, and the Nazi salute is placed side by side with a photograph of a Nazi gathering from the film "Confessions of a Nazi Spy" (which was having great success in Montevideo shortly before) and incidentally quite outshines it in general effect and rigour. The fairly lengthy text of a leaflet counterpart of the poster alleges subversive Nazi activities in Uruguay, said to be directed by the "Agent of Hitler" with a view to Nazi domination of the country and generally sounds a note of alarm.

Some thousands of these posters were issued both in Montevideo and the provinces, as were also many thousands of leaflets with the same photographs and the above-mentioned explanatory texts. A specimen of the leaflet is enclosed with the air mail copy of this memorandum and a specimen of the poster with the bag copy. [The diplomatic bag by international agreement allowed embassy correspondence to pass unopened through customs.]

Just after their appearance His Majesty's Minister heard by chance that the German Minister wished to make "an urgent representation" to the Minister of Foreign Affairs, which presumably was on this subject, but no more was heard of the matter, and it appeared to have "blown over" until yesterday "La Tribuna Popular", a "yellow" [?] journal with a relatively small circulation, published prominently on the front page an article quoting what appeared to be the most important passage of the said Note, as translated below, and in spectacular language called upon the German Ambassador to give an explanation: -

"I fatally am obliged to remind Your Excellency that on numerous occasions I have called your attention to the fact that owing to the unlimited attacks against the regime of my country and of my Government itself the day must fatally come when a situation will be reached in which the Government of the Uruguayan Republic will find itself unable to act with the necessary liberty of action".

Translation of the whole article is enclosed herewith.

It was evident that if the quotation were a correct one the copy of the Note had been obtained by improper means. Further, the passage quoted, though perhaps capable of interpretation in the sense of a threat, as "La Tribuna Popular" implied, was unlikely to have been intended in that way and probably was intended to mean that if the undue popular agitation were unchecked the Uruguayan Government might find themselves hampered in giving, as a neutral government, proper protection to German interests etc. For these reasons and because of the "yellow" character of "La Tribuna Popular" the Legation and Reuter's correspondent here did not think it desirable to report it to the Minister of Information or the B.B.C. [British Broadcasting Corporation], but it was apparently reported by the other press agencies, since it was quoted in the B.B.C. No. 5 transmission last night, which is recorded and distributed to the Uruguayan press.

You will observe that there is an implied criticism of the Minister for Foreign Affairs for having failed to send a rejoinder to the German Minister's Note or even to reject it. It appears to have been simply transmitted to the Municipality, where the competent office had authorised publication of the poster and the leaflet.

TRANSLATION OF A FRONT PAGE NOTICE FROM "LA TRIBUNA POPULAR" ON FRIDAY, DECEMBER 6TH.

To the German Minister

EXPLAIN YOUR WORDS.

Our country is small in size, and from a military standpoint weak, but spiritually it is far greater than one that considers itself sufficiently powerful to experience the unhealthy temptation of domineering the world. It is still more powerful because, with its conception of right, it will never run the risk of making but a fleeting appearance on the stage of History as have those numerous political systems which have pretended to carry their hegemony beyond the bound of what is tolerable.

We say this, Your Excellency, because a Note which was addressed by you to the Minister for Foreign Affairs has come into our hands, a paragraph of which contains certain terms whose sense we consider is not quite clear and may provoke suspicions and alarms that should not be allowed to continue.

These terms, Your Excellency, are contained in the paragraph of your Note which we quote with the object that the Uruguayan people should know them fully: -

"I am obliged to remind Your Excellency that on numerous occasions I have called your attention to the fact that owing to the unlimited attacks against the regime of my country and of my Government itself the day must fatally come when such a situation will be reached in which the Government of the Uruguayan Republic will find itself unable to act with the necessary liberty of action".

We do not know, Your Excellency, what are the grievances which the National-Socialist German Government has suffered in our country. If these were truly grievances it would have been sufficient for Your Excellency to have applied to the competent authorities for the proper punishment to be meted out, without adding counsels or menaces which are beyond the province of the action and words of Your Excellency.

We have laws and we have social ethics that do not allow publications offensive to anyone because sometimes excessive pride blinds the mind to the truth of the facts and it can find a grievance where there only exists a just anathema or bold word which expresses the collective feelings regarding an act which merits censure or condemnation.

In your country, Your Excellency, we know and appreciate in all its true value that conquest of civilisation which is called Liberty of Thought.

> In the course of our history the respect for this valuable liberty grows stronger and stronger. It was practised by our heroes; it is sung in the magnificent verses of our National Anthem; and in our Constitution that liberty of thought is solemnly recognised.
>
> Our judicial conception of organic force, Your Excellency, is born of that glorious transformation which is called the French revolution, and in a century and more of freedom we have never turned aside from these principles.
>
> Therefore, Your Excellency, here, in Uruguay, the spirit of the people is one with the spirit of liberty, whose highest expression is the written word or the word of mouth.
>
> We say it again; we do not know if Your Excellency considers that you have received a real offence. Offensiveness is not liberty of thought and should be punished as such. But in that unfortunate paragraph of the Note which Your Excellency addressed to the Uruguayan Minister for Foreign Affairs there is a menace or a line of conduct that cannot be allowed.
>
> We, therefore, invite your Excellency, as representative of the German National Socialist Government, to explain your words.
>
> It is for you to speak, Your Excellency. (Ibid.)

The following day, December 23rd, Ovey sent Halifax details of what was happing in Argentina.

> My Lord,
> With reference to my telegram No. 356 of the 19th instant, I have the honour to inform your Lordship that the principal Argentine newspapers have declared their approval of the issue of a Decree by the Argentine Government regarding the internment of the officers and crew of the German armoured ship "Admiral Graf Spee".
>
> 2. "La Nacion", which, as your Lordship is aware, is normally a faithful mirror of the views of the Government, states, in a leading article dated 21st December, that the Government's neutrality policy has been generally approved by the public, without prejudice to sympathies of individual citizens for one or other of the belligerents. The decision of the Argentine Government to take an active part in the Panama Conference, as also in the negotiations which are at present being conducted with other American states with a view to the adoption of measures designed to keep warlike activities away from the shores of the American continent, shows that Argentina is determined to see that the rights of neutrals are respected; she

will also, however, scrupulously respect International Law as exemplified by treaties such as the Hague Conventions of 899. The terms of these Conventions are elastic, in that neutrals are free to proceed in the manner which they consider most appropriate to achieve the objects of these instruments; for instance, the Convention signed at the Hague in 1899 for the application of maritime warfare of the Geneva Agreements of 1864 enjoins that the officers and men shipwrecked from belligerent warships and landed in neutral territory should be prevented from again taking part in operations in war. The geographic situation of the neutral country should determine the measures to be taken in order to achieve the above end, and it follows that the measures to be taken in a country far removed from the scene of conflict should be less strict than those which should be applied in European countries.

3. The article then goes on to urge that, should the dispositions of International Law regarding internment ever come to be revised, the distinctions now made between the treatment of officers and men should be abolished. However, it was in accordance with the traditions of Argentina that interned men, to whatever nation they happened to belong, should receive in this country the most hospitable treatment possible.

4. "La Prensa", in a leading article of the 22nd December, says that it should not be forgotten that the "GRAF SPEE" was a belligerent ship that had been destroyed in what the Argentine Government considered to be their territorial waters, and that her crew had been landed at Buenos Aires as a result of operations of war. It therefore followed that the rules of International Law governing the duties of neutral states should be strictly applied. The sailors of the "Graf Spee" were in the same position as troops of a belligerent power who had crossed the frontier of a neutral state. Article 57 of the Hague Convention of 1899, confirmed by Article 11 of the Hague Convention of 1907 regarding war on land, lays down that these troops must be interned and that a neutral country has the right of detaining them in camps, fortresses or other appropriate places. The writer adds that neutrals are also under an obligation to intern the crew of belligerent ships which remain in neutral ports for a longer period than that laid down by International Law, and to render the ships incapable of going to sea of the duration of hostilities.

5. The crews of belligerent ships do not, the article continues, lose their belligerent status by the fact of being shipwrecked or wounded, and it was quite certain that they did not cease to be belligerents by the mere fact of their ship having been voluntarily destroyed in the territorial waters of a neutral

state, article 13 of the Hague Convention of 1907 lays down that if sick or wounded sailors are picked up by a neutral warship they should not be allowed to take a further part in hostilities, and it therefore follows that they must be interned if they suceed [sic] in reaching neutral territory as a result of hostile action or the voluntary scuttling of their ship. Moreover, the fact that the "Graf Spee's" crew arrived in Argentina and Argentine tugs and lighters does not affect the juridical [legal] position. The method of their arrival is irrelevant, and the Executive Powers recognised this fact in deciding to follow the practice already adopted in the case of the gun boat "Eber" and of the auxiliary cruiser "Cap Trafalgar" during the war of 1914. The writer quotes other international precedents, such as the internment by the United States of various Russian ships during the Russo-Japanese war and of the German auxiliary cruisers "Kronprinz Wilhelm" and "Prinz Eitel Friedrich" during the Great War. Other South American countries, such as Peru and Columbia, had adopted measures to prevent the setting on fire of ships by their own crews with a view to avoiding capture and internment. China had interned German, French and British ships which happened to be in her ports at the beginning of the last War. In all these cases officers and men had remained interned for the rest of the war.

6. The conclusion of the articel [sic] is that the action of the Argentine Government was perfectly correct, and that the protest which had been entered against it by Germany had no foundation in International Law. It ends by stating that the crew of the "Graf Spee" were in a similar position to soldiers who had crossed a neutral frontier after blowing up the fortress which they had been defending,

I have etc.,
ESMOND OVEY

His Majesty's Ambassador at Buenos Aires presents his compliments to His Majesty's Principal Secretary of State for Foreign Affairs and has the honour to transmit to His Excellency the under-mentioned documents.

Reference to previous correspondence Buenos Aires telegram No. 356 of December 19th 1939.

<u>TRANSLATION OF ARGENTINE DECREE OF DECEMBER 19TH, 1939, REGARDING THE INTERNMENT OF THE OFFICERS AND MEN OF THE "ADMIRAL GRAF SPEE".</u>

Having regard to the disembarkation in the port of the capital of the Captain, Officers and crew of the German armoured cruiser "Graf Spee", sunk voluntarily in the waters of the River Plate and

Whereas, in accordance with the decree regarding the neutrality signed in general agreement of Ministers on the 4th September 1939, the rules to [be] applied are, firstly those contained in the Hague Conventions of 1899 which have force of law for the Republic.'

And whereas the question is governed in particular by Article 10 of the Convention signed at the Hague in 1899, for the Application of maritime Warfare of the Geneva Agreements of 1864, according to which the sick, wounded and shipwrecked from belligerent warships landed in neutral territory should be detained;

And whereas this criterion has already been applied by the Argentine Government in the course of the war of 1914 to settle the internment of the officers and crew of the gunboat "Eber" and of the auxiliary cruiser "Cap Trafalgar";

The President of the Argentine nation decrees:

Article 1. The Captain and Officers of the German armoured cruiser "Graf Spee" will be interned in the city of Buenos Aires, and will be subject to such measures as may be imposed by the police authorities, being required to promise upon their word or honour not to absent themselves without special written permission from that authority.

Article 2. The members of the crew will be interned in inland (mediterraneos) provinces or territories and will be subject to such measures as may be imposed by the local authorities charged with their supervision.

Article 3. The Ministry of the Interior will take the necessary steps to assure that the members of the crew, remain within the bounds to be fixed in accordance with the previous Article.

Article 4. The expenses arising from the internment measures provided for in the present decree will be chargeable to the German Government with which what is established by Article 10 of the Convention already quoted.

Article 5. The present decree will be countersigned by the Secretary of State in the departments for Foreign Affairs and Public Worship and of the Interior.

Article 6. To be communicated, published, etc.
(Signed) ORTIZ
Countersigned   Jose Maria Cantila [sic]
           Diogenes Taboada (Ibid, 23 December 1939)

On the same day, 23 December, the *Aberdeen Press and Journal* published the following article.

Under the Microscope
Nazis Claim Graf Spee Victory
By Edward F. Balloch
The Nazi papers containing the German version of the Graf Spee battle have now come to hand.
The "Berliner Zeitung am Mittag" interprets the "victory" as a big blow to Britain and something which will have a "tremendous effect on the neutrals, who have been impressed at last with Germany's mastery of the sea".
"Mittag" says there is great discomfort in Britain, both over the Bremen's "escape" and the Graf Spee "triumph". I await with interest the Nazi press accounts of Captain Langsdorff's suicide. The Leipzig radio is fuming at M. Campinichi [Cesar Campinichi was France's Naval Minister] for stating that two U-boats were sunk by the French the other day.
"The worst of it all is," says Leipzig, "that Campinichi's unfortunate listeners are expected to believe this utter rubbish."
(*Aberdeen Press and Journal*, 23 December 1939)

Dr Diogenes Taboada, Argentine Minister of the Interior in President Ortiz' Government 1938 to 2 September 1940

(https://second.wiki/wiki/dic3b3genes_taboada)

Miguel Jose Caraciati, Argentine Minister of the Interior from 2 September 1940 until the government overthrow on 4 June 1943 (https://es.wikipedia.org/wiki/Archivo:Miguel_Culaciati.jpg)

Sir Esmond Ovey, British Ambassador to Argentina between 1937 and 1942
(https://www.npg.org.uk/collections/search/portrait/mw19181/Sir-Esmond-Ovey)

Edward Wood, Viscount Halifax, British Foreign Secretary 1938 to 1940 and from 1941 British Ambassador in Washington (Yousuf Karsh, Dutch National Archives, The Hague, FotocollectieAlgemeen Nederlands Persbureau (ANEFO), 1945-1989 bekijk toegang. https://commons.wikimedia.org/w/index.php?curid=37130836)

On Christmas Eve, the Foreign Office sent telegram 227 to Ovey.

> Your telegram No. 359 (of December 21: Argentine decree interning crew of GRAF SPEE].
> My views regarding internment of crew were defined in my telegram No. 223 [of December 19th]
> Text of decree appears satisfactory as far as it goes but everything naturally depends on the actual precautions taken by the Argentine authorities to ensure that it is enforced in an effective manner. You should, as stated in the last paragraph of my telegram referred to above, leave the Argentine Government in no doubt of great importance we attach to adequate supervision of men.
> You may, should you think it desirable, express suitable gratification at the Argentine decision to intern. (Ibid, 24 December 1939)

Two days after Christmas, Ovey sent Halifax by air mail and Eden by bag a copy of the letter he had sent Cantilo.

>My Lord,
>I have the honour to transmit, herewith, with reference to Your Lordship's telegram No. 227 of the 22nd instant, copy of a private letter I addressed on Christmas Eve to senor Cantilo, Argentine Minister for Foreign Affairs.
>Your Lordship will observe that I used the discretion granted me to express gratification at the Argentine decision to intern.
>While feeling reasonably confident that the ARGENTINE Government would meet with reasonable firmness the somewhat whining appeals and misericordism [appeals for mercy] with which the German Counsellor and the German Ambassador were, according to the Press, regaling the Minister for Foreign Affairs and the Minister of the Interior I employed this method of informal address in the hope of being able with one and the same stone to kill the bird of suspicion that His Majesty's Government might in any way be dictating to this proud and independent nation, and at the same time to indicate that His Majesty's Government expects that every Argentine will do his international duty in that state of life to which Providence has called him.
>I have etc.

<u>Enclosure in Buenos Aires despatch No. 438 of December 26th 1939.</u>

24th December 1939

>My dear Minister and friend,
>When we were talking privately the other evening at your charming dinner-party, I told you that I had received no further news from my Government with regard to their appreciation of the measures so promptly taken by your Government in connection with the internment of the officers and crew of the ADMIRAL GRAF SPEE.
>My private view was, as I said at the time, that I felt hopeful that they would adopt the attitude that the decree issued by your Government would provide adequate safeguards against any possible evasion of the obvious intentions of your Government.
>I am happy to inform you that I am authorised to express the gratification of His Britannic Majesty's Government at your decision to intern. At the same time Lord Halifax expresses the hope that I have not failed, and shall not fail should occasion arise, to leave your Government in no doubt as to the importance which they attach to the adequate supervision of the men in

question. I feel quite sure that you will personally and readily acquit me of any such charge.

Not wishing to bother you at this season by asking for an audience, I take this opportunity of wishing you and your country – its government is not out of place in a letter tinged with a slight official character – your charming Lady wife and daughter, our very best wishes for Christmas and a happy New Year. (TNA ADM 116/4180, 26 December 1939)

Ovey sent telegram 372 to the Foreign Office on 27 December.

My telegram No. 369.
The Minister for Foreign Affairs tells me that:
1. In spite of German Ambassador's demand that the men should be kept together "in order to remain under the officers influence" they will be split up into parties of 200 or so and sent to the interior.
2. That the German suggestion (see last sentence of the penultimate paragraph of the above-mentioned telegram) was fantastic.
3. That he was countering point by point all the German arguments that these people were shipwrecked sailors.
4. That the Argentine Government were displeased with Delfino & Company and were taking legal action against them, their tug left port for a foreign country without my permission and apparently would be fined and warned that if they did this again they would lose their licence.
5. That the Argentine Government was contemplating concentrating German merchant vessels at some place such as Rosario in order to exercise better supervision, but ate doubtful as to their authority in view of the question of port dues. (Ibid, 27 December 1939)

On 28 December, Victor Perowne, an official at the Foreign Office, sent a note to Royal Navy Commander A.C. Stanford.

With reference to Buenos Aires telegram No. 369 of the 26th December (a copy of which is attached for convenience of reference), I enclose the draft of a telegram which, if you approve, we would propose to send to Ovey in connexion with the suggestion that the German Embassy at Buenos Aires are hoping to get permission for the officers from the "Graf Spee" to be sent out of the Argentine Republic as naval advisers to several South American Missions.

Will you let me know by telephone if you agree to its despatch? (TNA ADM 116/4180)

The same day, Ovey sent telegram 369 to the Foreign Office.

> My telegram No. 359.
> I have been unable so far to ascertain anything definite regarding proposed treatment of officers and internment of men although fingerprints and police registration are being done today. There seems to be consensus of opinion that officers will be on parole in the city and will even take up jobs. There is also a rumour that the German Embassy are hoping to get permission for the officers to be sent out of the Argentine Republic "as naval advisers to several South American Missions".
> I sent private note to the Minister for Foreign Affairs renewing warning given in your telegram No. 227 and thanking the Government for interning them. I have an appointment with the Minister of Foreign Affairs tomorrow. (Ibid.)

Also on 28 December, Ovey sent telegram 375 to London and the British Legation in Uruguay.

> My telegram 366.
> Press attaché has received information from La Prensa [Argentinian daily newspaper] under urgent request for secrecy that Captain Langsdorff's final letter, a five-page document addressed to the German Ambassador [Otto Langmann], which has been submitted to the court investigating the suicide contains a serious indictment of Nazi policy as a whole and a remarkable tribute to the British cruisers. La Prensa is endeavouring to obtain the text for publication but is doubtful as to the possibility. (Ibid, 28 December 1939)

Later the same day, Ovey sent telegram 377 to London.

> My telegram No.372 paragraph 3.
> The Argentine Government have published the texts of the German Ambassador's note protesting against the internment, and their own lengthy and reasoned reply rejecting the claim that Article 15 of the Hague Convention 1907 applies, and arguing that the fact that the Spee sank herself after arranging in advance for the presence of Argentine tugs vitiates the suggestion that the shipwrecked were rescued by neutral vessels. The reply seems very complete and firm. (Ibid.)

Another Admiralty file contains reports on the internment of the crew of 'Graf Spee' and a general summary of events of the action. An early report, dated 29 December 1939 and marked SECRET, was sent from McCall to Sir Eugen Millington-Drake, described as 'His Britannic Majesty [H.B.M.)'s Minister-Plenipotentiary in Uruguay'. Britain only had a Legation in Uruguay, not an Embassy so the Minister-Plenipotentiary had the same role as an ambassador. Copies of McCall's report were also sent to the Commander-in-Chief of the Royal Navy in the South Atlantic [?], the Rear-Admiral Commanding South American Division [?], the Naval Attaché in Santiago de Chile [?], the Assistant Naval Attaché at Rio de Janeiro [?] and the Civilian Assistant Naval Attaché at Montevideo (Captain 'Rex' Miller).

Sir,

Following on my War Despatch No. 4 (Serial No.45/74/39) of 21st December 1939, paragraph 26 thereof, concerning the events subsequent upon the embarkation of the crew of the "ADMIRAL GRAF SPEE" into tugs [boat which uses direct contact to push or a tow line to pull other often larger boats] and lighters, Pay-Commander Lloyd Hirst has given me the following report: -

TRANSFER OF CREW TO BUENOS AIRES.

The marine superintendent of the Hamburg South America Line, Captain Hope, informed the press that at 2 a.m. on Sunday 17th December, he received instructions directly from the German Embassy to send craft down to the entrance of Montevideo to bring the crew up to Buenos Aires as it had been decided to scuttle the "Admiral Graf Spee".

He despatched the large tugs "Coloso" and "Gigante" AND the lighter "Chiriguana", belonging to A.M. Delfino & Cia., from the new port at dawn without the necessary clearances [official permission].

Their sailing was reported to the Naval Attaché's Office about noon and I denounced the fact to the officer of the Guard at the Marine Prefecture, alleging that they were bound on some unneutral business, and suggesting that the Guardship "Libertad" at Recalada, the entrance to the dredged channel to Buenos Aires, should be told by W/T [Wireless Telegraphy] to investigate. On hearing by telephone from Montevideo that the German crew were embarking in the Delfino tugs, I again visited the Marine Prefecture to urge them to take every possible step against clandestine landing and escape of officers and men who should be interned. The officer of the guard reported the denunciation by telephone at the Ministry of Marine. For 45 minutes I could get no interview with an officer so eventually I left a written denunciation with a warrant officer. I then telephoned to the Federal Police

Headquarters and was provided immediate action and eventually at 0130 got in telephone communication with the Chief of the Intelligence Section of the Naval Staff who said that the coast was being watched and that a police boat had been sent to meet them.

For several days afterwards there were reports of clandestine landings but on investigation and on checking the total number of officers I feel certain that no great number, if any, have escaped internment.

The "Coloso" and lighter arrived in the port of Buenos Aires at 11.15 and at 15.00 came alongside and landed 785 officers and men. The "Gigante" came alongside an hour later and landed 254. Some others arrived in the motor launch of the Graf Spee. 56 officers and 263 men were lodged in the barracks of the Naval Arsenal and the rest in the Government Hostel for Immigrants.

2. The Argentine Minister of Foreign Affairs [and Public Worship] has informed the Ambassador [Sir Esmond Ovey] that the Argentine Government were displeased with the Delfino Co.; and were taking legal action against them for authorising their tugs and lighters to leave port for a foreign country without permission and that they would be probably fined; and that they would lose their licence if such an offence were repeated. The Ambassador has recommended that the Delfino Co. should be put on the Statutory List – and it is to be hoped that this recommendation will be carried out as this firm are thought by all out here to be working in enemy interests.

3. <u>INTERNMENT OF CREW</u> The Argentine Government have turned down protests from the German Ambassador that the crew of the "Admiral Graf Spee" should not be interned on the grounds that they are shipwrecked mariners. They have also refused to listen to pleas that the men should be interned close to Buenos Aires and under their own officers. The men will be split up into parties of about 200 and sent into the interior to work on the land – the Argentine hope being that they will elect to remain permanently in the country to the country's benefit. The officers will be allowed on parole. The Ministry of the Interior is preparing for each officer and man an identity card recording finger prints, photograph, personal data and the prescribed zone of residence.

4. A list is enclosed (Appendix I – to the Director of Naval Intelligence only) of the names ranks or ratings and dates of birth of all those landed in Buenos Aires from the "Admiral Graf Spee". From this list it will be seen that those labelled 'oficiales y aspirantes' are skilled workmen and are of a much higher average age that the remainder. It is these whom I fear may work themselves into positions where they can damage our interests

through sabotage. There is no question that this large number of Germans added to the community out here will cause constant anxiety on this score. Those who know the local conditions say that once they get into the interior it will be difficult for the authorities to keep a permanent check on them. Official circles are by no means pleased with the arrival of these uninvited guests who will be both a trouble and an expense. The crew of the ship are remarkably young looking and are of the clean country lad type. I fear that the general public will soon forget the ignominious flight and end of the GRAF SPEE and will sympathise and fraternise with them.

An analysis of the total complement of GRAF SPEE is given in Appendix 1.

5. SUICIDE OF CAPTAIN LANGSDORFF. The suicide of the Captain of the GRAF SPEE in the early hours of 20th December caused a great sensation as his demeanour on the previous day had given no hint of the tragic resolution he was about to take. He left behind a letter to the German Ambassador which according to the Embassy said that he had always meant to share the fate of his ship but that he felt that he must first see his men into safety and make his report on events. A "B" 2 report says that the suppressed letter, which had five pages, was a strong criticism of the Nazi regime and included words of praise for the way the British cruisers fought. Captain Langsdorff was given an impressive funeral, the Argentine Navy rendering the military honours. Part of the ship's company went to the cemetery in charabancs. The British ex-prisoners [who had been on board the Graf Spee] who were landed at Montevideo delegated Captain Pottinger to come to Buenos Aires to attend the funeral, which he did in a private capacity in plain clothes, a tribute which was appreciated by the German officers.

6. INTERNMENT OF GERMAN SHIP "TACOMA" in URUGUAY. This ship will probably be interned by the Uruguayan Government for having left the port without clearance on 17th December in order to act as an auxiliary to the "Admiral Graf Spee". Four seamen who came back to Montevideo in her are under arrest 'for blowing up a ship in territorial waters' but the charge may not be pressed. Twelve officers were also brought ashore by the "Tacoma" and avoided arrest by taking refuge in the German Legation and the German Minister has had the effrontery to notify the Government that he proposes to appoint them as naval attachés to the various south American countries and has claimed diplomatic privilege for them. [The last phrase was underlined in pencil with the note: Latest orders from H.M.

Minister are that these men may be given diplomatic recognition by Uruguayan Government. 17/1/40]

7. All conversation here still centres on the "Admiral Graf Spee" and the following questions are always being asked: -
(a) Why did the "Admiral Graf Spee" seek refuge in Montevideo?
(b) Why did she come out to blow herself up and not to fight?
(c) Why did her Captain commit suicide? Or did he?

No certain reply can be given to any of these questions, but after much discussion and reflection, I hazard these answers: -

Loss of nerve on account of the low state of morale of the crew after the ship had received much punishment and of false intelligence that led the Captain to believe that our cruisers had support near at hand.

The desire of a very kindly and idealistic Captain not to send to their probable death his very young crew for a cause which his heart was not in.

It is still more difficult question to answer and rumours and counter rumours are still rife. It is known that he had a telephone talk with Hitler after his arrival in Buenos Aires and rumour of some reliability says it was of a most violent nature; we may have more definite news of this later. On the other hand, a shrewd reporter of my acquaintance who saw him the morning before his death says that he never saw a man who less gave the appearance of contemplating suicide. The Minister of Foreign Affairs has told the Ambassador that he is perfectly certain it was suicide and not murder; also that the flag he was found on was the old German flag not the Swastika.

8. In the same conversation with the Ambassador which took place last night the Minister of Foreign Affairs made it quite clear that only the officers would be given parole and that the 'aspirantes' who are in reality artisans would be drafted into the interior. He also told the Ambassador that the German Ambassador had never expected anything but a flat refusal to his protests on the internment of the ship's company.

9. Enclosed as Appendix 3 to this despatch is a brief report made out by Mr. Garland on W/T Communications at Montevideo. A more detailed report will be given to the Rear-Admiral South American Division. In order to pay for "expenses" necessary to ensure the goodwill of those operating the Uruguayan Government Wireless Station and on whose goodwill we are entirely dependent for the rapid transmission of urgent signals, I have authorised expenditure out of my account "B" (Ref my 9/88/39 of 14th October) for the sum of $253.90 Uruguayan paper pesos: I am satisfied that this is by no means an extravagant amount and that it will make for good service in the future.

10. One reason advanced by the Germans for the "Admiral Graf Spee" not continuing the action was a lack of ammunition. This seems hard to believe. According to the account of the British captains on board [as prisoners after their ships had been sunk] the rate of fire was slow even when she was most hotly engaged by our ships. A very rough estimate they gave was something under 50 rounds per gun during the whole of the action. No doubt this can be more accurately checked from the Rear Admiral's account of the action. From the enclosed photographs (Under separate cover to Director of Naval Intelligence only) it can be seen that the after-main magazine may have exploded but the forward one has not. I witnessed all the explosions which took place; none of them in any way shook Montevideo. The ship was about five miles off. It is possible that one or both of the main magazines had been flooded to prevent undue damage. Enclosed as Appendix 4 is the German so called official of the action as published in the leading Buenos Aires daily paper.
11. Attached to this deposition as Appendix 5 is a copy of the official disposition taken by the Captain of the "Admiral Graf Spee" from Captain Dove late master of the British Ship "Africa Shell" sunk by the armoured ship off the coast of Portuguese East Africa on the 15th November 1949. (TNA ADM 1/10803, 29 December 1939)

Other documents related to the Graf Spee, not included in this account, are Captain Dove, the Master of M.V. AFRICA SHELL's account of the German response, Mr Garland's report on the interception of German wireless telegraphic messages to and from the Graf Spee before and during the Battle of the River Plate, and the account of the British Royal Navy's attack on the Altmark in Norway. (TNA ADM 1/10803; ADM 116/4180; ADM 223/27)

On 29 December, Ovey updated Halifax by sending him the following documents.

> My Lord,
> I have the honour, with reference to my telegram No.377 of the 28th Instant, to transmit to Your Lordship herewith, a free translation of the notes recently exchanged between the German and Argentine Governments, as published in the Press, with regard to the internment of the officers and crew of the "Admiral Graf Spee".
> 2, I took the opportunity of a private encounter yesterday to congratulate the Minister for Foreign Affairs on his note. His Excellency's impression was that the German Ambassador had presented his note of protest against internment more as a matter

of form, by instruction from Berlin, than with any hope that any results would derive from it.

3. The reference, under heading III of the Argentine note, to the auxiliary vessels being in principle subject to capture by the enemy, forms an interesting echo of the instructions issue to me in Your Lordship's telegram No. 221 Most Immediate of the 18th December.

I have, etc.

Enclosure in Buenos Aires despatch No. 446 dated December 29th 1939.

The Government of the Reich consider that the officers and crew of the sunken German armoured ship "Admiral Graf Spee", who arrived in the port of Buenos Aires on the 18th December, 1939, on board merchant ships under the Argentine flag, cannot be interned by virtue of the application of the prevailing and recognised rules of International Law.

In the view of German Government, the present case is not governed by the terms of Article 10 of the "Hague Convention of the 19th July, 1899, for the adaptation of maritime warfare of the principles of the Geneva Convention of the 22nd August 1864, the text of which corresponds to that of Article 15 of the Hague Convention of the 18th October 1907, for the adaptation to maritime warfare of the principles of the Geneva Convention." This interpretation of the legal situation is supported by the following reasons: -

1. The terms of the above mentioned Conventions are not applicable, either in letter or in spirit, to a case in which shipwrecked men arrive in the territory of a neutral country on board steamships also under a neutral flag. The officers and crew of the armoured ship "Admiral Graf Spee" were brought to Argentine territory on board vessels under the Argentine flag.

2. The circumstance that this special case is not covered by the above mentioned Convention is borne out by the fact that this particular topic has formed the subject in the negotiations of the Hague Conference of 1907, of a special resolution. (See "Rapport General dans les actes et documents de la Deuxieme Conference de La Hague", 1907, Volume 1, page 76).

3. According to this principle laid down in the above quoted "Rapport General" of the second Hague Conference, shipwrecked men must be set at liberty if they are disembarked in a neutral port from merchant vessels under a neutral flag by which they happen by chance to have been picked up.

4. According to this view, which has become part of recognised International Law, the Netherlands and other neutral states proceeded, during the World War, to set at liberty the shipwrecked crew of the warships "Cressy", "Aboukir" and "Hogue", who were disembarked in neutral territory from neutral merchant vessels.

The present case is exactly on a par with these precedents, and no parallel can be drawn between it and the case of the crew of the German auxiliary cruiser "Cap Trafalgar" who, during the World War, were brought to Buenos Aires on board a German ship and interned in Argentina.

5. The decisive point in the argument for making an exception is exclusively the fact that the shipwrecked Germans were brought to Argentina on board neutral vessels. The motives which induced those Argentine ships to proceed to the spot where the armoured ship "Admiral Graf Spee" was sunk appear to be irrelevant. According to the spirit of the rules in question a distinction cannot be drawn between neutral ships proceeding to a given spot in the normal course of their traffic and, for example, being called thither by requests for aid from the crews or by direction of any other outside authority.

In accordance with what has been set out above, the Government of the Reich having studied the facts, and their juridical implications, have come to the conclusion that the officers and crew of the sunken armoured ship "Admiral Graf Spee" should remain in Argentina in the full enjoyment of their liberty. December 23rd 1939.

Enclosure in Buenos Aires despatch No. 446 of December 29th 1939.

The Government of the Argentine Republic have received the memorandum dated the 23rd instant in which the Government of the Reich, for various reasons set out in that document, conclude that: "The officers and crew of the sunken German armoured ship "Admiral Graf Spee" who arrived in the port of this city on the 18th December 1939, on board merchant vessels under the Argentine flag, cannot be interned by virtue of the application of the prevailing and recognised rules of International Law.".

The Argentine Government regret that they cannot share this opinion, which is at variance with the higher duties imposed on them by the Conventions by which they are bound, and the general principles of International Law which they desire to respect and to see respected by others. These principles and Conventions, which were invoked in the neutrality Decree issued by this Government on the 3th September, 1939, were duly communicated to the German Embassy, so that when the officers and crew of the German cruiser disembarked in Argentine territory, by virtue of a purely voluntary act, they did so with a full knowledge of the principles which would govern the attitude of the Argentine Government in the fulfilment of their obligations of neutrality.

A careful examination of the memorandum communicated to them has not modified the view in accordance with which, after the due study and analysis of the present case, the Argentine Government have the honour to set forth below the reasons by virtue of which they have considered these measures to be appropriate within the framework of the general principles of International Law.

I. According to the view of the Government of the Reich, the present case is not governed by the terms of Art. 10 of the Hague Convention of 1899 for the adaptation of maritime warfare of the principles of the Geneva Convention of the 22nd August 1864, the text of which was reproduced as Art. 15 of the similar Convention of 1907.

This instrument of 1899, states the memorandum under reply, is not applicable, either in letter or in spirit, "to a case in which shipwrecked men arrive in the territory of a neutral country on board vessels under neutral flag. The officers and men of the armoured ship "Admiral Graf Spee" were brought to Argentine territory on board vessels under the Argentine flag".

In the first place, it must be observed that, although the case may be governed, by the Convention signed at the Hague in 1907, for the adaptation of maritime warfare of the principles of the Geneva Convention of 1906, the terms thereof do not allow of so general an interpretation. On the contrary, if an express ruling exists, it is that of Art. 13 which established the following: "In the event of wounded, sick or shipwrecked men being picked up by a neutral warship, precautions should be taken, so far as is possible, to prevent them again taking part in operations of war". This obligation to keep shipwrecked men under guard continues to bind the neutral state after the men have been disembarked.

II. "The circumstances that this special case is not covered by that instrument (that of 1899) – continues the memorandum - is borne out by the fact that this particular topic has formed the subject, in the negotiations of the Hague Convention of 1907, of a special resolution (See "Rapport General dans les actes et documents de la Deuxieme Conference de La Hague", 1907, Volume 1, page 76).

(Page missing]

In effect, it cannot be considered that tugs which, on behalf of the belligerent Government, arrive at the spot where the voluntary and predetermined sinking of a warship has taken place, are in a similar situation to that of a merchant ship which, in the course of their voyage along their normal route, are surprised by a warlike encounter between two enemy forces, and are obliged by their humanitarian duties to recue wounded and shipwrecked and bring them to a neutral port, independently of the will of the victims themselves.

For the latter to be set at liberty it is necessary, as it is admitted in the German Government's memorandum, that the ships should have happened "by chance" to pick up the wounded, sick or shipwrecked men, and that they should not be vessels which have been arrived "on purpose" and in anticipation of the event. That right belongs exceptionally to hospital ships, which are characterised by a number of requirements which, however, were not fulfilled in the present case.

Except in the case of hospital ships, the only applicable situation is that provided for in Art. 9 of the Convention according to which: "The belligerents can appeal to the spirit of mercy of the Captains of merchant vessels, yachts or any neutral ships to take on board, and care for the wounded and sick. Ships which have responded to this appeal as well as those who have spontaneously picked up wounded, sick and shipwrecked men, will enjoy special protection and certain immunities. In no event may they be captured owing to the fact of their being used for this purpose, but apart from promises which may have been made them, they are exposed to capture for any violations of neutrality which they may have committed.

As can be easily seen from the text, the article refers to vessels which "by chance" (as stated in the Commission's report) have happened to be in the spot where a combat was taking place, and have picked up combatants. But it must be observed that, in addition to this circumstance, the article also lays down that the shipwrecked men must have been "spontaneously" rescued.

The merchant ships involved in the present case were contracted and prepared in advance to be used by the crew of a warship, and their position is to a certain extent similar to that of an auxiliary vessel; and it is in this guise that they arrived in our port accompanied by a launch from the cruiser itself.

Moreover, they could not have demanded from the other belligerent – as would be the case in the event of casual and spontaneous aid – liberty of action and proper respect for their humanitarian and neutral functions. The vessels were contracted by one of the belligerents; they obeyed the orders of that one in whose interests they acted, and in principle they could have been subject to capture by the enemy.

This distinction becomes all the more certain after consideration of the fact that the tugs on board which the officers and crew of the "Admiral Graf Spee" were brought to Buenos Aires, besides having been prepared and having left the port expressly for that purpose, did so without conforming to the necessary port regulations, thus rendering themselves liable to legal proceedings.

IV. The German Government's memorandum goes on to say that, in accordance with the view which it sustains, the Netherlands [Page missing] (Ibid, 29 December 1939)

A couple of days later, New Year's Eve, the Foreign Office sent telegram 102 to Millington-Drake.

> Your telegram No. 173 [of December 19th].
> It is understood that Uruguayan Government have given "Tacoma" twenty-four hours in which to leave Montevideo.
> Please do whatever you can by informal representations to delay her departure as much as possible. From paragraph 3 of your telegram under reference and paragraph 7 of your telegram No.186 it would seem that Uruguayan Government were at one time thinking of interning this vessel a course which would suit us best. (TNA ADM 116/5474, 31 December 1939)

Leaving port when there were still British cruisers at anchor offshore waiting to attack the Tacoma may well explain why the Captain did not sail.

Millington-Drake responded later the same day with telegram No. 198.

> Your telegram No. 102.
> It is practically certain that Uruguayan Minister concerned decided yesterday afternoon before dispersing for two days of holidays to give such 24 hours' notice but it has been impossible to ascertain as from when notice runs.
> Tacoma this morning shows intentions of departure but there is now no possibility of making further representations and even if there were I feel they would do no good as Uruguayan

Government have taken their decision knowing full well our views about this ship.

Her capture would therefore be presumably in our view an attack on an auxiliary warship and not on a merchant vessel and indeed the Uruguayan Government also have recognised her character as an auxiliary by giving her 24 hours' notice.

Therefore aggression on her would not be within meaning of Ministry for Foreign Affairs' definition of aggression on merchant vessel given in my telegram No. 194 and would at the most be only an infringement of security zone as a battle zone. (Ibid.)

Chapter Three: Developments in 1940

Millington-Drake continued his message in telegram No. 199 sent on 1 January 1940 with copies to Washington, Rio de Janeiro, Santiago and Lima.

> My immediately preceding telegram.
> S.S. TACOMA has moved to ante port. It is understood that her time limit expires at 6.a.m. tomorrow Monday.
> I learn from a reliable source that efforts to obtain extension of time limit have been made by influential person on behalf of American owners [?Allen] but have proved unsuccessful. (Ibid, 1 January 1940)

Later that day, he sent the Foreign Office another telegram informing them that, according to announcements by local officials, the Tacoma has been interned. 'Owing, however, to the holiday, it has not been possible up to the present to obtain official confirmation of this. A tug of the Prefecture of the Port remains alongside the vessel and it is reported that a guard has been placed outside.' (Ibid.)

Also on New Year's Day, the *Portsmouth Evening News* published the following article.

> GRAF SPEE'S SUPPLY SHIP CHOOSES INTERNMENT
> ESCAPE BID FALSE ALARM
> Would Not Run Gauntlet
> BRITISH WARSHIPS READY OUTSIDE HARBOUR
> Marine Police Now On Board.
> THE Nazi steamer Tacoma, which acted as a supply ship for the scuttled German battleship Graf Spee, will be interned in Montevideo for the duration of the war.
> Two courses were open to the captain had he decided to leave Montevideo. He could have defied the British warships waiting in the Plate Estuary and made a dash for the open sea, or scuttled his ship, vessel of 8,268 tons, just as the Graf Spee did.
> As her time limit set by the Uruguayan Government expired 3.30 a.m., to-day, it was officially announced, here, that the German vessel would not be leaving and would therefore be interned immediately.
> Fifty Uruguayan marines boarded a naval steamer and headed for the Tacoma, which is anchored in the roads.
> The Tacoma left harbour late last night with the battle flag of the German Navy flying from her masthead. For a time it looked as though she might be about to run the gauntlet of the waiting British worships. But she slowed down and stopped near the spot where the Graf Spee was scuttled.

It then seemed that the Nazi supply ship might repeat the tactics of the German battleship and "commit suicide" beside the Graf Spee.

Nothing happened. And when the "zero hour" for her stay in Montevideo passed she became the prisoner of the Uruguayan Government, no more to carry fuel for the German raiders.

Half-an-hour before the expiry of the time limit there were no signs that the Tacoma was preparing to leave Montevideo; her bow was facing the Inner port.

More than the usual number of Naval Police are on the docks to handle the vessel. (*Portsmouth Evening News,* 1 January 1940)

On the same day, the *San Pedro News Pilot* included the following article.

Uruguay Interns Nazi Ship
Officials Board Tacoma
Vessel, Which Stood by Graf Spee Held as Naval Auxiliary

MONTEVIDEO (UP) - The German freighter Tacoma today was interned for the duration of the war by the Uruguayan government at the expiration of a 24-hour ultimatum demanding her departure from this neutral port. The 8,268-ton freighter, which stood by the scuttled pocket battleship Admiral Graf Spee in her final hours and therefore was adjudged a naval auxiliary, became the first victim in this war of a neutral's Interment regulations. The Tacoma was in the roadstead just inside the harbor breakwater where she had lain all night in apparent indecision, when a tug carrying Uruguayan officials pulled alongside shortly after expiration of the 24-hour period. Captain Hans Know signed the certificate of interment. Early today, upon the 8 a.m. deadline set by Uruguay for the departure, the government announced the Tacoma would remain and be interned. Fifty Uruguayan marines aboard the Uruguayan navy's steamer La Valleja went out to the Tacoma. Capt. Hans Know, charged by Uruguay with placing his ship in the category of a belligerent by standing by the Admiral Graf Spee when that German pocket battleship was destroyed by its commander Dec. 17, ran up a German naval ensign Sunday afternoon and steamed from the inner harbor, as the Admiral Graf Spee had done two weeks previously. Instead of going on to self-destruction as the warship did, however, the Tacoma dropped anchor just inside the harbor breakwater. There had been waterfront reports the Tacoma might go to Buenos Aires, where she might have been treated simply as a merchant ship. The

Anatolia and the Niemburg, owned by the same company, have been anchored at Buenos Aires since the war began. Before sailing, the Tacoma discharged a tug baggage which presumably belonged to the crew. Some of the men had been put ashore beforehand, and the number remaining aboard was not disclosed. One estimate said there were 60. (*San Pedro News Pilot*, Vol.12, No. 257, 1 January 1940)

On 3 January, Millington-Drake sent telegram No. 2 in his 1940 series to the Foreign Office.

> Decree giving reasons for ordering internment Tacoma failing departure within 24 hours was published in press this morning but I have waited to see Minister for Foreign Affairs before telegraphing further. He confirms that notification was made to German Legation Saturday evening and to Captain of vessel at 6.30. Sunday morning and that formalities of internment were proceeded with immediately on expiry of time limit yesterday.
>
> **Preamble of decree**, translation of which is being sent by air mail, a reasoned and exhaustive indictment of vessel's activities, showing that though the Uruguayan authorities grind slowly they grind exceedingly small. following are the principal points: that it has been evident throughout that Captain of Tacoma was acting under orders of Captain of Admiral Graf Spee: that vessel left the port of Montevideo following the Graf Spee and without proper authorisation and then acted as transport for military forces: that its operations within territorial waters are tantamount to making the port of Montevideo a base contrary to provisions of Hague Convention XIII and would therefore, failing action the part of the Uruguayan Government, constitute a breach of their neutrality: finally that it being clear that vessel acted as a naval auxiliary her stay in port should be limited to 24 hours in accordance with Hague Convention. (TNA ADM 116/4180, 3 January 1940)

Telegram 3 was sent later the same day.

> My telegram No. 1 and my immediately preceding telegram.
> Minister of Foreign Affairs states that the German Legation was pressing its protest but that he intended to disregard it. Nevertheless he was grateful when I handed to him actual cutting from Buenos Aires newspaper El Sol containing interview with one of the officers of the Graf von Spee which began with the statement that the battleship was approaching Uruguayan coast in order to re-fuel from the Tacoma. I enquired about internment

of the sixteen officers of the Graf von Spee and he said that that was the third matter he was studying "and seriously".

I have obtained audience with the President of the Republic for admiral Harwood at noon tomorrow after his visit to the Minister for Foreign Affairs. (Ibid.)

Enrique Dick, the son of Hein Dick, one of the sailors on the Graf Spee, wrote a biography of his father, *In the Wake of the Graf Spee*. In the chapter 'From Buenos Aires to Capilla Vieja [Cordoba]' he stated,

> It was official. They were to be interned. Their officers' eyes glittered with impotent rage then they heard the shameful word, but there was nothing anyone could do about it – not the German ambassador, nor the Naval Attaché, nor First Officer Kay. Internment! As the word went round the lower ranks, some even had to ask what it meant. It was the last thing those young sailors who until just a few weeks before had been proud servants of the mighty Third Reich ever expected, and another body blow so soon after losing their captain.
>
> They quickly realised they were going to be made to stay in Argentina instead of being allowed to return home which probably meant spending the rest of the war without purpose or direction, forced to simply bide their time until it was all over. The older ones who had seen direct action before and were used to the privations and sacrifice of life in the armed forces complained they were being treated like naughty schoolboys, about to be sent to a strict boarding school so they could be taught a lesson. They had done nothing wrong, had broken no laws, yet here they were, about to be interned on the orders of a weak government. The burning question was whether Argentina was pro-German? They drew some comfort to know that some of the local populace were on their side, at least if the number of arms raised in the Nazi salute at burial services and other public events were anything to go by. Unfortunately, they weren't the ones who made the rules.

Post-war photograph of Dr Roberto Ortez, Argentine President 1938 to 15 July 1942 (Diego Abad de Santillán, TEA, Tipográfica Editora Argentina. 1971, Buenos Aires, Argentina, https://commons.wikimedia.org/wiki/File:Roberto_Ortiz.jpg)

Ramon Castillo, Vice-President of Argentina from 1938 to 27 June 1942, then President to 4 June 1943 (Public Domain, https://commons.wikimedia.org/w/index.php?curid=1368718)

Jose Luis Cantilo, Minister of Foreign Affairs in Argentine Government from 1938 to 1940
(https://www.wikidata.org/wiki/Q1646739)

The decision to intern them had been spearheaded by the Argentine President, Dr Roberto Ortiz, a man who had primarily been elected to office because of his stated opposition to election fraud, a deeply-entrenched problem in "The Land of Silver". His decree had brought the shutters firmly down on any hope of their being allowed to leave the country, but while it may have satisfied the demands of the British and the French, it had incurred the inevitable wrath of the Germans.

There were some compensations, however. The German community in Buenos Aires soon rallied round the sailors, giving up their time to show them the city on foot, organising trips further afield, giving them small gifts, inviting them to concerts and dances and welcoming them into her own homes. My father remembered how the first time they had been allowed to leave the confines of the 'Hotel de los Immigrantes' for a few hours, thousands of people had lined up outside hoping to be assigned "their own sailor". They tried to put a brave face on it, but after the euphoria of surviving the battle, many were now in low spirits. They had lost their ship, the captain they so admired, their liberty, their future as fighting men. They had also lost many of their friends and comrades. And to cap it all, Christmas was fast approaching but instead of having to endure the bitter cold and snow, with short days and long nights, everything was topsy-turvy [disorganised] here. They suddenly found themselves in the middle of a heatwave as the sun beat down on them and the humidity sapped every ounce of energy.

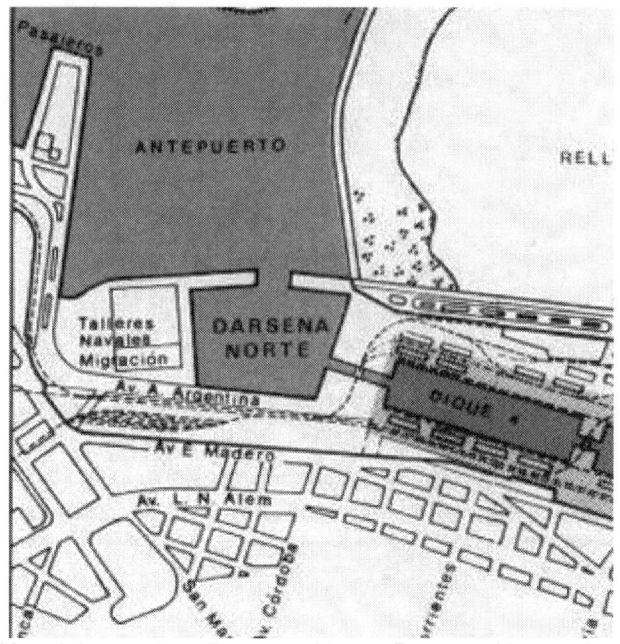

The Naval Arsenal ay Darsena Norte, Buenos Aires, where some of the Graf Spee were initially accommodated. (https://www.histarmar.com.ar/Puertos/BsAs/DarsenaNorte1-1897-1910.htm_

Hotel de Immigrantes in the port of Buenos Aires, where the Graf Spee sailors first stayed. Opened in 1912, it could accommodate up to 3000. (https://www.theguardian.com/world/2017/feb/09/argentina-macri-executive-order-immigration-hotel)

Bunk beds in the Hotel de Immigrantes
(https://www.loc.gov/item/2001704592/)

A group of German-Argentine families had got together and hurriedly organised a Christmas Eve celebration at the *Hotel de Immigrantes* to try to cheer them up. A huge fir tree had been erected in the grounds and decorated with hundreds of twinkling fairy lights. As dusk fell Captain Kay addressed the divisions lined up before him, as he did each day. Tonight, though, some of them didn't hear a word he was saying, their thoughts drifting instead to a far-away land where their loved ones were probably wondering whether they were alive or dead.

In the refectory, the ladies of the community had hung a traditional German Christmas wreath above the fireplace and decorated every table with candles, little sprigs of pine, silver and gold ribbons and tiny bunches of mistletoe. They had been laid with immaculate snow white table cloths and polished cutlery and glassware sparkled in the candlelight. Next to each wine glass there was a little tiny Christmas tree. In the background there was soft music playing similar tunes from the past. More than one sailor had a lump in his throat as he walked into that room with its reminders of the sort of traditional German Christmas they were used to. They were overwhelmed with gratitude for the effort that had gone into organising the evening. There they were, local people celebrating the birth of Christ with hundreds of young strangers who had suddenly found themselves here in circumstances beyond their control that none would have foreseen, let alone wanted. (Dick, Enrique, *In the Wake of the Graf Spee*, WIT Press, 2014, p.112ff)

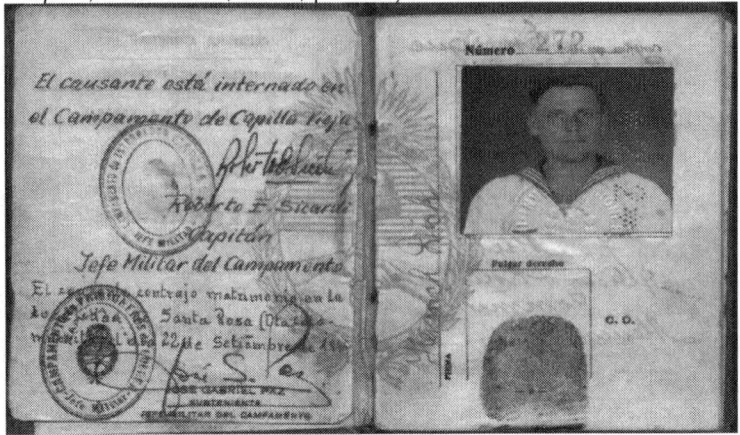

Hein Dick's internment card (Dick, Enrique, *In the Wake of the Graf Spee*, WIT Press, 2014, pp.112)

The beginning of 1940 saw a number of British newspapers publish accounts of the first escape attempts.

Graf Spee Men's Escape Bid
Five members of the interned crew of the Admiral Graf Spee made daring but unsuccessful bid to escape yesterday. The men, who were among those who boarded the Nazi tanker Tacoma shortly before the pocket battleship was scuttled, secured a motor launch and set out for Buenos Aires. Before they had gone very far, however, the motor launch developed engine trouble, and they had to abandon the attempt. (*Aberdeen Press and Journal*, 5 January 1940)

GRAF SPEE MEN'S ESCAPE BID
MOTOR LAUNCH DASH FAILS
Five members of the interned crew of the Admiral Graf Spee made a daring but unsuccessful bid to escape yesterday. The men, who were among those who boarded the Nazi tanker Tacoma shortly before the battleship was scuttled, secured a motor launch and set out for Buenos Aires. Before they had gone far, however, the motor launch developed engine trouble, and they had to abandon the attempt. Another vessel put out

from port and the men were brought back to land, where they were put under arrest. (*Dundee Courier*, 5 January 1940)

Five of Tacoma's Crew Try to Escape in Launch
Montevideo. Thursday. Five members of the crew of the Tacoma, the interned German supply ship to the late Nazi pocket battleship Graf Spee, attempted to escape to Buenos Aires today in a launch formerly belonging to the Graf Spee, the Montevideo harbour police state. They were intercepted about ten miles from the harbour.—British United Press (*Nottingham Journal*, 5 January 1940)

German Ships Trying To Run Gauntlet
Two German, ships, cargo liners, belonging to the North-German Lloyd Line, have left the principal port of Ecuador for "an unknown destination." The vessels are the latest of their type. Five members of the crew of the "Tacoma," the German oil tanker interned by the Uruguayan authorities at Montevideo on the ground that it acted as an auxiliary war vessel when it assisted the "Graf Spee," attempted to escape from Montevideo. On a launch which belonged to the "Graf Spee," they left Montevideo in an attempt to reach Buenos Ayres, but the launch developed engine trouble ten miles out and they were intercepted and recaptured. (*Derby Journal*, 5 January 1940)

NAZI SHIPS BOLT
It is known that 26 German ships lying in South American harbours are only waiting a favourable opportunity to make a dash for home.
Yesterday came this news:
The two German merchant ships, Quito and Bogota, which have been anchored at Guayaquil, a port of Ecuador, since September, left suddenly yesterday for an unknown destination. Five of the crew of the Tacoma. The interned German supply ship to the late Nazi "pocket" battleship Graf Spee attempted to escape to Buenos Aires yesterday in a launch, state Montevideo harbour police. They were intercepted ten miles from the harbour. British United Press. (*Birmingham Daily Gazette*, 5 January 1940)

Carlos Benemann commented that the five crew members that got stuck on one of the small Graf Spee Launches that left the Spee after setting the explosives two weeks earlier. They could not reach or find the Chiriguana the Colosso and the barge towed behind it in the dark. They turned around and went back to board the Tacoma. They were arrested by the Uruguayan port authorities and later released. It may have been these five that then tried it again on January 4th. (Email communication 21 December 2021)

AJAX CREW FETED
Reception "Bigger Than Biggest Cup Final"
SAILOR'S DESCRIPTION

(FROM OUR OWN CORRESPONDENT) Montevideo, Thursday. —The festivities to celebrate the visit of the Admiral, officers, and crew of the victorious Ajax continue. Rear-Admiral Harwood held a reception on board the Ajax at noon to-day in honour of Ben. Baldomir, President of Uruguay. He also invited guests of the British community.

The Uruguayan pro-Allies organisation, presided over by Senor Serrato, former President of the Republic, assisted by prominent Uruguayans, are holding a reception at the Parque Hotel this evening, in honour of the Admiral and officers of the Ajax. The crew, who were given shore leave today, were similarly entertained at lunch at the Sayago Polo Club this afternoon, and at dances given by the British community tonight. The local Press is enthusiastically eulogistic of the ship, officers, and crew. The papers are profusely illustrated, showing crowds waving British flags and acclaiming British sailors; stopping vehicles in which they are travelling, and handing them flowers. It would be impossible for the men to receive a more triumphal reception from their own people in England. Rear-Admiral Harwood's modesty and unaffected simplicity have completely charmed the Uruguayans, who contrast his demeanour with the stiff, formal attitude of the Germans. One sailor of the Ajax briefly described the triumphal reception of the ship and crew as " bigger than the biggest Cup final.

FORMER FOES MEET IN BUENOS AIRES
"British and German Sailors "Swap Stories"

[FROM OUR OWN CORRESPONDENT] Buenos Aires, Thursday. —Groups of British sailors from the Achilles, and groups of interned German sailors from the Graf Spee , met in bars at Buenos Aires last night and over glasses of beer swapped stories of the battle they fought three weeks ago. The fears of the Argentine authorities that such encounters might cause friction were not realised. Members of the Achilles crew, who have come here for two days to celebrate their victory, expressed regret that the Germans, who have to report to the naval arsenal before midnight, had to go home so early.

HELP FOR BRITISH SAILORS' DEPENDANTS
Achilles Men Give Up Day's Pay

Buenos Aires, Thursday. —Sir Esmond Ovey, the British Ambassador to Argentina, flew to Montevideo to-day to meet Rear-Admiral Harwood, Commander of the British Cruiser Squadron which fought the Graf Spee; taking with him a cheque for £1000 subscribed by the British colony here for the dependants of the British sailors who lost their lives in the engagement.

At a luncheon given by the Buenos Aires Jockey Club to-day, Captain Parry, of the cruiser Achilles, disclosed that the men on his ship voluntarily gave up last Monday's pay, raising £200 for the same purpose. — Press Association.

GRAF SPEE SAILORS
Escape Attempt Fails

Montevideo. Thursday. —Five members of the interned crew of the Admiral Graf Spee made a daring but unsuccessful bid to escape to-day.

The men, who were among those who boarded the nazi [sic] tanker Tacoma shortly before the "pocket battleship" was scuttled, secured a motor launch and set out for Buenos Aires. [To avoid showing respect, some writers do not use the capital letter N in Nazi.] Before they had gone very far, however, the motor launch developed engine trouble, and they had to abandon the attempt. Another vessel put out from port, and the men were brought back to land, where they were put under arrest. Press Association. (*The Scotsman,* 5 January 1940)

On 6 January, Millington-Drake sent telegram No. 4 to Halifax. It related to an earlier document which, although dated 2 January, was a copy of a telegram sent on 19th December about Germans sailors on the Tacoma being transferred by lighter to Argentina.

My Lord,

With reference to my telegram No. 2 of the 2nd instant and to previous correspondence relating to the German motor-ship "TACOMA", I have the honour to transmit, herein, a translation of the Decree issued by the Uruguayan Government on the 30th December last ordering the internment of that vessel as having been an auxiliary of the "ADMIRAL GRAF SPEE" if she did not leave within 24 hours, and by which Decree this ship was in fact interned on January 1st.

2. The preamble states that the Uruguayan Government's action is based on the Hague Convention XIII, in view of the

"TACOMA"'s activities, which are recited at length, and a summary of that preamble was given in my telegram No. 2 under reference, as follows: -

"That it was evident throughout that Captain of "TACOMA" was acting under orders of Captain of "ADMIRAL GRAF SPEE"; that vessel left the Port of Montevideo following the "ADMIRAL GRAF SPEE" and without proper authorisation and then acted as transport for military forces; that its operations within territorial waters were tantamount to making the Port of Montevideo a base contrary to provisions of Hague Convention XIII and would therefore failing action on the part of the Uruguayan Government constitute a breach of their neutrality; finally that it being clear that vessel acted as a naval auxiliary her stay in the port should be limited to 24 hours in accordance with Hague Convention."

3. The "TACOMA" is a passenger and a cargo liner of 8,258 tons displacement, built in 1930, with exceptionally large fuel tanks. She carried a crew of 60 and had been plying regularly from Hamburg to Valparaiso via the Panama Canal. Her trade being chiefly in fruit, there being unusually good cold storage facilities on board. She had remained in a Chilean port at the outbreak of the war, but together with the German steamer "LAHN", which was in a similar position in Chile, she undertook the voyage round by Magellan, reaching Montevideo on November 22nd last. The "LAHN" has remained under a commercial embargo for the delivery of cargo of minerals belonging to a British firm.

4. On or just before December 15th, the very day of the Battle of Punta del Este, the "TACOMA" had taken on board 400 tons of drinking water and 1,600 tons of fuel oil, together with 600 tons of diesel oil as utilised by submarines and which mixed with fuel oil forms fuels as used in warships.

5. I drew attention of the Uruguayan Government to this in a Note of December 15th and pointing out that such fuelling was more than enough to take her to Germany and would only be justified by Uruguayan regulations if this vessel had a full cargo of Uruguayan or at any rate River Plate produce for Germany, which was not the case. Copy of this note is enclosed for purposes of record.

6. The "TACOMA" was in fact preparing to go out to meet the "ADMIRAL GRAF SPEE", as is now confirmed by the statement of an officer of the latter ship in an interview which appeared in a Buenos Aires paper "El Sol" on December 23rd. He stated definitely that the "ADMIRAL GRAF SPEE" approached the

Uruguayan coast with the intention of refuelling from the "TACOMA".

7. As you are aware, the "ADMIRAL GRAF SPEE" had arrived at about 22.45 o'clock the night of December 1st and anchored in the ante-port, and at 7.30 the next morning the "TACOMA" moved to a position at anchor alongside the "ADMIRAL GRAF SPEE" and not 200 yards away from her.

8. In the early morning of Sunday, December 17th, the day on which the "ADMIRAL GRAF SPEE" was under notice to leave by 20 o'clock, it was observed that some 200 men and their effects were being transferred with some attempt at secrecy from the "ADMIRAL GRAF SPEE" to the "TACOMA" but later in the afternoon the number so transferred increased to some 800 – 900, the operation being carried on quite openly, thus leaving only some 200 – 400 men on board the "ADMIRAL GRAF SPEE"

9. I immediately went down to the Ministry for Foreign Affairs and informed the Minister's private secretary verbally of what was occurring at approximately 16 o'clock, and told him that in an hour or so I would return with a Note to that effect and confirming my request for the internment of the "TACOMA", since it would constitute a breach of neutrality to allow in the port of Montevideo the organisation of such a force and the equipment of such a vessel as a naval unit and to allow it to proceed to sea" (See telegram No. 168 of December 17th). I enclose for purpose of record copy of my note in question.

10. When the "ADMIRAL GRAF SPEE" left the harbour about a quarter past six, the "TACOMA", without authorisation from the port authorities, followed her out, and then the "ADMIRAL GRAF SPEE" anchored some 5 miles out, the "TACOMA" hove to [stopped] some 8 miles away from her, between her and the shore. Several boats left the "ADMIRAL GRAF SPEE" for the "TACOMA". As was reported in the Naval Attaché's War Despatch No.4 of December 23rd to the Director of Naval Intelligence (paragraphs 20 – 21), the crew of the "ADMIRAL GRAF SPEE" mustered on the decks of the "TACOMA" and gave the Nazi salute as the "ADMIRAL GRAF SPEE" blew up, and then immediately transferred to two Argentine tugs and a lighter which had meanwhile arrived from Buenos Aires, where they had left the port also without authorisation, being sent by A.M. Delfina y Cia., the agents of the Hamburg South America Line.

11. This transfer had taken place before a Montevideo Port Official arrived on the spot within 20 minutes of the explosion, on board the tug of our Naval Control Authorities, which has set out the moment the explosion had taken place. The Senior Port Official arrived in another tug soon afterwards and after some

parley and reference to the Port authorities by wireless allowed the Delfino tugs and the lighter to proceed to Buenos Aires, but directed the "TACOMA" to return to port which she did.

12. On her return she was searched and four ratings of the "ADMIRAL GRAF SPEE" who had remained on board and admitted to having been responsible for actually blowing up the ship were arrested, as their action was regarded as a criminal one. When I saw the Minister of Foreign Affairs on December 18th (see telegram No. 173) he informed me that in his view the "TACOMA" had acted as a Fleet auxiliary in every way, under the orders of the Captain of the "ADMIRAL GRAF SPEE", and would have to be interned. He renewed his assurance in the same sense of December 22nd (my telegram No. 185, paragraph 7.) It was clear to me that Dr. Guani wished the case to be very thoroughly sifted and that nothing should be done hastily.

13. When I saw him again on December 28th, he seemed impressed by the information which I had communicated to him, Meanwhile in my Note No. 121 of December 26th, to the effect that an officer of the "ADMIRAL GRAF SPEE" had informed a Buenos Aires newspaper that the pocket battleship had been approaching the Uruguayan coast in order to refuel and reprovision from the "TACOMA". He told me that internment was imminent. It may appear that there was unusual delay in this matter, but it must be borne in mind that the Uruguayan administrative departments concerned have nor a numerous or very efficient personnel and that moreover a certain dilatoriness in such matters is normal in these countries, not to mention the fact that the days in question were those of the Christmas and New Year holidays.

14. In effect the matter was decided on at a special meeting of the President of the Republic and the Ministers concerned on the afternoon of Saturday, December 30th, but the vessel was to be first formally notified that she was regarded as a Fleet auxiliary and was therefore given 24 hours in which to leave, failing which she would be interned. The German Legation was so informed that evening, and the Master, Captain Konow, was notified at 6.30 next morning, December 31st. At 17 o'clock the vessel moved to the outer part of the ante-port and there was every reason to suppose that she would sail and thereby created what appeared to be a delicate problem in connection with the security zone (see your telegram No. 2 to Buenos Aires of January 1st), since her capture by His Majesty's ships within that zone would have constituted aggression within that zone, but, because of her classification by the Uruguayan Government as a Fleet auxiliary, not an aggression against Uruguayan sea-borne commerce as

defined to me a few days previously by Dr. Guani (see my telegram No, 198 of December 31st). As the "TACOMA" failed to leave, the formalities of internment were proceeded with at 7 a.m. on January 1st, and the Master, Captain Konow, on being given the choice whether he and his crew should be interned on board or ashore elected to remain on board, to ensure the proper upkeep of the vessel.

15. On January 2nd the Minister of Foreign Affairs told me that the German Legation was pressing its protest against the internment, but that he intended to disregard it (see my telegram No. 3 of that date).

16. The 1,600 tons of oil taken on board by "TACOMA" as reported in paragraph 4 above has been transferred back to the National Fuel Administration, but it is understood that a reimbursement of its cost has not yet been effected.

17. An important part of the general cargo consisting of Californian fruit has had to be jettisoned because of deterioration, and another important part consisting of red pine is likely to be purchased by local firms.

I have, Sir. (Ibid, 6 January 1940)

<u>Enclosure No. 1 to Montevideo despatch No. 4 of 6th January 1940.</u>
<u>DECREE: PROVIDING FOR THE INTERNMENT OF THE GERMAN MOTOR VESSEL "TACOMA"</u> (Translation)

Having regard to the findings of the enquiry ordered by the Prefecture General of Ports, apart from other evidence relating to the arrival and stay of the German Merchant Vessel "Tacoma", in order to reach a decision as to the activities of that vessel on the occasion of the voluntary sinking of the German cruiser Admiral Graf Spee" on the 17th of the present month.

Whereas: Among the activities of the "Tacoma" it appears that the Captain of this vessel, in the events which took place, has evidently been obeying the orders of the Commanding Officer of the above mentioned cruiser, and has assisted in various ways to effect the scuttling of that Ship;

And Whereas: On the occasion of the sinking, the "Tacoma" served as a transport of armed forces, which were transhipped afterwards to other vessels, and still contains various property belonging to the sunken cruiser;

And Whereas: Ten more members of the crew of the "Admiral Graf Spee" remained in the obeying the orders of the Commanding Officer of the above mentioned cruiser, and were later landed on the orders of the maritime authorities;

And Whereas: All the activities in which the above mentioned merchant vessel engaged took place in the territorial waters of the Republic, on the occasion of the vessel's departure from the port of Montevideo to follow the cruiser "Admiral Graf Spee", without the authority of the General Prefecture of ports and without a pilot on board, for which act the fine authorised by Article 135 of the General Pilotage Regulations was applied;

And Whereas: One of the fundamental duties of belligerents, according to Article 1 of Convention XIII signed at the Hague on 18th October 1907, is the respect due to the sovereign rights of neutral powers which oblige belligerents likewise "to abstain in territorial or neutral waters from any act which may constitute on the part of the power which allows it a breach of its neutrality";

And Whereas: If acts such as those committed on the 17th day of December by the vessel "Tacoma" in territorial waters, acting under the orders of the Commander of the belligerent war vessel, were to be permitted, the Republic's neutrality would undoubtedly be violated, since Powers at war are expressly prohibited from making use of neutral Ports or waters as a base for naval operations;

And Whereas: Neutral governments are obliged in a specified manner to exercise the vigilance which the means at their disposal allow to prevent any violation of those rules in their ports, roadsteads, and waters;

And Whereas: Merchant ships which place themselves under historical precedents, laid themselves open to be considered and to be treated as auxiliary vessels of belligerent war fleets, from the very moment when they place themselves under such orders; giving rise in such cases to the application of the appropriate provisions of Convention XIII signed at the Hague of the 18th October 1907, which the Government of the Republic must observe in accordance with the decree of the 5th September 1939, declaring the neutrality of Uruguay in the present war.

NOW THEREFORE:

THE PRESIDENT OF THE REPUBLIC DECREES:

ARTICLE 1. The dispositions of Convention XIII of the Hague, signed on the 18th October 1907, referring to belligerent ships of war shall hereby be applied to the German vessel "Tacoma", and the time limit of 24 hours be fixed for that Ship to leave the port of Montevideo, together with the application of other corresponding measures laid down in the same Convention.

ARTICLE 2. The above-mentioned time limit shall count from the moment in which the Captain of the ship is notified of the present decree.

ARTICLE 3. Let it be communicated, etc.

SIGNED.   BALDOMIR.
A.   GUANI.
GENERAL ALFREDO CAMPOS.

Ministry of Foreign Affairs,
Montevideo. 30th December 1939.

Enclosure 2 in Montevideo despatch No. 4 of 6th January 1940.
No.107   BRITISH LEGATION,
                                                            MONTEVIDEO

Monsieur le Ministre,

I have the honour to draw your Excellency's attention to the fact that a German cargo boat, the "Tacoma", obtained the day before yesterday 1,600 tons of fuel oil, which would be sufficient for a voyage to Europe.

In accordance with the rules which Your Excellency was good enough to lay down, this supply would only be justified in the case of the ship referred to carrying a full cargo of Uruguayan produce or part of which only was from elsewhere in the River Plate, which I am informed is not the case of this steamer.

Further, the s.s. "Tacoma" took on board 300 tons of Diesel oil as utilised by submarines and which mixed with fuel oil forms fuel used by warships.

I have the honour to request Your Excellency to be so good as to take the necessary steps to prevent what would appear to be an infraction of Uruguayan neutrality.

I avail myself, etc.
E. MILLINGTON-DRAKE.

Enclosure No.3 in Montevideo despatch No.4 of 6th January 1940
No.115   BRITISH LEGATION, MONTEVIDEO
                                    17th December 1939.

Monsieur le Ministere,

As 703 Officers and men from the German battleship "ADMIRAL GRAF SPEE" have been transferred to the German Merchant Ship "TACOMA" with their effects and other equipment, etc., this steamer has become a military transport and I therefore have the honour to request that her departure be prevented, since it would be a breach of neutrality to allow, in the port of Montevideo, the organisation of such a force and the equipment of such a vessel as a naval unit and to allow it to proceed to sea.

It is my duty to draw Your Excellency's attention immediately to this very serious matter and to ask Your Excellency to take, urgently, all possible steps to prevent the departure of this vessel.

I avail myself, etc.

E. Millington-Drake. (Ibid.)

On 12 January, the Staff officer (intelligence) (SO(I)) at Britain's Legation in Montevideo, sent the following message to SO)I) Freetown (Sierra Leone, West Africa), the Commander-in-Chief (CIC) of South Atlantic Station, the Admiralty for the attention of DNI, the Rear Admiral Commanding South American Division (RACSAD), the America and West Indies Naval Squadron and the British Naval Attaches in Buenos Aires and Rio de Janeiro.

DIR 60 with a view to preventing possibility of German ship DHXD (TACOMA) sailing. Uruguayan Government has made her discharge her oil onto a lighter. (TNA ADM 116/4180, 12 January 1940)

Given Tacoma's role in the Battle of the River Plate, copies of the telegram were also sent to Sir Dudley Pound, the First Sea Lord, his Chief Security Officer (CSO), P.A.S.(S) (?), the Deputy Chief Naval Staff (DCNS), the Head of Naval Operations (Ops), I.P. (?), and M, the Admiralty's Military Branch.

On the same day, Ovey updated Halifax about the situation in Buenos Aires.

My Lord,
In my despatch No.372 of the 27th December last I reported a statement made to me by His Excellency, the Minister for Foreign Affairs, that the crew of the "Graf Spee" would be split up into parties of 200 or so and sent to the interior of the country.

2. So far, this action has not been taken; verbal enquiries by my staff at the Ministry of Foreign Affairs eliciting the reply that time was necessary for taking the fingerprints of each man, ascertaining his qualifications, and classifying him for inclusion in one of several parties.

3. Meanwhile, a certain number of the men of the "Graf Spee" are to be seen, smartly turned out and usually accompanied by women friends, both in the streets of Buenos Aires and at the waterfront bars. A few of them also watched the arrival of H.M.S. "Achilles" last week; two of them being seen to salute our officers and a few being reported by the press to have attempted to fraternise with some sailors of the British cruiser while the latter were drinking beer at a bar.

4. Two days ago my attention was drawn to advertisements in the local press of concerts to be given on Friday, January 12th, in German halls in the suburbs if Buenos Aires by the orchestra of the "Graf Spee"; the proceeds of which were to be allocated to

German charities. I therefore enquired of His Excellency, Senor Cantilo, with regard to the dispersal of the crew; only to receive a somewhat evasive reply.

5. The moment was not propitious for further discussion on this side-issue; but a further announcement of a boxing tournament between members of the ship's crew and Argentine amateurs having appeared in today's German newspaper I propose to renew this Embassy's pressure upon the Ministry of Foreign Affairs at the earliest convenient opportunity, lest the apparent dilatoriness in giving effect to Senor Cantilo's earlier and laudable intentions should be due to more than a natural propensity to hurry slowly in dealing with this large number of unwanted guests, reinforced by a combination of new year holidays and the unusual heat wave which has visited the city for the last 10 days.

6. I am sending a copy of this despatch to His Majesty's Minister (Millington-Drake) at Montevideo.

I have, etc.   (TNA ADM 116/4180, 12 January 1940)

A few days later, the Admiralty sent F.O.C. [First Officer Commanding] North Atlantic 221, the Commander in Chief of South Atlantic 22 and the Directorate of Naval Intelligence (DNI) the following telegram. Given the importance of the contents, copies were also sent to First Sea Lord, Chief Staff Officer to First Sea Lord, D.C.N.S., A.C.N.S. [Acting Chief Naval Staff], D.E.W.D. [Director of Economic Warfare Division], D.S.D. (Director of Signals Division), P.A.S. (?), M, M34, M35, M37, 70, Ops, O.D. (?) O.I.C. [Officer in Charge], and I.P. (?)

Information received that 180 ratings [junior member of the ship's crew] from GRAF SPEE may be on board Italian steamer OCEANIA who will call Teneriffe 18th January and Barcelona 21st January. French cruiser EMILE BURTIN has been ordered to board steamer before her calling at Teneriffe [sic]. (TNA ADM 116/4180, 15 January 1940)

On 16 January, Claud Waldock, the Head of the Military Branch I, the Foreign Relations section of the British Admiralty which dealt with questions of international law, commented that he,

Proposed to send the attached reply to the Foreign Office. Presumably the case for interning the vessel would have to be based on a claim that the harbouring by the merchant vessel of a belligerent of 7 fugitive members of its armed forces compromises the neutrality of a State in whose waters the vessel lies. It is true that fugitives who have not been made prisoners of war are treated much more harshly by the law than escaped prisoners of war. But it is a wholly novel point and it is questionable whether it is even desirable to put forward such a doctrine. We ourselves are not infrequently in the position of wanting to recover men from neutral countries and this doctrine might prove something of a boomerang, (TNA ADM 116/5474, 16 January 1940)

Also on 16 January, Dr Guani sent a note to Herr Langmann which Millington-Drake claimed 'vigorously and sarcastically' refuted the German minister's note claiming that the Tacoma had acted purely from humanitarian motives. The note shows 'the Uruguayan Government's energetic rebuttal of the German protest and their fearless attitude towards Hitler at this time when already the attitude of many governments was very different.'

Your Excellency,
I beg leave to differ from the view of the German Legation which are set forth above. One cannot consider as help of a philanthropic character, as Your Excellency affirms, the transfer and transport of the crew of the battleship ADMIRAL GRAF SPEE as was carried out before her sailing and sinking in Uruguayan territorial waters;
1. Because the acts in question were, as appears in the report of the relative enquiry, in accordance with indications made to the Captain of the TACOMA by the Captain of the warship in our port.
2. Because it is unquestionable that the said Captain had foreseen, when he ordered the Captain of the TACOMA to take such measures, the fate that a few hours later was to be that of the battleship GRAF SPEE - as is well known that was the sinking of that ship.
3. 3, everyone knows the request which with the obvious purpose of avoiding internment was made by the German Embassy in Buenos Aires at the time when the crew of the GRAF SPEE arrived there, in the sense that her crew should be considered by the Government of the Argentine Republic as shipwrecked sailors.
4. Such a view of the facts was definitely reported by the Argentine Government (see its decree of December 19, 1939). Therefore it is evident that in the act of transfer and transport of the crew of the said TACOMA in our port there was already the intention of avoiding, for the crew of the ADMIRAL GRAF SPEE, their probable internment in Buenos Aires by means of the interpretation given to the matter by the German diplomatic

Representatives which was not admitted by the Argentine authorities.

5. What, then, was the purpose of the action begun in Montevideo? It simply meant an attempt to secure the release of officers and crew of the ADMIRAL GRAF SPEE on arrival in Buenos Aires, enabling them in this manner to return without difficulty to their activities as members of the German armed forces.

6. In these circumstances was this or was in not a violation of the neutrality which governs us, viz. [which is] the refuge which the crew sought in the TACOMA? Was it or was it not an act of obvious complicity that took place in our waters in the circumstances mentioned, on the part of the German ship TACOMA?

To put the question is to reply to it in the sense that the merchant ship in queston was transformed by her acts during the time that she was in Montevideo into what was in fact an auxiliary warship. Neutral governments, such as that of this Republic, are obliged, according to Article 25 of the Hague Convention, to exercise a most efficacious watch so that the rules of neutrality should not be violated in their ports or territorial waters. In addition, there is the even earlier obligation of the Government, by its own Decree of September 5, 193, declaring its neutrality in the present war. In this circumstance ... the Uruguayan Government could not adopt any other attitude than that dictated by the foregoing occurrence and the principles that govern neutrality in war at sea. The Government of the Republic, however, is glad on this occasion to be able to repeat that, in applying the rules of the Hague Convention mentioned above, it has done so in the spirit laid down in Article 26 of the same, according to which the exercise by a power of the rights set forth in it cannot be regarded as an unfriendly act.

Comment. General Campos later records that the Captain and crew of the TACOMA were officially interned by a Uruguayan Government Decree of January 23, 1940, together with the thirty-two wounded landed from the GRAF SPEE on December 17 (and transferred to the Military Hospital) as well as a few other members of the GRAF SPEE crew who remained on board the TACOMA.

General Campos emphasises that the regime imposed on them was lenient and even hospitable, especially as regards the Captain, and recalls that nevertheless the Captain and his engineers were found to have sabotaged the engines when these were inspected in 1942. He refers with some bitterness to what he calls a lack of good faith.

This note was the last act of the Uruguayan Government dealing with the GRAF SPEE at the time. It should be noticed that its fearless and indeed sarcastic tone is characteristic of the courageous attitude of the Uruguayan Government in the whole emergency, especially as the Government knew there was a well-organised German underground movement. (Millington Drake, E. op.cit, pp.377-8)

The following day, 17 January, Jarrett at the Admiralty noted that,

> If the attached extract from the Daily Summary for the 15th January is correct, it would appear that the Argentine Government have failed in their undoubted duty to intern the crew of the GRAF SPEE, and we should, it would appear, ask the Foreign Office to make strong representation on the subject.
>
> Before the Foreign Office are approached, however, perhaps D.N.I. could say, or if necessary, ascertain from the Naval Attaché, whether there is any truth in this report.

> SECRET
> Extract from Daily Summary of Naval Events
> No. 134 of 15th January, 1940.
>
> According to a Transocean [A German wireless news agency] message from Buenos Aires on January 13 the band of the ADMIRAL GRAF SPEE gave a concert in the suburb of Vicente Lopez, which attracted an audience of four thousand, including many Argentines. The band played German march music which was greatly applauded, as were serious and humorous sailor songs sung by the ship's choir. The band of the ADMIRAL GRAF SPEE had four of its members killed in the action of December 13. (Ibid.)

Also on 17 January, the Commander in Chief of the South Atlantic Fleet contacted the Admiralty and the Flag Officer Commanding the North Atlantic [FOCNA]. A copy was sent to all the recipients of the earlier message.

> 158. Your 0921 15th January to F.O.C.N.A. On enquiry from B.N.A. [British Naval Attaché] Buenos Aires, he reports there is no repetition no evidence that any ratings from German armoured ship ADMIRAL GRAF SPEE sailed in Italian Ship IBJK (OCEANIA). Mistake may have arisen due to French Naval attaché

reporting 108 Chinese ex German Merchant Vessel sailed in Italian Ship IBJK (OCEANIA). (TNA ADM 116/5474, 17 January 1940)

Millington-Drake sent telegram 18 to the Foreign Office on 18 January with copies to Rio, Buenos Aires and Santiago.

> My immediately preceding telegram.
> In a subsequent conversation with the Minister of Foreign Affairs this morning I raised the question of the would-be attachés from the Graf Spee in a roundabout way. I referred to the information in your telegram Circular No. 4 that time bombs were being distributed in South America and said that it appeared to me that the fact the four specialists who had blown up the "Spee" remained in Uruguay was done with a purpose, and might be connected with sabotage.
> The Minister for Foreign Affairs told me that these men in their launch had reached Tacoma after the rest of the crew had transferred to the Argentine tugs which had hastened off. Their return to port on the Tacoma was therefore seemingly natural though of course premeditation was not excluded.
> I then spoke of the other men who were, I supposed, awaiting internment, and the Minister said that the time limit which he had given them to prove that they were accepted as attachés in other South American countries expired today. When I asked whether these countries had been warned by him of the whole position, he assured me that they had and that any acceptance by them was practically out of the question for the very reason that Argentina had interned the men of the "Spee". The Uruguayan decree of internment is now ready.
> In the circumstances I suggested that action should be suspended on my suggestion for a personal letter. (TNA ADM 116/4180, 18 January 1940)

The following day, he sent telegram 20.

> My telegram No. 18 and my telegram No. 12.
> I am relieved to be able to inform you that I got a good impression of the Minister of Foreign Affair's intentions. He did, however, [grp.und.] German Minister personally at least fully realise that in all these questions he had proceeded with justice and even consideration towards German interests. He seemed anxious to avoid giving cause for any change of this view, and I got the impression that though he felt convinced that there was no other solution than internment, he had nevertheless decided that this being so, he would at least by unhasty procedure show them such consideration as possible.

I also ascertained, as I surmised, that he knew the men in question who lodged in the German Legation and some of them in the Consulate. (Ibid, 19 January 1940)

He sent telegram 19 later the same day to London and Buenos Aires.

My immediately preceding telegram – my telegram No.11 – paragraph 9 and your despatch No. 157.

I referred to the wreck of Graf Spee and the Minister for Foreign Affairs said the Uruguayan Government had no plans regarding it for the time being but that he would certainly raise important question of the three mile limit and that he had intended to speak to me about this. Wreck lay exactly four and a half miles from shore and he believed Germans had done this with intention. He had been told by the German Minister that the question of its location and disposal was now being studied by the legal adviser to the German Foreign Office. He believed that the Germans would claim that the wreck was outside the three-mile limit and therefore, in accordance with British general acceptance of interpretation of territorial waters, in open sea and therefore the property of the German Government.

It would be a great satisfaction to the Minister for Foreign Affairs if he were able to reply that His Majesty's Government had made an exception in the case of the River Plate for special reasons.

He did not ask me to do so but would be glad if I would convey to you quite informally suggestion whether his Majesty's Government would not consider recognising River Plate as territorial waters because of many special circumstances. I abstained from comment and said that I would communicate to you what he had told me.

In this connexion I would of course refer to Buenos Aires telegram No. 381 paragraph 5 in which Sir E. Ovey hinted at the excellent effect that would be caused by the publication of such a concession which might be justified in this special case by the fact that the navigability of the river was due entirely to dredging carried out by the Argentine Government.

Since drafting the above I have received your telegram No. 11 addressed to Buenos Aires. Would decision of Argentina to ban submarines, this certainly turning the scale at Rio de Janeiro Conference, and following initiative of Uruguay in this sense be considered such quid pro quo [a favour or advantage granted in return for a similar favour or advantage] or have you in mind that in addition to the foregoing Argentina and Uruguay should take the lead in abandoning the security zone proposal, Cortes [?]

alternatively securing all desiderata [something needed or wanted] of His Majesty's Government concerning the same? (Ibid.)

Ovey sent Halifax another report on 20 January.

My Lord,
    With reference to my despatch No.16 of the 12th January, regarding the interned crew of the German warship "Admiral Graf Spee", I have the honour to transmit herewith a memorandum by the Counsellor to this Embassy recording an interview with the official in charge of the Ministry of Foreign Affairs which took place – by arrangement with the French Embassy – after my French colleague had again raised the subject with the Ministry.
    2. M. Peyrouton's representations appear to have resulted in cancellation of a second concert by the ship's company; and there is, on the whole, no material reason for believing that the Government is not gradually implementing its decree. Martin Garcia Island, on which the German sailors were interned during the last war, is, for instance, I am given to understand, being prepared to receive 200 of these men.
    3. But apart from the nervousness at their numbers, to which Sr. Santos Munoz alluded, the Argentine Government is faced with the problem of maintenance, the cost of which I hear from other sources is calculated at 89,000 pesos paper a month.
    4. I therefore propose for the present to maintain discreet and friendly pressure on the Argentine Government for the exact fulfilment of its decree; and shall take an early opportunity of warning the Minister for Foreign Affairs against falling in with the German plan for attaching apparent Gestapo agents from the ship's company to the German Embassies in Buenos Aires and elsewhere, as reported in telegram No. 11 of the 14th January from His Majesty's Minister in Montevideo.
    I have etc.

"GRAF SPEE"

    I drew Dr Munoz' attention today to the fact that the men of the "Graf Spee" were now lounging about the docks in the neighbourhood of British ships. Apart from the undesirability of this procedure on general grounds, there was the risk of an incident arising out of hot words between our more independent merchant seamen and these "internees". The Embassy therefore, hoped that the action indicated by Dr. Cantilo to the Ambassador – that is the early removal of this warship's crew to the interior, in batches – would soon be taken.

Dr Munoz told me: -
a) That the President himself was concerned in this question (I could get no more out of him as to the manner or extent of the President's concern).
b) That efforts were being made to have the men of the "Graf Spee" put in civilian clothes "as this would make them less able to go about posing as victims of a naval disaster". (To this I rejoined that in civilian clothes they might be more dangerous, in Buenos Aires, than in uniform; since they would be less conspicuous.
c) That the French Ambassador had made representations two or three days ago (as had been agreed between the Counsellor of the French Embassy and myself last Monday 15h) with regard to "Graf Spee" concerts; as a result of which the second concert advertised had been prohibited.
d) (On my again urging the early despatch of these men up country) That this would be done "as was specifically laid down in the Government decree concerning their internment"; but that their number presented a serious problem. (TNA ADM 116/4180, 20 January 1940)

On 23 January, the Foreign Office sent Millington-Drake telegram No. 15.

Your telegram No. 18 [of 18th January: internment of men from "Spee"].
Admiralty have now established, as a result of interrogation of masters made prisoners by Graf Spee, that one of the fourteen men is a very expert cryptographer who accompanied all boarding parties sent out from the warship [to collect whatever documents and coding machines he could find in the code room].
It is clear therefore that he must be regarded essentially as a member of the enemy forces.
Unless decree of internment has already been published and men have actually been interned, you should draw attention of Uruguayan Government to above considerations, informally. (Ibid, 23 January 1940)

The following day, Millington-Drake updated London, Rio de Janeiro, Buenos Aires and Santiago

Your telegram No. 15.
The Political Director of the Ministry of Foreign Affairs informs me confidentially that no reply having been received from the

Argentine Republic, Brazil, or from Chile and Paraguay, to who the Uruguayan Government had addressed similar communications, the internment decree has been signed by the President of the Republic but not yet published, and the information is confidential for the time being. I had already mentioned to the Minister for Foreign Affairs [Alberto Guani] that one party must be the semi-independent Gestapo agent known to have been on board (see my telegram No. 11 paragraph 4). (Ibid, 24 January 1940)

The *Belfast News Letter* reported on the Graf Spee crew on 24 January.

GRAF SPEE'S CREW
Demoralised in Battle With British Warships
YOUNG AND INEXPERIENCED

Some of the younger men the crew the Graf Spee had been sent to sea after only a few months' training ashore. They were inexperienced and unhandy about a ship. The crew were demoralised in the action against Exeter, Ajax and Achilles.

This is the information which the Admiralty have gained from interviews with British masters and wireless operators who were prisoners aboard the German pocket battleship.

"If, as has been said, the Graf Spee had picked crew then the standard of the Nazi Navy cannot compare with that of the German Navy of 1914-18," is the Admiralty conclusion. Interviews with British masters and wireless operators who were prisoners on Graf Spee show that German boarding parties invariably seized sextants, chronometers, binoculars, telescopes, and even typewriters.

ABNORMALLY YOUNG

All the British prisoners agree that the Graf Spee's crew were abnormally young. Most were between 17 and 22. Some had never been afloat before and were inexperienced and unhappy about a ship. The entire crew of the Graf Spee firmly believed that their ship was invincible. They thought most of the British Navy was already sunk, and said everyone knew that- the Mood, Renown, and Repulse were out of action, along with the Ark Royal, and that Mr. Churchill's speeches were all bluff, and the Germans could not be beaten. The German wireless had told them the week before that the British East Coast ports were blocked with mines that traffic had ceased to run.

The food served to the prisoners was exactly the same as that given to the crew. "It was very bad indeed. Insufficient," some of the captives said, to enable men to do a full day's work. The sausage, composed of goodness knows what, "could only be swallowed after hard mastication." (*Belfast News Letter,* 24 January 1940)

At the end of January, Sir Charles Bentinck, the British Ambassador in Santiago, sent the Foreign Office a note that the 'Head of political department of Ministry of Foreign Affairs told me that Chilean Government had been approached in connexion with proposed appointment of officers of "GRAF SPEE" to German Embassy at Santiago. The Chilean Government had replied throwing the whole responsibility of the decision on the shoulders of the Uruguayan Government. Obviously these men would only come to Chile if the Uruguayan Government permitted them to leave the country.' (TNA ADM 116/4180, 29 January 1940)

The Foreign Office's response to Ovey, telegram 231, was sent on 30 January.

> Your telegram No. 369 (of 26th December: crew of "Graf Spee".)
>
> Article 24 of Hague Convention 13 states that when a belligerent ship is detailed by a neutral Power the officers and crews are likewise detained and that the officers may be left at liberty on giving their word not to quit the neutral territory without permission.
>
> Similarly Article 11 of Hague Convention 5 in the parallel case of the internment of land forces provides that a neutral Power which receives in its territory troops belonging to the belligerent armies shall detain them and shall decide whether officers are to be left at liberty on giving their parole that they will not leave the neutral territory without authorisation. Furthermore, Article 12 of the same Convention provides that in the absence of a special convention the neutral Power shall supply the interned with food and that at the conclusion of peace the expenses caused by internment shall be made good.
>
> In view of these provisions it is not only obviously the clear duty of the Argentine authorities to intern the crew of the "Graf Spee" (which they have done) but, if the officers are released on parole, not to give them permission to leave the Argentine in order to carry on any type of naval work elsewhere, since the effect of allowing them to do so would obviously be adverse to our interests and inconsistent with the obligations imposed upon a neutral. Since the Hague Convention makes express provision for the cost of the upkeep of the internees there can be no justification for any attempt by the Argentine Government to evade their responsibilities and duties as neutrals to ensure that

these men do not leave the Argentine before the end of the war and do not have any opportunity meanwhile of engaging in activities which might be very prejudicial to our rights and interests.

I leave it to your discretion to draw the attention of the Argentine Government in whatever manner you deem desirable to the above considerations should a suitable opportunity present itself. (Ibid. 30 January 1940)

British Embassy, Dr. Luis Agote 2412, Buenos Aires (https://www.gov.uk/government/news/british-embassy-buenos-aires-launches-call-for-project-bids-for-2017)

Sir Eugen Millington-Drake, British Plenipotentiary in Uruguay 1937 to 1941 (https://www.pluna.uy/blog/sir-eugen-millington-drake-y-su-apuesta-por-pluna/)

British Embassy, Montevideo
(https://www.gov.uk/government/news/british-embassy-in-montevideo-closed-on-november-1st)

Hans Götz, one of the crew members, referred to the early days in Argentina in his diary which Millington-Drake included in his anthology.

> During the following weeks we were allowed to go out and about and meet the local population. Both Germans and Argentines received us cordially. Our Swabian fellow countrymen came and invited us to their homes. My comrade Hein Wild from Ulm and a few other Swabians who had always kept together, found that even in distant South America our fellow countrymen did make every sacrifice to assist us and so overcome the tragedy of our fate. The smart young sailors in their uniforms were very welcome guests. We look back happily to that time and think gratefully to the land of Argentina and her people. (Millington-Drake, op.cit. p.384)

Dick's biography shed light on the life of the internees in the early months of 1940.

> The next few weeks sped by. The German Cultural and Charitable Association arranged regular visits to places of interest, walks and outings and laid on great spreads of food. This routine continued throughout the Argentine summer, which they discovered ran from December to March. The guard detail was responsible for sweeping the communal areas, keeping the garden tidy and ensuring everything was spick and span. The other internees passed their days doing sport and physical

exercises, swimming and visiting some of the gym clubs around the capital such as the Villa Ballester, Quilmes and Los Polvierines, which were also an opportunity to enjoy a good lunch before they returned to their usual grind. Every four days they were give a pass that allowed them to leave the Hotel for a whole day.

One day the crew was split into several groups then called one by one into an office at the Hotel de Immigrantes where specially appointed police officials photographed them, took down their names in a register and took their finger prints before getting them to sign some papers. On the 29th December they were each given a tiny booklet. It had had to be printed in record time and had a grey cloth cover printed with the words "Cedula de Internacion" in black. It was an identity carnet that specified their status as internees. Even though only a few of them spoke Spanish at that time, they knew immediately what it meant and that it would go with them wherever they went for the foreseeable future. [...]

During that time of profound change, they were vaccinated on numerous occasions against diseases classified as "tropical", subjected to several health checks and given their first spending money in the form of pesos, the Argentine currency. Any comparisons with German prices were useless because their homeland was at war and inflation had in any case been rampant there for several years. Even so, the cost of meat, leather, some kinds of drink, and getting around by public transport struck them as ludicrously cheap.

The First Officer, who had by now been put in charge of the interned crew, had asked the authorities to find accommodation for the men at a naval base, but the request had been turned down. In fact, this may have been a stroke of luck for the internees as the base he had in mind was some distance from Buenos Aires and they also learned they might well have received less favourable treatment there. Various other possibilities were also discussed, however, because the fact was that neither the Naval Arsenal nor the Hotel de Immigrantes would be able to cope with such a large influx of men in the long term. Their facilities had been designed for short stays by frightened immigrants who were in transit elsewhere. In contrast, these lively young Germans hogged the bathrooms, the kitchens were not geared up to feed so many mouths and local officials were nervous at having to deal with so many people all in one go. Tongues were in any case beginning to wag and Benjamin Franklin's famous saying that "Guests, like fish, begin to smell after three days" was quoted on more than one occasion. The authorities discussed splitting them up and billeting them with German host families so they could get involved in business or in industry or in farming or fishing activities. Another alternative, one that gained ground at the beginning of 1940, was to spread them around the country in small groups that would be simpler to administer and monitor. [...]

The contingent was split in two and each man was given a little bit of spending money and something to eat. My father's group got back on the bus and were driven to the barracks run by the Mounted Police in Calle Lima, a few yards back from the river and about a mile away from the railway station. with its thick walls, crenelated watch towers and huge exercise yard the place looked like a 19th century Spanish prison, not dissimilar to the ones they had seen during their travels in North Africa. It had two floors. On the upper floor, the rooms stretched along a series of gallery-stye balconies. The far right hand corner of the exercise yard was where they kept the horses, 'noble brutes' as those who found horse more interesting than people used to say. These horses were shorter than usual and had an air of resignation as they waited to be taken out on patrol again.

Their new guards showed them where they would be sleeping. It was an untidy, unwelcoming place. The only furnishings were some iron beds, a big table made out of dark wood on which several previous inmates had carved their names, a few mismatched chairs that looked as if they might have come from some bar that the police had raided. The latrines were outside at the back.

They were beginning to feel hungry. "You'll be getting your midday meal shortly," they were told. By way of an entree, a loaf of bread was passed round inside a dented metal pan covered with an equally dented metal lid, a couple of plates and an empty sack, big enough to cover a bed, made of some kind of fabric that might at one time have been white.

"Later on, you'll be given one of these each and told to fill them with straw," explained one of the guards, seeing the looks of incomprehension on their faces. "They are your mattresses."

The food when it arrived comprised a dish of rice with chicken giblets, a few potatoes, beans and peas jazzed up with some local spices. They were so hungry they just dived in and wolfed the lot. They were given some late-season oranges, which at least helped quench their thirst.

As if of one mind, the sailors asked if they could have some cleaning materials, all anxious to return the hovel that was to be their new home to some sort of shape. It was already time for the local soldiers to take their daily siesta and to snatch a little sleep.

They looked through the windows and saw that the whole city appeared to have taken themselves indoors and out of the heat for a couple of hours. But as their guards rested, the sailors got busy sweeping, scrubbing, applying bleach and disinfectant, despatching ants and other bugs without mercy, and stowing away their meagre belongings. (Dick, op.cit. pp.112, 119)

At the beginning of February, Ovey sent telegram No. 6 'Saving' to London and Montevideo. The words 'Saving' and 'Savingram' appear to be a codename used for South American correspondence.

My despatch No. 16 of January 12th.
Minister for Foreign Affairs described to me yesterday the steps the Government proposes to take regarding the internees of the "Graf Spee".

His Excellency explained that he had been conversing with the German Ambassador about the question of payment. The Germans were prepared, first of all, to pay after the war, but I gathered from the reference to certain funds at the disposal of the Germans, some partial payment may be made before. (The German Ambassador was, however, going to put something in writing). The expense question evidently worried him as he referred to $5 a day for 1000 men as being a considerable sum.

The first thing to do was to get the men in civilian clothes which was being arranged. His Excellency then said that as far as possible they would attempt to give the men employment. I said "In the Interior, I suppose", to which his Excellency replied "Yes", but added "for instance, if employment were available a man might work in (here he mentioned an immediate suburb of Buenos Aires_".

I pointed out that many of these men might be experts and might find employment in German firms making time bombs [delayed action magnetic explosive devices used for sinking ships, etc.] for instance. He assured me that they would not violate the hospitality offered to them.

I gather there has been some difficulty with the Provincial authorities about these men.

His Excellency described the German Ambassador as being very forthcoming, which did not surprise me as he appeared to be obtaining the best possible terms.

As regards the proposal to send certain officers from Uruguay as Attachés to other posts, His Excellency had been awaiting events and said that the matter has now been settled as Dr Guani has interned them.

His Excellency seemed pleased that he had thwarted the German suggestion that they should be kept in groups under their own officers, but my general impression is that the measures His Excellency proposes will be the minimum consonant with the assurance that these men will not either return to Germany or engage in nefarious practices here. I did not press his Excellency strongly on the subject in view of the general question of the Rio Conference, regarding which see my Savingram No. 6 of February 2nd. (TNA ADM 116/4180, 2 February 1940)

The *New York Times* reported on 12 February.

11 INTERNED MEN ESCAPE URUGUAY; Former Officers and Sailors of Graf Spee and Tacoma Believed on Way Home HAD LIBERTY IN CAPITAL Authorities Checking to Find Whether Others Have Left-- Argentina Tightens Hold.
    MONTEVIDEO, Uruguay, Feb. 11--Eleven interned officers and sailors of the scuttled pocket battleship Admiral Graf Spee and the interned supply ship Tacoma have disappeared under circumstances that indicate they have escaped and are en route to Germany via Italy. The police are investigating to determine whether still others have fled. [Rest of article available on subscription. *(New York Times,* 12 February 1940)

The British *Newcastle Journal* reported the same day.

GRAF SPEE MEN ESCAPE
SEVERAL sailors and officers of both the scuttled pocket battleship Graf Spee and her attendant ship, the Tacoma, which has been interned, have disappeared from Uruguay, said the Montevideo newspaper "El Pais," yesterday. The newspaper says that although these men were interned it is suspected that they managed to escape to Brazil by air. and are trying to get back to Germany by way of Italy.—British United Press. (*Newcastle Journal*, 12 February 1940)

A few days later, Millington-Drake updated the Foreign Office with telegram 42.

Minister for Foreign Affairs informed me that press rumour of escape of some interned German officers and men is untrue. German Minister has published formal denial in El Pais, the only local paper which made the statement. See paragraphs 9 and 10 my airmailed despatch No. 22. (TNA ADM 116/4180, 13 February 1940)

On 14 February, S.H. Philips, the Principal Assistant Secretary in the Admiralty's Military Branch, sent a letter to Alexander Cadogan, the Permanent Under Secretary of State for Foreign Affairs throughout the war.

Sir,
　　I am commanded by My Lords Commissioners of the Admiralty to refer to the despatches from H.M. Ambassador, Buenos Aires, enclosed with Foreign Office printed letters No. A 508/22/2 of the 30th January, and No. A 738/22/2 of the 5th February.
　　2. H.M. Ambassador's report to the effect that members of the crew of the GRAF SPEE were still at liberty in the middle of January confirms information which Their Lordships had received from other sources, and the note that H.M. Ambassador proposes to maintain discreet and friendly pressure on the Argentine Government with a view to the enforcement of its decree of internment.
　　3. It is unnecessary to emphasise the importance of ensuring that the officers and men from this vessel are placed under such confinement as will certainly prevent their further participation in the operations of the war, and My Lords are somewhat apprehensive lest dilatoriness on the part of the Argentine Government in arranging for adequate detention may enable the potentially more dangerous members of the ship's company to evade all supervision.
　　4. While, therefore, it is recognised that H.M. Ambassador is best qualified to judge what tactics are most likely to prove successful. Their Lordships would urge that, unless the Secretary of State sees strong objection, Sir Edward Ovey should be reminded of the dangers of acquiescing in the slow and perfunctory methods which the Argentine Authorities appear to have adopted in this matter, and that he should be instructed to make strong representations at once unless the Argentine Government has by now effectively fulfilled their undoubted duty with regard to the internment of these persons, or unless he is fully satisfied that there will be no risk of any of them escaping supervision and confinement if his present policy of discreet and friendly pressure is maintained..
　　I am, sir,

Your obedient Servant, (Ibid. 14 February 1940)

Ovey updated London the same day.

My telegram No. 5 Saving.
Following is resumé of an obviously inspired press article today. The Minister of the Interior yesterday informed the German Ambassador that the Argentine Government now proposed to implement the internment decree by distributing internees in different parts of the country. The Ambassador produced a list of firms in the capital and provinces which had offered to employ 500 of the crew for the whole period of employment and the Minister promised to discuss the offer with the President of the Republic.

The sailors will be provided with civilian clothing by the Argentine Naval Authorities at the expense of the German Government. They will be obliged to report periodically to the Argentine Authorities who will also decide the measure of responsibility for them to be incurred by their employees.

If the Argentine Government accept the above offer, the remainder of the crew will be split up and sent to the provinces. The Governor of the Rioja (Northwest province west of Cordoba including the foothills of the Andes] has requested that as many as possible should be allotted to his province. (Ibid.)

Later the same day, Ovey sent telegram No. 76 with an update.

It is evident from my immediately preceding telegram and from my Saving telegram No. 5 of February 2nd that the Argentine Government are not apparently minded to implement fully Article 2 of their decree of December 19th 1939 (my despatch No. 435 December 23rd.)

Minister for Foreign Affairs is away on leave and the Political Director is reticent in conversation on this subject.

Please telegram instructions as to any representations you would wish me to make.

My general view is that unless there is any strong motive it would be difficult and even inadvisable to press the Argentine Government too hard. On the other hand we must keep possibilities of sabotage in our mind. Apart from this if important questions of principle and precedent are involved a formal protest (putting responsibility on the Argentine Government might not be inappropriate. (Ibid.)

McCall updated the DNI the same day with his views on the situation in Argentina. Given the content, copies were also sent to the First Lord, the First Sea Lord, CSO to First Sea Lord, DCNS, ACNS, Naval Secretary, Director of Military Intelligence (DMI), PAS(S), O.D, OPS, M, DOP, DDIC, DSD.9, IP, and FNLO (?French Naval Liaison Officer).

German Ambassador yesterday submitted to Ministers of Marine and Interior a scheme whereby 500 GRAF SPEE sailors would be employed by German firm(s) in capital and provinces. Publication of proposal by Government spokesman may be an attempt to discover our reaction which I recommend should be immediate and damnatory.

Article two of Argentine internment decree (see Ambassador's telegram 356 Dec. 19th) definitely provides internment in interior of country and principle of removal of internees from area of operations [northeast coast and River Plate estuary] is recognised convention of international law (see Manual of Military Law]. Ports of Argentine must be considered as potentially such. German factories in capital are principally engineering or chemical and this idea; as sabotage centres and I consider German sailors allowed to take civil employment in capital will be trained into active and subsequently dangerous sabotage agents. Secret source of information [probably intercepted and decoded German wireless messages] indicates that sabotage at present quiescent will break out simultaneously with Military activity in Europe. (Ibid, 15 February 1940)

Two days later, the Foreign Office sent instruction to Ovey in telegram 48.

Your telegrams Nos 5 Saving, 75 and 76 of 14th February: internment of crew of Graf Spee.

You should inform Argentine Government that His Majesty's Government have learnt with concern and disappointment of unsatisfactory nature of proposed measures which not only appear to be incompatible with Article 2 of the Argentine Internment Decree (see you despatch No. 435 of 1939(but also with the obligations of neutrals under international law to provide effective supervision so as to ensure that interned members of belligerent armed forces shall not escape to participate in belligerent activities. You should point out danger of sabotage mentioned in Naval Attaché's telegram to Admiralty 0230 of the 15th February, if German sailors are allowed to take up employment with German firms in the capital or even in the provinces and strongly urge the Argentine Government to recast measures contemplated so as to provide for some form of effectively supervised confinement of interned men in the interior.

Questions of principle and precedent are involved which make protest necessary and while I realise delicacy of seeming to teach Argentine Government their own business, we are certainly entitled, in the circumstances of the case, to do all we can to see that they fulfil their obligations and I would not like them to be under any illusion as to our feeling that their contemplated measures as so far reported fall far short of what we are legitimately be entitled to expect.

The Argentine Government must surely realise also that risk of sabotage is a very real one and that acts of sabotage, while directed against British interests, could hardly fail, given the circumstances, to injure them too both materially and morally. They would, for instance, find it very difficult to defend their position if sabotage did occur and the inevitable damaging inferences were drawn that they had either been incapable of complying or, whether through German pressure or from some less worthy motive, had not wanted to comply with their obligations under international law to say nothing of their own decree. (Ibid, 15 February 1940)

Ovey responded later the same day in telegram 82.

> Your telegram No. 48.
> I read in French to Political Director text of your telegram above mentioned repeating important points.
> He undertook to communicate at once protest of His Majesty's Government to Minister of Marine and Minister of Interior and would in the absence of Minister of Foreign Affairs in the country inform me of result.
> He made no particular defence of his Government's attitude except to point out minor difficulties (which I politely pooh-poohed [dismissed as of little importance] and rather implied we had not so far intervened with our views.
> I explained that in view of the delicacy [2 grps. und.] measures to which the Argentine Government had not actually committed themselves I had confined myself to verbal communication and gave him the opportunity of asking for something in writing which he did not take up.
> I submit that a note recapitulating the views of His Majesty's Government may nevertheless become necessary if the Argentine Government prove sticky [unwilling to change their position].

In view of my verbal representations I suggest such a note recording our attitude could be based on paragraph 1. (Ibid.)

Also on 15 February, Millington-Drake sent Eden telegram No. 7 SAVING. Copies were also sent to Buenos Aires, Rio, Santiago and Lima.

> My telegram No. 42 of February 13th.
> Following report from Buenos Aires newspaper "La Nacion" was reproduced in "El Pais" here on the 14th inst. "The German Minister visited Dr. Guani at the Ministry of Foreign Affairs and had a long conference with him. The interview took place at the suggestion of the Minister for Foreign Affairs and in it they referred to the versions that have circulated insistently since yesterday regarding the possible disappearance from Montevideo of several officers of the "ADMIRAL GRAF SPEE" and of the engine room artificers of the German merchant ship "TACOMA".
> The outcome of the conference was that only one of the officers of the German cruiser tried to leave Montevideo surreptitiously but was not able to do so owing to the intervention of the police in charge of Maritime passenger traffic. This incident, to which no importance is given in official circles, has nevertheless made known that none of the crew of the German ships, either war or merchant ships, are authorised to give their word of honour regarding their stay in the places of internment which have been established for them.
> In these circumstances the Ministry of Foreign Affairs has decided to take other measures to prevent another attempt of this kind. A resolution will also be taken on this occasion regarding the position of the crew of the "TACOMA", who are still on board that ship. The principal purpose is to prolong their stay on the ship and to give them at the same time the means to carry out other activities on land. Regarding this, three members of the crew have already requested authorisation to undertake to do rural work.".
> As regards statement that officers and men of the German ships are not allowed to give their word of honour regarding non-escape from internment, I have since ascertained from Ministry for Foreign affairs that this is correct, thus considerably complicating the whole question. (Ibid, 15 February 1940)

Eden's response to Ovey, telegram 53, which was sent on 20 February, instructed him to maintain pressure on the Argentine Government and, if necessary, use the sabotage argument mentioned at the beginning of the last telegram.

Dr Tomas Le Breton, Argentine Ambassador to UK 1938 – 1941
(https://upload.wikimedia.org/wikipedia/commons/2/24/Tom%C3%A1s_Le_Breton.jpg)

On 22 February, Ovey sent telegram 89 to the Admiralty.

> Your telegram No. 53.
> Discoveries that the Argentine Government sill appeared quite unrepentant as regards their internment plans I again saw Political Director and left him with aide-memoire [a reminder or memorandum] in the sense approved by you. He was [grp.undec.] polite and suggested I should see the Minister of the Interior with whom he arranged immediate interview.
> 2. I explained the views of His Majesty's Government and left the Minister translation of side-memoire. The Minister went over the same ground. He however entirely denied the suggestion that the Argentine Government were acting from motives of economy.
> 3. No new decree has been drafted and he advised me to talk the matter over with the Minister for Foreign Affairs on his return next week.
> 4. Although I could not pin him down in so many words to any immediate definite steps to implement their new plan before I can see the Minister for Foreign affairs it would seem unlikely [?grp.

omtd] particularly as the Government are very much occupied with the election.

5. I submit that the Argentine Ambassador [Dr. Tomas Le Breton] should be instructed as to the seriousness with which His Majesty's Government view the proposal so that he can inform the Minister of Foreign Affairs before I see him.

6. The Argentine Government will be very obstinate and if we are set on getting full pound of flesh as laid down in your telegram No. 48 strong pressure will be required. [an allusion to William Shakespeare's play Merchant of Venice in which the moneylender Shylock made an agreement for a pound of the person's flesh if the loan was not repaid on time. It is used when someone is determined to get what is theirs by right regardless of the consequences.]

7. I would be grateful for instructions and for information regarding any steps taken in London. (Ibid, 22 February 1940)

On 23 February, Millington-Drake sent telegram 35 to Halifax.

My Lord,
In my telegram No. 7 Saving, of the 15th February, I transmitted a report from the Buenos Aires newspaper "La Nacion" regarding the attempt to leave Montevideo made by one of the Officers of the "ADMIRAL GRAF SPEE" who had been interned in this capital in accordance with the decree of the 23rd January last (enclosure No. 7 in my despatch No. 22 of the 3rd February).

2. I now have the honour to report that, as a consequence of this attempt, the Uruguayan Government have adopted stricter measures in regard to the internees of both the "ADMIRAL GRAF SPEE" and the "TACOMA". The new regulations require the Officers and men concerned to present themselves every eight days to the competent police or maritime authorities in order to show that they have complied with the existing arrangements whereby they are lodged in the German Legation and the hotels or buildings belonging to the State to which they have been assigned. They are, moreover, obliged to wear civilian clothes, and only by a previous agreement between the Minister for Foreign Affairs and the German Legation may they appear in the street in uniform. Those members of the crew that wish to take up work outside the capital will be given facilities by the Ministry of Foreign Affairs, but in each case the necessary authorisation to absent themselves from Montevideo must be obtained.

3. details of these regulations appeared in the vernacular press on Saturday last, but have not yet been published in "DIARIO

OFICIAL". I have in the meantime applied to the Ministry of Foreign Affairs for a copy of the text of the regulations.

I am sending copy of this despatch to H.M. Ambassador at Buenos Aires.

I have etc, (TNA ADM 116/4180, 23 February 1940)

Casa de Gobierno, the Headquarters of Argentina's Executive Powers (https://es.wikipedia.org/wiki/Casa_Rosada)

The same day, Ovey sent Eden a translation of an article in that day's *La Prensa*.

Enclosure in Buenos Aires despatch No. 62 dated February 23rd, 1940.
Free translation of "La Prensa article of February 23rd.
BRITISH AMBASSADOR CONCERNED WITH THE INTERNMENT OF THE "GRAF SPEE" SAILORS.
HE WAS INFORMED THAT THESE PROCEEDINGS ARE A MATTER FOR THE ARGENTINE GOVERNMENT ALONE.

Yesterday evening the British Ambassador, Sir Esmond Ovey, was received in audience at the Casa de Gobierno by the Minister of the Interior, the visit having been previously arranged at the Ministry of Foreign Affairs. At the latter Department the Ambassador was received by the Under-Secretary, Dr. Roberto Gache, whom he informed that the object of the visit was to discuss the internment of the crew of the German battleship "Admiral Graf Spee", which has already been decided by the Argentine Government in accordance with the principles of

International Law, and which on the point of being properly carried out, as is generally known. the British diplomatist, after setting forth his views, left a memorandum putting those views on record. In accordance with the usual procedure, Dr. Gache proceeded to the Ministry of the Ministry of the Interior to introduce the Ambassador to the Minister. (sic. Untrue).

According to the information which we have been able to obtain, Sie Esmond Ovey told Dr. Taboada that the internment of the German sailors should take place, in his opinion, in the interior provinces of the Republic, according to the terms of the Internment Decree, and not in the capital or in towns near the capital, as has been lately announced.

To this request for the fulfilment of the Decree the Minister of the Interior replied that the Argentine Government are carefully attending to all the details of the internment, and that, as hitherto, without being influenced or turned aside by external factors, they will continue to carry out the obligations imposed upon them by their neutrality, the terms of the agreements to which they are a party and the principles of International Law which Argentina invariably upholds.

Further, he added that the despatch of the sailors to the interior involved certain difficulties which were derived from the difficulty of obtaining work for them in the provinces work which would allow them to earn their living and permit their being supervised at the same time in accordance with the police measure which the Government must adopt in this case.

After observing that the manner and time of the execution of the Internment Decree is the business of the sovereign country, the Minister informed the Ambassador that the proposal made by certain industrial establishments to take into their service one or more of the sailors will be carefully considered by the National authorities, who are trying to obtain the best guarantees possible. An attempt is being made to ensure not only that they shall not leave Argentina or carry out acts harmful to the country's neutrality, but also that they shall lead a life which does not involve a loss of human dignity or a derogation from the traditional hospitality of Argentina.

The Minister took the opportunity of also explaining to the Ambassador that a Decree such as the Internment Decree has in Argentina the nature of an expression of the private will of the Executive Power, and that for this reason it is susceptible of being modified by another decree, especially when the question is so simple as that of fixing the place of residence of the German sailors, which is a matter of internal policy and administration. (Ibid.)

The Times reporter in Buenos Aires must have read the article and have written a piece for his paper as Ovey reported it in his telegram 90 sent the same day.

My immediately preceding telegram.
Minister of the Interior [Dr Diogenes Taboada] published today account of my interview (see tomorrow's Times). There seems no malice in it – on the contrary it will (although Government recapitulate their own point of view only) probably do good. (TNA ADM 116/4180, 23 February 1940)

Times 24 Feb 1940.

GRAF SPEE CREW IN ARGENTINA

BRITISH REQUEST TO GOVERNMENT

FROM OUR OWN CORRESPONDENT

BUENOS AIRES, FEB. 23

The British Ambassador to Argentina, Sir Esmond Ovey, yesterday called at the Foreign Ministry and left a memorandum requesting the fulfilment of the Decree of December 19 last providing for the manner of the internment of the crew of the Admiral Graf Spee in the provinces and territories. As the Foreign Minister, Señor Cantilo, was absent, the Under-Secretary to the Foreign Ministry arranged an interview between the Ambassador and the Minister for the Interior, Dr. Taboada.

Sir Esmond Ovey explained that the British Government considered that the internment of the crew should be in the provinces according to the Decree, and not in the capital or neighbouring cities as had been later announced.

Dr. Taboada replied that the internment was an internal administrative matter of the Argentine Government, which took the greatest care to respect international law and treaties and to prevent the sailors from leaving the country while the war lasted or from committing acts of sabotage. Dr. Taboada added that there were certain disadvantages about sending the sailors to the provinces, an especial difficulty being the finding of suitable work, and, at the same time, placing them under the necessary vigilance. Proposals of industrial firms to accept one or two sailors each would be carefully considered by the authorities. As well as preventing escape, the Government wished the sailors to enjoy a life which respected human dignity and traditional Argentine hospitality. Dr. Taboada ended that if necessary the Decree of December 19 could be modified by another Decree, especially where such a simple matter was involved.

Uniformed German sailors are still walking about Buenos Aires.

The following day, Ovey reported on the reactions in the Argentine press.

> My telegram No, 89.
> Prensa Leader frankly criticises my intervention in matter which solely concerns Argentina as inexplicable interference.
> Nacion Leader expresses surprise my action stating matter is one of internal administration and Argentina capable interpreting international law without external assistance. Decree already issued may be modified if desirable.
> Bandera Argentina courteously critical insisting on Argentina's sovereign rights in application of decree.
> 2. Anti-British papers violently critical. (Ibid, 24 February 1940)

Later the same day, Ovey sent telegram 94.

> My telegram No. 89.
> Today the Press (see my immediately preceding telegram) carried leading articles which indicate that my demarche [political protest] regarding internees is not a matter for precaution but one of Argentine Republic Sovereignty alone.
> I made this point very carefully to the Political Director who seemed to agree with me that the principal raison d'etre [reason for being] of diplomacy is to avoid possible misunderstandings between two equal sovereign Powers, upon which he turned me over to the Minister of the Interior. The latter as well as today's "Nacion" indicated that at least 500 sailors may be found work in Buenos Aires.
> I adhered to the view that part of the excitement is for the purpose of election propaganda, but whatever be the motive the Minister of the Interior's publication will make appeal to the national touchiness, which is already to a certain extent arousing their controversies over the meat negotiations in which we rightly or wrongly are accused of petty-fogging [placing undue importance on unimportant details] methods.
> There seems only two possible lines of action.
> (1) To accede to the Argentine point of view, after creating considerable ill-feeling by our ineffectual and friendly representations. (This is obviously unthinkable).
> (2) To insist on the whole pound of flesh (which would have to be accurately defined in advance), failing which, to enter strong protest against the Argentine Government's unfriendly interpretation of neutral obligations, and to place full responsibility on Argentina for any unfortunate results.

> The second alternative, which I strongly recommend, if the principal [sic] is as important as I believe it to be, will require strong and unremitting pressure. It will require strong representations [to the Argentine Ambassador] in London, and what (in view of the fact that I cannot obviously involve myself in press polemics here) is more important still, strong explanatory newspaper propaganda in London to gain local campaign.
>
> If you approve, such a campaign should begin as soon as possible. It will be fully justified by the one-sided Argentine Republic's publication, which (see my telegram No. 90) had the advantage of showing the public that His Majesty's Government were pre-occupied by the Argentine Government's intentions.
>
> Please instruct fully.
> Obtaining details. (Ibid.)

Ovey sent the Foreign Office telegram 96 later that day.

> My telegram No. 94.
> I informed the French Ambassador of my first demarche regarding the internment demand (see my telegram No. 365 1939).
>
> His Excellency entirely approved and evidently informed His Government.
>
> His Excellency is now away and I learn in confidence that the Counsellor (who does not want the source to be mentioned) that the French Embassy have received a somewhat weak telegram from the French Government, indicating that, in view of the distance from the seat of war etc. strict fulfilment of the Hague Convention (grp. undec.) was not of major importance. (Ibid, 24 February 1940)

Also on the same day, McCall sent the DNI the following memo.

> My 1725 14th Feb please see Ambassador's 94 to Foreign Office. I continue to receive indications from source S Secret and otherwise that if the GRAF SPEE Sailors are allowed to remain in the vicinity of Buenos Aires they will menace to our shipping and British interests.
>
> I have already received complaints that whilst still in uniform they may try to contact Frigorifico [major meat processing and refrigeration company] workers. (Ibid.)

A few days later, Ovey sent Eden telegram 98.

> My telegram No. 98 [sic. 96]

Following is literal translation of the memorandum from the Minister for Foreign Affairs of February 26th begins:

"The Minister for Foreign Affairs has received the British Embassy's memorandum dated 22nd instant, by which it is pleased to indicate the measures which, in the opinion of the British Government, should properly be adopted for the effective operation of the decree of December 19th last, governing the internment of German sailors of the Graf Spee.

The international obligations created by the German conventions and accepted by the Argentine in the Decree under reference contemplate the retention of disembarked troops with the sole object of preventing them from further participation in warlike operations. It is a question of a measure of an administrative character, which each country fulfils at its discretion, within its own internal and sovereign organisation. In this same sense the inter-American neutrality committee of Rio de Janeiro has just declared that the liberty of personal activities of the internee is to be restricted only to the extent that this is indispensable to assure the measure being carried out in conditions which the neutral State alone should fix.

In the preservation of its own neutrality the Argentine Government has taken the necessary measures to arrange that the above personnel should remain in the country in accordance with the objects of their internment. This Ministry does not therefore see any justification for the concern of which the memorandum under reply gives evidence. For the rest, the internment decree of December 19th last, rendered effective from the start by the very fact of the retention of disembarked crew under police control, will be implemented by the finding of work and the

Placing of that crew, once the questions of an administrative order, which the case has raised, have been settled. Buenos Aires, February 26th 1940 (Ibid.)

The Graf Spee file included a draft of Ovey's note for Cantilo and the actual aide memoire delivered so the observant reader can detect what was omitted and what was included.

On the 19th December the Argentine Governments enacted a Decree providing for the internment in the City of Buenos Aires of Captain and officers of the German cruiser "Graf Spee" under which the members of the crew would be interned in the inland provinces or territories of Argentina subject to measures imposed by the local authorities charged with their supervision. Under this decree the Ministry of the Interior were charged with the responsibility of ensuring that members of the crew would remain within bounds to be fixed.

On the 14th February however an article apparently sanctioned by the Argentine Government appeared in the Argentine press to the effect that the German Ambassador had been informed that the Argentine Government proposed to implement the internment decree by distributing internees in different parts of the country and that the question of the employment of these men by firms suggested by the German Ambassador was under discussion. On the 15th March a press statement appeared to the effect that all sailors from the "Graf Spee" would receive civilian clothing and be interned within 10 days, but this was qualified by a further press statement on the 16th March indicating that 200 sailors would be distributed in the Province of Mendoza [Mid-Western Argentina] amongst farms and families willing to take them.

As the Argentine Government are already aware, from the representations made by His Majesty's Ambassador at Buenos Aires the most recent of which was on the 13th March, His Majesty's Government have learned with concern and disappointment of the unsatisfactory nature of the proposed internment measures which seem to be incompatible not only with the terms of the Argentine internment decree but also with the obligations of neutrals under Article 10 of Hague Convention No. X of 1899 which while in principle leaving it to the neutral state to decide on the precise nature of the steps to be taken, provides that internees must be guarded so as to prevent them from taking part in the operations of war. It appears to them moreover that the measures about to be adopted are the result of discussion and agreement with the German Ambassador and amount indeed to the acceptance of suggestions made by one belligerent only. If as appears to be contemplated, the German sailors are allowed to take up civilian employment in particular with German firms in the capital or even in the provinces there would in the opinion of His Majesty's Government be a serious risk not only that they might escape or indulge in propaganda, but also take part in acts of sabotage, which would affect Argentina's own interests.

His Majesty's Government hope therefore that the Argentine Government will recast the measures contemplated to provide for some form of effectively supervised confinement of the men in the interior. (TNA ADM 116/4180)

<u>Enclosure in Buenos Aires despatch No. 63 of February 27 1940</u>

AIDE MEMOIRE

His Majesty's Ambassador has the honour to refer to his conversation with His Excellency the Under-Secretary for Foreign Affairs on the 17th instant with regard to the question of internment of the officers and crew of the "Admiral Graf Spee".

Sir Esmond Ovey was, as he had the honour of informing Dr Gache, instructed to inform the Argentine Government that His Britannic Majesty's Government had learnt with concern and disappointment of the unsatisfactory nature of the measures which it appeared the Argentine Government were proposing to take in this connection.

These measures, if correctly reported, would appear not only to be incompatible with Article II of the Argentine Internment Decree of December 19th 1939, but also with the obligations of neutrals under international law to provide effective supervision so as to ensure that the interned members of belligerent armed forces shall not escape to participate in belligerent activities.

Sir Edmond [sic] Ovey was further instructed to point out the danger of sabotage which would arise were German sailors allowed to take up employment with German firms in the Capital or even in the Provinces and to impress earnestly upon the Argentine Government the desirability of recasting the measures contemplated so as to provide some form of effectively supervised confinement of the interned men in the interior.
Buenos Aires, 22 February 1940 (Ibid.)

On 28 February, Alan Ker, acting for the Head of the Admiralty's Military Branch, noted that,

It is clear that the Argentine Government are still grossly neglecting their duty of interning the crew. The Foreign Secretary is going to point out to the Argentine Ambassador how serious we think the situation is. The Foreign Office wish to know whether the Admiralty have any views on question raised at X on page 2 of Buenos Aires telegram No. 94 (tabbed d), i.e. whether we have any views on the exact measures we should expect the Argentines to take. The Admiralty views were expressed in the letter of 14th February tabbed (c), in which our demands were put in general terms.

2. It would seem best to inform the Foreign Office that we think that now that H.M. Ambassador is seriously disturbed by the situation we can safely leave to him to determine in consultation with the Argentine Government the exact measures to be taken to ensure that the internment is real. He alone can know how far

the Argentines can be pressed and what can be got out of them. But ii should be stressed that any arrangements made must exclude the possibility of sabotage by the members of the crew as well as of their escape from the Argentine.

3. It should perhaps be added that we cannot possibly accept X of the telegram under reference (tabbed d), and that we would press strongly for Y, leaving the definition of "pound of flesh" to the ambassador, if the Argentines continue to refuse to put them in internment camps.

Referred for early remarks. (Ibid, 28 February 1940)

On the same day, 28 February, C. Lamplugh acting for the Director of Naval Intelligence wrote the following minute.

> Concur with head of M. The following minute had already been prepared and an additional message is ordered.
>
> Reports are being received that the sailors of the "Graf Spee" are still at large in the vicinity of Buenos Aires, and it is apparent that the Argentine Government are not going the full length in segregating these men away from the coast. The danger of their being used for sabotage is becoming more serious, and it is suggested that M should take up the question with the Foreign office, with a view to the utmost pressure being brought to bear on the Argentine Government to implement fully its Internment Decree.
>
> 2. In a War despatch of the 29th December 1939, from the Naval Attache [McCall], Buenos Aires, some of 1,000 men from the "Graf Spee" were described as "officiales y aspirantes", skilled workmen, who are obvious material for saboteurs. In writing of them, the Naval Attache said "it is these men whom I fear may work themselves into positions where they can damage our interests through sabotage ... There is no question that this large number of Germans added to the community out here will cause us constant anxiety on this score.
>
> 3. The Ambassador in Buenos Aires was instructed by the Foreign Office on the 20th February to maintain pressure on the Argentine Government; but on the 22nd February he reported that the Government would be very obstinate, and "if we are set on getting the full pound of flesh ... strong pressure will be required". He asked for instructions and for information regarding any steps taken in London.
>
> Previously on the 14th February, he had expressed the opinion "that unless there is any strong motive, it would be difficult, and even undesirable, to press the Argentine Government too hard".

4. It is now submitted that the danger of sabotage supplies a motive strong enough, and Admiralty would be pleased if the Foreign Office took steps, both here and in the Argentine, to make clear to the Argentine Government the serious consequences of their present dilatory enforcement of the Internment Decree. The possibility of bringing commercial pressure to bear will no doubt be considered.

5. Following are the recent F.O. [Foreign Office] telegrams referring to this matter: -

Sir E. Ovey to F.O. Nos. 75, 76, 82, 89 and 90.

F.O. to Sir E. Ovey, No. 53. (TNA ADM 116/4180. 28 February 1940)

The same day, Ovey sent the Foreign Office telegram 106.

My telegram No.89, my telegram No.94.

Pending your instructions I have made no attempt to see the Minister for Foreign Affairs who returned to Buenos Aires yesterday morning.

Should there be delay in your final instructions there is slight danger (see paragraph 4 first telegram above mentioned) that absence of further demarches by myself be interpreted if not as acquiescent at least as sufficiently encouraging to entitle them to risk publication of regulations rescinding article 2 of their neutrality regulations and then face us with the fait accompli [something that has already happened or been decided before those affected hear about it, leaving them with no option but to accept it. (Ibid.)

Later that day, Ovey sent telegram 107 marked confidential.

My immediately preceding telegram.

A friendly Argentine has been told by member of German La Plata Zeitung that "British authorities had properly put their foot into it [made a mistake] by approaching the Argentine Government on the internment question" and that the internment decree has been ready for signature for three weeks or more. (Ibid.)

On 1 March, Ker stated that in view of the Argentine Government's 'insistence that they do not intend to concern themselves with any interests except their own, it would seem wisest for the F.O. now to stress the argument of the risk of sabotage.' In a note to the Admiralty sent the same day, he commented that,

The problem of internment at Montevideo is not so great as at Buenos Aires, but the Foreign Office wish to know our views on Montevideo telegram No. 7 Saving (tabbed A).

2. The suggestion at X seems just as dangerous as the proposal of the Argentines that large numbers of the internees should be allowed to work in factories. It is proposed to ask the Foreign Office to point this out to the Minister.

3. The difficulty of dealing with Y is that we can hardly protests against the absence of parole for the officers since we are ourselves not allowing our own officers to give parole.

4. It would seem best that H.M. Minister at Montevideo should be instructed in the same sense as H.M. Ambassador Buenos Aires: viz. that (a) the men ought to be properly interned in an internment camp; (b) if he fails to get this, he should come to some arrangement which will prevent any possibility of either escape or sabotage. (Ibid, 1 March 1940)

A note underneath by A. Stanford for DNI stated 'Concur with Head of M. It is considered most important that the potential saboteurs should be placed under restraint as quickly as possible.' (Ibid.)

On 2 March, the Foreign Office responded with telegram 61.

Your telegram 106 [of 1st March: internment of crew of Graf Spee).
We must not be taken as agreeing to rescission of article 2 of Argentine internment decree, and pending the receipt of further instructions which should reach you shortly you should leave the Argentine Government in no doubt about it. (Ibid. 2 March 1940)

Perowne sent the following letter to Ker the same day.

Will you please refer to Ovey's telegram No. 98 and previous recent telegrams from him on the question of the internment of the crew of the "Graf Spee".

It is quite clear from the Argentine Government's memorandum the text of which was telegraphed in Ovey's telegram No. 98 that the Argentine Government do not intend to meet our requirements in this matter. In his telegram No. 84 Ovey advocates that we should not accede to the Argentine point of view but exert strong pressure (1) through the Argentine Ambassador here (2) through himself and (3) by means of press publicity in this country with a view to obtaining our own requirements, failing which we should enter a strong protest against the Argentine Government's interpretation of neutral obligations and place full responsibility on Argentine for any unfortunate results.

We think that we should certainly instruct Ovey to place our views on record officially with the Argentine Government. Our note might in addition to re-stating our view of the legal situation (as set out in our telegrams to Ovey Nos. 223 and 48 of the 19th December, 1939 and the 17th February respectively together with any further points which it may be desirable to and) point out that the Argentine Government while asserting that under international law the neutral state is alone responsible for fixing the conditions of internment, appear to have negotiated with, and accepted the suggestions of the representative of one of the belligerent powers only. We might, to this connection draw attention to the (in our eyes) more correct behaviour of Belgium, the Netherlands and Denmark as regards internees (that is, if their behaviour is more correct) and finally lay, in quite unmistakeable terms, on the Argentine Government the onus [responsibility] for seeing that the men neither escape nor indulge in sabotage or propaganda.

We think that a note on the above lines to the Argentine Government through our Ambassador at Buenos Aires might be usefully backed up by a talk with the Argentine Ambassador here at which he can be handed an aide-memoire on the subject.

For political reasons, however, we are doubtful of the wisdom of being too insistent in this matter and consider that it will be best to confine ourselves to the presentations suggested above and not to indulge in a press campaign in this country as suggested by Ovey. The Argentine is or will shortly be in the throes of a general election and the moment is not therefore propitious for such action, which could only as we see it defeat in the circumstances its own object. In any case there seems very small prospect of bringing the Argentines from the position they have decided to take up.

As regards the French attitude reported in Ovey's telegram No. 96 we think we should, without giving away the fact that the Counsellor of the French Embassy at Buenos Aires has divulged his instructions, let them know through our Embassy in Paris of the importance which we attach to this matter and request their full support.

Will you please let us know as soon as possible whether you agree with the action proposed in this letter so that we can take the necessary action? (Ibid, 2 March 1940)

On the same day Millington-Drake sent a further update in telegram 14 (Saving).

My telegram No. 7 Saving.

I have received a Note from the Minister for Foreign Affairs informing me that details of the internment regulations will appear in the Official Gazette next week.

He adds that he has communicated confidentially to the Ministers of the Interior and of national Defence the allegation that some of the interned members may attempt to leave the country by the German merchant steamer "LAHN" which is preparing to leave for Germany with an exceptionally valuable cargo of wool and other products, but has at present been unable to obtain the necessary coal which the German Minister stated three or four weeks ago, was going to be obtained in the United States. (Ibid, 2 March 1940)

The *Nottingham Journal* reported a new development the same day.

Graf Spee Wreck Sold for £l,000
Wreck of the Admiral Graf Spee has been bought by Senor Julio Vega Helguera, head of a firm of importers of foodstuffs. Senor Helguera stated that he would use the wreck "for commercial ends.' The purchase price is not known, but it is reported not to exceed 10,000 pesos (about £1,000). The vessel cost £3,750,000 to build.— Reuter. (*Nottingham Journal*, 2 March 1940)

Four days later, 6 March, Ker replied to Perowne at the Foreign Office.

Your letter to me of 2 March about the question of the internment of the crew of the GRAF SPEE.

We agree with you that the strongest possible pressure should be put upon the Argentines both through the Argentina Ambassador her and through Ovey. It is clear, as you say, from Ovey's telegram No. 98. That the Argentines do not intend to meet our requirements. What exactly should be the measures Ovey should attempt to persuade the Argentines to adopt, is perhaps best left for him to determine. Our view is that since will apparently not intern them properly in an internment camp, he should aim at some arrangement which would ensure that sabotage will be impossible; and indeed we think that the risk of sabotage, since it effects the Argentines own interests, should be the argument most forcibly urged upon them, though of course we also lay stress on the prevention of escape. We would also suggest that the method of threatening commercial pressure should be seriously considered.

The problem in Uruguay I suppose is not so serious. But we are much concerned at the statement quotes on page 2 of Millington-Drake's saving telegram No. 7 of 15th February, that "three members of the crew of the TACOMA have already requested authorisation to undertake to do rural work.". and we would suggest that Millington-Drake should make representations in the same sense as Ovey. (Ibid. 6 March 1940)

The next document in the file was an undated note from DNI.

EXTRACT FROM NAVAL ATTACHE's BUENOS AIRES WAR DESPATCH No. 8 (W.D.8) Serial No. 90/74/40
5 GRAF SPEE INTERNMENT OF CREW. The crew are still walking about Buenos Aires smartly dressed in their uniforms – a fact that is causing much comment in the English colony, though it is obviously better that they should be conspicuous in their uniforms than free to do mischief 154uthorized154d in plain clothes. Much publicity was recently given to an alleged case of a British merchant seaman being battered by some Graf Spee men, but Argentine official enquiry revealed, whether rightly or not, that this man had been knocked down by a taxi. This case may have done something towards stirring up Argentine officialdom to get on with the work of internment, for such steps are now about to be taken. (Ibid.)

After repeating the McCall's note to Admiralty for the Director of Naval Intelligence of 15 February, he continued,

7. The French Naval Attache – now resident for some years in this country and who knows the conditions of Buenos Aires, expresses as much concern as I do at the suggestion that such a body of men should be loose in the River Plate ports. To acquiesce in such a demand is to ask for sabotage. We should consider nothing satisfactory short of all the men being put well into the interior with arrangements that they could not leave their district. (Ibid.)

On 7 March, Ovey updated the Foreign Office with the situation in Buenos Aires.

My telegram No. 96.
Continued absence of instructions regarding internment is making the position uncomfortable. The German controlled press

continues violent campaign against our treating Argentina as a colony.

The French Ambassador saw the Minister for Foreign Affairs last week and supported strongly His Majesty's Government's point of view respecting internment. In a long and friendly conversation this was the only point where the Ministry of Foreign Affairs was sticky.

Pampero and other papers today report the interviews between the Minister of Foreign Affairs and the Minister of the Interior in which the latter is reported to have said that all sailors "who do not find work in Buenos Aires" should come under the internment decree.

Pampero article continues "the opinion of the Minister for Foreign Affairs clearly indicates the defeat of the British Ambassador who demanded internment of all in order to prolong in these peaceful countries the hatred spread in Europe by His Majesty's Government", the articles add that the internment decree may appear at any moment.

Incidentally the President of the British Chamber of Commerce is preparing a list of Argentine citizens who will lose their jobs to make way for German sailors. This is a new argument which I hope to use.

Your telegram No. 61.

I sent polite private note to the Minister for Foreign Affairs regretting not having been able to welcome him back as I was awaiting important instructions and reiterating the importance His Majesty's Government attaches to the implementing of Article 2. His Excellency replied in equally friendly terms referring to the memorandum (see my telegram No. 98) and repeating that the matter is one for internal administration.

I can hardly believe that the Argentine Government will not await your reply to their memorandum particularly in view of my private letter to the Minister for Foreign Affairs, but would welcome early instructions as the position is interpreted not only in German controlled press but elsewhere as a diplomatic victory for Argentina over unscrupulous British Imperialism.

The government are more than ever taken up with electoral crisis. (see my telegram No. 111).

Confidential. The crux of ill-feeling (fanned by the Germans) is due to the unavowable disappointment that not only is Argentina not profiteering extravagantly but in view of the increase in prices of British commodities their favourable balance is liable to be even less than they expected. (Ibid, 7 March 1940)

On 11 March, the Foreign Office sent Ovey telegram 72.

My telegram No. 61 [of 2nd March: internment of crew of Graf Spee].

It is clear from the memorandum in your telegram No. 96 that the Argentine Government do not intend to meet our full requirement in this matter. I am doubtful whether insistence in this case will serve any useful purpose, and I do not propose for this reason to adopt your suggestion that a press campaign should be initiated over here. I propose however shortly to speak to the Argentine Ambassador and I request that you will meanwhile once more place our views officially on record [to Cantilo, the Argentine Minister for Foreign Affairs] in such a way as to leave the Argentine Government in no doubt that we hold them entirely responsible for seeing that no untoward consequences follow from the effects of their obstinacy.

You should now therefore restate in writing our views of the legal situation as set forth in my telegram No. 223 (of 19th December) and my telegram No. 48 [of 17th February] and express the dissatisfaction of His Majesty's Government at the measures proposed, adding that His Majesty's Government must reserve all their rights and that they meanwhile hold the Argentine Government entirely responsible for ensuring that none of the men escape or indulge in sabotage or other reprehensible activities, e.g. propaganda.

You should add, orally, that His Majesty's Government have observed that the Argentine Government in their memorandum of 26th February contended that the duty of internment is one which each neutral should fulfil at its own discretion, and that the measures decided on should be carried out in conditions which the neutral state alone should fix. They have also received from you accounts of the campaign in the Argentine press, as reported in your telegrams Nos. 93 and 94 [of 24th February]. It is therefore with all the greater surprise and regret that they have noted (see your telegram No. 75 9of 14th February] that the measures about to be adopted appear to be the result of discussion and agreement with the German ambassador, and amount indeed to the acceptance of suggestions made by the latter.

I am not clear whether there is any chance of the Argentine Government being ready to agree on some arrangement for the disposal of the crew which, while falling short of full internment and supervision in the inland provinces, would be more satisfactory to us than that now contemplated. If so, you are 156uthorized to endeavour to persuade the Argentine Government to discuss the matter. The most important object of any such arrangement would, from our stand point, be the prevention of sabotage. In any case, the risk of sabotage, since it affects Argentina's own interests as well as ours, should be the argument on which most emphasis should be laid by you in endeavouring to reach an agreement, though the prevention of escape and indulgence in propaganda are also important. (Ibid, 11 March 1940)

The following day, Ovey addressed the following note to Cantilo.

Monsieur le Ministre,
I have not failed to inform my Government of the contents of the memorandum from your Excellency's Department of the 25th February in reply to the aide-memoire from this Embassy of the 22nd February, in which is set forth the point of view of the Argentine Government with regard to the implementation of the Decree of the Executive Power of the 19th December last concerning the internment of the officers and crew of the "Admiral Graf Spee".

My Government now instruct me to reaffirm officially in writing their own point of view on this matter, namely, that the measures which the Argentine Government appear to contemplate remain in their opinion unsatisfactory and incompatible, not only with Article II of the Argentine Decree above mentioned, but also the with the obligations of neutrals under International Law (Art. 10 of the Hague Convention No. 10 of 1899) to provide effective supervision ensuring that the interned members of belligerent armed forces shall so be guarded by the neutral state as to prevent them from again taking part in operations of war.

While it is not contested that it is in principle for the neutral Government concerned to decide on the precise nature of the steps to be taken, those steps should, in the opinion of His Majesty's Government, clearly be sufficient to ensure the fulfilment of the above obligation, and in view of the size and organised nature of the body of men to be interned, of the great extent of Argentine territory and of the obvious possibility of the men escaping on board German warships, auxiliaries or submarines, a very considerable amount of strict supervision would appear to be necessary. In the view of His Majesty's Government, the material difficulties of guarding and feeding the internees cannot constitute a ground for not strictly confining the men, since the Argentine Government are explicitly bound to guard and feed them and are entitled to recover the expense from Germany, and it can hardly be regarded as beyond the capacity of a country of the strength and resources of the Argentine Republic to intern a thousand men. Switzerland, although not possessing any internment camps, is in the present war keeping any interned airmen in prison, and while His Majesty's Government would not suggest adopting such measures in this case, it is their view that nothing short of internment in camps under adequate supervision would suffice to ensure the fulfilment of Argentine's obligations.

My Government therefore instruct me again to impress urgently on Your Excellency's Government the desirability of recasting the measures contemplated so as to provide some form of effectively supervised confinement of the interned men in the interior. The questions of principle and precedent involved are of the greatest importance, and while my Government fully realise the delicacy of making these suggestions with regard to the nature of the measures which the Argentine Government are apparently about to take, they feel none the less entitled in the circumstances to leave the Argentine Government under no illusions as to their conviction that the contemplated measures, if correctly reported, would fall far short of what they expect.

His Majesty's government remain convinced and feel sure that the Argentine Government must be equally convinced that the risk of sabotage is a very real one, such acts, while directed against British interests, would not fail to effect both materially and morally Your Excellency's own Government, who would find themselves in considerable difficulty to defend their position should such acts of sabotage occur owing to lack of compliance with the general obligations of International Law, as well as with the terms of the Decree promulgated by the Argentine Government themselves on the 19th December.

I am therefore instructed to inform Your Excellency that His Majesty's Government feel constrained to reserve all their rights, and that they meanwhile hold the Argentine Government entirely responsible for ensuring that none of the men escape or indulge in sabotage or in any other reprehensible activities, such, for instance, as anti-British propaganda.

I avail myself of this opportunity, Monsieur le Ministre, to renew to Your Excellency the assurance of my highest consideration. (TNA ADM 116/5474, Graf Spee Internment, 12 March 1940)

The following day, 13 March, Halifax sent telegram 49 to Millington-Drake.

> Your telegram No. 14 (Saving) [of 12th March: Internment of crew of Graf Spee and Tacoma].
> While Uruguayan Government appear to be exercising fairly strict supervision to prevent escape of men it will not be clear

until you are in a position to inform me of the details of the Uruguayan internment regulations how far proposed measures of internment will meet requirements of His Majesty's Government. Proposal reported in your telegram No. 7 (Saving) and your despatch No. 35 that men should be allowed to work outside capital is clearly unsatisfactory and Sir E. Ovey has already been instructed to address a protest to Argentine Government against a decision taken by them to permit a large number of men to accept civilian employment in Buenos Aires.

In view of comparatively small number of men involved in Uruguay and of friendly attitude of Uruguayan Government towards his Majesty's Government in regard to whole of Graf Spee incident a protest on this matter is not contemplated at present. You should however refer Uruguayan Government to their obligation under Article 10 of Hague Convention No. 10 of 1899 to ensure that internees are guarded by the neutral State so as to prevent them from again taking part in the operations of war, stating that while in principle it is for neutral Government concerned to decide on the precise nature of the steps to be taken, those steps must clearly be sufficient to ensure fulfilment of the above obligation. You should point out that His Majesty's Government would have grave misgivings should it be decided to allow these men to take up work outside the capital, a course which in their opinion might give rise not only to the possibility of escape, but also to the danger that the men might indulge in sabotage and propaganda, both of which would affect Uruguay as well as His Majesty's Government. You should say that in the opinion of His Majesty's Government if all these dangers are to be adequately averted the Uruguayan Government should introduced measure providing for some form of effectively supervised confinement of the men. (TNA ADM 116/4180, 13 March 1940)

On the same day, Ovey sent telegram 122 to Eden.

> Your telegram No. 72.
> I had an hours intimate and friendly conversation with the Minister of Foreign Affairs.
> His Excellency first recapitulated his well know views: I then replied on lines of your instructions insisting particularly on the danger of sabotage.
> His Excellency said he would answer your note from the legal point of view. I explained more in sorrow than in anger that I had had an uncomfortable time during his absence what with press attacks which had influenced public opinion while I was

powerless to reply. In spite of his denials that the German Ambassador had influenced the Argentine Government's decision I told His Excellency that this was what the public understood from the press] see my telegram No. 75 and my telegram No. 76]. I added that I could quote eye witnesses of German sailor sticking illegal leaflets on railway trains and that I hoped soon to have the list of the Argentinians turned out of jobs to make way for Spee sailors etc.

I ended on the note that if the Argentine Government could not change their attitude the incident would end with our note leaving responsibility of them. This was not I felt an ideal solution for two countries so closely bound together as ours.

In reply to his hint and several attempts to draw him to suggest compromise he said he would telephone me later. I replied that I was going on a fortnight's leave for my health and Charge's d'Affaires would be at his disposal.

I feel he will probably return reply as indicated but study of your note and of the conversation which I told him Your Lordship proposes to hold with Argentine Ambassador may result possibly in some compromise or camouflage of existing intentions.

I lastly made earnest appeal to check [halt] German propaganda and left with him variety of examples or recent activities. (Ibid. 13 March 1940)

On 14 March, McCall, the British Naval Attaché in Buenos Aires, sent the Admiralty the following note with a copy to the C.in.C. South Atlantic, Rear Admiral South American Division (R.A.S.A.D.), S.O.(I) Montevideo and the Assistant Naval Attache in Rio de Janeiro. Ops, O.I.C, First Sea Lord, D.C.N.S., A.C.N.S., C.S.O.(S), O.D., D.T.D., D. of S.T., M,.D.N.I., Hydrog (?), D. of N., M.E.B and File X. As X was SOE's symbol for their German Section, it is possible that File X could have been the Admiralty's symbol for their file on German naval activity in South America.

> On night 6th March British Ship GCFK (FRESNO STAR) ran ashore whilst leaving San Julian 049o 20' South caused by extinguishing of Punta Pena Light but fortunately came off undamaged. If she had grounded south instead of north side channel she would likely have been total loss. Vice Counsel, Master and Pilot consider this to be attempted sabotage. I agree.
>
> Recommend all ships proceeding to ports in Southern Argentine were [sic] navigational dangers exist be warned to enter and leave harbour in daylight hours only. Am advising Vice Consul San Julian accordingly. (TNA ADM 116/4180, 14 March 1940)

On 15 March, Millington-Drake handed the British Government's note to the Uruguayan Government.

His Majesty's Minister at Montevideo presents his compliments to the Secretary of State for Foreign Affairs and has the honour to transmit to him the under-mentioned documents.
Reference to previous correspondence: Montevideo Telegram No. 49 of 13th March 1940.
"Enclosure in Montevideo Despatch No. 52 of 16th March, 1940)

DECREE, fixing place of internment and rules for the Officers and crews of the "ADMIRAL GRAF SPEE" and the "TACOMA" (Translation).
WHEREAS the internment of the Officers and crews of the German vessels "ADMIRAL GRAF SPEE" AND "Tacoma", now in territorial waters of the Republic has been decreed under date of 23rd January, 1940, and it is now necessary to establish the corresponding measures for the fulfilment of the aforementioned Decree;
The President of the Republic, Resolves and DECREES:
Article 1. The City of Montevideo is hereby established as the place of internment for the Officers and crews of the battleship "ADMIRAL GRAF SPEE" and the auxiliary vessel "TACOMA".
For specific reasons of health and for other causes, duly proved, the residence of the interned men in some other place of the Republic may be authorised, and the requisite measure of security be duly established.
Article 2. The Officers and men interned in Montevideo shall present themselves at the Police headquarters for the purposes of identification, with the obligation of stating to the Police authorities their place of residence.
Similar formalities shall be required for those who, in accordance with the condition mentioned in the foregoing Article, may be authorised to reside in the interior of the Republic.
Place of residence may not be changed without previous notice being given to the corresponding Police Office, to which the interned persons shall report every eight days, except in cases where the places of residence are under the jurisdiction of the Prefecture General of the Port, in which the interned persons must appear before the Authority at the intervals specified.

Article 3. Police headquarters shall provide the interned persons with a Permit of Internment in accordance with the corresponding process of identification.

Article 4. The cost of maintenance shall be paid in the manner and at the time agreed between the Ministry of Foreign Affairs and the German Legation.

Article 5. Permission may be given, when deemed expedient, for the internee himself to pay for his own maintenance by engaging in activities of a private nautre [sic], which must be outside the control or dependency of the belligerent country.

Article 6. As agreed between the Ministry of Foreign Affairs and the German Legation, the internees may only wear uniform on stipulated occasions, and after permission has been requested by the German Legation.

Article 7. Let it be communicated, etc.

(Signed) BALDOMIR – Alberto Guani – Manuael Tiscornia – General Alfredo R. Campos. Ministry of Foreign Affairs, Ministry of Interior, Ministry of National Defence, Montevideo, 16th February, 1940. (From "Diaro Oficial" of 10th March 1940).

The following day, 16 March, Ovey sent Eden telegram 129.

My telegram No. 122.

Yesterday the Press stated that all Spee sailors would receive civilian clothing and be interned within ten days.

Today inspired Press statement indicates the negotiations between the Ministry of the Interior and Provincial Authorities of Mendoza distributed 200 sailors amongst firms and families willing to take them; Government maintaining them for 60 days only.

The Ministry of Foreign Affairs inform the French Embassy that the matter is in the hands of the Ministry of the Interior and confirm report regarding Mendoza except as regards numbers. (Ibid, 16 March 1940)

On the same day, Millington Drake wrote the following note for Eden.

Your telegram No. 49.

I have addressed personal letter to Minister for Foreign Affairs conveying unofficially substance of your telegram but have been unable to see him owing to impending Easter holidays which here tantamount to ten days Bank holiday.

Decree mentioned in first paragraph of my telegram No. 14 Saving has now appeared and translation goes in despatch by airmail today.

Residence or work outside the capital will only be allowed for exceptional reasons.

Article 5 provides that men finding work and able to pay for their maintenance may do so provided such work is private and apart from any dependence or subordination to a belligerent country.

I will take early opportunity of discussing matter with Minister for Foreign Affairs. (TNA ADM 116/5474, 16 March 1940)

On 19 March Ovey updated Eden with telegram 135.

My telegram No. 129.

One hundred Graf Spee sailors left on March 18th by train for Mendoza. Under Secretary of State for Foreign Affairs informed me today

That further "important contingents" would leave shortly for station [grp. undec.]s where, according to the Press they must fend for themselves after a limited period but will remain under [grp. omtd.]. Officers are to remain on parole in or within fifty kilometres of Buenos Aires. (Ibid, 19 March 1940)

Cantilo's response for Ovey was sent on 20 March.

Sir,

I have the honour to acknowledge the receipt of Your Excellency's Note of 12th instant in which, reaffirming the representations made in previous memoranda, you were so good as to set out the views of the British Government regarding the position of the officers and crew of the "Graf Spee" who are detained in Argentine territory under the Decree of the Argentine Government of the 19th December last.

Your Excellency pointed out that the measure contemplated by the Argentine Government did not satisfy the British Government, and were incompatible both with the terms of their own internment decree and with the obligations imposed on neutrals by the Hague Convention of 1899. In consequence, Your Excellency suggested the desirability of reconsidering the measures contemplated on the assumption that only internment in camps under supervision can assure the fulfilment by the Argentine Government of their obligations and concluded by reserving the British Government's rights in the event of the interned men committing acts of sabotage or other illegal activities directed against British interests as a result of the Argentine Government not fulfilling the duties that devolve upon them in this emergency.

In reply, and reiterating the statements contained in this Department's memorandum of the 26th February last, I must at once inform Your Excellency that the Argentine Government do not accept the right of the British Government to intervene in a matter of internal order and of an administrative nature which must be settled without foreign interference by exercise of the country's sovereign rights.

Conscious of their responsibilities and of their rights, the Argentine Government have received and detained in Argentine territory the officers and crew of the "Graf Spee" in accordance with their duties as neutrals and solely with the motives laid down, as your Excellency will recollect, by the Hague Convention of 1899. In providing for the detention of the crew landed in neutral territory, the Convention, repeating the terms of the Geneva Agreements of 1864, was only intended to establish the general lines of internment. The methods of applying this measure are left to the discretion of the country that carries it out. Those Agreements did not provide for the belligerent nations continuing to exercise in neutral territory any kind of supervision or control in favour of their own interests, nor would my country have accepted such an interpretation.

The measures adopted in fulfilment of the Decree of the 19th December last, in accordance with a plan which is now being executed, after the administrative difficulties have been overcome are sufficient, in the view of the Argentine Government, to assure the peaceful status of the men disembarked in the conditions established by Article 10 of the above-mentioned Convention, i.e., "in such a way that they are unable again to take part in operations of war!

Neither the existing Conventions nor the theory of International Law interpret the act of internment – or detention, as the Hague Convention says – in the wide sense claimed in Your Excellency's Note, which suggests the setting up of concentration camps for the crew. This measure, which would deprive the men of their liberty, would conflict with elementary principles of International Law, applicable by analogy to the present case, according to which the captivity of prisoners of war ceases when they enter neutral territory. Moreover, it is also recognised that it detracts from the sovereignty of the State to admit a state of captivity which was not carried into effect within the limits of its jurisdiction, and that, as belligerent rights can have no force on neutral territory, military captivity, the consequence of these rights, cannot be maintained on neutral territory.

It is with a view to the observance of these general principles of international theory that the Inter-American neutrality Commission, at present in session in Rio de Janeiro, by the unanimous decision of the American Republics, after declaring that "the freedom of the personal activities of the internee should be restricted only in so far as it is indispensable to assure the observance of the measure (of internment) in conditions which must be decided upon exclusively by the neutral state", adds that "internment, in respect of the methods, forms and machinery of making it effective, is a matter of internal rights: therefore it is the duty of the neutral State; "I. to decide the district or place within its own territory where the internee must reside; II. To decide in each case if the internment is to be carried out individually or collectively; III. To decide upon the activities which may be permitted for the internees, as also the restrictions and prohibitions which may be placed on his liberties or actions; IV. To decide upon the measure of security or supervision which it may esteem desirable to exercise in order to render effective the dispositions referred to above; V. to decide whether those members of the crew indispensable for the up-keep of the ship must stay on board an interned vessel under proper guard; VI. To monitor, when it is considered necessary, the above-mentioned measures and dispositions". By Article 7 of the same recommendations – which in the absence of other Conventions the Argentine Government must accept as the principles to be applied in the present case – it is established that "the neutral state must be inspired "by the principle that it is desirable that the internee should gain his living for himself in activities of a private nature, free from any official dependence or subordination".

These are precisely the purposes which, in accordance with the free and humanitarian spirit of the country's institutions, are contemplated by the plan adopted by the Argentine Government in fulfilment of the Decree of the 19th December last for the internment of the majority of the men disembarked. Divided into groups in accordance with the suitability and possibilities of each district, the crew of the "Graf Spee" have begun to be distributed in the interior of the country, where they may be employed in all kinds of proper work, subject to the necessary measure of control by the local police, which will thus assure their remaining in the place of residence assigned to them. The Argentine Government consider that a system of greater strictness would be neither justified nor necessary. I must point out to your Excellency besides that, by virtue of the situation and geographical peculiarities of this country, there would in no case be reasonable grounds for the precautions which, according to your Note, have been adopted in parallel cases by Switzerland, a country with frontiers opening upon the belligerent countries.

I cannot end this reply without dealing with the reserves and fears expressed by Your Excellency regarding the illegal activities which, by reasons of the insufficiency of the measures adopted and with the intention of damaging British interests, may, according to Your Excellency, be indulged in by the members of the crew in question. Once more I must remind Your Excellency that the Argentine Government have adopted, and will continue to adopt, in accordance with their own legislation, those measures which circumstances may render necessary in defence of all the legitimate interests existing in the country, as required by their position as neutrals.

Without sharing, therefore, the doubts expressed in the Note under reply, I feel obliged to inform your Excellency that the Argentine Government, convinced that they have perfectly fulfilled their obligations, cannot modify the basic conceptions governing the steps being taken to give effect to the Internment Decree of the 18th December last, of whose terms and scope they claim to be the only judges. (TNA ADM 116/5474, 20 March 1940)

Later the same day, Mr Hadow, possibly in Ovey's absence, wrote telegram 139 for Eden.

> My telegram 135.
>
> Argentine Government has not returned a long stilted and legalistic reply and claims the disposition of crew is a matter of internal administration "which must be settled without foreign interference by exercise of this country's sovereign rights".
>
> (b) Justifying the Argentine action by lengthy references to the Hague Convention 1899 and recommendations of the recent Rio de Janeiro Conference.
>
> (c) stating that the crew would be sent in batches to earn their livelihood, under surveillance, up country.
>
> (d) Maintaining that their action gives effect to Argentine internment and that the Argentine Government – while not sharing our fears of sabotage – is taking adequate steps to defend all legitimate interests in this country.
>
> Our main demands, for the dispersal of the crew up country and the prevention of sabotage, seem on paper to have been met and the note savours mainly of bravado.

In view therefore of the somewhat excited state of the press over the internment of shipping and other Argentine "rights" I venture to recommend that no reply be returned at all events until [grps. Omtd.] which will reach you by next Thursday by air bag, has been considered in full. (TNA ADM 116/4180, 20 March 1940)

On the same day, 20 March, Richard Butler, Britain's Under Secretary of State for Foreign Affairs, sent the following message to the Admiralty.

1.   I spoke to the Argentine Ambassador this afternoon on the subject of the internees from the "Graf Spee". I also handed him a note, as attached. I need not detail the points I made, since they are included in the memorandum, but it is interesting to note that the Ambassador said that he had just received a message from the Under-Secretary for Foreign Affairs at Buenos Aires, who had told him that Sir Esmond Ovey was too persistent in pressing the British point of view about these internees. I replied that without wishing to be unpleasant I would remind him that Sir Esmond Ovey had been attacked in the Argentine press, and that he was only doing his duty, and further, that if the Ambassador wished to complain, he should complain to me. The ambassador said he had no wish to complain because he was a wise man; when a person was healthy it was no use taking patent medicines. He considered that to press upon his Government a different treatment of the internees would be extremely unwise and do more harm than good. He would therefore take home my memorandum with him to read. He would prefer not to send it to his Government until I had further opportunity of talking to the Secretary of State [Eden].
2.   I told Dr. Le Breton that he appeared to underestimate the importance which we attached to this question, that under Article 10 of the Hague Convention No. X of 1899 a neutral was obliged to pay more attention to internees that the Argentine Government appeared to wish to do. The Ambassador replied that that might be so, but that he would prefer to handle the matter in the following manner. He suggested that each case of unsatisfactory conduct on the part of the internees should be brought to his attention or should be brought to the attention of the Argentine Government by our Ambassador, but that a general broadside [naval expression for large scale attack] should be avoided. He reminded me that nine-tenths of the internees had the typical German characteristics of lack of initiative and education. The Officers might be dangerous, but were being kept on parole.

3.   I replied that however little initiative they might show, these internees might do harm to British interests if they became posted in the different industries in the country. Moreover I was not satisfied that in Mendoza they would be any more favourably placed than in Buenos Aires.

4.   The Ambassador was so insistent in pressing his point of view, and is so clearly desirous of furthering the interests of our two countries that I said that I would have a further word with the Secretary of State, and put to him the suggestion for a procedure under which definite cases of complaint are put rather that a general complaint submitted. Nevertheless I impressed on the Ambassador the need for reading the memorandum, which I insisted that he should take away, and told him that I should communicate with him after a short delay.

AIDE MEMOIRE.

On the 19th December the Argentine Government enacted a decree providing for the internment in the City of Buenos Aires of the Captain and officers of the German cruiser "Graf Spee", and of the members of the crew in the inland provinces or territories of Argentina subject to measures imposed by the local authorities charged with their supervision.

Under this decree the Ministry of the Interior were charged with the responsibility of ensuring that members of the crew would remain within bounds to be fixed.

On the 14th February however an article, apparently sanctioned by the Argentine Government, appeared in the Argentine press which stated that the German Ambassador had been informed that the Argentine Government proposed to implement the internment decree by distributing internees in difference parts of the country and that the question of the employment of 500 of these men by firms suggested by the German Ambassador was under discussion. On the 15th March a press statement appeared to the effect that all sailors from the "Graf Spee" would receive civilian clothing and be interned within ten days, but this was qualified by a further press statement on the 16th March indicating that 200 sailors would be distributed in the Province of Mendoza amongst firms and families willing to have them.

As the Argentine Government are already aware, from the demarches made by His Majesty's Ambassador at Buenos Aires, the most recent of which was effected on the 13th March, His Majesty's Government have learnt with concern and disappointment of the unsatisfactory nature of the proposed internment measures which seem to them incompatible not only with the terms of the Argentine Government decree but also with the obligations of neutrals under Article 10 of Hague Convention No. X of 1899, which while in principle leaving it to the neutral State to decide on the precise nature of the steps to be taken, provides that internees must be guarded so as to prevent them from again taking part in the operations of war. It appears to them, however, from the information at their disposal, that the measures about to be adopted are the result of discussion and agreement with the German Ambassador and amount indeed to the acceptance of suggestions made by one belligerent only. If, as appears to be contemplated, the German sailors are allowed to take up civilian employment in particular with German firms in the capital or even in the provinces there would, in the opinion of His Majesty's Government, be a serious risk not only that they might escape or indulge in propaganda, but also take part in acts of sabotage.

His Majesty's Government hope therefore that the Argentine Government will recast the measures now contemplated so as to provide for some form of effectively supervised confinement of the men in the interior of the country. (Ibid, 20 March 1940)

A couple of days later, the Foreign Office sent telegram 82 to Robert Hadow, Britain's Acting Counsellor in the Chancery, the office of the British Embassy, Buenos Aires.

Your telegram No. 139 [of 20th March: internment of crew of Graf Spee].

On 20th March Parliamentary Under Secretary of State spoke to Argentine Ambassador on lines of instructions to you in my telegram No. 72 and handed him aide-memoire. Ambassador said that Argentine Under Secretary for Foreign Affairs had telegraphed that Sir E. Ovey had been pressing British point of view too persistently. Mr. Butler reminded Ambassador that Sir. E. Ovey had been attacked in Argentine press and that he was only doing his duty. Ambassador said he had no wish to complain but expressed opinion that it would be extremely unwise for His Majesty's Government to continue pressure on Argentine Government in this matter, He would prefer not to send aide memoire to his Government until Mr. Butler had discussed matter further with me. He suggested that clash of opinion between His Majesty's Government and Argentine Government should be avoided and that matter could best be handled by His Majesty's Government drawing attention of Argentine Government to each case of unsatisfactory conduct of the internees.

Ambassador was told that his suggestion would be considered and the result communicated to him after a short delay. (Ibid, 22 March 1940)

Three days later, Hadow sent the Foreign Office telegram 141 concerning a new development. A copy was also sent to Rio de Janeiro as Saving telegram 2.

> Your telegram No. 82.
> Minister for Foreign Affairs being too busy to receive me I drew the attention of the Under Secretary of State today to the Prensa report of German Embassy's request for the exemption of fifty officers and men of Spee from internment as con-combatants under international law.
> Fearing legalistic quibbles as the result of further Rio de Janeiro conferences this week, I contented myself with leaving with him privately names of three officers and flotilla orderlies who alone I pointed out figured on the official list of ship's crew on their entry into Argentina: this number corresponding closely with similar personnel on our man of war.
> We must I said counter the dangerous possibility of invaluable specialists in modern warfare thus reaching Germany – as another newspaper has said, released men would be free to do – even at the risk of another incident in which Argentina might be involved: as might well be Germany's ulterior motive.
> I therefore urged the utmost vigilance and severest control over the lists before a single exemption from internment was granted.
> Under Secretary of State was receptive and promised utmost vigilance, pledging Argentine good-will in this matter. But trouble lies with Ministry of Interior which seemed [group undecipherable] already independent control over this question and is I learn on good authority partly pro-German if not worse.
> If therefore risk is considered serious I venture to recommend early exposition of our point of view to the Argentine Ambassador; avoiding international law which has a fatal attraction for south American legalists and enlisting Ambassador's utmost cooperation in recommending vigilance to the Argentine Government. (Ibid.25 March 1940)

On 27 March, Millington-Drake sent telegram 91 to Eden with a copy to Ovey.

> I discussed matter yesterday with Minister for Foreign Affairs who though expressing all goodwill strongly maintained his view

that in principle interned men were not prisoners and that he could not entertain the idea of confinement.

I replied that you had suggested confinement as the simplest means to the end of enabling the Uruguayan Government to comply with its obligation without constant preoccupation. He then expressed hope that the text of the regulations which I explained had crossed your instructions would give you some reassurance but I replied that I feared they would not do so much. I urged that control once a week was inadequate.

His Excellency agreed and was inclined to think that it should be at least twice a week though he assured me that the police had the men under observation. He would consider the matter further and consult with the Police Authorities.

Incidentally, the pro-German "Pampero" of Buenos Aires stated in its issue of the 19th March that the Uruguayan police pestered the interned men with surprise visits, etc. to give satisfaction to the British Legation. (TNA ADM 116/5474, 27 March 1940)

Somewhat belatedly, three months after the event, the *Dundee Courier* shed light on the demise of the Graf Spee.

Graf Spee Men Mutinied Before Scuttling
OFFICERS MADE EIGHT APPEALS ON DECK
CREW TIRED OF WAR, REFUSED TO PUT TO SEA
ONLY 60 VOLUNTEERED TO FIGHT

Refusal of the crew of the Admiral Graf Spee to take their ship out to meet the waiting British warships led to the decision to scuttle her, it was revealed by the Admiralty last night. Eight times officers, including finally Captain Langsdorff himself, appealed in vain for them to fight. When, in protest against the decision to scuttle the battleship, the officers called for volunteers to go out and fight, only 60 men stepped forward. The German sailors were tired of war.

Langsdorff's Appeal

The Admiralty received the news in authoritative report of the events immediately preceding the scuttling after the battle of the River Plate. An extract from this report reads:

The Graf Spee had been repairing at top speed from the morning of Thursday, December 14, onwards. Saturday, December 16. it was anticipated that repairs would be completed some time during Saturday night or early on Sunday morning. The Uruguayan officials were so confident that she would make a break some during that night that they prohibited all Allied ships from leaving the port.

MUSTERED ON DECK.

During the afternoon of Saturday, December 16, however, factor arose which the German command had not taken into account. The crew of the Admiral Graf Spee refused to take their ship to sea. Between p.m. and 7.30 p.m. on that day the crew of the Graf Spee were mustered on deck at least eight times and were harangued by one officer after another. The final appeal to the men was made by Captain Langsdorff himself, but still the men refused to return to duty. During these musters the crew of the Graf Spee broke ranks, shouted, and behaved in a disorderly manner verging on the mutinous.

HITLER'S ORDER.

Captain Langsdorff dismissed his men at 7.30 p.m., and came ashore at 8 p.m. to consult the German Minister. This advice must-have been cabled to Hitler about that hour, and a reply ordering the scuttling of the ship received about midnight. Captain Langsdorff returned on board the Graf Spee shortly after midnight and all repair work was suspended. At the same hour arrangements were made with Buenos Aires for two large German-owned Argentine tugs to tow a large barge over to receive the crew of the Graf Spee after the ship had been scuttled and take them to Buenos Aires.

During the previous afternoon, Saturday, December 16, large loads of provisions had been embarked by the Graf Spee and also a lot of lifebelts and other gear from the German merchant ship Tacoma. On Sunday morning this process was reversed. The lifebelts and gear were all returned to the Tacoma and the provisions embarked were transferred to that ship.

OFFICERS PROTEST.

From noon to 5.30 p.m. on Sunday about 900 of the Graf Spee s officers and men were also transferred to the Tacoma. The officers had previously protested against the order to scuttle the ship, and had called for volunteers from the crew to go out and fight. Only about 60 men of the crew stepped forward. The rest stood sullen and refused to volunteer. The crew of boys had had enough of war.

TROUBLE KEPT SECRET

The Germans kept this quiet until the Graf Spee was almost ready to go out and scuttle, and very few people knew about it even when the ship had actually left the harbour. Hence the surprise when she turned westward instead of to seaward. The German colony in Buenos Aires, who made much of the crew for the first two days after they had been landed there, boycotted them when news of their refusal of duty got around.

Reports of insubordination on the part of the crew of the Graf Spee and their refusal [to] obey orders have been confirmed by observers on board the merchant ships Lynton Grange and Trekieve and other vessels, both naval and mercantile, which were moored close to the Graf Spee in Montevideo harbour, including a tug which was alongside the German warship- These observers were witnesses of the occurrences on board the German ship. (*Dundee Courier,* 27 March 1940)

Also on the same day, Ovey sent telegram 147 to Eden.

> Your telegram No. 83.
> I have been very careful through my discussions regarding internment to acquire Your Lordship's exact instructions in advance and never to give Argentine Government opportunity of obtaining better terms in London than in Buenos Aires.
> 2. from paragraphs 4, 5 and 6 of my telegram No. 122 you will see I had strong hopes of some concession by Argentine Government of a face-saving nature if his Majesty's Government remained form and was gratified to learn that several hundred men have been sent inland in the last ten days. I hoped this would be compatible at least with a very much larger percentage than originally intended being sent to the interior.
> 3. I trust that last sentence in your above-mentioned telegram does not indicate any weakening of His Majesty's Government intention, as officially communicated to Argentine Government on March 14th (see my despatch No. 83 of March 14th (to leave responsibility to Argentine Government. While this is not the ideal solution for two very friendly countries, it is the only solution possible if Argentine Government (which I am not prepared to believe unless we show signs of weakening) refuse to meet us in any way at all.
> 4. a new feature has now been introduced by intrigues of the German Ambassador with the Minister of the Interior (see Mr. Hadow's telegram No. 141) on which Admiralty (see their telegram No. 1925 of March 25th to the Naval Attaché) have strong views.
> Please telegraph urgent instructions on this point and on general question. (TNA ADM 116/4180, 27 March 1940)

On 29 March, Perowne at the Foreign Office sent Ker the following note.

> Jarret [Sir Clifford Jarrett of the Admiralty's Military Branch] has already had copies of the record of the interview between Mr

Butler and the Argentine Ambassador on the 20th March and of Hadow's telegram No. 139 of the same date about the "Graf Spee" internees.

You will see form paragraph 2 of the record that the Argentine Ambassador made a not very happy suggestion that individual cases of unsatisfactory conduct on the part of the internees should be brought to his attention by us or to that of the Argentine Government by Ovey, and he seems (wilfully perhaps) to have misunderstood our purpose of sending for him. To adopt his suggestion would be very like agreeing to shut the stable door after the horse has gone, and to take upon our shoulders a responsibility which is properly that of the Argentine Government.

However, that may be, you will see from Hadow's telegram No. 139 that the Argentine Government have now provided a written reply to Ovey's latest representations on this matter, and that Hadow recommends that we should take no further action until we see the text, which is expected to reach us today, the 28th March.

We do not think that there is any further action we can usefully take until we see this note. When it is received we can consider whether any reply to it is required, or whether it is necessary to say anything further to Dr. Le Breton.

Meanwhile, the object of our latest demarche in London as well as in Buenos Aires, which was to impress on the Argentine Government our displeasure at their behaviour and to place squarely on their shoulders the responsibility for any untoward consequences which may follow from their obstinacy, seems to have been fully achieved. I should hope personally that the outcome of our study of the Argentine note would be to decide that both questions indicated above should be answered in the negative and that we can leave this matter alone, for the present at any rate. (Ibid, 28th March 1940)

On 29 March, Sir George Ogilvie Forbes, the British Ambassador in Cuba between 1940 and 1944, sent telegram 24 to Jarrett at the Admiralty informing him that 'A reliable friend in a Government department has just informed me that officers from GRAF SPEE have arrived at Havana' and that he was making further enquiries.

The following day, he sent telegram 26 to Jarrett in London and Ovey in Buenos Aires.

So far as I can ascertain there are about 12 staying at the Hotel Luz, Havana.

2. while the following may have no connexion with these men there are two German controlled schooners, ostensibly lobster

boats one in Almadares River, Havana, the other at Coloma on the south-west coast, named Marisco and Coloma respectively, in which these men might get away. The name of Cuban owners is given in Mr Grant Watson [the previous British Ambassador to Cuba]'s despatch No. 10 E.W. of November 7th 1939.
   3. I have informed my French colleague who confirms the above and adds that some of the crew of the Columbus [a German ocean liner] are there. (Ibid. 31 March 1940)

Eden's response to Ovey, telegram 91, was sent on 31 March.

   Your telegrams Nos. 141 and 147 [of March 25th and March 27th: Graf Spee internees].
   Object of recommendations made by you in Buenos Aires and by Parliamentary Under secretary in London was to impress on the Argentine Government our displeasure at their behaviour and to place squarely on their shoulders responsibility for any untoward consequences which may result from their obstinacy. We did not entertain any great hope that the Argentine Government would thereby be induced to alter their policy. Our object seems to us to have been fully achieved, and we are now awaiting receipt of text of latest Argentine note to you before considering whether it is necessary to say anything further to the arginine ambassador. For your own information, suggestion he made at interview with Parliamentary Under Secretary is not of course acceptable. To adopt it would be to agree to wait till the horse is gone to shut the stable door and ourselves to assume a responsibility which is in our view solely that of the ARGENTINE Government.
   As regards question of exceptions from internment we concur entirely in views set out in Admiralty's telegram to Naval Attache No. 1925 of March 25th. (Ibid, 31 March 1940)

Ovey sent a response to Montevideo with a copy to the Foreign Office on 1 April.

   I am grateful and relieved at your telegram No. 91.
   With regard to the second sentence I retain the hope that Argentine Government may compromise on their earlier attitude for following reasons.
      (a) Minister for Foreign Affairs while responsible, I imagine, for satisfactory Argentine decree, was in no way responsible for subsequent arrangement reached between the Minister of Marine, Minister of Interior and

German Ambassador. His Excellency cannot feel comfortable at the situation which he defends judicially.

(b) Argentine Government have taken no action regarding the rescinding of article 2 of their decree and since my interview, we calculate men have been sent inland.

(c) His Majesty's Government's solemn warning in the note of 12th March would not look well were it ever published especially if incident occurred.

(d) If, as I believe, Minister for Foreign Affairs was impressed by my arguments as to replacement of Argentine workmen by Germans and the behaviour of German sailors, effect will be still greater if the report in Sir. G. Ogilvie-Forbes's telegram No. 26 is correct and becomes known (I would welcome earliest information on this point).

(e) I feel [group mutilated – code indecipherable] insistence on the fact of one having left on record a note expressing dissatisfaction at the Argentine Government's attitude and delaying responsibility on them is not an ideal solution [Grp. Mut] may still produce concessions which, even if not 100%, will be much nearer to our original desiderata. (TNA ADM 116/5474, 1 April 1940)

The Foreign Office responded to Ogilvie-Forbes information about the escape of the Graf Spee officers in telegram 7 sent on 1 April to Havana. A copy was sent to Buenos Aires and Washington.

Your telegram No. 26 0of the 30th March: Officers of "Graf Spee"].

It is most important for us to know exact identity of these officers and whether they come from Buenos Aires or Montevideo. Please telegraph any relevant facts to Buenos Aires and Washington. (TNA ADM 116/4180, 1 April 1940)

Ovey sent telegram 159 to London on 5 April.

Newspaper "Nacion" states that only two "Graf Spee" sailors escaped on Italian ship "Neptunia" and been handed over by the latter to the Brazilian Authorities at Santos but certain officers who had not taken advantage of the arrangement made with the German Embassy whereby, in return for their word not to escape, they would be permitted residence and to take up work within 50 kilometres of Buenos Aires are reported to have left Argentina.

Some sailors had also shown their dissatisfaction at the subsistence allowance of three pesos a day agreed between the German and Argentine Government.

Argentine Government had therefore decided to act energetically and unless officers gave their word of honour within a week they would be interned on Martin Garcia island.

Other newspapers refer further to escapes from Santa Fe [north-eastern province, upriver from Buenos Aires]. (TNA ADM 116/5474, 5 April 1940)

The British *Midland Daily Telegraph* reported on 5 April that,

NAZI OFFICERS May be put on Island
BUENOS AIRES, Friday.
Annoyed at the escape of several men from the Graf Spee from places of internment, the Argentine Government was today reported to be considering transferring officers from the naval arsenal at Buenos Aires to the island of Martin Garcia in the middle of the River Plate.
The sailors are interned inland in contingents of 50 and 100 men. The officers will not promise not to escape if allowed similar freedom.
The men from the Graf Spee arrested by the police near Santos, Brazil, yesterday. They had escaped from Buenos Aires by sailing aboard the Italian steamer Neptunia. – Associated Press.
(*Midland Daily Telegraph*, 5 April 1940)

The location of Martin Garcia Island

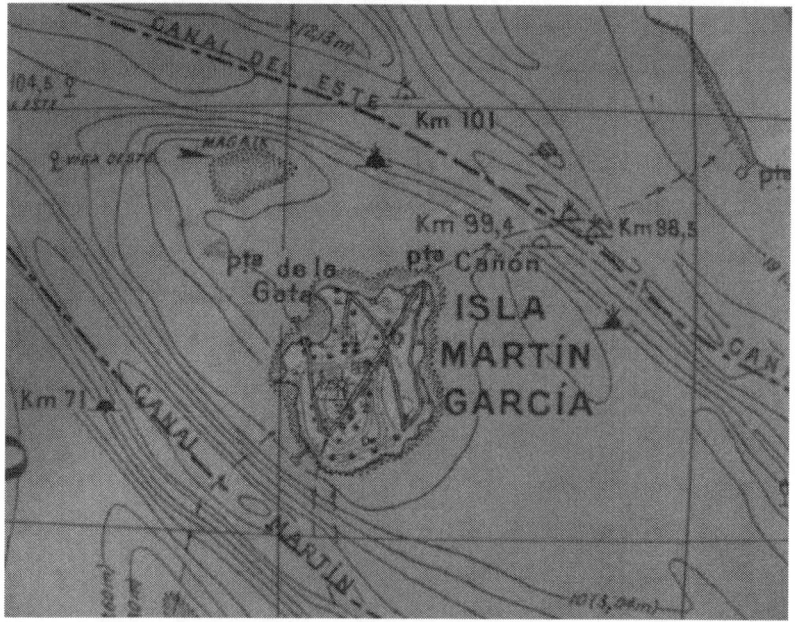

Map of Martin Garcia Island (Military Geographical Institute, Buenos Aires, 1943 (https://journals.openedition.org/corpusarchivos/1176)

On 6 April, the *San Pedro News Pilot* reported on the move to Martin Garcia.

Graf Spee Officers, Cadets to Be Interned on Island
BUENOS AIRES. (UP)—' The naval ministry announced today that 32 officers and 208 warrant officers and cadets of the scuttled German pocket battleship Admiral Graf Spee now in Buenos Aires would be taken Monday to the naval base on Martin Garcia island for internment. The remaining 400 sailors who have been in the Argentine capital will be kept in the naval arsenal here pending completion of a program to remove them to interior provinces. The officers so far have not been under detention but had been ordered not to go outside the federal capital without special authority of the Argentine government. Martin Garcia island is 80 miles off Buenos Aires in the river Plata. More than 400 members already have been sent to the interior. Today's measure reflected the irritation of the Argentine government over the escape or three officers of the ship. (*San Pedro News Pilot,* Vol.13, No.28, 6 April 1940)

The *Newport Daily Express* reported,

Argentina Agitated BY ESCAPE of Internees
Escape of Graf Spee Men Stirs Government to Take Steps to Stop More Flights. BUENOS AIRES, April 6. (AP)-The Government, disturbed lest the flight of three interned officers from the scuttled pocket battleship Admiral Graf Spee reflect on Argentine neutrality, was reported today to have advised the German ambassador that it is taking strict measures to prevent further escapes.

Unofficial reports said that one of the three officers already had reached Germany with papers of the Graf Spee, which was scuttled off Montevideo last Dec. 17 after she had taken refuge in Uruguayan waters following a running flight with three British cruisers.

Approximately 1,000 officers and men from the battle-scarred German warship later sought refuge in Buenos Aires and were interned for the duration of the war.

The German Ambassador, Edmund Von Thermann, was summoned to the foreign office yesterday shortly after the officers' escape had been disclosed.

Well-informed sources said Foreign Minister Jose Maria Cantilo had advised Von Thermann that the government was taking stringent steps to prevent further escapes.

These sources said that the remainder of the interned officers, held at the Buenos Aires naval arsenal, would be removed to safer places under close guard if they persisted in refusing to promise not to leave the country.

Several of the Graf Spee seamen previously were reported to have disappeared from interior provinces. (*The Newport Daily Express,* 6 April 1940)

The *Santa Cruz Sentinel* and the *San Bernardino Sun* ran the same story which gave more detail of the escape.

Nazi Officers of Graf Spee Flee Argentine

Buenos Aires, April 5, (AP) – The escape of three interned officers of the German pocket battleship Admiral Graf Spee was disclosed tonight and one of them was reported unofficially to have already reached Germany with documents of the scuttled man-o-war.

News of the escape of the officers from their quarters in the naval arsenal followed disclosure several Graf Spee sailors had disappeared from interior provinces.

More than 1000 officers and men of the Graf Spee took refuge in Argentina after scuttling their ship, loser in a running battle with three British cruisers, in Montevideo harbour last December 17.

The Argentine government decreed that the crew be interned in landlocked provinces and that the officers be requested to give their word of honour that they would not attempt to flee the country. Most officers refused to do this.

The government now is reported to be planning to intern the officers on Martin Garcia island in the Rio De La Plata and keep them under strictly military guard.

One of the escaped officers is believed to have been the third in command of the Graf Spee. The date and manner of their escape was not immediately learned.

Two seamen who eluded Argentine authorities were seized at Santos, Brazil, when they disembarked from the Italian steamer Neptunia. They will be returned here. (*Santa Cruz Sentinel,* Vol. 104, No.83, 6 April 1940)

The *Santa Ana Register* reported,

ARGENTINA MOVES TO BLOCK ESCAPE OF GRAF SPEE CREW. Buenos Aires, April 6. (INS)-The Argentine government today [?] to round up more than 1000 crew members of the scuttled German pocket battleship Graf Spee to be transferred en

masse to Martin Garcia island naval prison for the duration of the war.
    This decision was a result of the escape of several interned Graf Spee crew members, including three officers and refusal of the remaining seamen to take an oath not to leave the country.
    Six missing.
    The fugitive officers were said to be a lieutenant commander, who was third in command on the Graf Spee, and two lieutenants.
    Refusal to promise not to flee Argentine was based on the German military code which forbids imprisoned soldiers or sailors from pledging their honor not to take up arms again in defense of their country.
    Originally 1039 officers and men were interned last dec. 19, under orders of President Roberto M. Ortiz. At least six of these have escaped since, but officials would not reveal the exact number.
    Three captured.
    Martin Garcia island is 40 miles north of Buenos Aires not far from the scene of the running naval battle with British warships which resulted in the scuttling of the Graf Spee.
    Three Graf Spee seamen who eluded Argentine authorities were arrested aboard an Italian vessel at santos, Brazil yesterday. They will be returned to Buenos Aires. (*Santa Ana Register,* 6 April 1940)

The same day, the *Yorkshire Post* included the following article.

GRAF SPEE CREW
Some to Go to Prison After Others Escaped
New York, Saturday. All the officers and half the crew of the scuttled German battleship Admiral Graf Spee will henceforth be treated as prisoners instead of internees, according to a despatch from Buenos Ayres to the "New York Times."
    This step follows the escape of three officers and two sailors, and the refusal of the other officers to pledge their word not to escape.
    The officers and the men affected will be confined in the Naval Prison on the Island of Martin Garcia in the River Plate. Reuter. (*Yorkshire Post,* 6 April 1940)

The following day, *The Charlotte News,* reported,

    Argentine sends Nazis to Island. Escape of Graf Spee men Causes Anger. BUENOS AIRES, April 6,-The Argentine

Government, indignant over the escape of three officers and two sailors of the scuttled German warship Admiral graf Spee, today ordered the remaining officers and higher ranking members of the interned crew confined to Martin Garcia island, a naval base in the River Plata, 80 miles from Buenos Aires.

The Government, announcing the decision to send 32 officers and 208 warrant officers and cadets to the island on Tuesday, said:

"Argentina has been excessively generous to these officers and sailors who came to our country last December after their own ship was destroyed. But we canno continue to let our neutrality be jeopardized, therefore we have taken steps to ensure that they will not be able to return to Germany to resume belligerent action."

REPORTED IN GERMANY

Argentine authorities yesterday revealed that three of the Admiral Graf Spee's officers had disappeared. One, said to have been the third officer, was unofficially reported to have made his way to Germany. Two members of the crew were seized earlier in the week in Brazil.

The Ministry of the Navy said the 400 Graf Spee sailors still in Buenos Aires will be sent into interior provinces where a like number of their companions have already been transferred. (*The Charlotte News,* 7 April 1940)

On 8 April, Ovey sent Eden telegram 162 and Saving No. 8 to Montevideo.

> My telegram No. 159
> The press are in possession of and will probably publish this afternoon the story that an armed guard was called out on Sunday afternoon to prevent attempt by Graf Spee officers to escape from the naval barracks in Buenos Aires,
> Eight are said to have escaped; remainder confined on the naval transport Pampa pending transfer to Martin Garcia (TNA ADM 116/4180, 8 April 1940)

On the same day, Ogilvie-Forbes sent the Admiralty telegram 54 with copies to Montevideo and Washington.

> My telegram No. 30.
> It is officially denied that there are any officers of Graf Spee in Cuba on the ground that the immigration regulations which are applied more strictly to the Germans than to other foreigners

would make their entry impossible. Statement adds that the Secretariat of the state is making further enquiries.

2. My original informant who is Director of Public Health of Havana and controls port quarantine service is using his [?own] private police to ascertain real names of the officers of whom he says there are two here. He has not yet been successful.

3. I am informed also from another source, an American Jew resident in Hotel Luz, that there are three officers of the Graf Spee two of whom [grp. omt. : have] the following name, surname and false passport: 1. Perth Serger Estonian passport 2. Arthur Helmerson Norwegian passport. Name and address of third officer at present unknown.

Same hotel contains engineer from Columbus who has taken the name of Anderson and a Norwegian passport. (Ibid.)

The following day, the *Western Morning News* reported the escape.

GRAF SPEE OFFICERS ESCAPE. Eleven officers of the scuttled German pocket battleship Admiral Graf Spee are reported to have escaped, states P.A. [Press Association] special message from Buenos Aires. They are believed to be on their way to Chile in disguise. (*Western Morning News*, 9 April 1940)

The same story was reported in the *Belfast Telegraph*.

GRAF SPEE OFFICERS' FLIGHT. FEAR OF INTERNMENT. ARGENTINE PRESS ANGRY. BUENOS AYRES. Tuesday.— Eleven officers of the Admiral Graf Spee, who have been in Argentina since the scuttling of the pocket battleship, are reported to have disappeared. They are believed to be on their way to Chile in disguise. Their flight follows the unofficial announcement last week that it was intended to remove the officers and half of the crew of the Graf Spee to the naval prison on the island of Martin Garcia in the River Plate. Up till now the officers have been allowed full liberty though the crew have been interned. During the week-end it was rumoured that the officers were to be interned today. The flight of eleven of them has aroused indignation in the Argentine Press. "We cannot, probably, expect any other conduct from the terror stricken victims of Hitler," it adds.— Press Association War Special. (*Belfast Telegraph,* 9 April 1940)

The *Evening Despatch* had a similar article.

GRAF SPEE OFFICERS' ESCAPE

ELEVEN officers of the Admiral Graf Spee, who have been in Argentina since the scuttling of the pocket battleship are reported to have disappeared. They are believed to be on their way to Chile in disguise. Their flight follows the unofficial announcement last week that it was intended to remove the officers and half of the crew of the Graf Spee to the naval prison on the Island Martin Garcia in the River Plate. During the week-end it was rumoured that the officers were to be interned to-day.(*Evening Despatch*, 9 April 1940)

In Millington-Drake's anthology, he stated that the Graf Spee officers had been,

> ...quartered in the Naval Arsenal adjoining the port of Buenos Aires and were kept under a strict guard and not on parole. However, the then German Naval Attaché at Buenos Aires, Captain Niebuhr, stated that they were allowed out from the Naval Arsenal on parole, to visit friends in the town or even for excursions, but that in no case did they take advantage of these outings to escape.
>
> The first to escape was Gunnery Officer, Commander Ascher, in early January 1940 (who got to Germany by air via Buenos Aires, the Atlantic and Italy). Next came the escape of Lieutenants Dietrich and Blundau by the southern lakes on March 21. This was followed by the escape of a group of thirteen early in April which was undertaken when they learnt that they were to be transferred to the island of Martin Garcia, a naval station further up the estuary of the River Plate from which obviously escape would be more difficult. The group included Commander Wattenberg, Commander Klemp (as they then were), Commander Rasenack and ten other younger and very enterprising officers. Their escape from the Arsenal was facilitated by the electrical engineer officer of the party managing to cause a short circuit of the electric lighting. At this time there escaped two petty officers, Fieber and Wild.
>
> Captain Wattenburg wrote to me: 'The day of our flight coincided with the beginning of the Norwegian expedition (April 9), for I remember that at the house of the German friend who had taken me in I listened with the greatest interest to the news on the radio of the landing of our troops in Norway. Most of us met again in Santiago de Chile, which had also been reached by a small party which had crossed the Andes on foot. One group, including Klepp and myself, flew from Santiago to Germany via the Pacific, Japan and Russia.' (Millington-Drake, op.cit. p.385)

Lieutenant (later Commander) Frederick Rasenack who escaped in 1940, reached Germany and commanded a U-boat. (Millington-Drake, op.cit.)

After the war, Rasenack published *Panzerschiff Admiral Graf Spee* from which Millington-Drake included extracts.

I was interned three more months in Argentina. The hospitality the Argentinians and Germans gave us was extraordinary and I came to love that country and its inhabitants. But my thoughts and longings were in Germany. I could not accept the quiet life when I knew that my brothers continued fighting... when the crew was distributed to various Argentine provinces and when it was decided to intern the officers and petty officers in the island of Martin Garcia I felt no further obligation. With another ten officers we escaped from the Naval Arsenal in spite of a tight guard.

[Commander Rasenack supplemented this account in a letter to me in which he said the following:]

In spite of statements from enemy sources, not one of us had given his word of honour that he would not leave Argentine during the war.

I needed nearly half a year to reach Germany again! My adventures were not few! I reached Chile in the guise of a Czechoslovak engineer of the SKODA factory. From there I continued my journey as a traveller in wines, of Bulgarian nationality. In the Panama Canal zone I was interned in an Italian ship, together with one of my comrades, by the American secret police. With the help of the chief of that secret police, with whom we had made good friends, we managed to transfer to a Japanese ship by which we reached Mexico and the United States. From there we crossed the Pacific to Japan.

We went through Korea, Manchuria, Siberia and Russia as German commercial travellers and we arrived in Germany on September 1, 1940 – exactly a year after the outbreak of war. (Ibid, p. 386)

Estancia in semi-tropical northern Argentina where Fiebel and Wild hid while preparing to cross the Andes (Millington-Drake, op.cit.)

Chief Petty Officer Hein Wild who escaped over the Andes to Chile (Millington-Drake, op.cit.)

Fieber and Wild practising for their trip across the Andes into Chile (Millington-Drake, op.cit.)

Fieber and Wild crossing the Andes with a train of mules, when escaping from Argentina into Chile in 1940 (Millington-Drake, op.cit.)

Millington-Drake summarised Fieber's account of his escape written in *Flucht durch drei Kontinent,*

> ...He describes life in the Immigrant's Hotel in Buenos Aires and the assiduous hospitality of the local German colony. Soon the crew were forbidden to wear uniform except within the Arsenal. This turns out to favour attempts to escape.
> On 1 April 1940 Fieber fell ill and was taken to the German Hospital. He had been affected by some kind of virus, possibly caused by scratching a mosquito bite. This illness coincided with the order to go to the island of Martin Garcia in the estuary of the River Plate where there was a naval station; so his belongings were removed from the Immigrants' Hotel to be sent there, he only having on him a pair of trousers and a white jacket. On April 7 the doctor announced that he was cured and told him to hold himself in readiness to be taken the next day for internment in Martin Garcia. One of the nurses, a young woman from Hamburg, had been particularly kind to him and so he took her into his confidence

about his plan to escape. She arranged for civilian clothes to be delivered to the hospital and that very evening under the pretext of taking a bath he was able to put them on and slip out of the hospital to a car which was waiting to take him to his friend's house.

However he could not remain long as the Argentine police were keeping a special watch on Germans and German sympathisers. So another friend took him in his motor boat to an island on the Tigre (pronounced Teegry) [a much visited locality some 30 miles from Buenos Aires where the river of that name flows into the estuary of the Plate and makes a delta of intricate channels of semi-tropical vegetation producing many kinds of fruit. Amongst them are dotted remote summer bungalows not easy of access so it was a well-chosen refuge]. There he met three comrades who had already escaped, one of them a schoolmate from Augsburg. Their stay lasted about four weeks, during which they had at least one narrow escape when a police boat came looking for escaped prisoners from the GRAF SPEE. On May 1 they returned to Buenos Aires. Fieber had acquired a beard.... And a well-to-do German friend now fits him out from top to toe with new clothes. Whilst still in Buenos Aires the greatest care has to be taken not to give away their identities by careless talk and they go out as little as possible, taking their walks in the evening and only visiting places known as 'safe'.

The escapers from the Tigre, including the school friend from Augsburg, were furnished with false identity papers in a German bar where Fieber met Torpedo Chief Petty Officer Hein Wild at once realizes that he is the very man to share the great adventure with him.

Indeed on the same day they take train to Selta in the far north of Argentina, travelling as 'tourists' under the names of Johannes schiller and Heinrich Watter. In Salta they run into two other GRAF SPEE shipmates who are also planning to escape by this route; however, these two were caught next day!

So once more they need to lie low for a time and again a local German helps them to do so. Later he took them to the semi-tropical Chaco territory to his property there occupied by one man – a Finn. From there another German, a business man named Gross from Tucuman, took them back there in his car, and there in Tucuman the preparations for the expedition – it was no less - were made. They were given a Fiat, an old lorry and took a guide. They still figure as tourists, and Gross, as a member of the Argentine Automobile Club, can, when necessary, explain their enterprise as being a long planned one to attempt the crossing of the Andes from this northern region of Argentina from which it is rarely undertaken in winter. In fact the reason for choosing that particular point was that for the first part of the way there was an old track and then a road in course of construction, and above all up till now there had been no frontier patrol by the Argentine police (but this was established soon afterwards).

They reached the well-known but remote locality of Timogasata and once again took refuge with Germans, two farmers, brothers, from East Prussia. This was at their *estancia* near Chilecoto, another known locality, but near a hardly known village named Villa Union. Their reason for staying there some four months was that, because of the capture of yet more GRAF SPEE escapees in that region – no less than a group of twelve – all passes over the Andes were now controlled by the military as well as by the police. So Fiber and Wild helped with the work on the farm and as trained engineers were most useful with repairs, etc., and got paid for it. However, conditions were not too comfortable. Temperatures were high by day and low by night, there are sandstorms and they are tormented by mosquitoes and flying bugs. Meanwhile, with a view to the immediate future, they train themselves in riding horses, mules and donkeys, and continue to study Spanish.

All this time they were exploring the possibilities of a successful crossing to Chile, and in the end always came back to the plan of getting across on mule-back. But winter was now setting in and the high mountains were covered in snow.

Their hosts secured for them a dependable guide from the village of Villa Union. They knew him as 'Dom Fernando' and he had agreed to accompany them provided they equipped themselves adequately for the journey which might last four weeks. So they hire a horse and eight mules and load their gear on an old lorry from the farm. They were most favourably impressed by Don Fernando, an elderly man who inspired their entire confidence. He is told that they are tourists who want to make the sporting attempt to cross the *Cordillera* to Chile in the winter and then take the train to Puerto Montt in the far south, returning to Argentina by the usual route across to Mendoza. It was now nearly September. Meanwhile the whole village of Villa Union tried to dissuade the 'mad gringos' from their venture. Incidentally the local police *Comisario* who had been a frequent visitor to the *estancia* and must have had a shrewd idea of thenir identity nevertheless provided them with the certificate of good conduct always necessary when leaving Argentina for any frontier post.

They eventually set off, the party consisting of the author and Wild, one of the German brothers from the *estancia*, Don Enrique, the guide Don Fernando and a drover to look after the animals. Mostly riding at a gallop, they make their first halt at a weather station some 1,200 metres (say 4,000 feet) up, which they reach at midnight, very saddle-sore and already suffering from the altitude. The next day's ride brought them to a stone refuge hut. In the night the mules escaped, but the driver retrieved them from the weather station where they had returned and brought them back tin the late evening. The *contretemps* may have saved their lives as a heavy snowstorm came on and had they not had to wait for the animals they would probably have insisted on pressing on despite the advice of the guide.

On the fifth day the rode across a high plateau, a distance of 50 kilometres, which meant 16 hours in the saddle in the teeth of a gale. The night was spent in a hut. After this came the crossing of the high *cordillera* for which three days had to be allowed. The animals had difficulty in struggling through the deep snow, and yet by day the travellers are nearly blinded by the strong sunlight. The eighth day proved to be the culmination of their *tour de force* when at last they reached the frontier between Argentina and Chile, and on dismounting they literally collapsed. Here are Fieber's impressions at this crucial point of their adventure:

'We tarry for a moment and look into the silent immeasurable expanse, where there is no sound but the organ of the wind, nothing to see but snow-covered peaks and above them circling eagles with snow-white plumage, considerably larger than those to be seen in our German homeland.

'It is physically impossible for us to perform the dance of joy we had intended, but the feeling of happiness which arises within us causes all our sufferings to be forgotten. We know that the chain of hardships has not has not come to an end and that new dangers await us before we eventually reach home. But one thing imprints itself firmly in our consciousness... it is that we have survived the eight days climb over the high *cordillera*, we shall also overcome all further obstacles. A light touch to the reins and we are off again – step by stem downhill: we ride into freedom1

The first night is spent in the open and wrapped in their sleeping bags. Even now they might have perished in the snow had not the animals become restless and awakened them. On September 18 they reach the first habitation on the Chilean side and soon afterwards a village where they sadly bid farewell to their faithful guide Don Fernando and the animals. From here they get a lift to the little town of Copiapo. Don Enriquo takes them by train southwards to Santiago but leaves them there as he has to go back to meet up with the guide and make the return journey by the same arduous route over the *cordillera*.

In Santiago local Germans welcome Fieber and Wild and help them in every way. They decided to rest for a while to recover from the strain of the journey; and to get to know something of the country and the people. Their hope is to find a Japanese ship to take them further on their way, but this hope is dashed when they read in the papers that four men from the GRAF SPEE have been taken off a Japanese ship in the harbour of Valparaiso!. Details are given in the newspapers, and one of them was Fieber's school friend from Augsburg.

They were advised to disappear from Valparaiso and to take refuge on a vineyard, the property of a German =Chilean. They pass themselves off as engineers from a German merchant ship and take the names of Faber and Brandis. But their stay is unexpectedly cut short by the startling news that a census is about to be taken! So they take the train to the south (parting company at Chillan), Fieber goes to the better known Valdivia; however, there a drinking party at the German Club nearly brings disaster as his money is stolen and he is nearly arrested by the police as he tries to find his way home on foot, but he plays the part of a dead drunk and they leave him alone. Then in another well-known place, Osorno, he was put up for weeks in a comfortable villa by a German-Chilean and was able to recuperate from his many trying experiences. It was now December 1940 and he remained there over Christmas.

At the end of January 1941 he proceeded to Valparaiso and as a 'seaman on leave' stayed in a Seamen's Mission run by a German pastor. He then returns to Santiago and links up with Wild once more. Here they meet their Tucuman friend Gross, who is there with his wife on a business trip. He proposes to take them in his car northwards to Arica whence they can attempt to pass into Peru. Off they go through the arid wastes of that part of Chile, passing Antofagasta, Iquique, etc. sometimes the road runs along the coast and they can see a ship on the horizon, which later on arrival at Callao they learn is the Japanese RAKUJO MARU, in which in due course they were to embark.

But first they had to be smuggled into Peru and it is, in fact, through smugglers that this is arranged as there is a lively trade of tobacco and cinnamon across the frontier. The sum demanded was Peruvian $800 (half to be paid beforehand and the other half on safe arrival). The smuggler band of five duly turn up with one horse and some mules, already heavily laden with merchandise, so that the journey is uncomfortable in the extreme. The smugglers all look like villains in a melodrama; the leader turns out to be Italian-born. The journey lasts over 24 hours during which they had nothing to eat or drink as they had brought nothing with them, having been told it was a matter of some 8 hours, and during rests by the wayside they have to watch the smugglers eating and drinking heartily., and offering them nothing! They dod not take them to the appointed place where they were to meet Gross, but dumped them off near Tacna demanding the rest of the money. Through the help of an old Indian woman they manage to get a car and eventually turn up at the milestone, which was the rendezvous, and find Gross and his wife anxiously awaiting them.

They go to Lima in his car and arrive on March 13 1941. Here they learn that the above-mentioned Japanese steamer is the RAKUJO MARU and is sailing for Yokohama in four days time. A German who is employed in a shipping agency puts them up. Their identities are changed once more and they become Arturo Serrano Vergara and Enrique Gallardo, Chilean business men. The book says that how they obtained all the necessary documents, etc. must remain a secret. They replenish their wardrobes with clothing suitable for their part. They travel second-class and share a cabin with two Germans, a pastor and an engineer. The familiar sounds on board as the ship prepares to sail are joy to their ears and at last *'Wir sind wirder auf See'* ('We are at sea once more').

They thoroughly enjoy their life on board, travelling as passengers for the first time, and showing suitable interest as laymen when shown over the engine-room! The voyage lasts 38 days. Between Colombia and Panama Fieber falls ill with malaria and they take a German-Hungarian nurse into their confidence., Sister Carola, who had been for five years head of a hospital for tropical diseases in Guatemala. Fieber begins to improve, but as ill luck would have it, he has a relapse just when they reach San Diego, California, where there is a stringent medical inspection and anyone showing the slightest symptoms of malaria has to be taken ashore to a hospital. By a superhuman effort he manages to pass the inspection and walk out of the first-class dining room where it takes place with a firm step. Sister Carola has put a touch of rouge on his pallid cheeks! Once outside he collapses and she and Wild support him to his cabin where he loses consciousness. However he recovers his health and is able to land at Yokohama. The only other person thay had taken into their confidence was the Captain. Though they had no common language, he showed them every kindness and sympathy, being a great admirer of Germany. Indeed, during their stay in Japan he invited them to a dinner in Tokyo at which his wife and daughter were present.

They had reached Yokohama on April 24 and in the bustle on board they suddenly hear someone calling "Hullo, Serrano! Hullo, Gallardo!" He turns out to be a Dr Janson, a young German who has come to meet them in representation of the German authorities, who had had a cypher from Lima announcing their presence on board. They stay ina suburb of Yokohama for the next two weeks and Dr Janson takes them to Tokyo to call on the

German Naval Attaché, Admiral Wennecker, who receives them with open arms and hears the tale of their adventures. In the course of the conversation they learn that whilst they were in the GRAF SPEE in the South Atlantic he was in the DEUTSCHLAND in the North Atlantic. He promises them every help, including furnishing them with funds.

They took train to Fusan and then spent a day and two nights in Harbin [northeast Chinese port]. Sister Carola travelled with them and there were several other passengers from the RAKUJO MARU making for Germany. They travelled via Seoul, Mukden and Harbin to Moscow. There was an exhaustive search of luggage at the first town on Russian soil, Otpor, and a thorough interrogation and examination of papers. The questions were mainly in English which sister Carola interpreted for them (as they apparently did not know English), but from time to time questions were put in German to try to catch out these two Chilean business men. In due course they come to a station with a name in German letters, but not a very German one, viz, Malkinia. They make themselves known to the authorities, are told that neither their documentation nor their luggage will be further inspected and are given food coupons for two days.

At long last the moment when the train draws into the famous station 'Berlin-Friedrichstrasse'. They were now at the end of their journey which had lasted nearly 14 months. They step out of the train, deeply moved. The book ends with the words: "Ich bin daheim!" which can be translated "Home at last!".

Comment. Substantially the same story of the escape was written by Hein Wild and was published in instalments in the German illustrated weekly magazine *Bune* (circulation 1.240,000) in March, April and May 1963 under the title "Die Spee war mein Schicksal" ("The Spee was my Fate!). Wild in his account mentions Fieber's book. Wild, who was then 22 years of age, is today chief engineer of the Hamburg America Line (HAPAG).

One episode early on in Wild's story is amusing, in which he tells of staying in the flat of a wealthy pro-German lady in Buenos Aires, and that she gave a cocktail party to which came an important police official of her acquaintance, resident in the same building. He told of the escape of various GRAF SPEE internees, mentioning Wild and Fieber by name! (Ibid, pp.473-9)

Benemann commented that this escape included Hans Fuchs, Wattenberg, Rasenack and Klepp. 'Most of them went immediately back on duty, some on submarines. Most were separate escapes then with separate routes. ... I have the minute details that have never been published, including for example Rasenack's handwritten 200 page dairy of his escape via Air to Chile, on to Panama, San Pedro California, Yokohama, over Korea, China and Manchuria to the head of the Trans-Siberian Railroad over Moscow back to Berlin. Incredible! but not unique. Rasenack gave me his dairy in Cordoba Argentina about 20 years ago, shortly before he died there. He became then the artillery officer of the Tirpitz.' (Email communication with Carlos Benemann, 6 November 2021)

Commander Gunter Schiebush who escaped from Martin Garcia island (Millington-Drake, op.cit.)

Commander Günter Schiebush provided Millington-Drake with details of his escape from Martin Garcia.

> The launch was too small for seventeen of us and there was only a freeboard of perhaps 6-8 inches [15.24 – 20.32 cms] which gave us some anxiety in rough water. At the Tigre we all scattered and from there I reached Buenos Aires by the suburban electric railway and was hidden by a German family in another suburb till I got papers as a Lettish subject, Geraldo Schwarz, and so got by river steamer to Asuncion, Paraguay. Here I was hidden by a German resident, Herr Heckhausen, until I could get other false papers as a Paraguayan-born German (there were many) under the name of Federico Gunter, which would enable me to get the necessary Brazilian visa to fly to Sao Paulo.
> The day before the plane left, my German host took me to visit the Brazilian Consul. The Consul, who had been scrutinising me from time to time, finally gave me the required visa. However, the next day, an hour after my plane for Sao Paulo had taken off, he telephoned Herr Heckhausen and said that it was only to ask whether 'that GRAF SPEE officer' had got off safely! (Millington-Drake, op.cit. p.390)

Lieutenant Gerhard Ulpts escaped in 1940 (Millington-Drake, op.cit.)

Lieutenant Bruno Herzberg escaped in 1940 (Millington-Drake, op.cit.)

Millington-Drake included details of another escape found in Vice-Admiral Bernhard Rogge's *Under Ten Flags* based on information provided by Captain Bildingmaier and Captain Ulpts.

> The five "Prize Officers" (of the Merchant Marine Reserve) had been ordered to remain in Uruguay and were interned and allowed to live pleasantly for about two months in an *estancia* in the centre of Uruguay belonging to an Austrian (His name was Magerl and the estancia was called "La Estiria" and was near Trinidad, Department of Flores). In due course they were discharged (entlassen) from the German Navy and then, one more as marine merchant officers, were released from internment and in March [1940] were able to get away from Uruguay to Brazilian ports, Schünemann to Bahia where he joined a German ship which later got through to Germany, and Sörensen to Porto Alegre (where he eventually returned to Uruguay). Incidentally at the *estancia* he had married the owner's daughter.

But it is the subsequent services of Dittmann, Upts and Herzberg which are of special interest and should be told here. In March, the first two got away to the relatively near Brazilian port of Santos to join two German ships which had remained there for safety, namely the DRESDEN and the BABITONGA, Dittman joining the DRESDEN and Ulpts the BABITONGA. Another officer of the GRAF SPEE, Lieutenant Herbert Frölich (who had done such brilliant work as Wireless Chief Perry Officer notably in monitoring and decoding British wireless messages that Captain Langsdorff promoted him), Senior Wireless Operator, also joined the DRESDEN, having escaped from Argentina via Bolivia.

The DRESDEN of 5,567 tons was an auxiliary of the German Navy taken over from the Norddeutscher Lloyd, having been built in 1937. She was the same ship that was mentioned in Captain Bidlingmaier's book as having sailed from Coquimbo (northern Chile) in October with the much -needed supply of carbonic acid for the GRAF SPEE, but she failed to reach her and took refuse in Santos.

The BABITONGA of 4,422 tons was a much older ship built in 1922 for the Hamburg South America Line,

The DRESDEN was the first to leave Santos and did so in early April 1941, and in the South Atlantic she refuelled the famous merchant cruiser ATLANTIS which by Q-ship methods had become a most successful commerce raider under command of Captain (later Admiral) Bernhard Rogge. The ATLANTIS had been built by the Bremen Hansa Line as the freighter GOLDENFELS of 7,860 tons and had a speed of 17½ knots. Her elaborate conversion and fitting out, begun soon after the outbreak of war, took nearly four months.

Hers was to be an astonishing record.: Admiral Rogge and his crew were 655 days at sea (March 31 1940 to Christmas Day 1941) and sank 23 ships totalling 144,500 tons; they covered 110,000 miles – and the last thousand in lifeboats towed by German and Italian U-boats. The ATLANTIS herself had been sunk on November 22 by the cruiser DEVONSHIRE.

This story of amazing achievement was published in German under the title *Schiff 16* (as she was described by the German High Command, then in English with the title *Under ten Flags* (Weldenfeld and Nicholson, 1956) and was subsequently made into a film.

Part of this great adventure of the ATLANTIS was shared by Dittmann and Frölich, for they both chose to transfer to her instead of returning to occupied France in the DRESDEN with some two hundred passengers, including many American men and women from the Egyptian ship ZAMZAM, a former Bibby liner, which had just been sunk by the ATLANTIS, not knowing she was technically a neutral. This dramatic incident furnish abundant matter for the film.

Less sensational was the story of the BABATONGA which in early May, with Ulpts in her, also set out from Santos and, disguised as the Dutch S.S. JASPARA, likewise met the ATLANTIS in the South Atlantic and later took from her some ninety British prisoners from two British merchantmen, RABAUL and TRAFALGAR., sunk after the ZAMZAM. Ulpts, an experienced prize officer, was put in charge of them with the help of a small "prize crew" from the raider. In June, near the Equator, he and his men and prisoners were transferred to the German auxiliary supply ship ALSTERTOR. Shortly before the BABITONGA herself was scuttled on meeting H.M.S. LONDON on June 21.

The reason for the transfer had been that in the ALSTERTOR there was a much better chance of reaching a French port safely because she was a new and unusually fast "banana boat" of 3,500 tons and 18 knots which had been built in 1938 for the fruit trade from the West Indies. However, off the coast of Portugal, on June 23, 1941, she was held up by the MARSDALE and four other British destroyers. She then, according to Ulpts, scuttled herself, he getting the crew and the British prisoners into two separate lots of boats, a proceeding of which his captors showed appreciation, all being taken to Gibraltar. Thus Ulpts himself became a prisoner and was subsequently in P.O.W. camps in England and Canada. Ulpts states that he remembers that, for him, fateful day of June 23 well, as it was the day war broke out between Germany and Russia – and also his birthday!

To complete the record of GRAF SPEE officers who got away from internment it should be told that this was done the 'hard way' by Lieutenant Herzberg, the senior "Prize Officer" in the GRAF SPEE, in that he first got back to Germany across the Pacific. The extraordinary difficulties throughout such a journey have been sufficiently indicated in the accounts of Commander Rasenack and of petty officers Fieber and Wild. It need only be mentioned that Herzberg began it in an unusual way, viz. by going to Rio de Janeiro and then across to Chile and Peru, where, like Fieber, he boarded a Japanese freighter bound for Yokohama.

He arrived back in Berlin on August 10 1940, and went on the next day to Hamburg, where after a few days rest he reported for duty. [...]

Meanwhile Herzberg was put in charge of some specialised courses of training and was then appointed to command a fast reconnaissance motor boat (Vorpostenboot) and was confirmed in his hitherto temporary rank as First-Lieutenant... Then he was appointed to the KOMET for her second and ill-fated voyage under a new commander, Captain Brocksien, which started from Le Havre [northwest France] on October 13 but ended in disaster the next morning when at 2. A.m. she was torpedoes by the British motor torpedo boat, M.T.B. 236, commanded by Sub-Lieutenant R.Q. Drayson, This occurred off Cap de la Hague, the northwesternmost point of the Cherbourg peninsular. As the topedo caused the explosion of some of the many mines on board, the whole crew of 351 men was lost. Suring this daring and successful attack by the motor torpedo boat stopped at the outset what would have been another long and probably very successful cruise.

So Herzberg who was, according to Captain Wattenberg, a first-class seaman and "the best of fellows" – in short one of the most likeable officers in the GRAF SPEE, met his end after further valuable service to the Third Reich, which, like those of Dittmann, Frölich and Ulpts, afforded further evidence of the rightness of Langsdorff's decision after he had entered the fatal "trap of Montevideo" to save his crew by scuttling his ship. (Millington-Drake, op.cit. p.479-80)

Also on 9 April 1940, McCall sent the following telegram to DNI and the S.O.(I), Montevideo, to update R.A.S.A.D. (Rear Admiral South American Division), the America and West Indies Squadron and the Naval Attachés in Uruguay and Brazil. Given its importance, copies were also sent to the First Sea Lord, CSO of 1st Sea Lord, DCNS, ACNS, Ops, D. of P. (Directorate of Plans), DNI, O.D., M., and File 'X'.

My telegram 1120 April 8th entirely confirmed independent source. Morning press unanimously attacked GRAF internees for breaking parole given on getting leave and for abusing hospitality. Evidence from three sources report free fight took place in barracks Sunday and Monday between Nazi and Anti Nazi sailors latter blaming former for decree interning them Martin Garcia Island. Police announce that eleven officers and three sailors have failed to return from week end leave. (TNA ADM 116/4180, 9 April 1940)

On 10 April, Eden telegrammed Ovey.

Your telegrams Nos. 154, 159 and 162 [of the 2st, 5th and 8th April: internment of "Graf Spee" personnel] and Havana telegram No. 54.

In light of recent developments recorded in your telegrams under reference we consider that we can safely leave it to the initiative of the Argentine Government to compromise on their earlier attitude. You are therefore authorised, if you see no objection, to inform the Minister for Foreign Affairs semi-officially that, whilst fully reserving their attitude, His Majesty's Government do not propose to prolong the controversy by returning a reply to the Argentine Government's note of the 20th March, and that, since its receipt, they have been gratified to learn that more effective measures of supervision are being adopted. We propose to speak in the same sense to the Argentine Ambassador.

We see no necessity to refer to the presence of "Graf Spee" officers in Cuba especially as reports concerning them are so indefinite. Generally speaking it seems preferable to us unless you hold different views, to let the facts, or rather rumours, speak for themselves. (TNA HS 116/5474, 10 April 1940)

Ovey's response, telegram 166 of 9 April, stated,

Havana telegram No. 54.
Please inform when and if you would wish me to report to Argentine Government any definite facts regarding presence of Graf Spee officers in Cuba.

At present I am leaving the matter entirely alone as Germans seem playing entirely into our hands.

Repeated to Havana telegram No. 1 and by air mail Saving to Washington telegram No. 4 and Montevideo No. 9. (Ibid.)

Also on 10 April, the *Dundee Evening Telegraph* reported on the internment.

INTERNMENT ISLAND FOR GRAF SPEE OFFICERS Buenos Aires. Officers of the scuttled Nazi battleship Admiral Graf Spee, who are now on board the Argentine transport vessel Pampa, are to be interned this week on the island of Martin Garcia, in the River Plate. The Argentine police have announced that the 11 officers who escaped during the week end have been identified, and their arrest expected shortly. (*Dundee Evening Telegraph,* 10 April 1940)

A couple of days later, Eden telegrammed Millington-Drake.

Your telegram No. 25 (Saving), [of 27th March: internment of Graf Spee personnel in Uruguay].

Neither Uruguayan decree nor attitude of Uruguayan Minister for Foreign Affairs towards confinement of personnel give any reason to alter views expressed in my telegram No.49. in order to strengthen your hand, you may consider it advisable to refer to recent unfortunate escapes in Argentine resulting in decision of Argentine Government to adopt stronger measures and to impress the hope that the Uruguayan Government will in the circumstances revise their decision not to place these persons in confinement. As latest information from Havana is still somewhat indefinite it would appear undesirable to refer to alleged presence there of Graf Spee officers from Montevideo. (See Havana telegrams 29, 30 and 34). (Ibid.)

On 16 April, Ovey sent telegram 121 to Eden.

My Lord,
I took the opportunity of my conversation today with the Minister for Foreign Affairs to tell him of your decision – as set forth in your telegram No. 108 of the 10th instant - to let matters drop as regards the inter-Governmental correspondence on the subject of the internees from the "Admiral Graf Spee". I pointed out that the question appeared to be solving itself. His Excellency told me with pride that the two sailors who had reached Rio de Janeiro on the "Neptunia" were being duly returned.

2. We did not pursue the subject further and I acquired the impression that His Excellency was relieved, and perhaps even surprised, as the absence of further insistence on our part.

3. The mentality of Latin Americans, reputedly and correctly, I think, tinged with formal sensitiveness, is not always easy to gauge. His Excellency went on, for instance, to say – in a friendly and desultory conversation ranging over recent events – that we had committed a grave error in "giving way" to Italy over the coal ships. I said I thought it was a reasonable compromise and that weakness with them (not with the Argentine) was a mistake. We had, he opined, left them with the sting of our refusal to let the ships sail and an impression of our weakness in finally permitting them to do so.

I have the honour to be, with the highest respect… (Ibid, 16 April 1940)

On the same day, 16 April, a question was raised in the British House of Lords regarding the Graf Spee. Hansard, the official publication of parliamentary proceedings, documented the discussion.

5.55 p.m.
LORD NEWTON had the following notice on the Paper: To ask His Majesty's Government why the facts relating to the mutiny on the "Graf Spee," which occurred on 16th December, 1939, were not officially reported in this country until 27th March, 1940; and to move for Papers.

The noble Lord said: My Lords, this is a somewhat belated question, but I do not think it is quite so belated as the action, or rather inaction, of the two Departments concerned. Everybody here is well acquainted with the circumstances in connection with the "Graf Spec," but I must relate as shortly as I can what actually occurred. It will be remembered that in the middle of December the "Graf Spee" entered the harbour of Montevideo and at once proceeded to have repairs done, as quickly as possible took in large stores and provisions, and conveyed the impression that she was going to make a dash for liberty and engage the British cruisers outside. Well, as time went on it was evident that difficulties had arisen, and there were reports in the Press here and elsewhere of what I might call a serious division of opinion on board the ship. The upshot, as everybody knows, was that the "Graf Spec," instead of coming out and fighting, retired and ignominiously scuttled herself, and her captain, an honourable and gallant sailor who had won the respect of his opponents, was reported to have committed suicide, though I should think it quite within the bounds of probability that he was liquidated by one of the numerous Gestapo agents, of whom there are plenty to execute this kind of work.

My complaint against the Admiralty is this. Imagine, it you can, the reverse case. Imagine the case of a British ship which proceeded to a port which was blockaded by light cruisers—a very powerful ship. Remember, the "Graf Spee" was not vitally damaged and there was every reason to suppose that it would make an attempt to escape, more especially as the British cruisers waiting outside had been seriously damaged in the battle. Instead of that, as I have just said, it ignominiously disposed of itself and the captain committed suicide. Supposing that had occurred to a British ship, what would the Germans have done? In five minutes of the news reaching them, it would have penetrated the remotest corners of the world that the British had declined to go out and fight. It would have been an irretrievable blow to our prestige for the time being, and we should have earned the contempt of our Ally.

Well, now, what was our procedure? Instead of doing anything of the kind, the attitude of the Admiralty was to ignore all that was passing at Montevideo and to say practically nothing about it. One almost got the suspicion that they were afraid of injuring the feelings of the Nazi Government. This attitude was maintained for a long time, but three months afterwards—to be correct, on March 27—an official statement was brought out by the Admiralty announcing that they had been convinced that these allegations of mutiny and so forth were true, and that they had authoritative reason for making this statement. What I want to know is, why was not this statement made at the time? I suppose I shall be told it was necessary to verify the evidence. Well, that does not convince me in the least. It surely could not have taken three months to get evidence with regard to what actually happened. Montevideo is not an inaccessible place. Why, you could have gone and made two voyages there and back within the three months, and I would like to remind the House that there was every facility for obtaining the information. The place was probably full of correspondents, the Admiralty must have had agents there all the time, and we had a Legation and a Consulate in full working order. Now it is inconceivable to me, and absolutely incredible, that these people did not know everything that occurred within a very short time, and the information must have reached London, but was made no use of.

I am not a convinced believer in the virtues of propaganda. I rather disbelieve in its effects. There is a sort of superstition in the world at the present time that everything can be done by propaganda and that we can win the war by it. No one can cite a war which has been won by propaganda, and no war is ever likely to be won by propaganda, but somehow or other this idea has obtained firm root. The amazing statement that a war can be won or lost by propaganda was made by the Germans themselves. In 1918 Germany was deserted by her allies. The civilian population was demoralised, not by propaganda, but by the British blockade. There was a mutiny in the German Fleet, and the Army had been beaten and was out of control. Then the Germans, in order to conceal the truth, started the idea that they had been ruined by alien propaganda which had demoralised the civilian population. There was never greater rubbish talked in this world, yet that is the principle upon which the Nazi Government has existed and flourished for a long time.

I am not, as I have said, an implicit believer in the virtues of propaganda, and I do not think it is capable of performing much that is expected of it; but there are certain occasions, if you choose to make use of them, which are invaluable for destroying the confidence of your opponent. Here was a case in point. If the Admiralty had the insight to realise the effect, as I said at the beginning, we should have informed the whole world that the Germans had been afraid to fight. It really does not matter whether there was a mutiny or not. The crucial fact was that the Germans were afraid to fight, and we were apparently afraid to say so. I can only say I regard this as a most unfortunate example of inaction and want of insight. It is for that reason that I have brought the matter forward this afternoon, although I admit it is rather late in the day, and in any case the incident loses a certain amount of importance in view of the much more important events which are taking place. I beg to move for Papers.

6.3 p.m.

THE EARL OF LIVERPOOL

My Lords, I rise for one moment to support the principle the noble Lord has raised. It is not the first time that he and I have been associated on measures in your Lordships' House. The whole question of withholding news has been going on for some time. Although I understand that the noble and learned Viscount on the Woolsack is going to answer, I do not expect him to give a definite reply to what I have to say, but I hope he will take note of it. We lost a destroyer about six weeks ago—H.M.S. "Exmouth." [It was sunk by a German submarine off the coast of Scotland in January 1940.] The news came from the Admiralty at seven o'clock and also at eight o'clock in the morning, but it was not repeated again throughout the day. We heard no more about it. Unfortunately at that time the newspapers were handicapped, because trains were not running. It was the worst time of the winter, and a great many of the relatives heard nothing for sixty hours. I admit that parents did, by telegram. Since that day we have not heard anything about this destroyer.

In my work in my own county I have come into contact with a number of people who have lost sons and who would be grateful for some knowledge as regards the loss of this ship. After a certain time, as I did not wish to bother the First Lord of the Admiralty – [When Churchill was appointed British Prime Minister, his role as First Lord of the Admiralty was taken over by Albert Alexander] he has too much on his shoulders as it is—I wrote to the Admiralty, and the Private Secretary told me it was the fault of the B.B.C. I wrote to them, and they said the Admiralty had told them that this information was withheld so as not to discourage the public. All I can say is that we are quite capable of bearing the bad with the good. It is a very unfortunate thing for relatives of men who have been lost if bad news is to be withheld.

I would ask if anything can now be done to tell us something about what happened to this ship.

6.6 p.m.

THE LORD CHANCELLOR (VISCOUNT CALDECOTE)

My Lords, the question which has been raised by my noble friend Lord Newton obviously concerns the Admiralty primarily, and if circumstances were not what they are to-day my noble friend Lord Hankey would be replying. The question is as to the report which, I understand from my noble friend Lord Newton, was published on March 27, and he contrasts the lateness of that date with the date on which the mutiny occurred on the "Graf Spee"—namely, December 16, 1939. There has been no withholding of any information or intelligence in this connection, as will appear to your Lordships when I have stated the very simple facts. Nobody except the German authorities or persons on board the "Graf Spee" can give an authoritative account or explanation of the scuttling of the "Graf Spee," but it so happens that a resident in the town of Montevideo at the time of the scuttling observed from the shore certain incidents, from which he drew certain deductions, and set out the result of his observations and deductions in a letter addressed to a friend in England. His friend quite rightly thought that this narrative was of some special interest, and he thereupon conveyed it to the Admiralty, which, agreeing that it might be, and probably was, of peculiar interest, thereupon published it immediately the document was received. It was in no sense an official document, but a narrative of events as observed by a resident in the town. I hope that will dispose of my noble friend's fear that the Admiralty, having received or collected information, withheld it from the public until something or other occurred to make them release the information.

With regard to the question raised by the noble Earl, Lord Liverpool, I am not, as he expected, seized of the information which he would like now to be released to the public with reference to the loss of His Majesty's ship "Exmouth," but I am speaking within your Lordships' knowledge when I say it is not possible to complain of any withholding of information as to the loss of ships in connection with the naval events which have recently taken place. The First Lord has given the public, so far as I am informed, all the information which is necessary to prevent the public from being deceived as to the price that has had to be paid for the very great achievements of His Majesty's Navy. I hope my noble friend Lord Newton will be satisfied with this plain narrative which I have given of the circumstances in which this report was received and published.

6.9 p.m.

LORD NEWTON

My Lords, the noble and learned Viscount said nothing about whether he proposes to produce Papers. I presume I shall be told that there are none. I cannot help pointing out that the statement of the noble and learned Viscount seems to make the action of the Admiralty worse than I thought. What seems to have occurred is that for a long time they refused to do anything at all, then they published an official statement corroborating various reports which had come from Montevideo, and now they say they were misinformed. I am afraid the position of the Admiralty is rather worse than it was before. Can the noble and learned Viscount say whether there are any Papers that can be published?

THE LORD CHANCELLOR

My Lords, I am unaware of the existence of any Papers except the copy of the original document which was published by the Admiralty, as my noble friend says, on March 27. I am afraid I do not understand my noble friend's point that my statement has made the Admiralty's position worse. The information, as I said, was that of an observer. The only other information that could be obtained would be that of the persons on the ship before she was scuttled, and that, obviously, His Majesty's Government are not in a position to obtain.

LORD NEWTON

My Lords, I ask leave to withdraw the Motion.
(https://api.parliament.uk/historic-hansard/lords/1940/apr/16/the-graf-spee)

The Queensland newspaper, *The Worker,* reported in late April about the German internees.

> "Graf Spee" Internees. It is reported that all the officers and half the crew of the German pocket battleship, "Graf Spee," who are interned at Buenos Aires, will in future be confined to a naval prison and treated as prisoners instead of internees. - It is said that this drastic action is the result of the Government's irritation because three of the officers and two sailors recently escaped and the other officers have persistently refused to pledge their honour not to escape. One escapee is reported to have reached Germany with documents from the scuttled warship, and it has been revealed that numerous attempts have been made to escape by members of the crew who are interned in the interior. The Government of the Argentine has issued a statement explaining its action in regard to
> the crew of the "Graf Spee." "Argentina has been excessively generous to these officers," it declared. 'We cannot allow our

neutrality to be jeopardised, therefore we are ensuring that they will be unable to return to Germany to resume belligerent action."
It is now generally recognised that, while rancor and hate might have a prominent place in war, they are absolutely useless to the people of the world in regard to questions of economic reconstruction.
An idle factory is the last word in futility, and a system which from time to time renders factories idle is the last word in a futile system. — Bertram Benedict, England. (*The Worker*, Brisbane, Tuesday 23 April 1940, p.23)

On the same day, 23 April, the following document was included in the mail sent to the Foreign Office in London, the Argentine Government's modification of their decree on the Graf Spee sailors.

Enclosure in Buenos Aires despatch No. 127 dated April 23rd 1940.
DECREE No. 58,556 OF THE 16TH MARCH

With a view to the fulfilment of the Decree of December 19th, 1939, ordering the internment of the commanders, officers and crew of the German battleship "Admiral Graf Spee", -

The President of the Argentine Nation decrees:-

Article 1. The territory of the federal Capital, and that comprised within a radius of 50 kilometres from its boundaries, is fixed as the zone of internment for the commanders (jefes) and officers of the German battleship "Graf Spee".

Article II. Within 45 days from this date the above-mentioned commanders and officers must present themselves at the Central Police Department of the Capital for the purposes indicated by Articles I and III of the Decree of December 19th, 1939. After the completion of the formalities to be determined by the police authorities, the commanders and officers will leave their lodgings in the dependencies of the Ministry of Marine.

Article III. The Ministry of the Interior will determine in every case the zone of internment for the various groups or contingents which may be found from the crew of the battleship "Admiral Graf Spee" in whatever part of the country it may deem convenient.

Article IV. The police in the Capital shall adopt such measures as may be necessary for the transference of the crew to the zone of internment and for their lodging in the latter.

Article V. It is hereby declared that those members of the crew who formed part of the sick-bay staff of the battleship "Graf Spee" shall be exempted from the terms of the Internment Decree of the 19th December, 1939.

The police of the Capital will take the necessary measures for exempting them from the internment regulations.

Article VI. The following rates of pay, which will be issued in advance and for the account of the German Government are hereby fixed: -

Commanders	$350 per month
Lieutenants	300 per month
Midshipmen	250 per month
Petty Officers	4 per day
Sailors	3 per day

Article VII. This pay will be issued to the Commanders and officers by the police of the Capital, subject to the verification of the fulfilment by them of the Decree of the 19th December, 1939, and of such regulations as may be drawn up by the police authorities to put the Decree into effect.

Article VIII. The Directorate General of Administration of the Interior will delegate to the police official appointed for this purpose the duty of issuing to the contingents of the crew the pay due to them up to the 31st of the present month.

Article IX. As from the 1st April the pay of the crew will be issued directly by the various offices of the Department of Posts and Telegraphs, to which the crew will present their identity papers on the appointed date and hour.

Payments will be made in the presence of an officer of the local police appointed by the various competent authorities who will fill up special forms forwarded by the police of the Capital and will stamp the identity documents. The form will be transmitted in due course to the police of the Federal Capital.

Article X. Such expenses as are incurred by the application of the measures provided for by the present Decree shall be charged to the funds o the special account "Ministry of the Interior – Internment of the Officers and Crew of the "Admiral Graf Spee".

Article XI. All arrangements in contradiction to the present Decree are hereby revoked. The Decree will be counter-signed by the Ministers of State in the Departments of the Interior, Foreign Affairs and Public Worship and Marine.

Article XII. To be communicated, published, etc.

Enclosure in Buenos Aires despatch No. 127 dated April 27th 1940.

DECREE No. 59.459 of the 8th April.

In order to give effect to the Decree Nos. 50,826 of the 19th March, 1939, and 58,556 of the 16th March last, regarding the internment of commanders and officers of the German battleship

"Admiral Graf Spee", in accordance with the duties which are incumbent upon this country as a neutral, and in view of the fact that the commanders and officers have refused to fulfil the requirements set out in Article I of the Decree No. 50,826 and Article II of Decree No. 58,556 –

The President of the Argentine Nation decrees: -

Article I. The island of Martin Garcia is fixed as the zone of internment of the commanders and officers of the German battleship "Admiral Graf Spee".

Article II. The Ministry of Marine will adopt the necessary measures for the transport and lodgment of the commanders and officers in the zone of internment.

Article III. All arrangements in contradiction to the present Decree are hereby revoked; the Decree will be counter-signed by the Ministers of State in the Departments of the Interior, Foreign Affairs and Public Worship and Marine.

Article IV. To be communicated, published, etc. (TNA ADM 116/5474, 23 April 1940)

Whether the Germans in Cuba managed to get back to Germany or were returned to Argentina was not documented in the Graf Spee file. The fourteen who did not return from weekend leave were thought to have escaped.

One of the officials at the Chancery in the British Embassy in Washington wrote to the American Department of Foreign Office on 10 May.

Dear Department,

Buenos Aires telegram No, 166 of April 9th and previous correspondence about the escape of members of the "Graf Spee's" crew.

It may interest you to know that we have received an anonymous letter purporting to be written by a member of the crew of the "Graf Spee". The writer boasts that he has been in Canada since his escape as well as in this country. We are trying to trace the writer but have not much hope of succeeding. (Ibid, 10 May 1940)

The Foreign Office sent telegram 481 to Sir Robert Craigie who had been Britain's Ambassador in Japan since 1937. A copy was also sent to San Francisco.

1. Following are names and ranks of officers of Graf Spee who have escaped from internment: -

Commanders;	PAUL ASCHER
	KARL KLEPP
	JUGEN WATTENBURG
Lieutenant Commanders	FRIEDRICH WILHELM RASENSACH
	DETLEF SPIERING
Lieutenants	DIETRICH BLUDAU
	HANS DIETRICH
	ERICH HABELT
	HEINZ KUMMER
	DIETRICH MUMM
	HERMANN KOTTMANN
	GEORGE TATSCH
	WOLFGANG RICHEBERG
	HANS-JOACHIM

SCHEEBKE

2. I realise that these officers may travel under assumed names but it may nevertheless be possible to recognise them and prevent them from travelling on Japanese ships. (Ibid, 28 May 1940)

On 24 June, *The Scotsman* reported on one of the escapes.

GRAF SPEE MEN AS "MERCHANTS"
Travelling on Japanese Liner
[FROM OUR OWN CORRESPONDENT] New York, Sunday. — According to passengers on board the Japanese liner, Rakuyo Maru (9,419 tons, which arrived at Honolulu yesterday, the ship is carrying 17 members of the crew of the Graf Spee. After escaping from Argentina they embarked-at Peruvian and Chilean ports and are stated to be travelling as "merchants". (*The Scotsman*, 24 June 1940)

When Churchill became British Prime Minister in May, he appointed Eden his Foreign Secretary, a position he held for the rest of the war. Over a month passed before the next development in the Graf Spee story. At the beginning of August, the *Dundee Evening Telegraph* published the following article.

GRAF SPEE OFFICER ARRESTED
Buenos Aires, Friday. A former officer of the scuttled German battleship Graf Spee, whose name is given as Gottloff, has been arrested by the police. He had escaped from his place of internment, and was hiding in the Chaco [Argentine province north of Cordoba]. In his possession were found military maps

and photographs of Argentine oilfields. (*Dundee Evening Telegraph,* 2 August 1940)

The Indiana Gazette reported on 5 August,

INTERNED NAZIS ATTEMPT ESCAPE. Graf Spee Seamen Give Argentina Money and Social Troubles. BUENOS AIRES, Aug. 5. (AP) – The Nazi Seamen who last December scuttled the pocket battleship Admiral graf Spee outside Montevideo harbor and now are interned in Argentina are becoming a costly problem to their hosts.

Under international neutrality law the Argentine government must pay all unemployed seamen interned in this country their full naval salaries. Already this has cost upward of 500,000 pesos ($125,000), and so far Argentina had no word from Germany regarding re-imbursement.

Besides, the younger of the former Graf Spee crewmen are turning their guardians' hair gray with escapes and attempted escapes.

Four non-commissioned officers were found yesterday wandering near the heights of the Andes mountains apparently about o run away to Chile.

Originally the government planned to send only seamen in the interior and to keep the officers at Buenos Aires on their promise not to attempt escape.

But four months later, in April, wholesale efforts to escape caused the government to send the officers to Martin Garcia Island, in the River Plate 80 miles from Buenos Aires from where they are paroles for occasional visits to the capital.

The Graf Spee's crewmen were distributed among the cities of Mendoza, Cordoba, Rosario and Santa Fe.

Some 500, or about half those interned, have found employment with German firms in Argentina, thus easing the Argentine government's financial burden. But even they remain a problem because their whereabouts must be known at all times.

Occasionally – singly or in groups, in uniform or civilian clothes – the men of the Graf Spee may be seen at a cemetery in the heart of Buenos Aires, rending silent tribute before the grave of their commander, Hans Langsdorff. It was he who ordered the ship blown up outside Montevideo after its losing battle with three British cruisers and then after leading his men to Buenos Aires in tugboats, and launches and delivering them into internment, took his own life. (*The Indiana Gazette*, 5 August 1940)

On 6 August, *The Age* of Melbourne reported:

'GRAF SPEE SEAMEN TRY TO ESCAPE Australian. Associated Press. - BUENOS AIRES, August 5. Four German non-commissioned officers, formerly members of the crew of the "pocket" battleship Admiral Graf Spee, have been arrested at Rio Negro [Central Argentine province]. They were endeavouring to escape to Chile. (*The Age,* Melbourne, Tuesday 6 August 1940, p.7)

Two days later, the *Yorkshire Evening Post* reported on the same incident.

GRAF SPEE MEN ESCAPE
Buenos Ayres. Thursday. Thirty-five of the interned
German sailors from the Graf Spee. have escaped since they were distributed in the provinces last January, Argentine police investigation has revealed. Many of them have been caught near the Chilean and Bolivian frontiers. Thirteen Graf Spee men were detained last week at Bariloche, the Andes, while trying escape into Chile.—British United Press. (*Yorkshire Evening Post*, 8 August 1940)

On 16 August, the *Hampshire Telegraph* published the following article.

GRAF SPEE'S CREW Argentine Problem
BUENOS AYRES. Thursday. The Nazi seamen who last December scuttled the pocket battleship Graf Spee outside Montevideo Harbour, and are now interned in the Argentine, are becoming a costly problem to the Government. Under international neutrality law the Argentine Government must pay all unemployed seamen in this country full naval pay. Already this has cost 500,000 pesos (about £30,000) and so far the Argentine has had no word from Germany regarding reimbursement.
 The younger members of the former Graf Epee crew are turning their guardians' hair grey with escapes or attempted escapes.
 Thirteen men were captured yesterday after making an attempt to escape to Chile. They will be returned to internment. Four others who tried to run away were found wandering near the heights of the Andes mountains.
 Others are believed to have succeeded in crossing into Chile to escape their captivity which internment represents, while still

others have been found in Missions, the northern Argentine territory, where police seizure of an arms cache has been linked to a vague Nazi plot involving the Argentine's border with Brazil.

Some 500, or about half those interned, have found employment with German firms, thus easing the Government's financial burden, but even they remain a problem because they must report periodically.

Occasionally, singly or in groups, in uniform or civilian clothes, the men, of the Graf Spee may be seen at a cemetery in the heart of Buenos Ayres' rendering silent tribute before the grave of their commander, Captain Hans Langsdorff who obeyed Hitler's order to blow up the ship and then shot himself. (*Hampshire Telegraph*, 16 August 1940)

Engine room artificer Felix Eschner in Sierra de la Ventana
(Millington-Drake, op.cit.)

Millington-Drake used information provided by Commander Höpfner, Petty Officer Felix Eschner and other sources to produce the following description of Martin Garcia island.

The Argentine Government intended that the officers and petty officers of the GRAF SPEE with some ratings should be quartered at the naval station on the island of Martin Garcia, while the other ratings were to be distributed in the provinces in groups of about a hundred, one near Buenos Aires at Florencio Varela and others near the cities of Rosario, Santa Fe, Cordoba, Mendoza and San Juan, localities where many of them were to settle [...]. But [...] a group of thirteen officers escaped just before the transfer to the island in early April, and another group of seventeen later escaped from the island itself in August 1940.

There remained four officers with the Executive Officer of the GRAF SPEE, Captain Walter Kay, in command. These were to be joined later by Commander Robert Höpfner, who had had to undergo a severe operation for hernia followed by thrombosis and during his convalescence remained working in the office of the Naval Attaché in Buenos Aires, Captain Niebuhr, to whom he was of great assistance as the only officer of the GRAF SPEE who spoke Spanish fluently, and did much liaison work with the Argentine authorities and the internees of Martin Garcia. When transferred there he acted as Executive Officer to Captain Kay and they were in charge of twenty-five warrant officers, sixty petty officers and some twenty-five ratings. They remained on the island for four years, and during this time a carpenter among the crew, Feldwebel Brandt, with help from his fellows, made the decorated chest which was to contain Langsdorff's cap, dirk and decorations and which was presented to his widow when she was invited to visit Argentina in 1954.

The island is situated at the far northern end of the River Plate estuary and commands the mouths of the Rivers Parana and Uruguay, where they branch out respectively north-westwards and north-eastwards. It lies barely three miles from the Uruguayan shore and some five miles from the Argentine shore. The distance to the port of Buenos Aires as the crow flies is some thirty miles to the south, and so ten miles from the small delta of the River Tigre. In spite of the mud banks of the adjoining shores the island itself is formed of a mass of granite, almost circular, in the form of a flattened cone some hundred feet high, and it is about three miles in circumference, it is a naval establishment with a lighthouse and a wireless station. [...]

The name of the island is derived from the burial there in 1516 of one of the crew of the famous expedition of Juan Dias de Solis, which was the first [sic] to explore the country.

During this long internment at Martin Garcia each man was allowed a visit to Buenos Aires once a fortnight on parole, which was never broken. The men would proceed to Buenos Aires on the Friday by an old river gunboat which had been a German minesweeper in World War 1, named the KORMOZAN. On its return journey, on the Monday morning it left the north dock at 8 a.m. This vessel of course conveyed personnel, supplies etc. for the naval station. (Millington-Drake, op.cit. pp.485-6)

On 27 August, Hitler signed what was called the 'Axis Pacts' with the Italian and Japanese governments creating what the Germans termed 'a new world order' in Europe and Greater East Asia.

On 9 September, the *Birmingham Daily Gazette* reported another escape.

Fifteen Graf Spee men Escape
Buenos Aires, Sunday. Fifteen quarter-deck officers of the German battleship Graf Spee have escaped from Martin Garcia Island, where they were interned.
It is believed that to make their escape the interned officers had help from outside the island. – British United Press. (*Birmingham Daily Gazette,* 9 September 1940)

The Herald of Melbourne reported on 26 September:

GRAF SPEE ESCAPEES.
BUENOS AIRES, Wednesday. — A German source states that three of the 15 Graf Spee officers who escaped from internment in Uruguay recently have reached Germany. Four others are stated to be in Brazil awaiting a Spanish ship, from which they will transfer to a German flying boat at sea: Three more are on a ship on their way to Japan.— A.A.P.' (*The Herald,* Thursday 26 September 1940, p.3)

The *Maryborough Chronicle Wide Bay and Burnett Advertiser* in Queensland reported on 7 October that police in Valparaiso in Chile had 'arrested four members of the crew of the sunken German pocket battleship Graf Spee on a Japanese mail steamer. They had crossed the Andes and hidden in Valparaiso for several days.' (*Maryborough Chronicle Wide Bay and Burnett Advertiser,* Queensland, Monday 7 October 1940)

Three days later, the *Liverpool Daily Post* reported on the escape.

'GRAF SPEE PRISONERS – ESCAPES FROM INTERNMENT IN ARGENTINA. Argentina has already marked up a million pesos (about £60,000) bill against the Nazi Government for entertaining since last December the thousand or more hearty, hungry crew of the German raider Admiral Graf Spee. Despite such lavish hospitality, informed sources say that no less than 19 officers and 60 sailors have escaped from internment, apparently in attempts to reach the Fatherland. Attempted and successful escapes raising the need for more guards and costly searches, have added to the expense which Argentina, under the terms of international law, must bear until the end of the war. Argentina must provide pay as well as food for the sailors. Officers get pay equal to that of Argentine naval officers. The most sensational incident was the mass escape of a group of senior officers from the island of Martin Garcia, off the Uruguayan Coast. The number missing was reported to be from fifteen to nineteen.' (*Liverpool Daily Post*, Thursday 10 October 1940)

On 12 October the *Kalgoorlie Miner* of Western Australia added that 'The Chile Government has decided to hand over to Argentine the four members of the crew of the scuttled German pocket battleship who were arrested at Valparaiso recently while attempting to escape to Japan. The Government has also declared persona non grata [unwelcome] the German Consul at Valparaiso [Dr. Paul Barandon] who provided the men with false passports.' (*Kalgoorlie Miner*, 12 October 1940)

Further details were provided by Sir Charles Orde, the British Ambassador in Chile, who wrote to Halifax on 16 October.

No.196
My Lord,

I have the honour to transmit herewith a copy of a note which I handed to the Minister of Foreign Affairs on the 9th. instant regarding the attempted escape to Japan of four petty officers from the former German battleship "Admiral Graf von Spee", and in particular the action of the German Consul in Valparaiso in furnishing the men with passports containing false details. Particulars of these passports had been published in the local press by the Chilean police authorities, and I felt that, while it was evident that the Chilean authorities would not permit the men to sail for Japan, the opportunity should not be missed of striking a blow at German official machinations in this country.

2. Senor Mora [Senor con Marcial Mora Miranda was the Chilean Minister for Foreign Affairs] told me that he welcomed by note as it afforded him with further ground for action. He agreed with the view expressed in my note that the German Consul's action was most improper vis á vis [regarding] the Chilean Government and did not resent my intervention. He had, he said, as a matter of fact just told the German Ambassador that the Chilean Government would not view with pleasure the continuance of Dr. Barandon, the Consular Officer in question, in his functions. It had not been decided what to do with the men, but His Excellency hoped that they would be returned to the care of the Argentine Government.

3. I have now received an official note which passes over in silence the question of the conduct of the German Consul and merely encloses a copy of a long communication from the Ministry of Foreign Affairs to the Ministry of the Interior setting out the legal arguments in favour of returning the four men to the Argentine Government in accordance with that Government's request. The Chilean Government therefore avoid any acknowledgement of my right to intervene as between them and the German Government, but they have in fact taken action in the sense desired and have published the fact of their request that Dr. Barandon (who appears to be attached temporarily to the German Legation in Uruguay) should not resume his post in Valparaiso.

I have the honour to be with the highest respect, My Lord, Your Lordship's most obedient humble servant.

Enclosure in Santiago despatch No.196 of October 16th 1940.
COPY
BRITISH EMBASSY.
SANTIAGO.
October 9th 1940.

No. 192.
Your Excellency,

I have the honour to inform Your Excellency that His Majesty's Government have been seriously concerned at the escape from internment in Argentina of members of the crew of the German battleship "Admiral Graf von Spee". As Your Excellency will be aware, a case has just arisen in which four German seamen, of petty officer rank, formerly members of that crew, having escaped from internment, entered Chile and attempted to take ship for Japan, with the obvious purpose of eventually rejoining the German armed forces. The attempt was frustrated by the vigilance of the Chilean Authorities. If it had succeeded the Chilean Authorities would have been in the position of having rendered unneutral service to a belligerent Power by permitting the escape of members of that Power's armed forces who should under international law be detained.

2. A serious feature of the case, to which I have the honour to draw Your Excellency's special attention, is that, as would appear, an attempt was made by a German Consular Officer in this country to deceive the Chilean Authorities and to involve them in an unneutral act by furnishing them with passports containing false particulars. This action is one primarily of concern to the Chilean Government themselves. But it is also a

matter of great concern to His Majesty's Government that members of the crew of the "Admiral Graf von Spee" should not be enabled, contrary to international law, to rejoin the German armed forces. I feel therefore entitled to express the earnest hope, on the part of my Government, that the Chilean Government will take drastic action to prevent any similar attempt in the future to frustrate their efforts to preserve Chilean neutrality. The matter is one of particular importance since, according to my information, other members of the crew of the same German warship are likely to escape through Chile and from Chilean ports.

I avail myself of this opportunity to renew to Your Excellency the assurance of my highest consideration. (TNA FO 371/24182.4797, 9 October 1940)

Berkeley Square House, London, W.1, where the Foreign Office's Economic Warfare Department had offices.
(http://openoffices.com/upload/image/7510/gallery/192f19c3-51b3-417f-860e-c780cc8d25ca-0.jpg)

At the end of October, the *Liverpool Daily Post* published the following article.

GRAF SPEE OFFICERS ESCAPE Monte Video, Tuesday.— Five officers from the scuttled German pocket-battleship Graf Spee have disappeared from Monte Video, and police who are searching for them suspect that they have crossed the frontier into Brazil, where there is a large German population. The officers had given their word of honour to report periodically to the police. —British United Press. (*Liverpool Daily Post,* 30 October 1940)

In mid-November, the *Portsmouth Evening News* reported on the escape.

GRAF SPEE MEN ESCAPE Japanese Help?
BUENOS AIRES. Most of the officers and many of the men of the pocket battleship Admiral Graf Spee, scuttled off Montevideo last December, were reported here to have escaped from their enforced detention. Capt. Hans Langsdorff, who later committed suicide, led 31 commissioned officers up the River Plate to Buenos Ayres after the scuttling to avoid internment in Uruguay. Of that number only Capt. Walter Kay. the second in command, who succeeded Langsdorff, and a single assistant remain. The rest have gone. With them went at least 39 petty officers.

According to informed sources here, the majority received aid from Japanese ships, though Japanese officials declared that no belligerents would be carried on their vessels. Several of the former Graf Spee officers were known to have reached Japan, members of the German colony in Buenos Ayres having received letters from them in that country. They were said to be on their way back to Germany.

OFFICERS IN BRAZIL

Other Graf Spee officers have turned up in Brazil, apparently seeking to reach the Fatherland via the Italian Trans-Oceanic airline. At least four were reported to be hidden in Paraguay.

Of the crew of nearly 1.000 many were known to have taken similar leave of Argentine hospitality, though the actual number was not disclosed.

As contrast to the handling of interned Germans in the Argentine is the treatment they received in Uruguay. where strict supervision is maintained and only one out of 46 has escaped.

The Graf Spee officers in the Argentine were urged to give their personal paroles not to escape, but they refused. After one group disappeared the remainder were rounded up and taken to Martin Garcia Island in the River Plate, midway between Uruguay and the Argentine. Later a mass escape was staged, apparently with outside help, and when it was over only Capt. Kay and his assistant remained.

ENOUGH TO STAFF ANOTHER SHIP

Missing and apparently on their way back to Germany were the bulk of the Graf Spee's fighting brains, including airmen, gunnery officers, engineers and navigators. Among the escapees were six full commanders five lieut-commanders, lieutenants, numerous under-officers - in all enough trained veterans to staff another pocket battleship, group of destroyers, or a number of submarines.

British authorities were stated to have called the attention of the Argentine Government to the escapes. (*Portsmouth Evening News,* 13 November 1940)

The *Bradford Observer* published the following article at the end of November.

" GRAF SPEE " MEN Escape As They Like
Alleged Allegations that men of the Graf Spies crew can travel freely throughout Argentina and escape when they like are made in a manifesto by the National Democratic Party of Argentina which strongly criticises the Government.
"The Government takes a vacillating and contradictory attitude toward subversive armed organisations of foreigners, with whom groups of Argentine citizens. including Army officers of high rank, maintain open contact," says the manifesto. British United Press. (*Bradford Observer*, 30 November 1940)

Flag Lieutenant Commander Kirt Diggins escaped in 1940
(Millington-Drake, op.cit.)

Millington-Drake reported on the escape of Flag Lieutenant Commander Kurt Diggins

> He was one of the five officers retained in Montevideo with a view to their appointment to the German Embassies or Legations in other countries in South America, he had to report to the police once a week, but on seventeen occasions prepared plans for escape in one way or another., though in all cases something occurred to prevent it before he actually got to the point of leaving Uruguayan soil. He recalls that during the weeks of waiting he several times visited the nearby resort of Carrasco and had seen my teenage daughters out riding!
>
> Finally he did get to Buenos Aires as a stowaway on the nightly river steamer which was usually very crowded. In Buenos Aires Lieutenant Diggins, as he then was, secured false papers as Ricardo Teutsch, born in Siebenburgen, the centre of a large and united German community in Transylvania. As such he eventually reached Germany.
>
> Commander Diggins's submarine experience began in U-boat 751, which was stationed in the Atlantic. Later he became commander of U.458 and carried out a 'task' in the Atlantic, and then, in October 1942, he was sent to the Mediterranean. After some more or less successful raids, his vessel was sunk in 1943 in the neighbourhood of Malta by the British destroyer EASTON and the Greek destroyer PINDOS. As prisoner of war for five years he had experience of various camps in Malta, Algiers and Canada, and finally in various camps in England from 1946-47. In February 1957 Commander Diggins resumed his naval service. He is now on the Naval Staff of the Ministry of Defence in Bonn and in 1962 he was appointed to command one of the German Navy's finest frigates, the EMDEN. (Millington-Drake, op.cit. p. 388)

Nothing further was noted until in the Graf Spee files until mid-December when D. Sheridan, an officer in the Shipping Department of Britain's Ministry of Economic Warfare [MEW], Berkeley Square House, London, sent the following memorandum to E. Mather Jackson [?].

> Here is the story of the German ship "Portland", about which I spoke to you on the 'phone last Friday.
>
> On November 30th the "Portland" (H.A.L.7132 tons), sailed from Coquimbo [Chilean port about 500 km north of Santiago], and according to Captain Franklin of the Admiralty there was an unspecified number of officers and men from the "Graf Spee" on board.

On December 4th the "Portland" arrived at Talcahuano [Chilean port about 400km south of Santiago], and presumably the sailors were destined for the German ships "Frankfurt" and "Osorne" taking refuge there.

Clearly, the Chilean Government is bound by international law to intern the "Graf Spee" sailors, and I suggest that representations to this effect should be made. We are anxious to immobilise the "Portland", but it is impossible to arrest her unless evidence can be adduced [provided] that she is to be used as a base for some warlike operation; for example, provisioning a raider. Under Chilean law she would only be interned if she broke international regulations; for example, if she used her wireless telegraph installation while in port.

Two courses suggest themselves, firstly, to ask Santiago to press for the internment of the "Graf Spee" sailors and perhaps use that as a lever for taking action against the "Portland"; also to ask for fuller information about the international regulations; and secondly, to cable the nearest British Consul at Concepcion [Chilean port 500 km south of Santiago] to report on the movements and apparent intentions of the "Portland".

I have consulted Lieut-Commander Cohen here, and in his view this is a case which clearly calls for diplomatic treatment. He suggests that you should be asked to take the necessary action. (TNA FO 371/24182.4797, 15 December 1940)

Just before Christmas, the Foreign Office sent telegram 230 to Sir Charles Orde, the British Ambassador in Chile.

We are informed that the German ship Portland sailed on 30th November from Coquimbo to Talcahuahno having on board some twenty of the crew of the Graf Spee. We are most anxious to secure the internment of these men and to immobilise the ship. It occurs to us that since it would appear to be illegal for the Portland to secrete fugitive active service ratings it should be possible when applying to the Chilean authorities for the arrest and internment of the men to make a request for the arrest of the ship, unless you see strong objection therefore you should now press the Chilean Government strongly to act on the above lines. Please report by telegraph. (TNA ADM 116/5474, 24 December 1940)

Orde's response was sent on Boxing Day, 26 December.
Your telegram No. 230.

Information reached me on 4th December from Chilean sources that vessel named which reached Talcahuano that day, had on board 20 ex-Graf Spee men who had reached Coquimbo with gear from Graf Spee. I at once made strong representations to Minister of Foreign Affairs to prevent their sailing and suggested arrest pending full enquiry of all German ships at Talcahuano in view of the possible surreptitious transfer of men to another ship in better condition for sea. Naval authorities with whom we also got into immediate contact have made careful investigation and today state that it has led to no result. They are well disposed and it seems probable that original information was incorrect. But attempts of this kind are only too likely and we are keeping very careful watch with a view to immediate action.

Chilean Government have committed themselves fully to the proposition that ex-Graf Spee men when found, should be arrested and returned to the Argentine authorities. I have [Grp. Undec.] ed myself on this with general references to the need of avoidance of unneutral service. Can I if necessary argue 1) that above proposition is correct in International Law and 2) that departure of a vessel carrying ex-Graf Spee men would itself be contrary to International Law? (Ibid, 26 December 1940)
On New Year's Eve, Marshall made the following note,

"2". As regards point 1 in the last paragraph of this telegram, I am not aware of an exact precedent for the situation, but in as much as the men concerned would be members of a belligerent force who had escaped from internment and had entered neutral territory in the course of an attempt to rejoin their forces or to take part in military operations, I think that we should certainly content that the Italian [crossed out and replaced with Chilean] Government were bound under international law wither to return the men to the Argentine authorities or to intern them themselves.

As to 2, we could hardly argue [crossed out and replaced with maintain] that the departure of a belligerent merchant ship with members of the armed forces on board from a neutral port would in itself constitute a violation of neutrality, but it might be possible to argue in a particular case that the presence of these ex-internees on board was evidence of an intention on the part of the ship to convert herself into an auxiliary cruiser or armed vessel, which would make Articles 2 and 3 of the instructions contained in Santiago despatch No. 249 of September 11th, 1939, applicable, or might bring the case within Article 8 of the Thirteenth Hague Convention, which the Italian [crossed out and replaced with Chilean] Government (Santiago telegram No. 9 of September 7th, 1939) have announced their intention of applying. Such an argument would of course be strengthened if there were other suspicious circumstances attached to the ship, so that it might be possible, without laying down any general principle, for Sir C. Orde to make representations with the object of securing the detention of the ship in a case where the circumstances seemed to justify his doing so. (TNA FO 371/24182/4797, 31 December 1940)

Chapter Four: Developments in 1941

To obtain the official answer to Orde's two questions, on 8 January Perowne contacted Lord Croft and Sir Edward Grigg who together acted as the Under Secretary of State for War. A copy was also sent to the Secretary at the Admiralty.

>I am directed by Mr. Secretary Eden to transmit to you herewith to be laid before the Lords Commissioners of the Admiralty copy of a telegram from His Majesty's Ambassador in Santiago requesting guidance on certain points of international law, which arise in connexion with his representations to the Chilean Government against the presence in Chile of fugitive naval ratings from the "Graf Spee".
>
>2. Mr. Eden is advised, as regards the first question asked in the last paragraph of Sir Charles Orde's telegram, that there appears to be no exact precedent for the situation. Insomuch, however, as the men concerned would be members of a belligerent force who had escaped from internment, and had entered neutral territory in the course of an attempt to rejoin their forces, or to take part in military operations, it should certainly be contended that the Chilean Government were bound under international law, either to return the men to the Argentine authorities, or to intern them themselves.
>
>3. As regards the second question, it could hardly be maintained that the departure of a belligerent merchant ship with members of the armed forces on board from a neutral port would, not in itself, constitute a violation of neutrality, but it might be possible to argue in a particular case that the presence of these ex-internees on board was evidence of an intention on the part of the ship to convert herself into an auxiliary cruiser, or armed vessel, which would make applicable Articles 2 and 3 of the instructions enclosed in Santiago despatch No. 249 of September 11th, 1939, a copy of which was transmitted to the Lords Commissioners of the Admiralty in Foreign Office letter No. A 6569/156/9 of the 27th September 1939, or might bring the case within Article 8 of the Thirteenth Hague Convention, which the Chilean Government have announced their intention of supplying. Such an argument would, of course, be strengthened if there were other suspicious circumstances attached to the ship, so that it might be possible, without laying down any general principle, for Sir Charles Orde to make representations with the object of securing the detention in a case where the circumstances seem to justify him doing so.
>
>4. I am directed to enquire whether the Lords Commissioners of the Admiralty concur in the despatch of instructions on these

lines to his Majesty's Ambassador at Santiago. (TNA ADM 116/5474, 8 January, 1941)

On the same day, there was a note stating 'Fugitive members of Armed Forces on Merchant ship in neutral port' but no details were provided.

On 17 February, the *Newcastle Evening Chronicle* reported another escape.

> GRAF SPEE MEN "ESCAPE"
> Two more members of the crew of the former German pocket battleship Graf Spee have disappeared from where they were working near San Juan [city in mid-western province with same name] in the direction of the Chilean border, it is learned in Buenos Aires, reports British United Press. Another disguised as a mountaineer and carrying a radio set is reported to have been caught in the Northern Andes. It will be recalled that several members of the crew of the scuttled pocket battleship have escaped previously, although all members of the crew were freed from internment on condition that they did not leave the Argentine. (*Newcastle Evening Chronicle*, 17 February 1941)

On 22 January, Phillips, writing on behalf of Alexander Cadogan, provided the requested response.

> Sir,
> With reference to your letter No. A.4297/4797/9(2) of the 8th January 1941, I am commanded by My Lords Commissioners of the Admiralty to acquaint you, for the information of the Secretary of State for Foreign Affairs that they concur in the despatch of instructions to H.M. Ambassador, Santiago on the lines proposed in the letter under reference.
> Their Lordships would, however suggest that in replying to the second question asked by H.M. Ambassador it should be made clear that, in addition to the difficulty of maintaining in law that the departure of a merchant vessel belonging to a belligerent from a neutral port with members of the armed forces on board, constitutes in itself a violation of neutrality. It is not considered advantageous to our own interests that such a contention should be put forward. (TNA ADM 116/5474, 22 January 1941)

Lieutenant Hans Dietrich escaped from Buenos Aires and crossed the Andes by the southern lakes (Millington-Drake, op.cit.)

Millington-Drake was provided with details of another escape by Dr Hans Dietrich.

In March 1942 [sic – 1941] I escaped from the Naval Arsenal together with another lieutenant, Dietrich Bludau, soon after the First Artillery Officer, Commander Ascher, who was the first to return to Germany. We received secret instructions which way to return home not from the Embassy but from Admiral Canaris's organisation [Abwehr]. So my friend and I managed to get to Bariloche, some 500 miles west of Bahia Blanca at the foot of the Andres where we rode up the Argentine side and walked down the Chilean side.

As we were the first using this way my friend got orders to return in a boat via Japan and from there by train through the Soviet Union, as both countries were at that time still neutral. I was ordered to take the way through Bolivia and Brazil to Rio de Janeiro. From there I flew in an Italian transport plane, still operating once a week, via the Cape Verde Islands and Seville to Rome and Berlin. (Millington-Drake, op.cit. p.390)

In mid-March, London was sent several reports related to escaped Graf Spee sailors. The Vice Consul in Natal [port city on Brazil's northeast tip] sent the following note to the Admiralty, Staff Officer (Intelligence) (SO(I)) Freetown, the British Consul in Pernambuco, northeast Brazil, DSD.9, OIC, DNI and M, M.34 and M.36.

I am informed by Chief of Civil Aeronautical Department Natal that 14 of ADMIRAL GRAF SPEE passed through here yesterday Sunday aboard special Condor plane for Para [northern Brazil] to form part of crew of German steamer there. (TNA FO 371/25736, 18 March 1941)

Pencilled underneath by someone signing themselves 'E' was the comment, 'Let us with Adty [Admiralty] and if need be collected soon in one memo, all [illegible[available about Graf Spee escapes; about our replies to the Argentine Govt on the subject hitherto and the Argentine reactions in order that we may consider whether it is worthwhile taking the question up again.'

The following day, the Foreign Office was sent a translation of an intercepted Transocean news report.

GRAF SPEE CREW NOT ON CABO HORNO.
    MONTEVIDEO: - CAMERA MEN AND SECRET POLICE HAD LINED UP AT THE PIER TO CATCH SIGHT OF MEMBERS OF THE CREW OF THE POCKET BATTLESHIP "GRAF SPEE" WHO WERE SAID TO BE ON BOARD THE SPANISH STEAMER "CABO HORNOS" STEAMING INTO PORT. BUT THEY HAD WAITED IN VAIN, FOR THE MEN WERE NOT ON THE STEAMER. AN AMERICAN NEWS AGENCY HAD REPORTED THAT NUMEROUS MEMBERS OF THE CREW OF THE "ADMIRAL GRAF SPEE" WERE TRYING TO ESCAPE FROM BUENOS AIRES AND TO RETURN TO GERMANY ON BOARD THIS VESSEL. ITS ARRIVAL HERE WAS THEREFORE AWAITED WITH UTMOST INTEREST AND EVERYTHING HAD BEEN PREPARED FOR THE ARREST OF THE FUGITIVES. BUT INVESTIGATIONS OF THE VESSEL AND A CLOSE EXAMINATION OF THE SHIP'S PAPERS MERELY SHOWED THE PRESENCE OF ONE GERMAN ON BOARD. SHE WAS A GERMAN WOMAN TRAVELLING WITH A BRITISH VISA. (Ibid, 19 March 1941)

Pencilled underneath was the unsigned comment, 'Let us enter and then discuss with Admiralty question of a protest to the Argentine Government.' There was then a handwritten note by Rodney Gallop who worked in the Foreign Office's South American department,

> The memo within shows that the Argentine Govt have consistently resented any representation from us regarding the practical steps taken to intern the officers and crew of the 'Graf Spee', on the ground that the matter was one exclusively within their domestic jurisdiction. It might have been expected that they would take all the more care to see that we have no ground to complain that our interests have not been injured by the matter in which they carry out their neutral duties. And the contrary has been the case. Although there was some slight improvement a year ago, there has been a singular epidemic of escapes. Unfortunately our information as to these is not very detailed. In

particular, we do not know whether the 14 "members of crew" who passed through Natal by plane on March 17th had come from Argentina and whether they are the same as the 15 officers who escaped last August. Sir E. Ovey would, I imagine, only return to the charge with reluctance. But we might ask him (repeating our tel[egram] to Rio and Montevideo) if he can throw any light on the most recent incident and if he is satisfied that precautions are being maintained, since the departure of axis ships from Brazilian ports would be an obvious incentive to renewed attempts to escape. I submit a draft which I have sent over the phone to Mr Downie (D.N.I.) who concurs.

There followed a heavily annotated document with suggested edits. What follows is the much shorter and more diplomatic version.

<u>Internment of Officers and men of the Graf Spee in Argentina</u>.
Mr Gage's memorandum of February 27th gives an account of the differences between H.M.G. and the Argentine Government regarding internment of the officers and men of the Graf Spee from the original incident up to that date.

2. On February 26th 1940, Sir E. Ovey was handed a memorandum by the Argentine M.F.A. [Minister of Foreign Affairs], contending that the duty of internment is one which each neutral state should fulfil at its own discretion and that the measures decided on should be carried out in conditions which the neutral state alone should fix. The Argentine Government had taken the necessary measures to arrange that the personnel of the ship should remain in the country and the internment decree would be implemented by the finding of work for the crew. Sir E. Ovey was instructed in F.O. telegram No. 72 of March 11th to restate to the Argentine Government in writing H.M.G.'s views on the legal situation and to express their dissatisfaction, adding that they must reserve all their rights and that they meanwhile held the Argentine Government entirely responsible for ensuring that none of the men escaped or indulged in sabotage or other reprehensible activities such as propaganda. The telegram authorised Sir E. Ovey, if there was any chance of the Argentine Government agreeing to some arrangement which while falling short of full internment and supervision in the inland provinces would be more satisfactory than what was then contemplated, to discuss the matter with the Argentine Government, laying most emphasis on the sabotage argument. Sir E. Ovey accordingly

addressed a note (No. 30 of March 12th) to the Argentine M.F.A. in the above sense.

3. On March 20th Mr. R.A. Butler held somewhat similar language to the Argentine Ambassador in London and gave him a memorandum setting forth British desiderata [decisions]. The Argentine Ambassador stated that he had heard from the Argentine Ministry of Foreign Affairs that Sir E. Ovey was too persistent in pressing the British point of view on this matter and suggested that it would do more harm than good to press upon his Government a different treatment of internees. He proposed that each case of unsatisfactory conduct on the part of the latter should be brought to the attention of the Argentine Government, but that a general broadside should be avoided.

4. Advice on these lines was promulgated on March 6th. On March 20th the Argentine M.F.A. replied in writing to Sir E. Ovey's note. The Argentine Government claimed that the matter must be regarded as one of internal administration "which must be settled without foreign interference by exercise of this country's sovereign rights" and justified the steps they had taken by lengthy reference to the Hague Convention of 1899 and the recommendations of the recent Rio de Janeiro conference. They further stated that the crew would be sent in batches to earn their livelihood under surveillance in the interior and maintained that the action taken gave effect to the internment decree and that the Argentine Government, while not sharing British fears of sabotage, was taking adequate steps to defend our legitimate interests in Argentina.

5. Meanwhile Sir E. Ovey's telegrams Nos. 129 and 135 of March 16th and 19th, 1940, showed signs of an improvement in the situation. Although the matter was in the hands of the Ministry of the Interior, who had been reported to be "pro-German if not worse", 100 sailors had left on March 18th for Mendoza and it had been stated that "important contingents" would leave for the provinces where they would remain under supervision. Officers were to remain on parole in or within 50 kilometres of Buenos Aires.

6. In his telegram No. 154 of April 3rd Sir E. Ovey gave reasons for hoping that the Argentine Government might compromise on their earlier attitude and that our note might still produce concessions which, even if not fully satisfactory, would be much nearer to our original desiderata. He was informed that H.M.G. considered that in view of this they could safely leave it to the initiative of the Argentine Government to compromise on their earlier attitude, and was authorised to inform the M.F.A. semi-officially that, while fully reserving their attitude, H.M.G. did not

propose to prolong the controversy by returning a reply to the note of March 20th and that since its receipt they had been gratified to learn that more effective measures of supervision were being adopted. Sir E. Ovey carried out these instructions on April 16th and reported that the M.F.A. appeared relieved and perhaps even surprised at the absence of further insistence on our part.

7. Even more effective measures were taken as a result of reports that two Graf Spee sailors had escaped on the Italian ship "Neptunia" (which handed them over to the Brazilian authorities at Santos, whence they were returned to Argentina) but that certain officers had broken parole and left the country. Other escapes were reported in the Argentine Press from Santa Fe. On April 8th a further decree No. 59459 was promulgated providing for the internment of officers on Martin Garcia Island in the River Plate.

8. On April 8th Sir E. Ovey reported that some days previously an armed guard had been called out to deal with an attempt by Graf Spee officers to escape from the Naval barracks in Buenos Aires. Eight were said to have escaped and the remainder to be confined on a naval transport [boat] pending transport to Martin Garcia Island. On April 18th the Assistant Naval Attaché at Rio de Janeiro reported that Graf Spee officers, who has arrived on board the S.S. "Windhuk" on April 17th had been removed by Brazilian Police for internment in Buenos Aires.

9. On August 12th 1940, Sir E. Ovey reported that the Argentine Government had laid hands at various frontier posts on escaped members of the Graf Spee crew, the last lot, who had been sent to Cordoba, having been caught near the Chilean frontier and brought back to Buenos Aires. Sir E. Ovey expressed doubts as to whether deterrent action had been or would be taken, but added that they appeared to have been sent to Martin Garcia.

In the middle of September further escapes on a substantial scale have taken place, but reports varied as to the exact dates, the numbers involved and the mode of escape. The Argentine Minister of Marine informed the press on September 7th that 15 out of the 16 officers interned on Martin Garcia had escaped on August 31st, while the press explained that the men had failed to return from week-end leave in Buenos Aires expiring on September 1st. a number of them were reported to have sailed in the Spanish ship "Motomar" while another report suggested that they were hidden in Uruguay. Sir E. Ovey has asked for a full report on September 19th and replied on Sept 20th that the reports regarding the escapes were still conflicting, that the

Argentine authorities were showing touchiness [unease], and until it could be established that the men had left Argentina, the escape was considered to be an internal matter. The Commandant of the detention island had been relieved [replaced] and the authorities were believed to be pursuing the search with genuine zeal. He had, therefore, avoided any official demarche pending the result of the Naval Attaché [McCall]'s enquiries but had spoken privately to M.F.A., who appeared grateful that he had not taken up the matter officially and added that "it had no political importance." On September 21st Sir E. Ovey added on the authority of the M.F.A. that the evasion had taken place by night in small boats from the Uruguayan side of the River Plate, and that suitable punishment would be inflicted on anyone found guilty of collusion.

On October 2nd Sir E. Ovey was instructed to request the Argentine M.F.A. unofficially to furnish him with a complete set of photographs of the escaped officers, adding if necessary that this was the least the Argentine Government could do in view of the breakdown of their precautions and of their failure to furnish [provide] prompt information of the escape, such as would have enabled H.M.G. to take timely steps to minimise the resulting injury to their legitimate interests. On October 14th he replied that he had failed to obtain a favourable reply. He begged, however, not to be instructed to press the matter in view of the Argentine Government's sensitiveness to any intervention as being derogatory to their national pride. He was nevertheless instructed on October 23rd to return to the charge on the ground that, although there was no precedent for our request under international law, it was fully justified by reason of the failure of the Argentine Govt to fulfil their obligations under international law to detain the officers in question so that they could no longer participate in the war. On October 31st Sir E. Ovey reported that he had reverted to the matter without success although he "thought he detected signs of absence of opposition other than official non possum's." [we cannot] but that in practice we possessed sufficient data.

On March 17th 1941, H.M Vice Consul at Natal was informed by the Chief of Civil Aeronautical Department there that 14 members of the crew had passed through on the previous day on board a special Condor plane for Para to form part of the crew of a German steamer. (TNA FO 371/25736, 9 April 1941)

Gallop queried the following day, 'Have you any information to show whether these men escaped recently and what was their point of departure? Or are they the officers who escaped in August from detention island? Since preparations for departure of axis ships from Brazil provide additional incentive to escape, in view of the generally unsatisfactory attitude of Argentine Govt in this matter, please report whether presentations have in any way been relaxed. I leave it to you to decide whether unofficial enquiries of MFA would do good or harm. Please respond by air mail to HMRR [?representatives] Montevideo & Rio for similar action should they see no opposition.' (Ibid, 10 April 1941)

On 15 April, Ovey sent telegram 258 to the Foreign Office.

> Your telegram No. 216.
> Men may be either officers who escaped last August, whose photographs were sent to Naval Attaché, Rio de Janeiro, last October, or fifteen men reported to have sailed on S.S. [?Cabo] de Hornos which called at Rio March 22nd.
> Suggest Consul at Para [Northern Brazil state, capital Belem] be sent photographs by Rio for confirmation. (Ibid, 15 April 1941)

Gallop commented the following day that, 'Sir E. Ovey has told us nothing of the report that 15 men sailed on the "Cabo de Hornos". Nor has he repeated his telegram to Rio although it contains a suggestion for action by that port.' This led the Foreign Office to send telegram 235 to Buenos Aires. 'I assume that you are repeating to Rio your telegram No. 258 [of April 15th. Escape of internees from Graf Spee]. Have you no information regarding means and place of escape of men mentioned in second half of your first paragraph? (Ibid, 16 April 1941)

A similar telegram was sent to Knox in telling them to 'Please act as suggested in Sir E. Ovey's second paragraph if you have not done so already and telegraph all the information you can obtain regarding the report in the second half of his first paragraph.' (Ibid.)

Ovey's response, telegram 278, was sent on 20th April. 'Your telegram No. 235. [Grp.undec. ?Story] probably escaped from interior where it is very difficult to obtain information. Embarkation on Spanish vessel not certain.' (Ibid, 20 April 1941)

The following day Knox sent telegram 175 to the Foreign Office, repeated to Buenos Aires and Montevideo. 'Foreign Office telegram No. 216 to Buenos Aires. Natal story appears to be garbled report of a Condor flight which took 12 members of "Lech" crew to Para on March 15th. I am asking for report.' (Ibid, 21 April 1941)

Knox replied to the Foreign Office in telegram 181 sent on 26 April, repeated to Buenos Aires. 'Buenos Aires telegram No. 278 to Foreign Office. Out information is that prisoners were not on board the Spanish ship.' (Ibid, 26 April 1941)

On 24 April, there was another report that some escaped Graf Spee sailors had reached Chile and boarded a German ship bound for Europe. Waldock contacted Perowne at the Foreign Office.

I enclose a copy of Naval Attaché, Washington's 1841/23 which appears to raise much the same problem as that dealt with in your letter dated 8th January, No. A.4797/4797/9(2) and our reply of 22nd January, M.0894/4.

2. We do not think on the information available that it is very likely that the S.S. ERLANGEN is in a condition to sail at short notice, though the possibility of her sailing cannot of course be ruled out altogether. On the other hand, we think it quite likely that ratings from the GRAF SPEE may have gone on board the German vessel. We therefore suggest that the attention of the Ambassador should be drawn to this report and instructed, if he considers the report well founded, to press for the internment of the GRAF SPEE ratings.

The attached telegram read:

From Naval Attache Washington
Addressed: Admiralty
IMMEDIATE:
Following from Navy Department.
From Buenos Aires April 21st.
Many ratings from GRAF SPEE have joined crew of German ERLANGEN which is expected to sail from Puerto Montt between April 20th and April 26th to supply German raiders south of Cape Horn. (TNA ADM 116/5474, 24 April 1941)

Given its importance, the Washington telegram was also sent to the 1st Lord, 1st S.L., 4th S.L., V.C.N.S., A.C.N.S.(F), A.C.N.S.(T), Nav. Sec., Ops, O.D., D.N.I., D.T.D., Cdr. Holbrook, O.I.C., D. of P., D.S.D., I.P., W.D., D.P.D., M., M.34 and M.36.

The Foreign Office sent telegrams 120 and 258 to Santiago and Buenos Aires informing them about the Erlangen's imminent departure adding that 'Many ratings from the Graf Spee are reported are stated to have joined crew.' (TNA FO 371/25736, 24 April 1941)

On 26 April, Ovey sent the Foreign Office telegram 306, with copies to Washington and Montevideo.

Your telegram No. 258.
I informed Minister of the Interior privately of rumour regarding this vessel/

Minister recently informed me of the fact that further men of Graf Spee had escaped and is investigating matter. He was evidently taken responsible police severely to task.

He promises a full account as soon as detective returns. [not found in the Foreign Office file].

I shall try to extract information of number and whereabouts of remaining interned men and of precautions which Minister hopes to take to prevent further escapes.

Minister asks that we shall meanwhile not weaken his position by awkward official demands. (Ibid, 26 April 1941)

On 9 May, the Foreign Office asked Orde whether he had been able to confirm the report and if so whether he had been able to secure the internment of the men. The following day, Orde sent the Foreign Office telegram 139.

Your telegram 141.

Ship in question is not ready for sea and appears to be in no hurry, though she has received permission to ship 400 tons of coal. Maximum on board estimated at 750. No confirmation of any new forces among crew except some from German training ship at Valparaiso. Report of proposed sailing came from so many quarters that it is suspected of being purposely circulated. (Ibid, 11 May 1941)

On 19 May, he wrote again stating that 'Erlangen Frankfurt Quito Bogota Rhakotis all sailed late on May 17th.' (Ibid, 19 May 1941) The outcome of the incident was not reported in the Foreign Office or Admiralty files examined but the cargo ship Erlagen is included in the list of shipwrecks as having been scuttled by her crew off the mouth of the River Plate on 25 July when it was approached by HMS Newcastle. (https://en.wikipedia.org/wiki/List_of_shipwrecks_in_July_1941)

Whether the Graf Spee crew had been transferred to another German ship or submarine beforehand is unknown but, according to the sixtant website, the captain and crew were taken first to Scotland where they were interned until transferred to Canada where they were released in 1946. (https://www.sixtant.net/2011/artigos.php?cat=ships-hit-germany-25*&sub=blockadebrecher &tag=10)erlangen-(scuttled)).

In early August, the *Liverpool Daily Post* published the following article.

Argentine Action

Informed quarters in Buenos Ayres said that Argentina intended to withhold her support of the black list. [Details of German companies or companies trading with Germany that British and later American companies were forbidden to do business with]. At the same time the Argentine Foreign Office demanded that the Germans either destroy or remove the controversial wireless transmitter found in the diplomatic bags opened by the committee investigating anti-Argentine activities. Meanwhile Argentine Congressional circles discussed plan to request the removal of the German Ambassador. Edmund von Thermann. The Argentine Government studied the Nazi plot discovered in the Entre-Eios province—reputed hot-bed of pro-German activities—but stated that, so far, it considered that it did not provide any national threat. Chile ordered the German Consul- General at Valparaiso for the second time to leave the country on charges of falsifying a passport to help Graf Spee men escape Argentine internment. Chile said that the Consul-General had overstayed the original time allotted to him to conclude his affairs. The ex-Minister to Bolivia, Ernest Wendler, prepared to-day to sail to Japan from Chile where he went after being expelled from Bolivia. - The Associated Press. (*Liverpool Daily Post,* 2 August 1941)

The *Belfast News Letter* had a similar story the same day.

GERMAN "ADVICE" TO U.S. MINISTER'S VIEW "No Less Than Barefaced Impudence"
NAZI PLOTS DISCOVERED
MR. SUMNER WELLES. U.S. Acting Secretary of
State, yesterday accused Germany of "barefaced impudence" in urging Mexico to protest to the United States over the Washington "black list" of Latin-American firms aiding the Axis. Mr. Welles said that Germany had destroyed and violated the sovereignty of many countries and, therefore. It was nothing less than barefaced Impudence for Germany to try to tell Mexico or any other country what it should do to protect sovereign rights.
ALIVE TO DANGER
Mr. Welles praised the action of several Latin-American nations in taking energetic measures recently against Axis moves in harmony with inter- American solidarity. The measures | demonstrated, he said, that fee Independent republics of the Western Hemisphere were fully alive to the existing danger. In rejecting the German Note, the Mexican Foreign Minister told the German Minister that Mexico refused to accept the insinuation that Washington's action violates Mexico's liberty of

commerce and even her sovereignty. The Mexican reply called the German Note a threat which the Government regarded as Imperious and unacceptable.

The Latin-American nations yesterday displayed an almost unbroken anti-Axis front in face of German provocations, but informed quarters in Buenos Aires said that Argentina intended to withhold her support of the "black list".

MAY SEVER RELATIONS

Argentine M.P.s are expected to urge the Government to break off diplomatic relations with Germany as the result of disclosures by the Parliamentary Committee investigating totalitarian activities. Senor Damonte chairman of the Committee, said at Press conference yesterday: "I understand that some members of Congress are going to advocate this course. The Committee has proved the existence of totalitarian activities with important ramifications abroad. These actions constitute serious threat to the integrity of this country and its institutions." At the same time, the Argentine Foreign Office demanded that the Germans either destroy or remove the controversial wireless transmitter found in the diplomatic bags opened by the committee investigating anti-Argentine activities.

SEVEN ARRESTED

A Nazi-engineered plot for the stirring up of a seditious movement in the province of Entre Rios has been discovered by the police. Seven persons have been arrested. Police raided the headquarters of the German Culture and Welfare Association at Rosario, Argentina, and arrested 30 persons after neighbours had complained that young men were engaged in secret military training at night. Monies, "Mein Kampf" and propaganda leaflets were seized. Chile has ordered the German Consul-General at Valparaiso, for the second time, to leave the country on charges of falsifying a passport to help Graf Spee men escape Argentine internment. The Government said that the Consul-General had over-stayed the original time allotted to him to conclude his affairs. The ex-Minister to Bolivia, Ernst Wendler, prepared yesterday to sail to Japan from Chile, where he went after being expelled from Bolivia. The existence of a Nazi organisation in Bolivia, which met secretly under the name of the German National Socialist Labour Party of Bolivia, is proved in documents published by the police. —Reuter and Associated Press. *Belfast News-Letter,* 2 August 1941)

Benemann commented that this was 'mostly breathless British yellow press bunk.' The *Northern Whig* reported on the incident the same day.

Chile Orders German Out
Argentine Congressional circles are considering requesting the removal of the German Ambassador, Von Thermann. The Government is studying the unearthed Nazi plot M.P.s are expected to urge the Government to break off diplomatic relations with Germany. It is understood that the Government has asked the German Embassy to explain why wireless transmitting set was found in the diplomatic baggage of high German Embassy official. Chile has ordered the German Consul-General at Valparaiso to leave the country charges falsifying a passport to help Graf Spee men escape Argentine internment. (*Northern Whig*, 2 August 1941)

Benemann admitted that there was 'some truth to this. Therman was constantly undermined by Müller and his nazi spooks. This was one of the reason why TH. went back for "consultations" with Ribbentrop shortly thereafter. There was also a fizzled bombing attempt. Pretty dumb all of that!' (Email communication with Carlos Benemann, 6 November 2021)

Nothing further was mentioned in the Graf Spee files until the end of August when the Military Attaché in Buenos Aires sent the following telegram to the Directorate of Naval Intelligence (DNI), the Commander in Chief South America and the Rear Admiral Submarines and Destroyers Staff Officer 1 in Montevideo.

Consul Rosario who had previously reported GRAF SPEE sailors were stowing away in Spanish ships from that port and landing at Las Palmas reports that a (?GRAF) internee denounced personally at Consulate on August 27th that eight more including one mechanisian [sic] Franz Gillhaus born 1919 sailed on Spanish ship end of July possible URUMEA or MONTEDURIA and other sailed about August 20th possibly in MONTEINCHORTA. (TNA ADM 116/5474, 30 August 1941)

In mid-September, R. W. Spraggett, the Admiralty's Director of Plans, wrote the following note,

The last protest to the Argentine Government – the last of a series – was made about November 30th, 1940.
2. From the fact that no occasion to make further protests has arisen between then and now appears to indicate that these protests achieved some result in tightening up the supervision and custody of the GRAF SPEE internees, in all probability this has in the last months, in the absence of further incidents, been

relaxed and the present escape may well be the first of a new series.
3. It is considered, therefore, that the Foreign Office should be requested to make a strong protest.
4. As R.A.S.A.D. been omitted in the Addressees of so many messages in Part I it is suggested A.C.N.S.(F) [Assistant Chief Naval Staff (Foreign)] would be interested. (Ibid, 15 September 1941)

A note at the top of the letter read: 'We seem to have done all the protesting possible to the Argentines about these escapees. See case 5784 attached. Propose no further action.'

Naval Commander Henry Johnston, the Staff Officer (Intelligence) in Montevideo, reported on 25 September on the 'Escape of ex-Graf Spee sailors.'

> H.M. Consul, Rosario, reports that attempts are still being made to smuggle "Graf Spee" sailors out of the Argentine in Spanish ships. The premium for this has now been increased to two thousand Argentine pesos per head.
> H.M. Consul confirms that five German sailors left in s.s. "ARGESTONA" which sailed from Rosario on 25th February 1941. Since then however the Spanish Consul has warned all captains of Spanish ships that they must not take such stowaways.
> Information is requested whether there have been any reports of these sailors arriving at Las Palmas or ports in Spain. (Ibid, 25 September 1941)

At the end of September, the *Daily Advertiser* of Wagga Wagga, Australia, reported on the Graf Spee escapees.

> 'BUENOS AIRES, Sunday (A.AJP.) Acting-President (Senor Castilo) informed the Argentine senate investigation committee to-day that 128 of the 1056 interned crew of the German pocket-battleship Graf Spee, had escaped from a concentration camp during 21 months. (*Daily Advertiser*, 30 September 1941)

The *Belfast News Letter* had a similar story.

MEN FROM GRAF SPEE
128 Escape From Internment (From The Times Correspondent) BUENOS AIRES, Monday.—In a message sent by the Argentine Government to the Senate replying to a questionnaire about the landing and internment of sailors from the Admiral Graf Spec is shown that of the total of 1,046

internees 128 have escaped.— Per Press Association. (*Belfast News Letter,* 30 September 1941)

At the beginning of October, Rear Admiral Jack Salmond, the Director of Naval Intelligence at the Admiralty, sent the following letter to the Naval Attaché, East Coast, South America. Copies were also sent to the British Ambassador in Buenos Aires, C. in. C. S. Atlantic, R.A.S.A.D.,S.O.(I), Montevideo, A.S.O.(I) Montevideo and the U.S. Naval Attaché, Buenos Aires.

I attach a translation of a written reply to the Minister of the Interior to a request from the Senate to be informed about the present state of the interned crew of the German battleship "Graf von Spee".

The reply is obviously based on the secret police report dated May 30th, 1941, a summary of which I telegraphed to you on June 4, 1941. It is therefore out of date and reports have been received from the Rosario and Mendoza Consulates that further escapes from their districts are suspected.

The actual date of the escape of 16 officers from the Naval Barracks in the Island of Martin Garcia is still concealed. The escape was announced on September 7, but it is believed to have taken place early in August a few weeks after the French Naval Attaché had warned the Minister of Marine that an escape had been planned.

The reply mentions that subsequent attempts to escape from Martin Garcia in November 1940, February and May 1941 were frustrated.

ARRIVAL OF "GRAF SPEE" CREW AT BUENOS AIRES
(Government reply to Senate question)

Question 1. Who contracted the craft which left the port of Buenos Aires to bring to Buenos Aires the officers and crew of the German battleship "Admiral Graf Spee"?
What part did the German Embassy take in this matter?

Reply. The report of the maritime sub-prefecture of the port of Buenos Aires states that at 03.00 on December 17th, 1939, Rudolph Hope, Director of Towage Company "La Portena," which is administered by A.M. Delfino & Cia., Florida 439, was telephoned by one Muller, and asked to get ready urgently 3 or 4 tugs to embark in them about a thousand shipwrecked men in the neighbourhood of the roadstead of Montevideo.

	Hope accordingly ordered to proceed there the Argentine tug "Gigante" which sailed at 06.00 and picked up in the Buenos Aires roads the Argentine lighter "Chirguana". At 08.00 the tug "Coloso" also sailed and all the draft proceeded to Montevideo roads where they arrived approximately at 19.20 the same day.
Question 2.	Did these vessels take down the explosives for the sinking of the "Admiral Graf Spee"?
Reply.	No. The tugs "Gigante" and "Coloso" and the lighter "Chiriguana" never went alongside the German battleship. When they reached her vicinity they were told from on-board that the crew were on board the German merchant ship "Tacoma" anchored close by, so the tugs went straight to the latter ship. Consequently, if the craft had brought explosives, they could not have been used to blow up the German battleship.
Question 3.	Did the said craft leave with the authorisation and under the control of the Argentine Authorities? If not, what port regulations were thereby violated?
Reply.	The said craft sailed without authorisation or knowledge of the Argentine Authorities, thereby infringing Articles 337, 349 and 1679 of the "Maritime and Fluvial Digest of Laws".
Question 4.	Were proceedings commenced in this matter, what facts were proved and conclusions reached, and what penalties were decreed and applied?
Reply.	The proceedings instituted proved the departure of the craft mentioned without clearance or knowledge of the maritime authority. The carriage of passengers without permission and mission to notify the change of route of the lighter "Chitiguana". The following penalties were imposed: Master of the "Coloso" fined $100. – for sailing without clearance and $50. – for carrying passengers. Master of "Gigante" fined as above plus $50. – for failure to notify the change of route of the lighter. Master of the lighter fined $50. - for carrying passengers. ['Nominal fines' was pencilled in the margin.]

Question 5.		Who is the owner of the craft mentioned, and does he fill any Argentine government post? If the owners were a company, who were the directors?
Reply.		The craft mentioned figure as the property of the Hamburg South American Company, Florida 439,whose representatives are the Cia. A.M. Delfino. The Board of the latter is formed by: Antonio M. Delfino (President), Eduardo B. Delfino (Vice President), Bernardo L. Delfino (Secretary) and Carlos O. Marenco (Secretary).
		Senor Antonio M. Delfino has been Director of the Banco de la Nacido, Argentina since March 2nd 1932, having been appointed by the Executive in agreement with the Senate.
Question 6.		Where are the ex-officers and crew of the ex-German battleship "Admiral Graf Spee" interned? What steps are taken to watch over their activities? Are all their places of interment or have some escaped? What punishments have been inflicted? Have they taken, or are they taking part in activities harmful to this country or violating our neutrality? Give details of any such cases and of the penalties applied.
Reply		The officers and crew were mustered [concentrated] at the Naval Workshops in the North Basin of Buenos Aires on arrival on December 18, 1939, and were placed at the disposal of the Minister of the Interior.

The total complement was: -

Senior Officers	39
Warrant Officers	47
Petty Officers	199
Seamen	751
Civilians	19
Total	1055

On December 19, 1939, Decree 50,836 interned them in conformity with existing conventions and with the neutrality Decree dated September 4th, 1939.

Decree 58,556 of March 16, 1940 fixed the zones of the internment but only 1046 men came under its rules, since the Commanding Officer, Captain Hans von Langsdorff, had committed suicide on December 20, 1939 at the Naval workshops, and, in accordance with the conventions, the following medical personnel were excluded: -

Officers	2
Petty officers	2
Seamen	3
Total	8

The refusal of the ex-officers to give their word of honour not to absent themselves without special written permission from the police authorities of Buenos Aires (as required by Decree 508826) caused the Executive Power to dictate Decree 59459 of April8, 1940, fixing their place of internment as the Island of Martin Garcia.

When the movement of the crew to the places of internment fixed for them had been completed, the distribution of them on May 17, 1940 was as follows: -

Federal Capital	148	
Province of Cordoba	207	
San Juan	47	
Mendoza	92	
Santa Fe	181	
Total Capital and Provinces	675	
Island of Martin Garcia	241	936
Escaped		108
Died		2
		1046

A nominal list of the persons interned, grouped according to the residence assigned and a list of deaths is attached.

244

Some of the Graf Spee crew arriving at San Juan railway station 1940
(https://www.maritimequest.com/warship_directory/germany/pages/cruisers/admiral_graf_spee_friedrich_bachmann_page_11.htm
Courtesy of Hugo R. Sochi)

Arrival at San Juan internment camp 1940 (Ibid.)

Meal time in the San Juan internment camp (Ibid.)

Friedrich Bachmann in San Juan internment camp 1940 (Ibid.)

Friedrich Bachmann and fellow internee at San Juan 1940 (Ibid.)

Internees at San Juan 1940 (Ibid.)

Friedrich Bachmann, 2nd from left, with other Graf Spee internees (Ibid.)

Graf Spee internees at San Juan, Argentina in 1940 (https://i.pinimg.com/564x/6c/c3/0c/6cc30ca7598fc1f31dca405aa161c485.jpg)

Measures adopted to supervise their activities.
When it was decided to disperse the crew from the Naval Workshops, as a first precaution instructions were given to the Police to have their photographs and finger prints taken.
Each person was given an identity card and contingents were distributed to the places fixed for their residence where

they are subject to local police vigilance in accordance with Article 2 of Decree 50826.

In accordance with this arrangement the authorities of the Ministry of Marine in the Island of Martin Garcia, and the police of the Federal Capital and the Provinces watch their activities.

Payment of the allowances fixed by Article6 is made by the local post offices in the presence of a police officer who verifies identity by means of the card.

As regards those interned at Martin Garcia, the Minister of Marine has issued the following special regulations: -

Treatment: Identical with that of Argentine personnel of the same category.

Jurisdiction: Under the orders of the Military Command of Martin Garcia.

Occupation: Officers, petty officers and men may take up any occupation they wish. The seamen and civilian servants will attend as necessary to the rest of those interned.

Leave; Officers may have leave every 7 days, and ratings every 14 days. Period of absence: 3or 4 days, according to the itinerary of the vessel communicating with Buenos Aires. Warrant officers and petty officers must give their word of honour to return punctually.

Seamen and civilians: To be instructed by their officers to return, and to be warned that failure to do so will lead to restrictions on the leave of the rest of their category.

The maximum number allowed from the Island is 43.

Correspondence: Postage paid and no restrictions.

Telegrams may be sent in Spanish with the authorisation of the Commandant of the Island.

Visits: Visitors up to the number of 30 may come to the Island on Sundays. Those invited by internees will obtain passages at the Ministry on proving their identity.

Uniform: Will be worn exclusively on the island and civilian clothes when on leave.

ESCAPES: All internees are at their correct residences except nine at the German hospital, and 128 who have escaped. While the internees were lodged at the Naval Workshops and at the

Immigrants Hotel the following escapes took place:

Officers	14
Warrant Officers	6
Petty Officers	31
Seamen	5
Civilians	-
	56

Of the above 4 Warrant Officers, 16 Petty Officers and 6 seamen subsequently surrendered or were arrested.

Since April 9, 1940, on which date, in compliance with Decrees 50556 and 59459, the personnel destined for Martin Garcia were sent there, up to the present date the following escapes have taken place: -

Officers	16
Warrant Officers	1
Petty Officers	6
Seamen	3
Civilians	-
	26

Moreover, on the following dates, frustrated attempts at escape from Martin Garcia were made: -

1st November, 1940
28th February, 1941
2nd May, 1941.

Various escapes have been made by those interned elsewhere. Some of these have been arrested here or in neighbouring countries.

Those still absent are: -

Province of Cordoba	24
Province of Mendoza	4
Province of San Juan	2
Province of Santa Fe	12
Federal Capital	29
	71

[Pencilled in the margin was the sum '56-26=30 +26+71 = 128']

Penalties Applies.
45 Seamen have been sent to Martin Garcia for attempting to escape.
5 others have been sent there for disregard of discipline or misconduct.
Those attempting to escape from Martin Garcia have their leave stopped for 3 months.

Those leaving their zone of internment have their leave stopped for 2 months.
Those missing the liberty steamer lose 2 or 3 turns of leave.

Illegal Activities or Violations of national neutrality.
A nil return except as regards those interned in the Province of Cordoba. The Governor of the Province reported in general terms that they were spreading totalitarian ideas and urged their removal to Martin Garcia.

Expenses. $
   Disbursed by Argentine Government   1,297,621
   Claimed so far   875,672
   Reimbursed by German Government   732,387
   Unpaid   123,375 (Ibid, 2 October 1941)

A few days later R.G. Henderson at the Foreign Office sent DNI a summary of the above adding,

Measure taken to control internees
   In the first instance the City police carried out the identification of all the crew who each received an identity card. They were then transferred to their various places of residence where they remain under the vigilance of the local authorities. The payment of the allowance to the crew is carried out by the Post Office in the presence of a police official who vises [sic] on the men's identity card.
   Special regulations govern the treatment of these internees in Martin Garcia Island. They come under the Military Control of the Island and receive the same treatment as the Argentine personnel of similar categories. The senior officers are given leave every 7 days, the others every 14 days. The period varies between 3 or 4 days according to the schedule of the craft which takes them to the mainland. The officers are allowed leave on parole. The ratings and civilians are given leave on the recommendation of the officers and warned that failure to return will lead to restrictions on the remaining personnel. The maximum ashore at one time is 40. Visitors are allowed to the island on Sunday up to a maximum of 30 persons. Uniform may be worn on the island but plain clothes must be worn on leave.
   The following are the details of the 128 who have escaped: -

                        Senior   Junior   Petty

	Officers	Officers	Officers	Ratings
During internment in Buenos Aires City	14	2	15	0
From Martin Garcia Island	15	1	5	3
Buenos Aires City				29
Cordoba				24
Mendoza				4
San Juan				2
Santa Fe				12
	20	3	21	74

There are also 8 who are at present in the German Hospital.
<u>Nazi activities</u>. The Government states that there have been no reports of violation of neutrality or activities contrary to the Argentine except in the Province of Cordoba. (TNA ADM 116/5474, 2 October 1941)

On 7 October, the *Dundee Evening Telegraph* published the following article.

Graf Spee Officers Arrested
Porto Alegre, Brazil, Tuesday. Karl Leopert and Alfred Kroen, officers on the former pocket battleship Graf Spee, were arrested yesterday while attempting to return to Germany.
They escaped from a concentration camp in Argentina. (*Dundee Evening Telegraph*, 7 October 1941)

A few days later, Philip Broadmead, who had been appointed Counsellor at the British Embassy in Rio de Janeiro in April 1941, informed the Foreign Office and the British Embassy in Montevideo that,

> Acting Consul Porto Alegro reports two sailors from Graf Spee have arrived there and are detained by the police. Awaiting instructions from Rio de Janeiro.
> I told Secretary-General today that I was sure that His Majesty's Government would be interested in fate of these men. He said that Ministry of Foreign Affairs had not yet been approached by Ministry of Justice on the subject and he could not say offhand what the legal position was likely to be. I added that essential thing was that they should not be at liberty in Brazil. (TNA ADM 116/5474,10 October 1941)

A handwritten but unsigned note dated 11 October stated,

Reference attached telegram, M Branch is anxious to share all possible information examining escapes of the crew of the Graf Spee from internment, in order to judge whether the position is sufficiently serious to warrant a protest to the Governments concerned, on the subject of their duty to prevent such escapes.

Will DNI please relate the number of men from the Graf Spee who are interned in the various countries concerned, the numbers of men who have escaped from these countries and the dates of escape, if such information is available? (Ibid, 11 October 1941)

A comment written at the bottom of the note read:

Reference B.N.A. [British Naval Attaché] Buenos Aires 1505/3 Oct (tabled A) a detailed statement by the Government of Argentina has been obtained and is enclosed in NID 2706/41 (behind). From this statement it will be seen that out of a total of 1046 officers and crew of Graf Spee originally interned in Argentina, 128 have succeeded in escaping. From BNA Buenos Aires 2015/14 Oct, however, the number would appear to be higher, but as no dates are available it is impossible to say whether the number of escapees has substantially increased since the last protest was made to the Argentine Government: - apparently in November 1940.

It is to be remembered that previous protests have been met with little or no success. Indeed the Argentine Government has stood on its dignity and replied that it cannot accept the right of the British Government to intervene in a matter of internal order and of an administrative nature, which must be settled without foreign interference.

In these circumstances, and in order not to weaken our position should we wish to extricate British seamen from the Argentine in future, so Branch is of opinion that no further action is to be taken. (Ibid.)

On 12 October, NID.2 acting for DNI sent McCall in Buenos Aires and the Commander Henry Johnston, British SO(I) in Montevideo. the following message. Copies were also sent to DNI, O.I.C. D.S.D.p, M.34 and D. of P.

Reference N.A. Buenos Aires 1505Z/3.
Please report by signal
   (i)   Total numbers of officers and men ex GRAF SPEE who were interned.
   (ii) Total numbers who have escaped.
   (iii) If possible dates of escape and numbers in each case.
   (iv) Similar report also required for TACOMA.

This information is required in order to judge if the position is sufficiently serious to warrant a protest to the Governments concerned. (TNA FO 371/25736, 13 October 1941)

The same day, William Marshall, Head of the Admiralty's Military Branch with the symbol M.34, wrote the following note.

> This point has come up before, and I think it must have been in connexion with the "Graf Spee" internees, though I do not recall which was the country concerned. I believe I expressed the view that we could, if we wanted to, argue with some force that internees who had escaped to another neutral country ought to be either interned there or returned to the country which had originally interned them, but I do not recall what, if any, action was taken about it. These papers might be looked up.
>
> I appreciated of course that it may not be to our interest to raise the point, and as to this the Admiralty will no doubt have something to say. In point of fact, under Articles 1 and 4 of the Brazilian decrees of January 25th, 1941 (I think the number is R 985, but my copy is somewhat illegible) if literally interpreted, the Brazilian Government are clearly bound to intern these men. These provisions go beyond the accepted rules of international law, because they provide for the internment of all members of belligerent armed forces who enter Brazilian territory, whatever the circumstances in which they got there, and I think that we made a reservation about them for this reason. This had better be looked up, but if we do not want to argue that the Brazilians are bound to intern these particular individuals, we could rely on the provisions in question, unless it were thought undesirable to do so in view of the terms of the reservation which we made. (Ibid, 13 October 1941)

A handwritten note beneath Marshall's comment was 'Then let us look up the precedents (which I think may be found to relate to Chile) and subject to anything which may thereby be brought to light, write to Adty [Admiralty], urgently, on the lines of the 2nd para of Sir W. Malkin's minute. Sir W. Malkin [William Malkin was Legal Adviser to Britain's Foreign and Commonwealth Office] and Govt. Dept. should see draft before it is submitted to me.'

McCall included the updated figures about escaped seamen in a telegram dated 15 October. 'Escapes acknowledged by Argentine Government Officers 30 Warrant Officers 7 P.O.s [Petty Officers] 37 seamen 79. Statistics probably only up to May 30th 1941. With reference to my 2152X Aug.29th if you have confirmation that escapes have been made in Spanish vessels I recommend action against S/S

[?Spanish Shipping] Lines. In view of (i) delicate political situation (ii) excellent personal relations between Naval Attaché and Ministry of Marine Ambassador assumes no action will be taken as to a protest without further reference to him.' (TNA ADM 116/5474, 15 October 1941)

On the 16 October, P.B. Gilby at the Foreign Office, outlined the legal position.

> In his telegram No.304 of December 26th, 1940 (A 4797 addition (2) of 1940) Sir C. Orde reported that a ship had reached Talcahuano with twenty Graf Spee men on board. The Chilean Government had committed themselves fully to the view that the men when found should be arrested and returned to the Argentine authorities. Sir C. Orde enquired if he could, if necessary, argue that this view was correct in international law, and that the departure of the vessel would be contrary to international law. In our telegram No. 17 of January 25th (A 417) we informed him that in the case of Germans who had escaped from internment and entered neutral territory in the course of an attempt to rejoin their forces or take part in military operations, the Chilean Government were bound under international law either to return the men to the Argentine or to intern them themselves, but that we could not maintain that the departure of the belligerent merchant ship with members of the armed forces on board from a neutral port would in itself constitute a violation of neutrality, nor would in itself be advantageous to our own interests to do so, except in certain special circumstances detailed in the telegram. Characteristically enough, we do not appear to have heard from Santiago what eventually happened.
>
> We should therefore be on strong ground in pressing the Brazilian Government either to intern these men or return them to the Argentine. Whether it would be in our interest to do so may be affected by the following circumstances: Brazilian neutrality legislation goes rather beyond provisions of ordinary international law in that it prescribes internment for all members of the armed forces of belligerent powers whatever might be the occasion for their presence in Brazilian territory, and more specifically it implies internment of the officers and crews of belligerent warships or aircraft who through shipwreck or accident or for any other cause reach or are brought to Brazilian territory (A 3016). These provisions are based on the recommendation of the Inter-American Neutrality Committee, the attitude of H.M. Government towards which was stated as above in Foreign Office telegram No. 966 of June 1st 1940, to Washington repeated to Rio de Janeiro. In our telegram No. 242 of May 26th, 1941 (A 3824) we instructed

Sir G. Knox [George Knox was British Ambassador in Brazil between 1939 and 1941] had reported in his telegram No. 256 of May 13th (A 3564) that the Brazilian Government had instructed the local authorities on humanitarian grounds to treat them as shipwrecked mariners, and that he was endeavouring to arrange for a ship to remove them. Here again Sir G. Knox has failed to report the eventual departure of these men, or the action, if any, which he took on receipt of our telegram No. 242.

It seems to me that while the internment of the survivors of the Britannia required only by those provisions of Brazilian neutrality legislation which go beyond those of ordinary international law, the internment or return to Argentina of the Graf Spee sailors is required by general provisions of international law which we have already decided in the case of Chile that it is in our best interest to press, and that she should therefore instruct Mr. Broadmead to put this view to the Brazilian Government. In order to save time might it not be best to put this view orally to the Admiralty and enquire whether they agree? (TNA FO 371/25736, 16 October 1941) [The Ocean liner HMS Britannia was attacked by German raider Thor on her way to India in March 1941. Passengers and crew were put into lifeboats, the liner was then sunk. 28 sailors rescued by a Spanish ship were taken to Brazil where they were interned.]

Handwritten comments by others in the Foreign Office whose signatures were illegible included 'I agree: we put the case not on the Brazilian neutrality regs [regulations] but on our view of int. law.' 'I confess I am somewhat astonished at legal adviser's verdict. Prisoners of war who escape into a neutral country are not interned so why internees. However, on practical grounds I don't think we should be wise to press this. We are always sneaking people away from S. America (the 'Britannia; lot, sea plane crew from the 'Liverpool' etc.) and we may severely weaken our ground in future cases if we go heavily on record over this. The governing factor is that the Brazilian Govt. won't really do anything – at least nothing permanent – whatever we say.' 'I'm not quite so sure as Mr Steel about this. However, consult Admiralty as proposed and submit draft to Rio, bearing Mr Steel's minute in mind.' (Ibid, 16 October 1941)

The following day, 17 October, Marshall wrote a note for 'Kit' (?).

I rather sympathise with the puzzlement in the first two sentences of your minute, but the explanation is as follows. There is no doubt that (a) members of belligerent armed forces who take refuge in neutral territory to avoid capture by the enemy are interned; (b) prisoners who escape into neutral territory are not.

Logically, it is rather difficult to reconcile these two propositions, but it can I suppose be done on the ground that if a prisoner who is actually in the hands of the enemy succeeds in escaping into neutral territory it is not the business of the neutral to deprive him of the fruits of his ingenuity. In any case, such being the law, the question is which of the two principles should apply to escaped internees, and I think that since it is the duty of the neutral to prevent the internees from taking further part in the war, it would be contrary to the principles of neutrality for another neutral (which would be equally bound to intern the men if they had arrived direct in its own territory) to let them go and thus place the other neutral in an invidious position. In other words, neutrals ought to scratch each other's backs [support each other] in such matters. (Ibid, 17 October 1941)

The Foreign Office's response for McCall was sent in a telegram on 19 October.

> Your telegram No.487 [of October 10th: escape of Graf Spee internees].
> I approve your action. For your information Brazilian Government are in our view bound under international law either to return to the Argentine or to themselves intern Germans who have escaped from internment and entered neutral territory in the course of an attempt to rejoin their forces or take part in military operations. We are however uncertain how far we should be wise in our own interests to press this view too strongly on the Brazilian Government since it might weaken our ground in future cases where we may wish to extricate from Brazil, British subjects whom the Brazilian Government might be required by domestic if not be international law to intern, e.g. the "Britannia" survivors. Admittedly there is a distinction between the two cases since internment of Graf Spee men is required by international law and those of "Britannia" crew only by domestic law in regard to which our views are or should be on record with the Brazilian Government. [...]
> We hope that the Brazilian Government will spontaneously carry out their obligations under international law. Please report position. If Brazilian Government are disinclined to act as above you should refer to me for instructions adding whether you think representations would in practice be likely to make the Brazilian Government take up a less helpful attitude in cases like that of the "Britannia". (TNA ADM 116/5474, 19 October 1941)

On 21 October, Sir Paul Butler, the British Consul General in San Francisco, sent telegram 164 to the British Embassy in Tokyo. A copy was also sent to the Foreign Office, Callao in Peru, Quito, Panama, Washington, Los Angeles and the Canadian Staff Officer (Intelligence) in Esquimalt for the Naval Authorities.

British Naval Attaché, Buenos Aires, telegram 1740 September 30th, not to Panama, Foreign Office, Quito.

I am informed that a number of officers and men from the GRAF SPEE recently assembled in Ecuador with the intention of embarking for Japan on NOTO MARU, A.2. (TNA FO 371/24188,4626, 21 October 1941)

Japanese Ija Noto Maru (Ueda Kihachiro, http://www.combinedfleet.com/Noto_t.htm)

Whether the ship was intercepted was undocumented. The combinedfleet website reported that between January 1939 and 21 December 1941, the Ija Noto Maru carried silk, cotton, potash, steel and oil-based products between Yokohama and Europe calling at Singapore, British Malaya, Saigon, French Indo-China, New York, Rotterdam and the Netherlands. (http://www.combinedfleet.com/Noto_t.htm)

The Office of Strategic Services (OSS), was the United States' equivalent of SOE. Like the SOE, they engaged in subversive activities, some of which were detailed in John Bratzel and Leslie Rout's 1984 article, 'FDR an the 'Secret Map'.

As the United States' continued isolationist policy weakened Britain and its Allies' effort, William Stephenson, a Canadian industrial entrepreneur was instructed in 1940 to open offices on the 35th and 36th floors of the Rockefeller Centre, 5th Avenue, Manhattan, New York. Given the cover name of the British

Passport Control Office, the 'British Security Coordination' (BSC), was responsible for the security of Britain's shipping, helping to protect ports handling materials bound for the UK. Its other function was to influence American public opinion and the Roosevelt government on the risks of a certain Nazi invasion of South America.

Stephenson had arranged for US General William Donovan to visit Britain to study the role of their secret intelligence services, including agent training, propaganda and clandestine warfare, including forgery. When Donovan convinced President Roosevelt that the United States needed a similar intelligence organisation separate from the military and the Federal Bureau of Investigation, he was appointed Coordinator of Information. The Office of Strategic Services (OSS) was set up with an agent training school in Whitby on the banks of Lake Ontario. [Staffed by SOE instructors, it was referred to by the British as Special Training School 103 and by the Americans as Camp X.] Stephenson and Donovan liaised and with BSC help created fake documents and maps detailing the Nazis' invasion plans for South America. The intention was to persuade the United States Government to take a stronger line against Germany. Roosevelt was told that they were obtained following a staged car accident in Buenos Aires to capture a German spy. (https://www.infobae.com/opinion/2021/10/23/el-dia-que-churchill-engano-a-roosevelt-con-una-supuesta-invasion-nazi-a-sudamerica/)

The documents were shown to Roosevelt who made a speech at the Navy Day dinner on 27 October 1941 that was broadcast by radio to the American people. He stated that 'Hitler has often protested that his plans for conquest do not extend across the Atlantic Ocean. I have in my possession a secret map, made in Germany by Hitler's government – by planners of the new world order ... It is a map of South America and a part of Central America as Hitler proposes to reorganize it.' (Bratzel, John and Rout, Leslie, 'FDR an the 'Secret Map', *The Wilson Quarterly,* New Year 1984, p.167)

Roosevelt's speech was reported in *The Evening Post.*

THE LAST SHOT-AND AFTER! History, says President Roosevelt, "'already has recorded who fired the first shot. In the long run, however, all that will matter is who fired the last shot. . . . When we have helped to end the curse of Hitlerism, we shall help to establish a new peace which will give to decent people everywhere a better chance to live . - . ." In this looking-forward sentence the President foresees what did not happen in 1918: the successful co-operation of both worlds—the Old World and the New—in civilisation's peaceful reorganisation. Roosevelt has the bitter experience of Woodrow Wilson to guide him. Woodrow Wilson, father of the League of Nations that the U.S. Congress repudiated, has been described as prophet rather than politician. But Roosevelt is doubly armed, being both politician and prophet. Warned by the failure in 1918 of President Wilson and Congress, the President of today and the American people of today will not fail again. Their weight will be behind the last shot and behind the first total effort to rebuild the world of nations, a natural corollary of the first total war. The totality of the economic damage of this' shattering conflict demands a similar and Roosevelt totality pledges in reconstruction that America—

Fake map showing Germany's plans for South and Central America (Franklin D. Roosevelt's Digital Archives, https://www.globalsecurity.org/military/world/europe/images/german-ambitions-1941-1.gif)

- will be there. Roosevelt the politician has for three or four years led America's uncertain footsteps up the steep path of combat, which, however unpopular, is the only known antidote for combat. Roosevelt the politician has been faced with the task of outmanoeuvring at home his own anti-war factions, and of working up against Hitlerism a war that cannot be called war. Both in the external and in the internal aspects of this complex task Roosevelt has shown astounding political astuteness and patience. First of all, he managed to make America the Allies' arsenal. Then, notwithstanding his domestic enemies, he was able to add to the arsenal policy a pledge to deliver the goods. His principle of national defence gradually became "total |national defence," having as its objective the stopping of Hitler. "Stop Hitler!" is by no means a voice of aggression; the President in his Navy Day broadcast proves—with German maps and other Nazi documents—that Nazi aggression has already remapped South America into "five vassal States," wherefore "Stop Hitler!" means "Stop German aggression in the Americas!" 'and also means for the United States "total national defence." With this logic the President successfully confronts Lindbergh and other pro-Nazis who cling to the legend of the Atlantic moat. Following Roosevelt's placing of a temporary garrison in Iceland, Hitler attacked American ships and warships. Roosevelt replied with "shoot at sight!" Thus naval belligerence has developed—but still it is not called war. Hitler, that celebrated exploiter of the initiative, has been manoeuvred into a position which compels him to take Atlantic initiatives which he would dearly love to avoid, and to use his torpedo tubes in such a way as to justify Roosevelt's logic and confound the Lindberghs, the Wheelers, and other isolationists. Hitler, the greatest opportunist of his age, has been compelled to do things in the Atlantic that "give Roosevelt the vital opportunity to say: "We have wished to avoid shooting, but the shooting has started," and history has recorded that the shootist is Adolf Hitler. Further, Roosevelt has been enabled by Hitler to say: "Hitler has attacked shipping in areas close to the Americas." Thus Hitler has supplied America with an excellent reason for amending and ultimately repealing the United States Neutrality Act, with its restrictions on the movements of American shipping, its "combat zones" and other zones, and its other clauses reminiscent of a period when the United States Congress was seeking any means, however futile, of keeping out of the coming war. When President Roosevelt began, a year or more ago, to reaffirm the principle of freedom of the seas, he at once broke, in principle, with the Neutrality Act and its zoning devices and other restrictions. That Act was a step away from freedom of the seas. It follows, therefore, that either the Act, or freedom of the seas, must give way; and Congress now faces the question of how much is to be removed from the Act and how much left. Hence, in part, the explanation of this Navy Day broadcast. The futility of American-fixed "combat zones" at a time when Hitler is sinking ships "close to the Americas" must influence those Congressmen with whom isolation has ceased to be a fixed idea. Hitler's secret maps of his revised Americas will help them to recant, and-his written plan to re-create religion in his own likeness seems to be solid evidence that cannot be destroyed by mere shouts of "Liar!" from Berlin. America's present position is thus summed up by the President: It is the nation's will that America shall deliver the goods. In open defiance of that will our ships have been sunk and our sailors have been killed. We do not propose to take this lying down. Our determination not to take it lying down has been expressed in orders to the American Navy to shoot on sight. Further steps of great importance will disclose themselves if Congress deals with the Neutrality Act in the way desired. Are the Germans listening when President Roosevelt recalls 1918? The facts of 1918 are proof that the German army and tired German people can crumble and go to pieces rapidly when faced with successful resistance. And are the Japanese-listening when the President confirms the policy of aid to China? Upon American "production falls the colossal task of equipping our armed forces and helping to supply the British, Russians, and Chinese in the performance of defeating Hitler. We will not fail. If it is true, as Mr. Cudahy told the Senate Foreign Relations Committee, that the German people "fear a peace of vengeance," whom, other than the hostage-murderer Hitler, must the German people blame? According to Cudahy. Hitler looks very ill. But the futility of waiting for Hitler to die will surely proclaim itself even to the most rabid isolationist. Summed up, the President's broadcast is, as one commentator remarks, a logical and legalistic step leading the American people to "the last brink of peace." Legalistically. it may not be the last brink; much still depends on Hitler's reluctant initiative. But the broadcast is one more piece of poisoned meat artfully thrown to the mad dog of Europe. Whether he bites at it or merely snarls, the end of the chapter will be the same. (The Evening Post, Wednesday, 29 October 1941)

Henderson hand wrote a note on 11 November that 'On reading rear Admiral Salmond's enclosure it seems quite clear that the escape of any of the "Graf Spee"s crew can only have been due to gross and even deliberate negligence on the part of the Argentine authorities.' Gallop added, 'The Senate asked some very pertinent questions. Departmental memoranda on our attempts to bring the Argentine Govt to a proper realisation of their responsibilities are available if required. It is some comfort that recent attempts from Martin Garcia Island have been frustrated but it looks as though 200 had escaped successfully (and possibly only 128).' (TNA FO 371/25736, 11 November 1941)

A typed report from the Director of Plans (DOP), dated 15 November, stated,

> I view with considerable concern the laxity of control which has been exercised by the Argentinian Government in respect of the internees of the GRAF SPEE, and am unable to agree with the attitude expressed in Head of M's minute dated 11.11.42., which amounts to a suggestion that we should do nothing. We need not necessarily concern ourselves with the hypothetical possibility of extricating British seamen from the Argentine in future action since the whole of the Americas are moving not only in sympathy towards our cause, but towards action.
> 2. In a note in the Argentinian Government dated March 1940 (Tabbed A) in which H.M. Ambassador complained of the measures which the Argentinian Government intended to adopt with regards to the internment of the GRAF SPEE's Officers and ship's company, he also stressed the fact that the risk of sabotage by these German Naval internees was very real. The Argentinian Government in their reply (tabbed B) stated that they could not accept the right of the British Government to intervene in a matter of internal order, and of an administrative nature, which must be settled without foreign interference by exercise of the country's sovereign rights.
> 3. The Argentinian Government have already acknowledged the escape of some 30 Officers, 7 Warrant Officers, 37 Petty Officers and 79 seamen up to about 30th May 1941. Whether there have been any subsequent escapes we do not appear to know. It is, however, material that in allowing this large number of internees to escape the Argentinian Government has not properly fulfilled its obligations under International Law, and we are entitled to complain of the existing unsatisfactory state of affairs, and of the fact that by not properly supervising the activities of these internees escapes which have already taken place may certainly be expected to continue.

4. In M.013797/41 (tabbed C) wherein a telegram from Naval Attaché Buenos Aires inferred that the GRAF SPEE internees were stowing away in Spanish ships and reaching Las Palmas and, presumably, eventually Germany, I suggested that a strong protest should be made to the Foreign Office. No action, however, appears to have been taken on that proposal.

5. I now submit that the Foreign Office should be urged to make very strong representations on this whole question to the Argentinian Government. They might also be reminded that by having allowed certain of these internees to escape and thereby to enter Brazil, H.M.G. have been obliged to make complaints to the Brazilian Government of such a nature as are not calculated to improve the somewhat delicate relations which have existed between the two countries.

6. In view of the recent trend of events in the U.S.A., of the extent to which they are concerned over Nazi activities in South America and of the fact that this large number of German Officers and ratings is virtually at large in no less than six different districts in the Argentine and consequently of the fact that plenty of scope seems to exist for German ingenuity to devise means to affect further escapes, I consider that the [American] State Department should be fully informed of this unsatisfactory state of affairs. (TNA ADM 116/5474, 15 November 1941)

Marshall responded on 20 November.

In view of the points raised by D. of. P. in his minute of 15th November, 1941, with which M. branch now concurs, it is now proposed that the Foreign Office should be requested to obtain the fullest possible information from the Ambassador. In the light of the Ambassador's report, and if the report justifies this course, Foreign Office would be pressed to make strongest representations to the Argentine Government asking them to exercise a much more strict supervision of internees to prevent further escapes. Parallel action would also be taken through B.N.A [British Naval Attaché] Buenos Aires. (Ibid, 20 November 1941)

The following day, DOP agreed, commenting that he felt that 'we ought to adopt a strong attitude with the Foreign Office in this important matter.'

A.S.N, the initials of a British resident official in Rosario, wrote the following note to the Embassy in Buenos Aires on 25 November.

Minute
   KURT RODZERSKI, one of the German seamen interned; Cedula de Identification No. 326, Buenos Aires, December 29th, 1939.
   The above-named seaman called to see me and volunteered the following information.
   That in the house at Alberdi [a neighbourhood of Rosario] occupied by about 76/77 of the interned German seamen, the place is run by a German foreman under a form of military discipline.
   The men pay rent and lodging and are expected to work in the grounds, repair and painting of the house. For this each man receives from the German Consulate (in addition to $90 paid by the Argentine authorities) the sum of $50 per month.
   Kurt stated to me that he had incurred the displeasure of the foreman by becoming engaged to an <u>ARGENTINE GIRL</u> and that he Kurt abandoned the house at Alberdi on the 22nd of November 1941, forfeiting thereby his $50 per month. He added that he is now living at the home of his sweet-heart at Calle San Luis 916 and that he does not intend to return to Germany either during or after the war.
   The visitor appears to be a quiet inoffensive type and although he did not get a loan of $10 which he ended by asking for, I anticipate he may call again. (TNA ADM 116/5475, Graf Spee Crew, 25 November 1941)

On 27 November, Ker noted that 'The First Lord thinks a stiff official letter might have the effect of alienating the F.O. rather than spurring them to action. Perhaps a strong semi-official letter, or even better from the First Lord to the Foreign Secretary, would be more effective. The First Lord would like to see a draft.'
The draft stated that 'Further action will presumably be taken to ensure that NA Buenos Aires takes an active part and provides a better flow of information than there has been in the past. First Lord also observes that D of P proposed that the Americans should be brought into the picture. No doubt this will also be followed up.' (TNA ADM 116/5474, 3 December 1941)
The day before, 2 December, the Admiralty expressed their concern to Eden in a letter stamped SECRET.

   Dear Anthony,
      The Naval Staff are extremely concerned at the increasing number of officers and men from the GRAF SPEE who have escaped from internment in Argentina.

2. From telegrams which have passed recently between the Admiralty and the Naval Attaché, and also from a statement issued by the Argentine Government, it appears that out of a total of 1046 officers and men originally interned, between 128 and 193 officers and men have now escaped. It is reported moreover, that these figures probably do not include any escapes which may have taken place since 30th May, 1941.

3. The last occasion on which the Argentine Government were urged to show greater zeal in fulfilling their obligations under International Law with regard to internment, appears to have been September, 1940. You will appreciate that in the absence of precise information as to the dates of the escapes and numbers involved, the Admiralty are unable to assess whether there has been any deterioration in the position since these representations were made.

4. The Naval Staff, whose views I must whole-heartedly endorse, point out that the Officers, petty officers and ratings who have already escaped from the Argentine are, at the present time, invaluable to the German Navy as submarine and raider crews. There can be no doubt that the German Government will go to the limit to get away as many more as possible, since we know that the efficiency of their submarine crews is already on the decline. The Naval Staff, further, express great disappointment that there have been no opportunities in the past of arranging for the interception of such men as have escaped, since timely notification has not been received.

5. A further point which arises is that the escape of internees to Brazil is raising delicate issues which are not likely to improve relations with the Brazilian Government. This point is clearly brought out in telegram 477 and 487 from Rio.

6, The Admiralty, therefore, cannot but be most seriously disturbed at the failure of the Argentine Government to carry out their duties in this matter, and if their past laxity is continuing, we feel strongly that every endeavour should now be made to persuade the Argentine Government to apply stricter measures of supervision in order to prevent further escapes, and further reinforcement by trained seamen of the German U-Boat and raider fleets.

7. If, as I hope, you agree, I suggest that as a first action a telegram should be sent to H.M. Ambassador at Buenos Aires informing him of the serious view taken by the Admiralty and requesting him to report urgently.

    (i)   the total numbers of GRAF SPEE internees who have, to date, escaped from the Argentine;

    (ii) The dates on which these escapes have taken place;

> (iii) The date on which this matter was last raised with the Argentine Government'
> (iv) The measures at present enforced by the Argentine Government to fulfil their obligations in this respect, and also his personal views as to the effectiveness of these measures, and
> (v) His personal views on the advisability of making a further protest, together with any suggestions he may have, and which could be represented to the Argentine Government, for the purpose of preventing further escapes. (Ibid, 2 December 1941)

In early December, the Foreign Office sent telegram 815 to Buenos Aires.

> Your despatch No.220 [of October 8th: escape of Graf Spee crew from internment in Argentina.]
> Admiralty are extremely concerned at escape of "Graf Spee" officers and men from internment in Argentina. Petty officers and ratings who have escaped from the Argentine are invaluable to German Navy as submarine and raider crews, and German Government will strain every nerve to get away as many more as possible, since efficiency of submarine crews is on the decline. Lack of timely notification of escapes has made it impossible to attempt interception of escapees. Admiralty feel strongly that every endeavour should now be made to persuade Argentine Government to apply stricter measures of supervision in order to prevent further escapes.
> 2. Please now report urgently
> (1) total numbers of "Graf Spee" internees who have to date escaped from the Argentine;
> (2) dates on which these escapes have taken place;
> (3) date on which matter was last raised by you with Argentine Government;
> (4) measures at present enforced by Argentine Government to fulfil their obligations, and your personal views as to the efficacy of such matters;
> (5) your personal views regarding advisability of further protest, together with any suggestions which could, in your view, advantageously be put to the Argentine Government to prevent further escapes. (TNA FO 371/25736, 3 December 1941)

Gallop wrote the following memo on 4 December.

In order to save time a telegram was sent to B.A. [Buenos Aires] in the sense of paragraph 7 of Mr. Alexander's letter last night. [Albert Alexander was the First Lord of the Admiralty.]

Our representations to the Argentine Government up to the Spring of this year are summarised in my minute in A 2369 which shows that (i) Argentine supervision of the internees has been very lax, but (ii) the Argentine Government have been very resentful of our representations on the ground that this was a matter which concerned Argentine sovereignty alone, and Sir E. Ovey has felt that little would be gained by pressing our views strongly.

Mr. Alexander's letter is inaccurate on one or two points.

(1) Page 2 of the Argentine Government's statement in A 8997 shows that 128 had escaped by May 1940 (not 1941). Page 4 shows that 71 are "still absent", and although the point is not made quite clear the presumption is that these are in addition to the 128 which brings the total to 199.

(2) The last occasion on which Sir E. Ovey approached the Argentine Government was not in September, 1940, but in April, 1941. When the Minister of the Interior appeared to adopt a satisfactory attitude but asked that we should not weaken his position by awkward official demands (A 3041).

(3) Rio telegram No. 524 in A 8729 shows that the Brazilian Government are returning escaped internees to Argentina without any prompting on our part, and the escapes are not therefore "raising delicate issues which are not likely to improve relations with the Brazilian Government." (TNA FO 371/25736, 4 December 1941)

A telegram was duly sent to Buenos Aires listing the five requests. Ovey's response to the Foreign Office was sent a week later.

IMPORTANT.
Your telegram No. 815.
"Graf Spee".
1. It is impossible to state exactly the total number or dates of escapes as the Argentine Government refuse official information and even attempts to obtain it privately from friendly Ministry of the Interior, who is directly concerned.

2. Only official statement made to the British Consul on [3 grps.undec.] when Minister of the Interior confessed that 30 officers and 36 men had escaped up to May 9th.
3. Unofficial reports bring the total up to 37 officers or warrant officers and 116 men.
4. No official communication has been made to the Minister for Foreign Affairs since my note of March 12th 1940 based on your telegram No, 72 March 10th and my conversation with the Minister for Foreign Affairs reported in my telegram No.122 of March 13th 1940; but the matter has been kept continuously before the Minister of the Interior.
5. Measures taken for internment of officers and men – whether on Martin Garcia Island or under police supervision in the provinces - are <u>anything but effective.</u> But the Argentine Government based its attitude upon legalistic fulfilment of international statutes or conventions regarding internment and any official protest which might hinge upon admission in (2) above would have also to be based upon the Argentines responsibilities, <u>under such conventions</u>, for preventing interned men from escaping. <u>Unless there is any renewed case</u> of escape I would strongly deprecate reverting to the matter now. We should cause irritation, gain nothing and presumably not have American support. (TNA ADM 116/5475, 9 December 1941)

Two days earlier, 7 December, the Japanese launched their surprise attack on the American Fleet in Pearl Harbour, Hawaii. As well as intercepting, deciphering and translating German military messages, the British were doing the same with Japanese naval messages. This led some historians to suggest that Churchill withheld intelligence on Japanese intentions in the Pacific in the expectation that it would convince public opinion in America to join the war against the Axis.

Sir Ralph Stevenson, British Ambassador in Uruguay from 1941 to 1943 (https://imuseum.im/media/Photographic_Archive/People_surname_S_T/large_PG_13293.jpg)

Also on 9 December, Sir Ralph Stevenson, who replaced Millington-Drake as British Minister-Plenipotentiary to Uruguay in 1941, sent telegram 320 to the Foreign Office, repeated to Buenos Aires and Santiago and Rio de Janeiro as telegram 586.

Secret.
Your telegram No. 93 to Buenos Aires.
   I am grateful for the warning and will certainly convey to the necessary authority, S.O.E. representative, provided local situation permits. This proposal however opens up the whole question of S.O. [Special Operations] activities in this country.
2.   While I consider it essential that His Majesty's Representative should be consulted in view of possible

repercussions of actions of this kind, I do not think it suitable that S.O.E. representatives should have direct contact with him,. These men are operative and the possibility will always exist that they might be caught red-handed [in the act of carrying out subversive work]. His Majesty's Representative must therefore be in a position to deny all knowledge of them.

3. I recommend, therefore, that the intention to embark on specific operations in this country should be communicated to me through S.I.S. representative here whose functions are informative rather than operative, who is already a member of my staff and who is in constant touch with me. This will entail some degree of liaison between S.O. and S.I.S. and I realise that the latter may not wish to run the risks of exposure which might be involved.

4. I believe such risks can be reduced to a minimum provided S.I.S. have fore-knowledge of S.O's local organisation and plans that S.O. (who have probably less local knowledge than S.I.S.) are instructed to defer to S.I.S. Counsel, observing that such Counsel will be the outcome of the latter's knowledge and experience coupled with a knowledge of my views.

5. I understand that some liaison between S.O. and S.I.S. already exists out here; I should feel happier regarding the activities of the former in Uruguay if I were to be assured that this liaison would be manned with more experienced S.I.S. as senior partner. (TNA HS8/113, 9 December 1941)

It is worth noting that SOE had proposed sabotaging ships carrying goods from Brazil destined for the Germans earlier in 1941. The action was opposed by SIS as they argued that increased police and the security forces' action would make the work of their agents more dangerous. The British Ambassador agreed. The Foreign Office imposed a ban on 'special operations', arguing that as the British Government was encouraging South American governments to take action against German saboteurs, it would be politically embarrassing if pro-British sabotage was exposed.

Orde's response was that he was very largely in agreement and was prepared to have an SOE representative in Chile with official status,

> ...in view of the close interlocking of his work and S.I.S. and of the fact that far greater proportion of the former here at least would as I understand it be of unspectacular nature either, contributing to the latter or essentially defensive (obstructing enemy sabotage) which is carefully conducted should not be

indefensible. Purely offensive work by anyone on the Embassy staff might be impossible to approve. (Ibid.)

On 10 December, a Foreign Office note stated 'Escapes among the interned crew of the "Graf Spee" refers to Foreign Office telegram No. 815 of 4th December. It is impossible to state exactly the total number or dates of escapes as the Argentine Government refuse to give official information. The Minister of the Interior confessed to the British Consul that up to the 9th May, 20 officers and 36 men had escaped. The measures taken for internment of officers and men are very ineffective.' (Ibid.)

A handwritten note by A. Henderson commented that 'Although the Argentine Govt. have been consistently difficult as far as H.M.G. is concerned about the escapes of "Graf Spee" sailors, it would hardly seem politic at the present moment, when Argentine foreign policy is likely to undergo a considerable change, to revert to the matter.' Someone with the initials R.G. wrote underneath, 'This is exactly as expected. The Argentines have behaved thoroughly badly and their supervision over the internees is inadequate, But escapes are not reducing at present, and, in the circumstances we should lose more than we should gain by renewing representation. We can therefore wait and see whether the Adly [Admiralty] press us for further action'. (TNA FO 371/25736,10 December 1941)

The following day, 11 December, the Foreign Office sent Buenos Aires telegram 854.

> Your telegram No.842 (of Graf Spee escapees)
> In view of possibility that Germans may make increased efforts to get Graf Spee internees home for submarine crews please instruct all Consular officers to be keenly on the lookout for escapees.
> Please repeat to Rio de Janeiro, Montevideo and Santiago. (Ibid, 11 December 1941)

Also on 11 December, Ovey sent the following telegram to Eden with copies to Washington, Rio de Janeiro, Santiago and Montevideo.

IMPORTANT
My telegram no 850 and Montevideo telegram No.319
> Reaction of South America, including the Argentine, to Japanese aggression appears remarkable. The United States Embassy are swamped with messages of goodwill and all prominent politicians, including the late president Justo, late Minister for Foreign Affairs Cantilo, late Minister of Finance Pinedo

and President Ortiz, have expressed themselves in terms of complete solidarity.

2. The United States Ambassador told me confidentially this morning that he had reason to think that even Vice-President Castillo's mind had been shaken and that he may become a different man. I do not wish to indicate, as yet at any rate, that this means that the Argentine Government are anxious to declare war for a long while to come. Incidentally I see from Washington telegram No. 5676 that the United States Government appear to be hopeful that they will do so.

3. America's rough programme for Rio de Janeiro conference seems perfectly sound but much time must elapse before this meets. Caribbean states down to Bolivia seem to have gone the whole hog [completely] and presumably to our advantage. Uruguay at the mouth of our river is apparently feeling the way.

4. Our joint desiderata appears to be:
   (1) Cessation of all pro-enemy propaganda;
   (2) Cessation of all trade with the enemy and every facility for providing us with the necessary goods;
   (3) Treating United States allies as far as possible on the same lines in regard to non-application (2 grps. Undec.] administration of neutrality laws;
   (4) Cessation of all means by which the enemy can use this country for reporting movements of ships, sabotage etc.

5. While (1) and (2) are perfectly feasible if the United States are merely firm now and at Rio Conference and while (3) can possibly be obtained either openly or by connivance to a limited extent in every state except Argentina. (4) can presumably only be acquired by internment of enemy nationals and breaking off of relations to the extent that no enemy missions or consulates whatever remain. But this would be equivalent to war.

6. Arguments against war are (a) joint responsibility of defence involving [grp. undec.] force (b) greater justification for Axis raids on or sabotage of important industries working for us [e.g. Fray Bentos which was supplying Britain with tinned corned beef for her troops fighting in North Africa] (c) drain on our joint resources through [grp. omtd.] difficult if not impossible of fulfilment, for armament, aircraft and other means of self defence (d) Argentine care of our interests in Japan.

7. Arguments in favour of war, (a) equality of naval and other facilities for British and Americans (b) better Argentine co-operation in every field (c) moral effect of Continent united versus Axis.

Please telegraph guidance. (TNA FO 371/25736, 11 December 1941)

The same day, 11 December, a message was sent to Stevenson in Montevideo, probably by the Foreign Office.

PERSONAL AND SECRET
Your telegram No. 320.
We have discussed your views with S.O.E. and a circular telegram on the functions of the latter will shortly be despatched to all posts in South America affected.
In the meantime S.O.E. would like you to consider the following points:
(1) Subversive work so far as this country is concerned has only been carried out for a comparatively short period and S.I.S. as such has no experience of it at all. It demands a new technique which has been gradually formulated during the last 18 months.
(2) In any case the whole of S.O.E.'s organisation in South America comes directly under their head representative in New York, who is also the head representative of the S.I.S. in the United States of America.
(3) One of the principal reasons for dissociating subversive action from the S.I.S. lay in the fact that the latter, as you rightly point out, are concerned with intelligence and their whole instinct is to oppose any such activities, seeing that from their point of view it tends to disturb the ground and hence to render the collection of secret intelligence more difficult. This point is frankly admitted by S.I.S. themselves.
(4) In other countries and notably in Sweden, Portugal, Spain, Turkey, Tangier (and before the occupation in Yugoslavia, Roumania, Greece, Bulgaria, and Thailand [latter crossed out]). It is, or was, recognised that the head S.O.E. representative should in some way be attached to the staff of the head of the Mission, and have direct contact with him. This may involve some slight risk but it is a risk which we must take in time of war. In any case it has been recognised both by us and by S.O.E.
   (a) that S.O.E. has a definite role to perform in neutral countries, and
   (b) that this role can only be carried out if mutual confidence prevails in the relations between the local

S.O.E. representative and the head of Mission, who should be made aware personally of all important S.O.E. projects.

We hope that you had an opportunity for discussing the whole subject with Mr. Evelyn Baring, who is now engaged in a tour of south America on behalf of S.O.E. and in whom we have every confidence. Naturally, without prejudice to the principles stated above, it is often possible for the local S.I.S. and S.O.E. representatives to make some special arrangements as between themselves, and I have no wish, of course, to upset any arrangement in Montevideo if it is approved by the head S.O.E. representative in New York. (TNA HS8/113, 11 December 1941)

The following day, the Admiralty sent telegram 854 to Buenos Aires and copies to Rio de Janeiro, Montevideo and Santiago. 'In view of possibility to get Graf Spee internees home for submarine crews, please instruct all Consular officers to be keenly on the look-out for escapees.' (Ibid.)

On the same day, Peter Wilding, an officer in the DNI, commented about the Graf Spee internees that, 'this matter has been discussed verbally with the U.S. Naval Mission. The impression was gained that this subject should be taken up with the State Dept. through the Foreign Office. (Ibid, 12 December 1941)

On 14 December, the Directorate of Naval Intelligence was sent a note that the Argentinian Minister of Foreign Affairs had confirmed that eleven ex-Graf Spee prisoners had escaped on 16th October and that their names would be forwarded by mail.

Two days later, Naval Commander Henry Johnston sent the following reference sheet to the NID stamped SECRET in red.

From	Staff Officer (Intelligence) Montevideo
Date	December 16th, 1941 Ref. No. 1302/4/41
To	Director of Naval Intelligence, Admiralty
	(Copy to Commander-in-Chief South Atlantic.
	Rear Admiral Commanding South American Division
	British Naval Attaché, Buenos Aires
	British Naval Attaché, Montevideo
	Staff Officer (Intelligence), Rio de Janeiro
	Staff Officer (Intelligence), Jamaica
	Staff Officer (Intelligence), Callao.

Subject: Crew of Graf Spee interned in Montevideo

The attached list gives the present situation of the ex-crew of the Graf Spee in Montevideo, as supplied by the Montevideo Police to the Minister for Foreign Affairs on 12th December 1941.

Eleven men are shown to have escaped which agrees with the information previously obtained from secret sources.

Montevideo Police
Chief of the Department of Investigation

Ministry for Foreign Affairs
12 December 1941

SITUATION OF EX-CREW OF "GRAF SPEE" INTERNED IN MONTEVIDEO
Exempt from Internment
Physically unfit

1.
Name	Address
Heinrich Kostecki	Timote No. 4600
Ginter Trettin	Timote No. 4600
Walter Buttner	La Paz (Lung trouble)
Leo Bylicky	Timote No. 4600
Paul Lubeck	Timote No. 4600
Gottried Link	Timote No. 4600

2. (Names of internees who have escaped leaving no trace).

Friedhelm Niemetyes	Heinz Taubner
Kurt Diggins	Alfred Fennekol
Gerard Fromme	Heinz Necker
Ernst Klette	Hans Walden
Heblunt Hiersmann	Rolf Schauenburg
Friedrich Hinz	

3. (List of internees under vigilance of police).
   Address – Timote No 4600

Heinze Hermann	Fritz Buthehkau
Walter Muller	Friedrich Kuik
Gunter Zoufall	Reinhard Gossling
Johan Heiss	August Bremes
Helmunt Frunw	Josef Meulemberg
Heinz Heerlin	Herbert Pach
Franz Swarz	Jose Huber
Erich Mayer	Karl Kratch
Walter Weidmann	Wille Kegel
Fritz Schewer	Gerhard Zarksewski
Kurt Holzer	Walter Brosel
Hans Jhan	Gabriel Hurt
Alfred Hermann	Kurl Kalinjus
Franz Bongartz	Hebert Meyer
Hebert Jacob	Bruno Skibee
Hermann Lurs	Martin Jacob
Otto Walchuss	Erich Schlegel

Paul Ries   Otto Zentow
Heinrich Christiansen   Walter Harmann
Rudolf Haag (TNA ADM 116/5475, 16 December 1941)

An SOE report, probably written by Baring on 'The position of Latin American States in relation to the War', stated:

Argentina.
On December 7th, Vice-President Castillo made a "very neutral" declaration to the press, but the Government later issued a decree stating that the Argentine position with regard to the United States would be based on pan-American obligations as regards solidarity, reciprocal assistance and defensive co-operation, and that the Argentine Government would not consider the United States as a belligerent.
The Argentine Central Bank have blocked the external movement of Japanese funds and securities.
<u>Uruguay</u>.
The Uruguayan Government has declared solidarity with the United States and the decision not to regard the United States of America as a belligerent. The transfer abroad of Axis funds has been prohibited and controllers have been installed in Axis banks. (Ibid, 16 December 1941)

Evidence confirming *Graf Spee* sailors managed to return to Germany was found in the Imperial War Museum in London which has three certificates and one affidavit issued to Sub-Lieutenant Heinz Kummer, one of the escaped men, in Valparaiso and Lima in 1940. He was travelling with a false German passport under the name of 'Max Werner.' He subsequently commanded U-boat 467 and died when the submarine was sunk in the North Atlantic in May 1943. (https://www.iwm.org.uk/collections/item/object/1030012334)

Waldock expressed his concern about Ovey's attitude as British Ambassador in Argentina to Gallop at the Foreign Office on 17 December.

> The First Lord is much concerned at Sir Esmond Ovey's reply in your telegram No. 818 concerning the Graf Spee internees in the Argentine. Paragraphs 2 and 3 of H.M. Ambassador's telegram No. 842 suggest that we have official notice of the escape of only 20 officers and thirty-six men, whereas the Government Spokesman, in reply to a question in the Argentine Parliament on June 5th, stated categorically that thirty officers and ninety-eight mean had already effected their escape. It may confidently be assumed that there have been further escapes

during the past seven months, and it is probable that the correct figure is in the region of at least 150.

Nor does the reply show any realisation that the laxity of the Argentine Government in discharging its international obligations is doing substantial damage to our interests. The First Lord pointed out in paragraph 4 of his letter to Mr. Eden that Graf Spee prisoners who escape are invaluable as reinforcements for German Submarine crews. At this distance of time, the memory of the Graf Spee incident may have been blurred, but we, in the Admiralty, have not forgotten that the crew of the pocket battleship were the picked men of the German Navy, and although their long idleness may have affected them temporarily, their old training will soon reassert itself. The Germans are now building submarines at a great rate, and are finding the utmost difficulty in providing crews for them with sufficient professional experience. This fact, and the possibility that Argentine may soon become involved in the war on the side of the Democracies, will, we think make the Germans strain every nerve to get as many of the Graf Spee men away whilst they can. It is, therefore, essential in our view that all possible steps should be taken, and taken at once, to prevent their escape.

We appreciate that Sir Esmond Ovey's reply, though despatched on the 9th December, may have been prepared before Japan entered the war. It is difficult to believe that he would have concluded his paragraph 5 as he did if this were not the case, and we feel that his telegram No. 856 gives us strong grounds for hoping that he will now be less reluctant to approach the Argentine Foreign Minister on this subject.

We are not, of course, wedded to any particular form of approach so long as our object is achieved, nor are we asking that an official protest should be made, though the facts, in our opinion, fully warrant the strongest protest. We suggest, that the line to take now, is that we have good reason to think that with the risk of South America becoming involved in the war, the German Admiralty will move heaven and earth to recover men of such great value to their Submarine and raider campaign. It cannot be doubted that whether South America is involved in war with Germany or not, the enemy are now sure to direct their submarine attacks against trade between South America and the United States. Consequently, GRAF SPEE men who make their way back to Germany will contribute materially to the power of the German Admiralty to execute attacks on Argentine trade, and indeed on Argentine ships. We cannot think that any approach on these lines will cause irritation to the Argentine Government, or that it would not have the support of the United States.

The First Lord, therefore, hopes that you will agree to telegraph at once to Sir Esmond Ovey, requesting him, in the altered circumstances, to make an approach to the Argentine Government on the above lines. We suggest that this telegram should also be repeated to Washington.

P.S. Since writing the above, I have received a copy of S.O.(1) Monte Video's 1956/15 in which he reports the escape of 11 GRAF SPEE internees from Uruguay. This shows that the fear we expressed that Germany will now do everything possible to recover these men from the GRAF SPEE was fully justified. We, therefore, hope that you will either repeat to Monte Video the telegram you sent to Buenos Aires, or else send a telegram to Monte Video requesting H.M. Minister to represent to the Uruguayans the vital importance of preventing any further escapes. You may also think it advisable to repeat to Rio de Janeiro your telegram to Buenos Aires.

S.O.(1) [Johnston] Monte Video's signal emphasises the need for very early action. (TNA ADM 116/5474, 17 December 1941)

Waldock added further details of his concerns a couple of days later.

The reply of H.M. Ambassador in his telegram No. 842 is exceedingly unsatisfactory. He does not appear to have consulted the dossier, because in paragraph 2 and 3 the figures he quotes are wildly wrong. Nor does he show any realisation of the importance of preventing the escape of these seamen. The Naval Attaché would not appear to have brought home to him the very real damage done to the Admiralty's interest by escape of these men. It is understood from Private Office that the First Lord has directed that the matter should be taken up again with the Foreign Office.

2. It is felt that although telegram No.842 was despatched on the 9th December, it was probably before the Japanese attack on Hawaii. Otherwise it is almost incredible that he should have ended his telegram as he did suggesting that any approach to the Argentines on this question would have a bad political effect, cause irritation and lack U.S. support. It is therefore thought that he is likely to have changed his view by now, and this belief received support from his telegram 856 attached. Obviously an official protest would be likely to cause irritation but there is no reason why representations made on the proper lines should have this effect. Our cue would seem to be to represent to the Argentines the menace these men may in the future be to Argentine trade and to Argentine ships, since with the entry of the

United States into the war, it is a certainty that the Germans will now attack Inter-American trade. (Ibid, 19 December 1941)

Johnston sent another note to DNI on the same day, 19 December.

The attached copy of a report dated 25th November by the Vice Consul, Rosario, which was forwarded to me by H.M. Consul, Rosario, is passed for your information.
From intercepted correspondence and other sources it has been confirmed that the Germans are doing all they can to prevent the internees marrying local girls whether of German descent or not as they consider that girls born and raised in South America are not fit specimens for life in Germany when the war is over. (TNA ADM 116/5475, 19 December 1941)

Waldock enclosed a draft of a semi-official letter to the Foreign Office and proposed that the American Navy Department to take appropriate action.
Four days before Christmas, the Foreign Office sent Buenos Aires and Washington the following telegram.

My telegram No. 834 [of December 11th: Graf Spee internees] not repeated to Washington.

Unless you see the strongest objections you should now approach the Argentine Government in whatever manner appears to you most suitable and inform them that in our view the most recent international events will cause German Admiralty to do all in their power to recover Graf Spee internees who would be of greatest value to the submarine and raider campaign among aims of which is destruction not only of Anglo-Argentine but also of United States-South American trade. Return of such men to Germany would contribute materially to power of German Navy to attack not only Argentine trade but Argentine ships. His Majesty's Government earnestly trust that Argentine Government will accordingly neglect no precaution to prevent escapes renewed attempts of which may be confidently expected.

You should not act on these instructions until his Majesty's Ambassador Washington [Viscount Halifax after Philip Kerr's death on 10 December], to whom this telegram is being repeated informs you that State department consider that such a representation would not prejudice their aims at forthcoming Pan-American Conference and that they see no objection.

Please repeat to His Majesty's Minister Montevideo who should take similar action in terms suitable to the more friendly attitude of the Uruguayan Government. (TNA ADM 116/5474, 21 December 1941)

Ovey's response was sent two days later.

> IMMEDIATE
> Graf Spee internees.
> I mentioned this matter to my United States colleague. On the assumption that the State Department will welcome such action we both agree it would be much more forcible and useful if it came from both United States and ourselves.
> United States are just as interested now as we are and joint warning such as you suggest in the form of a note or aide-memoire, and asking for number of men who have escaped would I think have an excellent effect.
> My United States colleague promised to telegraph to his Government. (Ibid, 23 December 1941)

Stevenson confirmed to the Foreign Office that the U.S. Ambassador, William Dawson, had also contacted Washington and that he proposed to include those German seamen interned on the "Tacoma". (Ibid.)

On 26 December, Ovey telegrammed the Foreign Office 'and by safe hand to Montevideo', mentioning that he had received reports of possible disturbances with the internees and that he and Dawson had given details of the reported plot to the Argentinian Ministry of Foreign Affairs and the Ministry of the Interior. 'I still hope for instructions for sending joint notes of warning.' (Ibid.)

Two days later Washington telegrammed the Foreign Office, repeated to Buenos and Montevideo.

> Your telegram No. 7125.
> Matter was mentioned to the State Department on December 24th. They were entirely sympathetic and promised to consider the matter further as soon as they received the telegram from United States Ambassador Buenos Aires, referred to in Sir E. Ovey's telegram No. 921. The State Department have now telephoned to say that they are to-day instructing the United States Ambassador to approach the Argentine Government on lines of your telegram No. 862 to Buenos Aires. The State Department did not seem yet to have received the telegram from United States Ambassador in Montevideo referred to in Mr Stevenson's telegram No. 334 but promised to consider sending

similar instructions to Montevideo on hearing from their representative. (Ibid, 28 December 1941)

It is worth noting Atrevida's 2011 post on the Axis History Forum which stated that,

> From the outbreak of war until the end of 1941, regular transmissions were made from very close to "the Cape Polonia lighthouse"[on the mile-long island of San Gabriel about 35 km from Buenos Aires] providing details of all movements of naval and merchant traffic arriving in and leaving the River Plate. (If requested I will produce full details of this allegation). Uruguayan and British naval intelligence cooperated in a huge search around Cape Polonia which even today is bleak and very sparsely populated (in 1941 five fishermen's houses). The searchers knew that they were looking for a powerful transmitter which would have been large and difficult to conceal, and equally difficult to operate while the search was proceeding and finally they decided that the lighthouse men must be responsible and the two of them were arrested. During their remand in jail in Montevideo the transmissions continued even when the lighthouse was operated by accredited naval intelligence personnel and so the original light housemen were released and it was assumed that a U-boat must be responsible.
> At the end of 1941 the transmissions suddenly ceased. By the strangest coincidence the Argentine island of Martin Garcia upstream from Colonia del Sacramento was used from early 1942 [sic] as a prison camp for Graf Spee internees, and there now began a series of mysterious escapes from the island for which no explanation could ever be found. All that is known is that these men disappeared from Martin Garcia island, and a few months later were in Germany in the U-boat Arm. These escapes are described very fully by Professor Ronald Newton in his book El Cuarto Lado del Triangulo, and mentioned in his CEANA report to the Argentine Government during the period in which he was commissioned by that Government to investigate U-boat activities in Argentine waters. [CEANA was the official Argentine Board of Enquiry into Nazi Activities in Argentina.] (https://forum.axishistory.com/viewtopic.php?f=110&t=222586&p=2102377&hilit=cape+polonia#p2102377)

Benemann's comment on the above quote was that 'it is a statement from someone that is profoundly ignorant of the facts and insinuating a history that is unsupported by any of the known facts. The escapes were not mysterious at all. There are plenty of

Argentine reports (In Spanish) but of course they did not have the German side of the story.(In German) I do. I am having a lot of fun working on it. The amount of Graf Spee men that escaped, and later were assigned to the U-Boot arm is perfectly understandable. However, they were in the German Navy so they ended up on all kinds of German ships, the Tirpitz, The Bismarck, and any number of S boats, raiders, even as teachers in Mürwick. Nothing mysterious about it. (Email communication with Carlos Benemann, 15 November 2021)

Benemann commented that most of the Argentine books about escaping prisoners are "full of it" regarding "reported" sightings of U-boats on the Argentine Coast down to Patagonia.

> There is a lot of nonsense written about U-boat activity in the Rio de la Plata. First of all, the only way to get to Colonia [the headland on the River Plate in Uruguay which is closest to Buenos Aires] submerged in a U-Boat would have been through the fairly narrow "Canal del Infierno" with heavy traffic by cargo ships through this long channel even back in the early forties. It required dredging in spots and still is not very deep at all. Marked by buoys. That would have been an absurd approach by a U-Boat. Inevitable disaster. And for what purpose pray tell? To pick up Graf Spee sailors? Nonsense!! The stories about a transmitter in the area of Colonia are equally silly. However, there was a transmitter set up on the Argentine side of the Tigre Delta. It was of short duration. Mutti wrote about it recently. The stories about Gesell and the rail line on the beach allegedly to unload U-Boat cargo or drydocking discovered later are also nonsense. (Ibid.)

Another post from Ohrdruf on the Axis History Forum stated that,

> Although initially ashore in Uruguay, the crew of "Admiral Graf Spee" were accepted into internment in Argentina at Sierra de la Ventana in Buenos Aires province and on one of the islands in the Rio Uruguay. The Argentine Government was pro-German and so escapes were frequent. Eventually half [sic] the survivors returned to Germany to resume naval service over the 1940-1941 period, mostly assisted by the excellent German espionage network, a series of farms, estancia warehouses and stores throughout Patagonia run by the Lahusen family of Bremen. The escape route was through Neuquen province across the Andes to Chile, and then outward bound by ship.
> Those members of the crew who indicated their intention to remain in Argentina were ordered by the [German] Foreign Office

to form into loose espionage teams and given tasks from time to time. The German naval espionage HQ in Argentina was in a large office building close to the Buenos Aires merchant docks.

One of these teams, composed of two "Graf Spee" NCOs, Dettelmann and Schultz, gave evidence to a CEANA commission in 1952 that on the night of 28 July 1945 they assisted at the unloading of two U-boats near Necochea. Other evidence has now emerged that FW 200 aircraft made numerous flights to Buenos Aires from Madrid between the autumn of 1944 and the spring of 1945 and possibly "Graf Spee" crewmen would have been involved here too. (https://forum.axishistory.com/viewtopic.php?t=66505)

In the Autumn of 1941, the wreck of the *Graf* Spee was examined at great cost which led A. J.D. Winnifrith at the British Treasury Chambers in Great George Street, London, to contact Mr Higham at the Admiralty's Military Branch on 9 October.

> I gather that the position is that £14,000 plus Ward's expenses have gone down the drain [been wasted] finally without any return [benefit], unless the fact is that you have obtained valuable technical information from examining the wreck.
> Before the file is finally put away, would you be good enough to let us know whether in fact you did get anything useful out of the examination. I imagine that this is the sort of case which might come up for scrutiny later. (TNA ADM116/5475, 9 October 1941)

The examination report was not included in the examined Graf Spee files, but there was a note stating that it had been sent to E. in C. [Engineer in Charge], D.E.E. [?Directorate of Electrical Engineering], D.T.M. (?), D.S.D., D.S.R. D.N.I., D.N.O., the Controller, Assistant Controller and the U.S.N. Authorities. S. V. Goodall, Director of Naval Construction (DNC) stated that 'the enterprise was well worth-while, much useful information being obtained.' J. S. Pringle, DEE, commented that 'Only a small amount of electrical information is contained in the report because it was not possible to examine the vessel below decks. (Ibid, 16 October 1941)

Mira Denis, Director of Naval Ordnance, commented that 'The report on shell damage rendered by DNC's representative was of great value in assisting to determine whether our shell and fuses functioned correctly or not. In DNO's opinion, it is essential that such information should be obtained whenever opportunity offers. (Ibid, 3 December 1941)

C.L. Frith, Director of Signal Department noted that 'The examination of the GRAF SPEE by Admiralty Signal Establishment representative was most valuable in establishing the use of R.D.F. [Radar Direction Finding] by the enemy. It also provided sufficient technical detail in this matter to guide us in the search for enemy R,D.F. in general and in the devising and preparation of equipment for counter measures. (Ibid, 14 December 1941) G. Abbot of DTM commented that 'no information of any importance has been gained so far as this department is concerned.' (Ibid, 12 December 1941)

Chapter Five: Developments in 1942

On 1 January 1942, the Foreign Office informed Washington and Montevideo that 'the competent authorities had been urged to reinforce existing vigilance to keep this personnel in their places of internment and, if necessary, to adopt any other measure which may be considered applicable to prevent their flight from the Republic'. (Ibid.)

On 17 January, McCall informed the Admiralty and SO (I) Montevideo that on 6 December 1941, Fritz Notzel and Karl Kruse, both GRAF interned sailors left their billets on 31st December. They were recaptured by Argentine police attempting to cross Andes and were returned to Mendoza. (Ibid.)

The Protocol of Peace, Friendship, and Boundaries between Peru and Ecuador, or Rio Protocol for short, was an international agreement signed in Rio de Janeiro on 29 January 1942, by the foreign ministers of Peru and Ecuador, with the participation of the United States, Brazil, Chile, and Argentina as guarantors. The Protocol was intended to finally resolve the long-running territorial dispute between the two countries, and brought about the official end of the Ecuadorian–Peruvian War of 1941-1942. (https://en.wikipedia.org/wiki/Rio_Protocol)

Following an investigation of Nazi sympathisers in Uruguay which began in 1940, the Uruguayan Government terminated diplomatic relations with Germany on 25 January 1942. All the other South American countries followed suit except Argentina. The German Embassy in Montevideo was closed and its staff left. It is thought that documents related to Graf Spee and Tacoma personnel and the activities of their secret agents were destroyed.

Marshall was the last person to comment on the value of examining the wreck of the Graf Spee. On 29 January, he stated that,

> I am glad to be able to tell you that much valuable information on naval construction, ordnance, electrical, radio and other scientific matters was obtained. On the whole the Departments

concerned feel that the enterprise has been well worthwhile. If it had not been for the fact that so much of the ship was under water we are convinced that even more important technical and scientific information could have been obtained. (TNA ADM 116/5475, 28 January 1942)

In early February, Edward L. Reed at the American Embassy in Buenos Aires, sent Hadow a translation of a memorandum dated 27 January from the Argentine Foreign Office for his 'confidential information;'

CONFIDENTIAL   Relating to the Confidential Report of the Ministry of the Interior No. 296 – Year 1941. Ministry of Foreign Affairs and Worship Division of General Policy
MEMORANDUM.

This Ministry addressed the Ministry of the Interior on December 26, 1941, requesting the adoption of urgent measures in view of a confidential report received by the Chancellery from the Embassy of the United States of America, according to which a movement has allegedly been planned for the release and escape of the 207 sailors, former members of the crew of the "Graf Spee" interned in the Province of Cordoba.

The denunciation having been referred to the Police Headquarters of the city of Cordoba, the latter ordered the inspection of several houses. The only result of this investigation was the finding, in the house inhabited by Horst Brandt in Villa General Manuel Belgrano, of a letter (dated Buenos Aires, May 17, 1941) addressed to Horst Brandt and Heinz Abendroth – both interned sailors of "Graf Spee" – by Jose Kohlhaupt, telling them of the impossibility "for the time being", of their running away from the country in accordance with their wishes.

On June 16, 1941 members of the staff of the Division of Investigations of the same Police headquarters arrested the interned sailors Gunter Richter and Sigfrido Petersen when they were attempting to run away to Santa Fe. In this connection, in the premises of Union Germanica, there was a meeting attended by the German Consul in Rosario Mr. Hans H. Allfeld, the German Consular Agent in Cordoba Mr. Hans Behr, Kurt Bohmer and other ex-sailors of the "Graf Spee". During that meeting Consul Allfeld apparently told the ex-sailors that experts in Diesel motors should leave the country because they were wanted in Germany to take part in war operations, and it is gathered from this – according to the report of the above-mentioned Division of Investigations – that what was denounced by the Embassy of the

United States is a plan which was intended to be carried out more than a year ago and which may possibly have been abandoned or which was left pending by its organisers in view of the difficulty encountered in preparing the escape, as proved by the arrest of Scholz and by the fact that Brandt, Abendroth and Knuttel are still in Cordoba. However, owing to the fact that a flight is always possible, as shown by statements made by the sailors accused, the Cordoba police has established daily control exercised without fixed schedule over the sailors living in the city of Cordoba and it has addressed the chiefs of police in the various localities of the interior of the Province, requesting that they observe strict measures of vigilance and control over the interned sailors. (TNA ADM 11/5475, 2 February 1942)

On 6 February, Marshall made a note on a different matter.

The escapes mentioned in the S.O.(I)'s report are up to 12 December 1941. Our representations were made to Buenos Aires on 30 December. Foreign Office was requested to make similar representations to Montevideo. This action appears to have been delayed until the U.S. State Department hear from their representative in Montevideo. It is preferred, subject to remarks of D. of P., to request Foreign Office to expedite matters. (TNA ADM 11/5474, 6 February 1942)

Stevenson replied the following day in telegram 120, repeated to Washington as telegram 100.

Your telegram No. 129.
Following are my views on the three points mentioned in your first paragraph.
- (1) So far as I am aware, none of these men are physically incapacitated from working against the Allied cause either in Uruguay or in Europe. The deciding factor, however, is, surely, that the German authorities conclude that they would be of far greater service to the German war effort in Europe than in Uruguay, otherwise, they would not have been chosen for repatriation out of the large number of Germans who desired to return home. This is borne out by the fact that of the eight in question, four are trained sailors, two employed in the Rio Negro hydro electrical works, and two are agricultural experts.
- (2) These men are, I believe, under observation, but unless they misbehave themselves they are not likely at present to be put under any particular restraint. No decisions are likely to be

taken by the Uruguayan Government on the treatment to be accorded to Axis nationals in general before the forthcoming meeting at Montevideo of the Committee for Political Defence of America established as a result of the Rio conference.

(3) They might well be fitted into any subversive schemes which the German Government may have in mind. But again, the fact that they are selected for repatriation shows that their presence in Uruguay is not vital for any such schemes. It should be remembered that the German community in Uruguay (not counting Jewish and other refugees) is some 5,000 strong.

(4) As regards second paragraph, my United States colleague's instructions were to agree to the repatriation of any Axis nationals in whose departure the Uruguayan Government concurred, and he shared the latter's desire to see as many of them leave the country as possible. On the other hand, in his discussions with me, he fully appreciated the force of the points made under (1) above. I would not venture to guess, however, whether he would put them forward to the State department. (Ibid, 12 February 1942)

Also on 12 February, Marshall added another note.

Foreign Office has been consulted. It is stated that no further representations have been made to Uruguay either by us or by U.S. it is also stated that in view of our present relations with Uruguay, the offers of facilities to our ships, etc, it is felt that Uruguay fully appreciated the necessity for preventing further escapes. In these circumstances, further representations might be a cause of some irritation to Uruguay and it is proposed that the matter should be allowed to best for the time being. (TNA ADM 11/5474, 12 February 1942)

A further note underneath, unsigned and undated, stated,

Our object is to do everything possible to prevent escapes. This can be done if our Minister makes tactful representations, points out how sure we are that the Germans with their ingenuity will be certain to make attempts to escape and that only by exercising the most thorough vigilance and maintaining it, will they be prevented from succeeding. The Uruguayans should be informed of the escapes which have already been made from the Argentine and how short the Germans are of naval personnel and man power of every kind. The U-boat war has already been extended to American waters and raider activities must also be expected. The F.O. must be urged to request our Minister to make representations on the above lines. The Uruguayans must not misunderstand. (Ibid.)

Also on 12 February, Charles Dodds, the Chargé d'Affaires at the British Embassy in La Paz, informed the Foreign Office and the British Embassy in Madrid that the Spanish Chargé d'Affaires had informed him that the Spanish Government had instructed him to request the Bolivian Government permission 'to allow a member of the crew of the Graf Spee now under supervision in Bolivia to be repatriated with diplomatic staff of German Legation. The latter leave Bolivia later this month. The Spanish Government add that the German Embassy at Madrid state that His Majesty's Government have agreed to repatriate such persons under treaty regarding prisoners of war. I request urgent instruction as to the line I should take with the Bolivian Government.' (TNA ADM 116/5474, 12 February 1942)

On 14 February, Stevenson sent telegram 45 to the Foreign Office repeated to Washington as telegram 35.

> My immediately preceding telegram (not repeated to Washington).
> Group F (7 members of the crew of the Graf Spee). These men were excused internment by the Uruguayan Government owing to their wounds and are said to be entirely unfit for military service. Spanish Legation here has informed the Uruguayan Government that His Majesty's Embassy in Madrid notified the Spanish Government that His Majesty's Government in the United Kingdom would place no obstacle in the way of their return to Germany. Is this so? I understand from the United States Ambassador [John Winant] that the United States Government suggests that these men should be examined by a joint medical board before a decision is reached to allow them to go. (TNA ADM 116/5475, 14 February 1942)

The same day, Stevenson sent telegram 37 to Washington with a copy to the Foreign Office as telegram 46.

> Your telegram No. 2 Circular.
> It is doubtful whether the Uruguayan Government will be able to take advantage of the United States Government's offer (see paragraph 4 of my telegram No. 43 to Foreign Office) except in case of one Japanese national. If and when they take decision I will telegraph again. (Ibid.)

Two days later, the Foreign Office assured Stevenson with telegram 57 that there was no truth in the Spanish Legation's story and that the Admiralty's views were being sought on the United States' Ambassador's suggestion.

J. D. Higham of the Military Branch of the Admiralty responded to Dodds in La Paz on the same day informing him that there was no such agreement and suggested he tell the Spanish Government to raise the issue with him. He added that 'You should refuse all facilities, and you may inform the Bolivian Government that in our view a proper interpretation of their obligations should lead them to intern this man. (TNA ADM 116/5474, 16 February 1942)

On the 18 February, J. G. Ward acting for C.E. Steel at the Foreign Office wrote to Harold Schutz, the First Secretary at the American Embassy, Grosvenor Square, London.

> My dear Shantz,
>
> Your letter of the 3rd April about the wounded men from the "Graf Spee" at Montevideo has been fully considered here but I am sorry to say that we still consider our refusal to give them safe-conduct for Europe not only technically justified but also well founded in expediency.
>
> To take the legal aspect first, as you do, we consider your analogy from Articles 68-73 of the Geneva Prisoners of War Convention misleading for the following reason. The Convention provides for the treatment of severely sick and wounded prisoners of war in two ways only namely (a) by direct repatriation between the belligerents (as we have recently arranged with the Italians) and (b) accommodation in a neutral country.
>
> It does not provide for repatriation from a neutral country of such persons or of internees. On the other hand under Article 24 of Hague Convention XIII the Uruguayan Government is clearly bound to keep these members of the crew of the "Graf Spee" in detention "as long as the war lasts". We find ourselves unable to agree that any suggested analogy drawn from the Prisoners of War Convention can cut down or overrule the express provision of this Article 24.
>
> As regards your suggestion that our present attitude towards these men is inconsistent with our request to the United States Government to help us in obtaining the repatriation of forty-three of our own severely sick and wounded from Vichy [city in Southern France that was not occupied by the Germans until November 1942], your Government will be aware that as between His Majesty's Government and the Vichy Government repatriation on both sides has grown out of an ad hoc [for a specific not general purpose] arrangement which came into being during 1940 and

continued until June 1941. Moreover His Majesty's Government have consistently maintained that though the Prisoners of War Convention does not and cannot apply de juro [by right] its provisions shall so far as possible be applied to military personnel and civilian internees at present detained in British territory. The Vichy Government seem to have adopted a similar attitude on the provisions of Articles 68-74 of the Convention have been applied by analogy to the repatriation of sick and wounded British personnel from France. This is fully in accord with our consistent view that Vichy France is not neutral territory as being in a position to apply strictly the provisions of the Hague Conventions dealing with the rights and duties of a neutral state in land and sea warfare. On the other hand Uruguay is neutral and we consider ourselves entitled to insist as between ourselves and the Uruguayan Government that they strictly apply the provisions of Article 24 of the Hague Convention XIII. So much for the legal side which is however by no means the sole or even principal ground for our attitude in this matter. The following is based on more practical considerations.

Our information from Montevideo is that none of these men are physically incapacitated from working against our joint cause either in Uruguay or in Europe. Our view of course is that from their calling they would be more likely to prove effective in connexion with their own profession in Germany than as political or subversive agents in Uruguay. Nevertheless the important thing to us is the fact that the German Government obviously think as we do since they deliberately chose those eight men for repatriation out of the large number of other Germans who desired to return home. We are in fact confident that while these men might fit into any German subversive scheme in Uruguay they are not the chosen instruments and would play so larger a part than the other Germans in Uruguay who are some 5,000 strong, excluding Jews and refugees. The real German organisation is likely to be formed from among the 5,000.

Apart from the above there is the very important consideration to which I have previously alluded, namely the public feeling in this country with regard to the German attitude to our own severely wounded prisoners. I need not enlarge on it here, but I can assure you that on this ground alone it would be extremely difficult for Ministers to make a concession at the present time.

Finally your last sentence raises an issue which has already been under discussion in Washington for some time. As you know we are most anxious to reach a workable solution of this question and, so far as I know the reservations of our Embassy in Washington have been on a most modest scale. At the same time

I think these negotiations had better be pursued there and I can only hope that your government will after all feel able to take some account of our point of view. (TNA ADM 116/5475, 18 February 1942)

A summary of the Foreign Office's response to the United States was sent to Stevenson in Montevideo.

An extract from Montevideo intelligence notes dated 23rd February stated,

> Original in N.I.D. [Naval Intelligence Division] 01771/42.
> 126. <u>GRAF SPEE SAILORS IN MONTEVIDEO</u>
> The German sailors interned in Montevideo are living just outside the city and have up till now had complete liberty. Since breaking off relations with Uruguay, they have only been allowed to visit the city for urgent reasons and accompanied by a member of the secret police. (TNA ADM 116/5475, 23 February 1942)

Marshall noted on 24 February that,

> Although representations have been made to Argentina regarding the tightening up of the internment measures against Graf Spee internees, nothing has yet been said in Montevideo. In view of recent attempts at escapes from Argentina (fortunately frustrated), events off the American coasts, and the underhand diplomatic ruses being adopted by the Germans to secure repatriation of certain Graf Spee survivors (see MO2121/42 and MO2218/42 attached) it becomes necessary to bring home the seriousness of the matter to the Uruguayans. (TNA ADM 116/5475, 24 February 1942)

Three days later, Stevenson sent telegram 63 from Montevideo, repeated to Washington as telegram 50.

> Your telegram No. 57 second paragraph.
> Uruguayan Ministry of Foreign Affairs have suggested verbally to my United States colleague that examination by Uruguayan military medical board would probably be the best solution. He and I are inclined to agree, as we consider the findings of such a board could be relied on. Joint medical board would, according to the Ministry of Foreign Affairs, entail the participation of German medical officer. (Ibid, 27 February 1942)

At the end of February, Marshall contacted the Foreign Office.

Dear Gallop,

You will remember that in December last we wrote you on the subject of GRAF SPEE internees in Argentina and Uruguay, as a result of which an aide memoire was presented to the Argentine Government on 30th December last.

At that time it was intended that similar representations should be made in Montevideo, but this action was apparently suspended until the state Department was in a position to take parallel action. So far nothing further has been done.

From the information in our possession 11 internees had escaped from Uruguay up to 12the December last. Of the remaining internees it is understood that seven of them have been exempted from internment on the grounds that they are physically unfit while the remainder are under police supervision.

Our views on the absolute necessity of preventing any GRAF SPEE internees escaping from American countries have already been stated most strongly on several occasions, and these views are now fortified by recent events.

We learn from Naval Intelligence Officer, Montevideo, that recently two GRAF SPEE internees – Karl Kruse and Fritz Notzel, who had been interned at Mendoza, Argentina – had been caught by the Argentine police while attempting to cross the Andes and had been returned to Mendoza.

In addition, Montevideo telegram No. 44 makes it clear that the German Government is leaving no stone unturned [doing everything it can] in its efforts to secure the recovery of these invaluable skilled personnel, of whom Germany is in dire need. The Spanish Legation in Uruguay has apparently informed the Uruguayan Government that H.M. Embassy at Madrid notified the Spanish Government that H.M. Government in the U.K. would place no obstacle in the way of the return to Germany of 7 wounded GRAF SPEE survivors who have been excused internment in Uruguay. This statement of the Spanish Embassy, as Foreign Office has rightly pointed out, is entirely without foundation.

It is noted that the United States Ambassador has suggested that these men should be examined by a mixed Medical Commission before they are allowed to leave. Foreign Office was informed in Admiralty letter of 8th September, 1941, M.3035/41, that we are opposed to the repatriation of sick and wounded members of the armed forces of the belligerents who are interned in neutral countries, and that we can only agree to repatriation of such classes of sick and wounded as we are legally bound to repatriate under the Geneva Convention. I understand that the War Office and the Air Ministry share this view. We still hold this view. And are most anxious that the men concerned should not be repatriated since while they might be quite unfit for active service, they would be most useful as instructors for the German Navy, at the same that time releasing fit men for active service. with this point in mind we are strongly opposed to the repatriation of any GRAF SPEE survivors or to their examination by a mixed Medical Commission with this end in view, and we are anxious that the State Department should be fully informed.

La Paz telegram No. 9 also shows that the German Government have been making further false statements through diplomatic channels with a view to securing the repatriation of another member of the crew of the GRAF SPEE from Bolivia along with the staff of the German Legation. This should certainly be prevented.

In view of the importance of his matter and the concern shown by the First Lord and the Naval Staff, I shall be glad if you will agree to prepare a draft telegram for communication to Mr. Stevenson requesting him urgently to make representations to the Uruguayan Government similar to those recently made to Argentina and stressing in addition the above points. We are anxious that Mr. Stevenson should be instructed to inform the U.S. Ambassador that we strongly oppose any suggestion for repatriation of sick and wounded members of belligerent forces who are interned in any neutral country and that, as a result of this, we cannot agree to the examination by a mixed Medical Commission of the seven men mentioned to him. Indeed, we would prefer that the Uruguayan Government should be requested to exercise a strict supervision of the seven men previously excused from internment.

We also suggest that as a safety measure all the appropriate British representatives in the South American states concerned should be warned at all times to deny any suggestion that H.M.G. agrees to the repatriation of German Naval personnel, whether fit or unfit, unless specific instructions are issued by the Foreign Office.

Will you please let me know as soon as possible of the action you are taking. (TNA ADM 116/5474, 28 February 1942)

Sir Samuel Hoare, the British Ambassador to Spain, sent telegram 45 to the Foreign Office on 4 March with a suggestion.

Foreign Office telegram No. 57 to Montevideo.
Releases from St Hippolyte Camp near Nimes (Southern France) of disabled British prisoners (passed unfit by joint medical board) are now being resumed, after being stopped in

the Autumn by German pressure. Forty five such men are expected in Spain this week.

In view of this might it be of advantage to keep the question of similar facilities for disabled members of the Graf Spee crew as a possible bargaining counter. (TNA ADM 116/5475, 4 March 1942)

Five days later, the Foreign Office sent telegram 80 to Montevideo, stamped Secret in green ink. It was repeated to Washington as telegram 1516.

> Your telegram No. 45 (of February 13th, repatriation of sick former members of crew of Graf Spee).
> Please inform Uruguayan Government that His Majesty's Government regret that they are unable to agree to repatriation of these persons who, even though pronounced unfit for active service by an impartial medical commission, might be of assistance to the enemy e.g. as instructors, thus releasing fit men for active service. You will also doubtless explain this action to your United States colleague. (Ibid, 9 March 1942)

Ovey provided Eden with up-to-date intelligence on the Graf Spee internees in telegram 75 on 17 March

> Sir,
> The importance attached by His Majesty's Government to prevention of all kinds of further escapes from Argentine of the interned crew of the German cruiser "GRAF SPEE" has, since my telegram No. 3 of 1st January was despatched, been kept constantly before the Argentine officials concerned.
> 2. As a result of private representations of this nature by the Press Attaché to this Embassy – who is a close friend of the Minister of the Interior – Senor Culaciati has today given Mr Robertson the following figures, which he claims to be authentic and based on up-to-date official enquiries by his Department, which is responsible for the custody of this crew: -

Officers still in Argentine	7	
Petty Officers and men		916
Officers escaped		29
Petty Officers and men escaped		92 (Senate report 99)
Died		2
	925	121
Total		1046

3. Included among the interned men is R. Goesch; whose return to Argentina was reported in La Paz telegram No. 15 of 26th February to you.

4. The numbers given above are substantially those given in the Ministry's report of September last to the Senate. If exact, as stated, they therefore indicate that no further escapes have taken place since that date.

5. The continued employment of a number of this crew in a German-owned factory in Buenos Aires, and a report by a British subject (which I am having investigated) of un-wanted leave-conditions for the men interned on Martin Garcia Island point to the need for continued vigilance; which is being exercised in so far as is possible by responsible British Subjects in various parts of the country.

6. I am sending a copy of this despatch to His Majesty's Ambassador at Washington.

I have the honour to be, with the highest respect,

Sir, Your most obedient, humble Servant. (Ibid, 17 March 1942)

On 25 March, following the American State Department's response to Marshall's letter, he commented,

A memorandum from the American Embassy containing a reply to Foreign Office telegram No. 80 to Montevideo, in which we strongly oppose the repatriation of unfit members of the GRAF SPEE crew from Uruguay, is enclosed.

2. The reasons put forward by the State Department appear to be unsound. It is also considered (and semi-officially agreed by the Foreign Office) that the U.S. appreciation of the political situation is not quite accurate. It is considered that the political situation should be clarified before replying to the U.S. memorandum. The attached draft letter is therefore submitted for approval through D. of P. (TNA ADM 116/5474, 25 March 1942)

A handwritten note underneath read, 'It has just been learned by telephone from Foreign Office that they had already replied to the American Embassy before receipt of the Branch letter, flatly refusing the U.S. contentions and adhering strictly to our attitude of refusing to accept repatriation.'

On 31 March, Marshall wrote to R. Talbot at the Foreign Office.

Dear Talbot,

Will you please refer to a Memorandum dated 16th March from the American Embassy, of which you sent us a copy under

reference W.4106/34/39 of 17th March, relating to our refusal to repatriate certain unfit members of the GRAF SPEE crew from Uruguay. We note that the State department, in spite of our views, are in favour of repatriating these unfit men, stating as their reasons: -
(i) that the continuing delicate political situation in Uruguay makes repatriation desirable, and
(ii) that the potential danger to the common cause that may be done by this group if repatriated to Germany is much less than that which would result from their continued presence in Uruguay or elsewhere in the Western Hemisphere.

2. The Board are most anxious to ensure that these men are not repatriated for reasons which have already been sufficiently addressed. They feel also that the second of the United States reasons is not sound, since, if the unfit men are subjected to proper surveillance in Uruguay they must obviously be potentially less dangerous to the common cause that they would be if repatriated. Accordingly, we feel that not only should we resist the United States contentions but also that the State Department should be asked to co-operate with us in pressing Uruguay to subject the men in question to the restrictions which they are entitled to impose under Article 24 of the 13th Hague Convention. It might also be advisable to point out to the United States that there is no provision in International Law for the repatriation of sick and wounded members of belligerent countries who are interned in neutral countries, and that we have until now refused to agree to the repatriation of any class of sick or wounded other than those whom we are bound to repatriated under the Conventions.

3. From such information as we have it would appear that, while there has been political unrest in Uruguay, the situation is not so delicate as the United States would give us to believe. In fact, the sinking of the MONTEVIDEO and the seizure of the TACOMA by the Uruguayans would appear to justify the hope that the Uruguayans would appreciate our point of view and would be willing to cooperate in restricting the activities of men who are a potential danger to themselves and to us.

4. We suggest, therefore, that a telegram should be sent to Mr Stevenson at Montevideo asking him to confirm that there is no political obstacle to our adhering to the position stated in Foreign Office telegram No. 80 to Montevideo and also asking him whether, in view of recent Uruguayan measures against the Axis, the political situation would permit us to press for stricter supervision of the sick and wounded GRAF SPEE men and, where necessary, of the remaining internees.

5. Presumably you will not reply to the United States Memorandum until we hear from Montevideo. (TNA ADM 116/5475, 31 March 1942)

Further handwritten notes from Marshall followed but none of the documents he mentioned were found in the file.

On 4 April, Marshall stated that the U.S. had objected to the U.K.'s attitude to repatriation and that the Foreign Office did not intend to depart from their present position and would communicate with the Admiralty's Military Branch when they had considered it carefully.

Whether the International Red Cross initiated discussions about repatriating sick and wounded prisoners is not known but on 11 April, the Foreign Office sent telegram 128 to Montevideo, repeating it to Washington as telegram 2379.

My telegram no 80 [of March 8th: repatriation of sick members of Graf Spee crew.]

United States Embassy, having already once under instructions appealed to us to reconsider our attitude, which we declined to do, have now returned to the charge, basing their argument on grounds of (a) international law and (b) the local political situation. We are sure of our position on (1) but I should be grateful for your urgent views on (v) and in particular
(i)   To what extent these 8 men are incapacitated from work dangerous to allied cause either in Germany or in Europe, bearing in mind shortage of German man power and need of trained instructors in matters when physical disabilities would be no handicap.
(ii)   Under what degree of restraint they are now and are likely in future to be kept.
(iii)   Whether their capabilities are such that (to quote United States Embassy) they would "be willing and ready tools for such subversive activities as the German Government may plan in Uruguay."
2. It would also be useful to know how you think your United States colleague would report to his Government if asked the same questions. (TNA ADM 11/5475, 11 April 1942)

Another note, dated 21 April, stated 'Foreign Office reply of 18th April to the U.S. note of 5th April, relating to the repatriation from Uruguay of sick members of the Graf Spee crew, is enclosed. The American note is, at the moment, not available, but it endeavoured to persuade F.O. that we are legally bound to repatriate these men, and also argued that we are obstructive and inconsistent in refusing to repatriate these men on the one hand, and requesting. U.S. assistance to secure repatriation of sick and wounded men from France. Foreign Office reply gives adequate answers to the U.S.' (TNA ADM 116/5474, 25 April 1942)

Ten days later, McCall sent DNI repeated to Johnston a telegram stamped MOST SECRET in red. Given its importance, copies were also sent to A.C.N.S, D.D.I.C., D.S.D., D. of P. and M.34 for F.O. (Mr. Gallop).

Secret sources reported on 24th April that 5 GRAFS interned at Martin Garcia Island on night of 10th April tunnelled from quarters to shore and were taken off by launch. Minister of Interior confirmed escape of 4 officers to Press Attaché 4th May promised to communicate names and said police authorities were endeavouring to arrest.
2. An Argentine yacht HALCON cleared (?Cape) Oliveos for Punta Del Este about 1st February and arrived Tenerife 14th April with crew of 4 Germans. Captain was German owner Meybohm. Crew Helmut Griessmann, Kurt Werner and Kurt Doil. Last name figured as GRAF internee. Other names may be false. (TNA ADM 116/5475, 5 May 1942)

On 7 May, Marshall's typed letter for the Admiralty read,

A letter from the British Embassy, Buenos Aires, is enclosed. Attention is directed particularly to para. 6. Telegram 1300z/6 May from B.N.A. Buenos Aires is also enclosed, confirming the state of affairs on Martin Garcia Island and reporting four or five escapes. It is obvious that the aide memoire of 30th December, contained in M.03497/42, has not had sufficient effect. A draft letter to Foreign Office, requesting further pressure on the Argentine Government, is submitted for approval. (TNA ADM 116/5474, 7 May 1942)

There were several handwritten comments agreeing with Marshall's views. One with an illegible signature stated, 'Concur in letter. I have never yet met a German who was so incapacitated as to be unable to indulge in further villainy.'
On 7 May McCall identified the escapees from Martin Garcia Island as Petty Officers Heinrich Khedimeller 36, Otto Muller 32, Albert Sansonst 35, Willi Swaczyna 36 and Alfred Tetzner 30. (TNA ADM 116/5475, 7 May 1942)

On 11 May, Stevenson sent the Foreign Office telegram 149, repeated to Washington as telegram 132 and to Buenos Aires as Saving regarding another development.

My telegram No. 148.

My United States colleague has given me a copy of the Spanish note. Translation following by air [diplomatic] bag. It asks for repatriation of: -

(a) 269 Germans who desire to return to Germany, and

(b) Germans now interned or imprisoned including twelve members of Tacoma crew interned in Isla de Flores [21 miles [34 km] south-east of Punta Carretas, Montevideo], seven men in prison (presumably those detained as a result of exposure of "Fuhrmann plot") and seven disabled members of Graf Spee crew (see your telegram No. 80).

(c) "As a matter of just reciprocity German Government is disposed to grant analogous facilities to all nationals of Central and South America residing in its territory", including those interned or detained (see in this connexion paragraph 1 of my telegram under reference). Sufficient guarantees would have to be obtained from other interested countries for unhindered journey to Lisbon of respective groups and assent of interested belligerent countries would have to be obtained to release of persons interned.

2. Note adds, with obvious irrelevancy, that agreement has been reached between United States Government and German Government for reciprocal repatriation of their nationals, including persons interned or detained and that His Majesty's Government are in agreement with repatriation of such persons, subject to provisions of the Convention for Treatment of Prisoners of War.

3. Note is a fantastic document, as exchange idea embodied in it implies that belligerent Germans are on same basis as non-belligerent South Americans and infers that United Nations would adopt a similar attitude towards both groups.

4. I have not yet been approached on the subject by Uruguayan Government, if and when this occurs, I trust that there will be no question of His Majesty's Government giving way as regards interned and imprisoned Germans. Moreover, I suggest in the event of His Majesty's Government finding it expedient to yield as regards Germans mentioned under paragraph (a) above, they should do so only in return for some definite advantage such as that suggested in last paragraph of my telegram under reference and on condition that other Germans [?civilians] whom we know to be dangerous locally should be repatriated at the same time (these would amount to about 40 or 50 persons). In this latter stipulation

we would probably have support of United States Government. (TNA ADM 116/5475, 11 May 1942)

The 'Fuhrmann plot' was referred to in a Tasmanian newspaper report from summer 1940.

NAZI PLOT IN URUGUAY
BUENOS AIRES, Aug. 11- Police have arrested Arnulf Fuhrmann, confessed author of a Nazi military plan for the seizure of Uruguay as a German colony. The Uruguayan police have seized correspondence showing that Fuhrmann was the international leader of an anti-Semitic agitation in South America, and leader in plans for armed action whenever and wherever desirable.
A document outlining military plans for the seizure of Uruguay was found in Fuhrmann's files. He admitted that it was in his handwriting, but claimed that it was merely a joke.
The German Minister in Montevideo issued a statement to the Uruguayan newspapers that Fuhrmann was an Argentine citizen of weak mentality and could not be taken seriously. (*Examiner* (Launceston, Tasmania, 13 August 1940)

On 12 May, Marshall wrote a letter marked SECRET to the Foreign Office.

Dear Gallop,
Will you please refer to Sir Esmond Ovey's letter of 17th March concerning internment conditions at Martin Garcia Island, and to telegram 1500s of 6th May from B.N.A., Buenos Aires reporting the escapes of five members of the GRAF SPEE crew.
You are, of course, fully aware of my views of the First Lord and of the Naval Staff regarding the question of tightening up internment conditions in Argentine and Uruguay.
It is obvious that the Aire Memoire which was presented to the Argentine Minister of Foreign Affairs on 30th December last has not had the desired effect. We most strongly urge, therefore, that the Foreign Office should send a further telegram to Sir Esmond Ovey requesting him to take up this question again with the Argentine Government, re-emphasising the seriousness of the position and pointing out that the events have fully justified our fears and complaints in this matter. So long as conditions at Martin Garcia Island remain as they are, these escapes must be expected to continue as a matter of course. In addition, the continued employment of certain of the internees in a German owned factory is a potential menace both to the Argentine and to

ourselves. We must therefore press most strongly for increased vigilance and restrictions on these internees in terms of Articles 24 and 25 of the 13th Hague Convention.

Will you please take the necessary action as soon as possible and let me have a copy of your letter to Buenos Aires. (TNA ADM 116/5475, 12 May 1940)

On the same day, 12 May, Ovey sent telegram 481 to the Foreign Office, repeated by air to Montevideo.

My telegram No. 4.
I have officially drawn attention of the Argentine Government to the escape of 5 further Spee sailors (of which the Admiralty have details) and suggest careful search of out going ships. Should I request requesting photographs of the fugitives in order that our patrols can operate in their apprehension? (Ibid.)

The next day, Commander Harry Johnston, the Staff Officer (Intelligence) in Montevideo sent a note to the Staff Officer (Intelligence) in Gibraltar with a copy to DNI at the Admiralty.

Argentine Yacht "HALCON"
With reference to your telegram 1858A of 28th April 1942 (not to Director of Naval Intelligence) in which you gave details of the arrival of an Argentine yacht "CHELDE at Teneriffe which may have been the yacht "HALCON", I enclose report received from secret sources.

According to a yachting journal, the "Halcon's" length was 10.8 metres, beam 2.8 metres and a displacement of 6.5 tons, no bow sprit. She was built in 1933.

It appears very probable that some ex-"Graf Spee" sailors formed part of her crew and have been able to reach Germany. (Ibid, 13 May 1942)

The enclosed report stated,

Yacht "HALCON" recently reported in the Standard to have arrived at Teneriffe under Argentine flag after 79 day crossing of North Atlantic without having sighted another vessel during trip – stated to have left last February.

Double ender – sloop – Marconi sail – approximately 8/10 tons – was registered in the Yacht Club Buenos Aires, San Fernando, but usually anchored in the Port of Olivos due to draft – hull was recently reinforced, apparently for the trip – had a heavy one cylinder auxiliary motor.

Co-owners Meybohm – Bosemberg – understood first named holds German Marchant Marine Captain's ticket – sailed in race to Bermudas and from there to Cuxhaven [Germany] about time of last Olympic games.

Usual sailing companions: man named Grosmann and another name unknown.

Maybohm: big features and build – fair hair and bronzed complexion – speaks quietly and as though measuring every word.

Bosemberg: about same height, but slim – very marked red and white complexion – big sharp nose (like caricatures of Crown Prince of Germany) might be a Jew.

Grosmann big features and build – rather brutal looking – bit pock-marked – black hair and moustache.

Fourth man, name unknown – small build – looks like a corpse.

From conversations overheard Maybohm has gone in charge of the boat with a crew made up of men from Graf Spee, number unknown, but there are supposed to be a total crew of five.

Maybohm has a coffee business in B.A. and has left a wife here.

Bosemberg evidently did not go as he was seen in Tigra [?] a fortnight ago – he has a shop in B.A. (sells watches and clocks). (Ibid.)

Two days later, Marshall wrote the following note.

A note from the Embassy, Buenos Aires, is enclosed (of date 18th April) showing precautions taken by the police with regard to Graf Spee internees in Argentina.

A telegram No. 481 from Buenos Aires is also enclosed showing that Sir Edmond [sic] Ovey had already made official representations about the escape of 5 internees before MBr [Military Branch] letter of 12 May could be acted upon by the Foreign Office. Foreign Office feel that we cannot now ask Sir E. Ovey to do any more than he has done since he has taken the initiative and an official representation is a strong [illegible]

2. it is proposed to request Foreign Office to concur in the suggestion that the Argentine Government should be requested to institute careful searches of outgoing neutral ships in future, and that photographs of the 5 latest fugitives and any other information which may assist in their identification should be supplied to facilitate the apprehension by our patrols. Will departments please state whether they have any other suggestion which might facilitate the work of our patrols?

3. With regard to Montevideo telegram No. 149, Mr Stevenson obviously has a firm grip of the situation and it is not proposed to do anything more than ask the Foreign Office (1) to confirm that

they have no intention of departing from the attitude adopted by them in their very strong letter of 18th April to the U.S. Embassy, and (2) to requests Mr Stevenson to inform his U.S. colleague that H.M.G. will not agree to the repatriation of interned or imprisoned Germans for the reasons contained in the above latter (if 15th April). (TNA ADM 116/5474, 15 May 1942)

On 16 May, Ovey sent the Foreign Office. copies of the note verbale [unsigned diplomatic note written in third person] he had presented to the Argentine Minister of Foreign Affairs on 12 May and the Minister's reply.

Enclosure in Buenos Aires despatch No. 125 of May 16th 1942

No. 226   NOTE VERBALE

His Britannic Majesty's Embassy present their compliments to the Argentine Ministry of Foreign Affairs and have the honour to inform the Ministry that it has come to their knowledge that certain further members of the interned crew of the German battleship "Graf Spee" have made good their escape from the island of Martin Garcia.

His Majesty's Embassy cannot but view with distress this unfortunate occurrence; and they venture to suggest that, apart from the other measures which the Argentine Authorities are no doubt already taking to apprehend the fugitives, most particular care should be taken to search all outgoing ships from Argentine ports, particularly those wearing Spanish, Portuguese or other neutral flags.

Enclosure in Buenos Aires despatch No. 125 of May 16th 1942
Ministry of Foreign Affairs.
D.A.P. (G)   NOTE VERBALE

The Minister of Foreign Affairs present their compliments to the British Embassy and have the honour to acknowledge receipt of their Note Verbale No. 226 of the 12th instant, in which reference is made to information received regarding the escape from the island of Martin Garcia of several interned ex-members of the crew of the German battleship "Admiral Graf Spee".

The Argentine Chancery have to inform the British Embassy that the text of the note verbale under preference has been communicated to the competent authorities, with a request for information on the subject. (Ibid, 16 May 1942)

The following day, Marshall stated that 'M. Branch shares D. of P's concern at these escapes, but hesitate to demand further representations by Sir Edmund Ovey lest this should result in considerable irritation and deterioration of our relations with the Argentine Government. As, however, Sir Edmund Ovey has in mind a further approach for the purpose of obtaining photographs, etc. it would probably be well that he should take the opportunity to reinforce his representations at the same time, in the hope that measures will be adopted, which will produce satisfactory results and obviate [remove] the necessity for future recurring protests.' (TNA ADM 116/5474, 17 May 1942)

The following day, the *Coventry Evening Telegraph* published the following article.

"Graf Spee" Prisoners Escape
VICHY. Monday, Ten members of the crew of the German battleship Graf Spee, who escaped from an internment camp, arc being sought by Argentine police, says Vichy News Agency. - Reuter. (*Coventry Evening Telegraph,* 18 May 1942)

On 20 May, Spraggett as the Directorate of Plans, noted that,

The efforts of H.M. Ambassador at Buenos Aires have been singularly unsuccessful and indeed unsatisfactory.
The Germans by their persistence and ingenious methods will no doubt continue to outwit the so-called vigilance of the Argentine authorities unless something is done about it.
D. of P. is therefore of the opinion that notwithstanding the action already taken by H.M. Ambassador vide [see] Buenos Aires telegram No. 481, he should be instructed to reinforce his protest on the lines of the draft already approved by A.C.N.S. (F) with the addition of the points raised in paragraph 2 of Head of M's minute dated 15/5/42. D of P would like to see the draft letter to the F.O. (TNA ADM 116/5474, 20 May 1942)

At the end of May, Marshall wrote again to the Foreign Office.

Dear Gallop,
Will you please refer to my letter of 12th May reference L.C.2790/42 on the subject of GRAF SPEE escapees, and to Sir Edmund [sic] Ovey's telegram No. 481 of 12 May.
It is, of course, satisfactory as far as it goes, that Sir Edmund Ovey should have taken the initiative in this matter, but at the same time we feel that merely to draw the attention of the Argentine Government officially to the escape of 5 further seamen does not go far enough. We feel that the matter should

not be allowed to rest at this stage without putting forward the points mentioned in my letter of 12th May.

We fully appreciate that you will be anxious not to arouse hostility on the part of the Argentine Government by continually raising this matter. It is, however, to be remembered that if stricter measures are not speedily adopted, escapes are bound to take place with regularity and it will be necessary on each occasion to address further protests. We feel therefore, that it would be much more satisfactory of the strongest representations were made now in the hope that this would result in the adoption of satisfactory measures and would obviate the necessity of an unending series of notes.

The Board have therefore, instructed me to ask you to take action by instructing Sir Edmund Ovey to present a further Aide-Memoire in terms of my letter of 12 May, making the representations as strong as possible.

We are in full agreement with the suggestion that the Argentine Government should be requested to institute careful searches of outgoing neutral ships in future and that photographs of the five latest fugitives together with any other information which may assist in their identification and apprehension, should be supplied. Will you please instruct Sir Edmund Ovey accordingly?

With regard to telegram 149 from Montevideo, we presume that you will not depart from the attitude adopted by you in your letter of 18th April to the U.S, Embassy. We suggest that you should request Mr. Stevenson to inform his U.S. colleague that H.M.G. will not agree to the repatriation of interned or imprisoned Germans for the reasons contained in your letter referred to above. (TNA ADM 116/5475, 29 May 1942)

A week later, Marshall contacted M.J.R. Talbot at the Foreign Office.

Dear Talbot,

Will you please refer to Montevideo telegram 149 concerning a Spanish note asking for the repatriation of, inter alia [among other things], Germans now interned or imprisoned including 12 members of the TACOMA crew interned in the Isla de Flores, 7 men imprisoned and 7 disabled members of the GRAF SPEE crew.

I note that Mr. Stevenson has not yet been approached on the subject by the Uruguayan Government.

I had referred to this matter, amongst others, in a letter to Gallop some time ago, and he has telephoned to me suggesting that I should pass my comments by separate letter to you. I shall be glad if you will confirm that you have no intention of departing from the attitude adopted in your letter of 18th April, W.5169/34/49, to the United States Embassy.

We suggest that you should request Mr. Stevenson to inform his U.S. colleague that H.M. Government will not agree to the repatriation of interned or imprisoned Germans for the reasons contained in the above letter. (Ibid, 6 June 1942)

On the same day, the Foreign Office sent telegram 498 to Buenos Aires stamped SECRET in green.

> Your telegram No. 481 [of May 12th: escape of Graf Spee internees].
> Your representations are approved and you should act as suggested in the last paragraph of your telegram.
> 2. These escapes show that our previously expressed fears are wholly justified and that unless supervision is tightened up there will be further ones which we shall naturally not be able to pass over in silence. As a result there will be repeated representations by His Majesty's Embassy which will be liable merely to irritate without attaining our real object, viz. increased vigilance by the Argentine authorities.
> Do you think it would be useful for Secretary of State to mention question to Argentine Ambassador and for Admiralty to take it up with Argentine Naval Observers here, or can you think of any other _effective_ action we can take? If matter is to be taken up by Secretary of State or Admiralty, what line of argument is most likely to induce Argentines to take action we desire and so prevent a repetition of these escapes each one of which causes painful impression here and inevitably affects our relations in a wider sphere. (Ibid.)

Ovey's response, also stamped SECRET, was sent in telegram 548 on 9 June.

> Your telegram No. 498.
> Lack of response here makes frank talk by Secretary of State to Arg Ambassador infinitely most useful line of action. I suggest the following approach:
> (a) [Grp. Undec.: ? Remember] that we originally pressed for strict internment but were told that the matter was the private concern of Argentine Government which assumed full responsibility for keeping interned men in the Argentine.

    (b) Senate report and admission by Chief of Police that 40 had escaped, with additional 15 since last September.
    (c) Possibility of a repetition of Victoria incident [?] (my telegrams No. 534 and No. 545) by these very men.]
    (d) Request therefore that names and photographs of all who escaped may in future be supplied privately at once to their Embassy; in order to facilitate identification on neutral vessels or elsewhere.
    (e) Inevitable harm to Anglo-Argentine relations is steady trickle of escapes should continue; particularly if some escaped men should be proved to have sunk meat ships as essential to Argentina as to Britain.

2. Maximum suggested for Argentine naval officers would be a hint of the view taken by the Admiralty for these escapes.

3. To prevent crossing wires I prefer not to take up the question of taking of photographs here until Secretary of State has had time to ask the Argentine Ambassador – at some subsequent date – for results of his representations. (Ibid, 9 June 1942)

The following day he added a sixth point that 'up to date numbers and names of escaped men must also be requested.'

On 11 June, McCall sent a note to DNI and Johnston. Copies were also sent to A.C.N.S., D.N.D., O.I.C., D. of P., M.34 for F.O. and File X.

> Please see Ambassador's telegrams to Foreign Office numbers 548 and 551 re protest against escapes of interned Graf Spee sailors. Senate report of 26th September 1941 revealed statistics of escapes up to 30th May 1941. It acknowledged 24 escapes from Cordoba region but Chief of Police, Cordoba, has just informed via consul that present number is about 40.
>
> 2. Have you any evidence of subsequent war activities of escaped men? (Ibid, 11 June 1942)

Two days later, Gallop replied to M. Branch.

Dear Marshall,

Your letter M.02790/42 of May 29th on the subject of Graf Spee escapees.

You will have since seen our telegram to Buenos Aires No. 498 of June 's reply No. 548 of June 9th. The latter unfortunate arrived too late for the Secretary of State's interview with the Argentine Ambassador [Dr Miguel Angel Carcano] which took place on June 8th, and at which no mention was made of the Graf Spee question, as you will see from the record which is being copied to Admiralty under our No. A543/23/2. The Secretary of State is unlikely to have another opportunity of speaking to Senor Carcano in the near future, or to wish to create one for this sole purpose. Although his undertaking to look again into the question of the passage through the blockade of the powder factory [explosives] materials could be made the occasion for asking Senor Carcano to come and see him, there are special reasons, with which I need not bother you, which make it desirable that he should avoid rather than seek further oral discussion on this subject, and confine himself to a letter informing the Ambassador that after re-examination of the matter it has been decided that we cannot alter our decision. The Ambassador's hint at the possibility of a bargain in paragraph 5 makes it particularly undesirable that the Secretary of State should raise the Graf Spee question in this context. Otherwise we shall have the Argentines attempting to make play with any concession they may make in this respect, just as they did last year with their belated ban on belligerent submarines.

Kelly, our Ambassador Designate, has already mentioned the Graf Spee question to Senor Carcano, and we see no reason why on his arrival in the Argentine he should not himself speak more or less on the lines suggested by Ovey. Meanwhile you may like to impress your views, the expression of which might be somewhat more than the hint suggested by Ovey in paragraph 2 of his telegram No. 548, to the Naval Observers before they leave this country. When this action has been taken we shall feel that we have done all that we usefully can to press our views on the Argentine Government. If you will let me know that you concur we will draft instructions to Kelly accordingly. (Ibid, 13 June 1942)

Sir David Kelly, British Ambassador to Argentina 1942 - 1946
(https://collectionimages.npg.org.uk/large/mw174769/Sir-David-Victor-Kelly.jpg)

Three days later, Sir David Kelly, the new British Ambassador in Argentina, made the following note before his departure for Buenos Aires.

At my farewell visit to the Argentine Ambassador yesterday I told him I had just learned that, according to our latest information, 56 [sic] of the "Graf Spee" internees had escaped. It was clear that many of these might already be back at their old job of sinking ships carrying Argentine produce or English supplies to the Argentine, and possibly Argentine ships as well. The Argentine Government had told us that the supervision of these men was their private affair, to which we had agreed, but it was their affair to ensure that the supervision should be adequate. He could not be surprised if such obvious negligence was interpreted as indicating a positive bias in some official quarters in the Argentine. The Ambassador was very shocked at the figure given, saying he had imagined it was a case of half a dozen, and said it seemed inexplicable. I said that while the first point was obviously to ensure real detention, we wished also to suggest that whenever escapes did occur, particulars including photographs should be privately given to H.M. Embassy in order to assist our controls in identifying the subjects on board neutral vessels. He promised to take the matter up. (Ibid, 16 June 1942)

This report was not forwarded to Marshall until 18 June as the day before, 17 June, Marshall wrote another note for the Graf Spee file.

As the result of M. Branch letter of 29th May, Foreign Office despatched the telegram tabbed 1 to Buenos Aires which speaks for itself. The telegram tabbed 2 and 3 were received in reply.
2, It will be seen from Foreign Office letter tabbed 4 that the reply from Sir Esmund [sic] Ovey arrived too late to enable the Foreign Secretary to put the matter to the Argentine Ambassador. The Foreign Office do not wish to create another meeting between the Foreign Secretary and Senor Carcano solely on this matter and probably fear that another meeting would involve further discussion of the thorny question of permitting the passage through the blockade of machinery from Germany for the Argentine powder factory. In view of the fact that the Argentine Ambassador has suggested that the powder factory question might be the subject of a bargain, M. Branch fully concurs that it would be unwise to raise the question of the GRAF SPEE internees in any correspondence relating to the machinery for the powder factory. It is in addition undesirable to make a question such as internment a matter of bargaining.
6. In these circumstances M. Branch agrees with the Foreign Office suggestion that this matter should form the subject of representations by the Ambassador designate to Argentina on the lines indicated in telegrams 2 and 3. A draft letter to Foreign Office is submitted through D. of P. for approval.
7. With regard to the suggestion that our views might be impressed on the two Argentinian naval observers now in London, it is considered that we can probably make a good impression on these officers in their present pro-British frame of mind. The extent of their influence in Argentine official circles is not known. Probably the best method of approaching these officers would be an informal visit to their hotel by D.D.N.I. [Deputy Director of Naval Intelligence] to take action in terms of the enclosed draft personal minute, which is also submitted for approval.
8. It is requested that early consideration be given to this paper. Action by D.D.N.I. if approved, will require to take place within the next 8 or 9 days, as the officers concerned are leaving the country at the end of this period. (TNA ADM 116/5474, 17 June 1942)

Spraggett commented, 'Concur generally with M Branch, and in the draft letter as amended. An addition has been made to the details which have been proposed to D.D.N.I., who may think it less pointed if arrangements could be made for the two officers to come and say good bye to him before they leave. (Ibid, 18 June 1942)

When Gallop sent Marshall Kelly's report, he added 'As Kelly preferred not to have to take this disagreeable question up with the Argentine Government immediately on his arrival in Buenos Aires, he took the opportunity of a farewell visit to the Argentine Ambassador her to speak on the lines agreed.' (Ibid.)

Marshall replied with the following note the same day.

Dear Gallop,

Will you please refer to your letter of 13th June reference A.5467/55/51 on the subject of the GRAF SPEE internees in Argentina.

2. I have seen the various telegrams referred to by you. We appreciate the undesirability of raising this question with the Argentine Ambassador in the same context as the Powder Factory question. We also note that it is considered undesirable to create a special interview solely for the purposes of discussing this question.

3. In these circumstances we agree that the Ambassador Designate should be instructed to raise the matter on his arrival in the Argentine and to make the strongest representations. We would also like to see included in the instructions the points mentioned in the third paragraph of my letter of 12th May, M.02790/42. The Admiralty would like to see a draft of your proposed instructions for any comments we may have.

4. We welcome the suggestions that this matter should be mentioned by us to Commander Brunet and Lieutenant Fisher [The Argentinian Naval officers in London]

With this end in view we are making arrangements for a Senior Officer of the Naval Intelligence Division to meet these officers and discuss the matter informally.

P.S. Since writing the above the undernoted information concerning the subsequent activities of escapees has come to hand. I suggest that it would be most valuable ammunition for the Ambassador Designate in his representations. I may therefore suggest that this information should be included in the instructions to Kelly.

(1) Korvette Kapitan Wattenberg is now a successful U-Boat C.O.
(2) Kapitan Leutnant Schiebusch is now a U-Boat C.O.

(3) Ober Leutnant Kummer now serving in U-Boat probably as C.O.
(4) Ober Leutnant Murrim now U-Boat C.O.
(5) Ober Leutnant Rotsch is now a Prisoner of War from 8.38 [?].
(6) Ober Leutnants Spiering and Hosenach known to be in Germany/
(7) Leutnant Zue See Dietrich known to be on active service.
(8) Korvette Kapitan Ascher, now escaped, was, when interned, recipient of anti-British propaganda from Kapitan Zur See von Euler. (Ibid.)

Marshall sent a note to DDNI the same day with an up-to-date report.

>The attached minute, which is more or less a brief, has been approved by the Board. Will you please make the necessary arrangements to speak to these officers, presumably by inviting them to visit you in your office.
>Lt. Cdr. Stubbs, R.N, is acting as conducting officer to the South American party as is resident with them at Claridge's Hotel. Perhaps you could make arrangements through him to have Commander Brunet and Lieutenant Fisher visit you.
>If there are any other points in which you wish assistance or further information, M. Branch will be only too pleased to help. It is to be noted that the Argentine Officers are expected to leave this country within the next 8 to 10 days. Thus, action would require to be taken at the earliest possible date.

>D.D.N.I,
>The Admiralty, since December 1939, have been greatly concerned over the question of the measures taken by the Argentine Government to prevent the escape of the members of the GRAF Spee crew who were interned there in that month.
>Since early 1940 until now the Foreign Office has made regular representations with regard to the measures adopted but despite all notes and verbal protests, escapes continue. The Ambassador Designate to the Argentine is being instructed to make further representation on his arrival in Buenos Aires, but it is not unlikely that these representations will produce no greater results than past efforts unless additional pressure is brought to bear from other quarters.
>The Foreign Office are agreeable to the Admiralty impressing their views on the two Argentine Naval Officers who are at present staying at Claridge's Hotel as guests of the Admiralty. These officers are Commander Ramon Brunet and Lieutenant

Benno Fisher. D.D.N.I. is requested to arrange an informal meeting with Commander brunet and Lieutenant Fisher and to discuss the matter with them on a man-to-man basis. It is requested that these officers may be impressed with the fact that the spreading of the Naval war and intensification of U-boat warfare make it imperative that Germany should avail herself of the services of every trained seaman on whom she can lay hands. Accordingly, no stone is left unturned in the efforts to secure escapes of these highly trained men from the Argentine who were once the cream of the German Navy. In these circumstances, it is essential that Argentina should increase her internment restructions [sic] and the Admiralty is deeply concerned in this question, not only from the legal point of view but also to the end of denying to the enemy the services of as many men as possible.

The presence of U-boats in American waters makes it fairly certain that increased efforts will now be made to assist escapes. The Argentine officers will appreciate that these U-boats are a danger to Argentine shipping, as well as to Allied shipping trading with the Argentine and other American states. In addition, the extraordinary amount of liberty enjoyed by the internees must constitute a menace to Argentine internal security as well as to Allied interests. In this connection is should be noted that the interned members of the GRAF SPEE are situated in not less than 6 areas viz: -

Buenos Aires City	148	Mendoza	92
Cordoba	207	Santa Fe	181
San Juan	47	Martin Garcia Island	241

The legal aspect of the matter need not be discussed in view of the forthcoming diplomatic representations. It would, however, be greatly appreciated if Commander Brunet and Lieutenant Fisher would mention the Admiralty views in such quarters as they feel able, and stress the seriousness of the position, with the object of having internment restrictions greatly increased.

The undernoted points will be of use to D.D.N.I. in his conversation.

(1) The crew of the GRAF SPEE were concentrated in Buenos Aires on 18th December 1939 numbered 1,055 officers and men.

(2) According to official statements and admissions of the Argentine Government, the number of internees who escaped up to 31st May, 1941, was between 128 and 153.

(3) In October 1941 a further 11 internees succeeded in escaping.

(4) In April 1942 five internees escaped from Martin Garcia Island.

(5) Other GRAF SPEE men had actually escaped but been recaptured in December, 1941.

(6) The fact that about 15% of the internees have escaped shows that the internment measures adopted to date are far from satisfactory and that much more strict supervision is required; possibly the only effective method is the establishment of internment camps.

(7) Official notes and an aide-memoire have been presented to the Argentine Government on various occasions, but the escapes continue.

(8) The Germans have even gone so far as to make untruthful diplomatic representations with a view to persuading the Uruguayan Government to repatriate certain internees held in Uruguay. In this instance, the Spanish Legation in Uruguay informed the Uruguayan Government that H.M. Embassy at Madrid had notified the Spanish Government that H.M. Government in the U.K. would place no obstacle in the way of the return to Germany of seven GRAF SPEE survivors from Uruguay. This statement was far from being the truth; not only had H.M. Government made no such statement, but in point of fact they were strongly opposed to repatriation of any GRAF SPEE internees. This case, however, illustrates just how far the Germans are prepared to go in their efforts to secure the services of GRAF SPEE internees. (Ibid.)

When more than three million German and Axis troops invaded the Soviet Union in April 1941, the German High Command began a programme of encouraging men from occupied territory to go and work in German farms, mines and industries to release German men to join the armed forces. With the Allied Navies and Air Forces sinking German U-Boats and other Kriegsmarine shipping, there was also an increased demand for men to replace those drowned or captured sailors.

The following day, 19 June, Marshall wrote again to the Foreign Office.

Dear Gallop,
Your letter of 18th June A.5632/55/2 crossed with my letter of same date, M.0290/42.
2. It is greatly to be hoped that it is not intended that Kelly's conversation with the Argentine Ambassador should take the

place of formal representations immediately after his arrival in Buenos Aires. Should, however, this be the intention, then we cannot regard the position as being satisfactory. It was understood from your letter of 13th June that we were to have an opportunity of seeing your draft instructions to Kelly. With this in view we had been endeavouring to obtain the additional information contained in the postscript to my letter of 18th June.

3. I wish to emphasise that Kelly's information as to numbers of escapees is by no means accurate. Instead of 56 escapes having taken place, the numbers are believed to be no less than 160 and probably more. That is, about 15% of the total number of internees. Of the original number of officers about 85% have escaped.

4. In addition we are of opinion that Kelly might have laid greater stress on the obligations of Argentina under International Law. Particular reference should also have been made to:

(a) the conditions at Martin Garcia island.
(b) The potential menace to internal and Allied interests constituted by the employment of the internees in a German factory.
(c) The wide areas over which adequate supervision extremely difficult and actually inviting escape.

5. When, added to these points, account is taken of the evidence of subsequent activities of escapees vide [see] my letter of 18th June, it is obvious that the present state of affairs cannot be allowed to continue. We feel, therefore, that Kelly should as soon as possible after his arrival in Buenos Aires, make formal representatives [sic] to the Argentine Government. We should be glad to see your instructions in draft.

6. I understand that Colonel Spraggett [Admiralty's Plans Division] has spoken to [Rear Admiral] Sir David Scott, emphasising the feelings of the Naval Staff on this matter. (Ibid, 19th June 1942)

On the same day, McCall was sent the names and details of the eight men escapees who had returned to active service so that he might use them as evidence with his Argentine contacts.

The following day, 20 June, the Foreign Office sent telegram 521 to Buenos Aires.

Your telegrams Nos. 548 and 551 9of June 9th and 10th: Graf Spee internees in Argentina[arrived too late for my interview with Argentine Ambassador whom in shall have no opportunity of seeing again for the present. Accordingly Sir D. Kelly discussed matter with Argentine Ambassador on June 15th on lines that many of these men might be sinking ships carrying Argentine produce or British supplies to the Argentine, and possibly Argentine ships too. Argentine Government had told us that supervision of these men was their private affair. We agreed but it was also their duty to ensure that supervision should be adequate. He must not be surprised if such obvious negligence was interpreted as indicating a positive bias in some official quarters in the Argentine. Ambassador was very shocked at figure of 126 which Sir D. Kelly gave him on basis of your despatch No. 75, saying that he had imagined not more than half a dozen were in question. Matter seemed to him inexplicable and he undertook to telegraph to his Government. Sir D. Kelly said that besides ensuring effective detention we wished also to suggest that whenever escapes occurred particulars including photographs should be privately given to his Majesty's Embassy in order to assist our controls in identifying escaped internees on board neutral vessels. (Ibid, 20 June 1942)

A couple of days later, McCall sent DNI a query. 'Our record number 4 as MUMM number 6 as RASENACH [corrected to RASENACK] and TATSCH [corrected to RATSCH]. Please verify.' The following day. the Admiralty informed McCall that 'Ober Leutnant Bluxlau certainly active probably in U-boat.' On the same day, Gallop wrote to Don Ricardo J. Siri, the Charges d'Affaires at the Argentine Embassy in London. A copy was sent to Marshall as requested.

My dear Siri,
On June 16th I took advantage of a visit from you here to correct the figure which, as the result of a typing error, Sir David Kelly had given your Ambassador of the number of officers and men of the "Graf Spee" who had escaped from internment in Argentina, and to let you know, on the basis of official Argentine statements, that the total amounted to at least 126, and not 56 as Sir D. Kelly had said. I also mentioned that no less than 29 out of 36 of the officers had escaped.
I am now able to give you information which has reached use in regard to the subsequent activities of these officers. Korvette Kapitan Wattenberg, Kapitan Leutnant Schiebusch and Ober Leutnant Murrim are now known to be Commanding Officers of U-boats, and the first of them a particularly successful one. Ober leutnant Kimmer is known to be serving in a U-boat, most probably as Commanding Officer. Ober-leutnant Bludau is now on active service, probably on a U-boat. Leutnant Zue See Dietrich is also known to be on active service. Ober Leutnant Rotsch, who was serving in a U-boat, is now a British Prisoner of

War. Ober Leutnants Spiering and Hosenach are known to have reached Germany. There is no reasons to suppose that this information is complete, and there is on the contrary every reason to suppose that other of the escaped officers are, as we have from the first feared, now, as a result of their escape, taking an active part in the German war effort. Indeed, as Sir D. Kelly pointed out to your Ambassador, there is every likelihood, in view of their experience in the "Graf Spee", that many of these officers are now operating <u>inter alia</u>, against Argentine shipping, in the South Atlantic, and the possibility must by no means be excluded that they have themselves been responsible for the torpedoing of the Argentine ships "Victoria" and "Rio Tercero".

A further detail of reliable information which has reached us is that one of the escaped officers, Korvette Kapitan Ascher, was, while interned in Argentina, receiving anti0British propaganda from Kapitan Zur See von Kuler.

I hope that your Ambassador will see his way to supplement any report he may have made, as a result of his conversation with Sir D. Kelly, with this information, which should go far to explain to the Argentine Government the interest which we have always shown in the effective internment of these men – an interest which at times they have appeared to resent, but from which they no less than we stand to gain owing to the ever-increasing threat which the recruiting by the Garman Navy of submarine crews constitutes to international trade at sea, whether belligerent or neutral. (Ibid, 23 June 1942)

Telegrams in late June from Buenos Aires to Foreign Office reported 'ship sunk off New York not Brazil.' 'Argentine Ministry of Marine communique states German submarine Innsbruck torpedoes Krio Tercero without warning, killing give, wounding one.' Commander Dillon Robinson, Director of the Admiralty's Plans Division added the comment 'This may be of use to you in your propaganda about Graf Spee.' (Ibid, 23-24 June 1942)

Also included in the Graf Spee file was the following transcription with the comment 'On instructions of AD of C' (Assistant Director of Communications).

<u>EXTRACT FROM GERMAN BROADCAST 20.6.42</u>

Asked how he came by a small black pig as the result of an Atlantic cruise, U-boat Captain says he was operating in waters fairly familiar to him from his cruise in the Graf Spee at the beginning of the war.<u> They sank a British tanker under ballast and then an armed Brazilian</u> – a welcome find, for armed neutral ships are no longer neutral. After one torpedo, launched in an underwater attack, the Brazilian broke in two, "a particularly fine spectacle" – and the U-boats crew collected some hens, two pigs, despite the oil on surface. A few days later, they sank a freighter, then a British three-mast schooner, which hove to after shots had been fired across her bow. The Captain, in white drill and his negro crew held up their hands. The U-boat Captain shouted, in English; "Leave your ship, I sink you" and they all took to their boat. After sinking the schooner with a few shells, the Germans picked up a little pig, and christened it "Florence Doublas" – the Schooner was the Florence Douglas of Demarar. Hardly was the ceremony over, when a plane arrived and they had to crash dive.

It is known that among the many many officers of the Graf Spee who escaped from internment in the Argentine ten officers made their way back to Germany. Of these, one, Ober-Leutnant Ratsch, has been made prisoner of war after the small craft was sunk under him by British forces in the North Sea. Of the other nine who reached Germany, six are known to be on active service, three of them Commanding Officers of U0-boats.

It is possible that it is one of these who sank the Brazilian steamer referred to in the broadcast above.

The Ministry of Information, Latin-America Section, will arrange for this to appear in the press and local broadcasts in the following countries: 0 Brazil, Bolivia, Peru, Uruguay, Chile. Under no circumstances will this information be quoted as from a London or official source.

The M.O.I. [Ministry of Information] think that if it is desired for this to be put out in the Argentine itself, it would be better done by S.O.E. they will leave this matter for the Admiralty to arrange direct. They suggest that if planted on the Uruguayan Correspondent of "Efe" it may well draw some remark from Germany. (Ibid, 24 June 1942)

The Special Operations Executive (SOE) had been established in August 1940 under Winston Churchill's order 'to set Europe ablaze by sabotage'. The British Cabinet authorised it 'to co-ordinate all action by way of subversion and sabotage against the enemy overseas.' As well as training agents and infiltrating them for sabotage and subversion missions, they also arranged supplies to be parachuted to resistance movements and were involved in manufacturing and disseminating propaganda.

In early June, the British Chiefs of Staff sent memo W 198 to the Joint Staff Mission.

MOST SECRET
1. We are anxious to see an end of Axis machinations in Latin America which constitute serious potential threat to Allied supplies and are a dangerous fount of espionage and general fifth column [group of people who undermine others in support of the enemy - i.e. pro-Axis civilians] work
2. United States policy has been to rely on normal relations and economic hold over Latin American Governments to keep such activities in check. Donovan has been prevented from operating there and only activity has been limited security control by Federal Bureau of Investigation.
3. Our policy in regard to secret anti-Axis activity has been one of laisser-faire [let it happen], to avoid risk of upsetting Latin American States or acting against wishes of [US] State Department although over security measures to prevent sabotage to ships and cargoes have been organised in all major ports by British Security Co-ordination.
4. Except for above security organisation in paragraph 3, Axis have virtually had a free run. It is therefore highly important that secret work should start quickly before Axis increase their lead.
5. It would obviously be preferable for U.S. to initiate this work and that it should be controlled un Washington, but if they are reluctant to act we must try to obtain permission to act alone.
6. To enable work to start quickly and efficiently we have recommended to Ministers concerned that resources of both I.S. and S.O.E, should be made available, making clear that our help would be directed solely against enemy or enemy-controlled nationals and organisations.
7. We have also recommended that British Security Co-ordination should extend their over security measures in collaboration with U.S. authorities. This would be entirely separate from secret organisations although intelligence would be contributed to common pool.
8. We understand Marshall intended to discuss whole subject with President on return but do not know whether he has yet done this.
9. Above is for your information only. We are asking for necessary Ministerial authority. (TNA CAB 122/1587 9 June 1942)

The 'overt security measures' included 'bringing up employees of the various British firms in South America for training in this country in anti-sabotage arrangements. A good deal of work has already been sone in this respect. (Ibid, 1 July 1942)
Hadow sent the Foreign Office telegram 585 on 24 June.

Your telegram No. 521.
 I addressed today personal letter to Under Secretary of State giving names and details supplied by [grp undec:?Portuguese] naval Attaché of escaped Graf Spee officers now commanding or serving in U-boasts etc and asking on basis of recent sinking of Argentine vessels for reinforced precautions to prevent the escape of men dangerous to Argentine as well as ourselves.
2. Pending written reply Under Secretary of State informs me verbally that Minister for Foreign Affairs will at once take up matter personally with the Minister of Marine and that "most vigorous" measures will be taken.
3. Photographs of all escaped men also requested. (TNA ADM 116/5474, 24 June 1942)

The following day, McCall was sent the names of the three Germans, correctly spelt. On 25 June, he contacted DNI welcoming 'any evidence that four ex GRAF officers now U Boat commanders have attacked Latin American shipping.' Copies were also sent to the Naval Attaché in Washington, S.O.(I) Montevideo, 1st Lord, 1st S.L., V.C.N.S., A.C.N.S., P.A.S., D. of P., O.D. M, O.I.C. and File X. (Ibid, 26 June 1942)
On 27 June, the Foreign Office sent telegram 541 to Buenos Aires, repeated to Washington as No. 4022.

Your telegram No. 585 [of June 24th: Escape of Graf Spee internees in Argentina].
 Following for Sir D. Kelly.
   You should take an early opportunity of reinforcing Mr. Hadow's representations and your remarks to Argentine Ambassador in London by drawing attention of Argentine Government by deplorable impression which has been created here by the ineffectiveness of measures to intern officers and men of "Graf Spee". You should begin by recalling Sir E. Ovey's note to Argentine M.F.A. of March 12th 1940 in which he referred to the Argentine's obligations under Article 10 of the 10th Hague Convention and pointed out that the measures which the Argentine Government were taking were insufficient to secure the fulfilment of the obligation to guard internees "so as to prevent them from again taking part in the operations of the war." Argentine reply of March 20th admitted their obligations under the Convention but maintained that it was for them to decide "the methods of applying this measure" (which His Majesty's Government have never contested), and that what they were

doing was sufficient to fulfil their obligation to ensure the peaceful status of the internees "in such a way that they are unable again to take part in operations of war." This statement subsequent developments have signally failed to confirm as a result of which His Majesty's Government have been obliged over a period of 2 years to address frequent representations to the Argentine Government.

2. On the latter's own admission (your despatch No. 75 and your telegram No. 481), escapes amount to at least 126 including 29 out of 36 officers, of whom as you are aware many have taken active part in hostilities, in some cases as commanders of U-boats.

3. You should accordingly press the Argentine Government to take vigorous measures to secret the effective internment of those officers and men who have not yet escaped, drawing their attention at your discretion to (a) the conditions at Martin Garcia Island, (b) the political menace to internal and Allied interests constituted by the employment of the internees in a German factory, and (c) the wide areas over which the internees are spread, rendering adequate supervision difficult. You should make what play you can with sinkings of Argentine ships and possibility that escaped internees may themselves have been responsible for them, and you should endorse Mr. Hadow's request for photographs of escaped men and ask for up-to-date figures of escapes. (Ibid, 27 June 1942)

Two days later, Marshall contacted the Foreign Office again.

Dear Gallop,

We spoke recently regarding the exact number of escapes of GRAF SPEE internees from Argentina. We have previously maintained that the number amounted to approximately 160, whereas in your instructions to Buenos Aires the figure had been given as 126. You pointed out that the figure of 126 was that officially admitted by the Argentine Government.

On checking through my files, I find that I received a telegram from the Naval Attaché at Buenos Aires on 15th October 1941 in which, in reply to queries as to the original number of officers and men interned and number of escapes which had taken place, he stated that the escapes acknowledged by the Argentine Government numbered 153. I enclose a copy of this telegram for your information. Will you please make the necessary alteration in your instructions to Sir D. Kelly. (Ibid, 29 June 1942)

The following day, the Admiralty contacted McCall, repeating the telegram to Washington and Johnston.

> Your 2025/25. No evidence to identify these officers as having attacked Latin-American shipping. A German broadcast on 20.6.42 stated that a U-boat captain who was operating in waters fairly familiar to him from his cruise in the Graf Spee at the beginning of the war sank a Brazilian tanker – "a particularly fine spectacle." Name of this officer not known. (Ibid, 30 June 1942)

On 1 July, DNI informed McCall, the Naval Attaché in Washington and Johnston that the name of the U-boat Commander who sank the Brazilian Parnahyba in early May 1942 was Korvetten Kapitan Wattenberg. The following day, the Foreign Office updated Kelly with telegram 548, repeated to Washington as No. 211 Saving. 'According to Naval Attaché's telegram of October 15th escapes acknowledged by Argentine Government totalled 153 probably up to May 30th 1941.'

On the same day, McCall sent 1950Z marked SECRET to DNI, BNA Washington, BNA Rio de Janeiro and Johnston. It was also copied to 1st Lord, 1st Sea Lord, VCNS, ACNS, PAS, DNI, DOP, OD, M for FO and OIC.

> Your 22 B/30th June. Since repeated to Rio de Janeiro para 2 – suggest this information be issued by Admiralty to the press who will cable it out here. State Provincial Regulations will not repetition not permit publication here of such a statement if issued from Embassy sources. Effect is bound to be good.
> Charge d'Affaires is communicating para 2 to Argentine under-secretary for foreign affairs. (Ibid.)

Kelly sent telegram 604 to the Foreign Office and Washington the following day.

> At my reception by the Minister for Foreign Affairs this morning His Excellency, after stating that the Argentine Government valued very highly the traditional relations with Great Britain, made lengthy defence of their attitude. He said they had promised "assistance" in Pan-American scheme and would keep all their agreements, but that the country was in so sense prepared for breaking off relations with the Axis. He thought Mr. Cordell Hull [U.S. Secretary of State throughout the Second World War] understood their position but Welles [Foreign Policy advisor to Roosevelt and Under Secretary of State from 1936 to 1943] was "very hard" on Argentina and there had been an unfair propaganda against Argentina in the United States. I would soon

find out that the Argentine Government had the full support of the country whatever might be personal sympathies for one or other of the belligerents. He did not see any likelihood of change of policy unless some grave attack on Argentine Sovereignty took place.

2. I said both in Washington and London the activities of Axis Embassies were regarded as real practical danger and secondly that the Argentine Ambassador in London must have informed him of the serious anxieties which existed as to the reality of the Argentine Government's neutrality. The most serious case was that of the Graf Spee internees (see your telegram No. 541) of whom far more than 100 had admittedly escaped and eight had already been identified as engaged in commerce destruction. German radio had even boasted that one of them had sunk a Brazilian ship. It would assist me greatly if Argentine Government could let us have without delay effective guarantees on the lines requested in recent notes by Mr. Hadow.

3. The Minister for Foreign Affairs said that he had been speaking with the Minister of Marine and that the matter was under close study. He thought that the eight officers had escaped last year but that most of the other ranks who had escaped were still living in Argentina. They had at first been given liberty allowed to internees but guards had been greatly tightened and two who had escaped had been caught. He gave me to understand in a general way that we should get satisfaction. (Ibid, 3 July 1942)

Almost a week later, Marshall sent Secret message 1757B to McCall, NA Washington, BNA Rio de Janeiro and Johnston. 'Your 1950/1. Ministry of Information consider suggestion impracticable. Other steps are being taken to ensure that story obtains currency [gets publicity] in Argentina. (Ibid, 9 July 1942)

Another week later, the Foreign Office sent telegram 576 to Buenos Aires asking 'Have Argentine Government taken any concrete steps?' Kelly's response, telegram 638, was sent the following day, 18 July.

Your Telegram No. 576.

They have not informed me but the Minister of the Interior assured me there have been no recent escapes. The Under Secretary of State for Foreign Affairs has also promised list of al Warrant Officers and men remaining and their photographs. Prensa [Argentine newspaper] had strong leading article on the subject 17th July (inspired by ourselves) which has perturbed the Government. I am continuing the pressure at every opportunity. (Ibid, 18 July 1942)

On 18 July, the *Dundee Evening Telegraph* reported that,

GRAF SPEE OFFICERS NOW IN U-BOATS
Buenos Aires, Saturday. Several officers of the German pocket battleship Graf Spee sunk in the River Plate in December 1939, who escaped from Argentina, are now in command of submarines operating in the South Atlantic, according to well-informed circles here.
Among the Graf Spee's 29 officers were several submarine experts. (*Dundee Evening Telegraph,* 18 July 1942)

On the 21 July, *The Baltimore Sun* reported,

Personnel escapes. It is known that by last September 128 members of the Graf Spee personnel, including twenty-eight officers, had already escaped and left Argentina.

Unofficial but reliable information from Allied circles indicates that several former Graf Spee officers and men are among prisoners taken from German submarines which have been captured or sunk.

It is also reported that Jergens Wattenberg, a junior officer on the Graf Spee, commanded a submarine which sunk at least one Brazilian ship before being put out of action by United Nations forces off the north Brazilian coast.

Call Attention to Escapes.

It is also known that United Nations diplomatic missions here have called the matter of the continual escapes of Graf Spee personnel to the attention of the Argentine government.

The Argentine Navy Ministry responsible for guarding the internees, refused today to indicate how many of them had left Argentina since its last report, delivered to Congress last September. Sailors and petty officers were scattered throughout Argentina, most of them on parole. Fourteen of the officer staff had escaped before confinement was finally enforced in May, 1940, five months after the battle.

Sent to Island.

Those still in Argentina were sent to the Island of Martin Garcia, forty miles north of Buenos Aires in the river Plate at a point where the river is only ten miles wide. At least fourteen others had escaped from there when Congress received its information ten months ago.

This afternoon the Buenos Aires paper Critica demanded that the Government reveal how many of the original number are still in Argentina and what measures are being taken to see that those still here remain.

The *Liverpool Daily Post* reported the incident on 23 July.

GRAF SPEE SAILORS ESCAPE
TAKEN OFF BY U-BOATS
By a Political Correspondent
The escape of considerable numbers of German sailors interned in the Argentine after the Battle of the River Plate, in which the Graf Spee was sunk, has not passed unnoticed in London. There is a distinct possibility that they are being taken aboard U-boats operating off the North and South America.
Information in London last night is that 153 Germans have escaped including 29 of 36 officers. It may be assumed that careful watch is being kept on the situation and upon the conditions under which these enemy naval men are interned.
(*Liverpool Daily Post,* 23 July 1942)

Similar stories were included in the *Yorkshire Post and Leeds Intelligencer* and the *Aberdeen Post and Journal.* Benemann's comment was, 'NOW THERE IS A TALL "TAURINE FECAL MATERIAL" STORY. A bit cramped quarters for another 36 men to be taken over 6000 miles. There were no more officers on the "request to escape" Kriegsmarine list by mid-1942. Just a couple of administrators, the Musical band director, Riedel who was just got the promotion as officer for trying but failing to escape and one officer that was in and out of the German hospital and unfit for the escape stress.' (Email communication with Carlos Benemann, 6 November 2021)

Graf Spee Men Escape
Argentine Government statement that 33 of the interned Graf Spee officers and men have escaped has caused surprise here. I learn authoritatively that the correct figure is 153. This includes no fewer than 29 out of 36 interned Graf Spee officers. The escapers are believed to have been picked up by U-boats.
(*Yorkshire Post and Leeds Intelligencer,* 23 July 1942)

153 Graf Spee Men Escape
Escape of considerable numbers of German sailors interned in the Argentine after the Battle of the River Plate, in which the Graf Spee was sunk, has not passed unnoticed in London. There is a distinct possibility that they are being taken aboard U-boats operating off the coasts of North and South America. Information in London last night is that 153 Germans have escaped, including

twenty-nine of thirty-six officers. *Aberdeen Post and Journal* 23 July 1942)

The Graf Spee crew file included an article from the *London Evening Standard*.

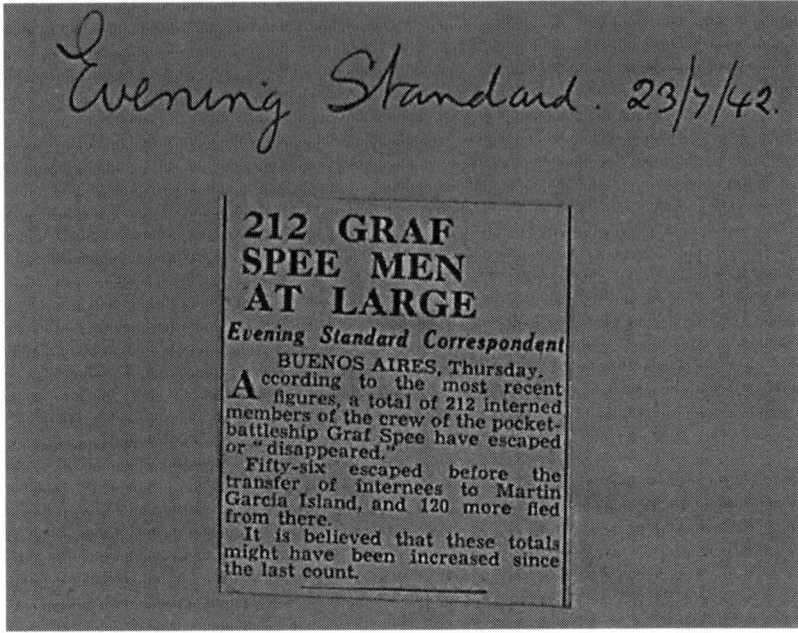

> *Evening Standard. 23/7/42.*
>
> **212 GRAF SPEE MEN AT LARGE**
>
> *Evening Standard Correspondent*
>
> BUENOS AIRES, Thursday.
>
> According to the most recent figures, a total of 212 interned members of the crew of the pocket-battleship Graf Spee have escaped or "disappeared."
>
> Fifty-six escaped before the transfer of internees to Martin Garcia Island, and 120 more fled from there.
>
> It is believed that these totals might have been increased since the last count.

(Newspaper article in the Graf Spee file (TNA ADM 116/5475)

The *Belfast News-Letter* also reported on the escapes.

Graf Spee Prisoners Escape by U-Boat?
THE escape of considerable numbers of German sailors interned in the Argentine after the Battle of the River Plate, in which the Graf Spee was sunk, has not passed unnoticed in London, says the diplomatic correspondent of the Press Association.

There is a distinct possibility that they are being taken aboard U-boats operating off the coasts of North and South America.

Information has reached London that 153 Germans have escaped, including 29 or 36 officers. It may be assumed that careful watch is being kept on the situation and upon the conditions under which these enemy naval men are interned.

Argentina's "Fear"
The position and the policy of Argentina was submitted to the U.S. Secretary of State, Mr. Cordell Hull, yesterday for comment

at his Press conference, says the Washington correspondent of "The Times". The question arose from a Buenos Aires despatch to the "New York Times".

According to this, the news about the secret session of the Argentine Chamber on July 16 establishes as the reasons for the failure to carry out the recommendations of the Rio de Janeiro conference for the rupture of relations with the Axis are that the Government thinks that Argentina still belongs to the European economic sphere, and regards the expansion of the military, economic, and political strength of the United States on the American continent with greater alarm than even the possibility of a German victory.

Mr. Hull said that he would not discuss the question unless and until he was more fully informed of what had actually happened when the Foreign Minister, Dr, Ruiz Guinazu, appeared before the Chamber.

Dr. Ruis Guinazu is said to have complained bitterly that the United States was trying to dominate the whole continent, to have aroused criticism when he declared that other American Republics have been "led by the nose," to have implied that the further development of the strength of the United States was in conflict with the best interests of Argentina, and by contrast to have been studiously friendly in his references to Axis nations.

The Government's case, as submitted by Dr. Guinazu, was strongly controverted by many deputies in the sitting, which lasted for more that 18 hours. Yet the Government feels that the failure of the Chamber to introduce and pass a resolution calling for a breach of relations with the axis amounted to a victory. Per Press Association. (*Belfast News-Letter*, 23 July 1942)

The *Birmingham Daily Gazette* published an article on the escapes the same day.

Graf Spee Men Escape to Germany by U-Boat
From Our Diplomatic Correspondent
SOMETHING in the nature of a U-boat passenger service has been run from South America to Germany. It has just been announced that 33 of the Graf Spee crew, officers and men, interned in the Argentine, have escaped, and many of them, skilled sailors are working in U-boat crews. I understand that the true figure of escaped Graf Spee sailors of all ranks is 153, and that out of 36 officers interned no fewer than 29 have managed to escape the vigilance of the Argentine authorities and made their way to freedom. The activities of U-boats on the eastern seaboard of the Americas has [sic] made it possible for these

officers and men to be picked up and taken home for further training and employment, either in new German surface vessels or in U-boats. (*Birmingham Daily Gazette,* 23 July 1942)

At the end of July, the escapes were commented on in the British House of Commons.

ESCAPED CREW OF GRAF SPEE. ARGENTINE ATTITUDE. In the British Parliament, Captain GRAHAM (C., Wirral) asked if Mr. Eden would cause to be conveyed to the Government of the Argentine Republic the surprise felt by the Government and people of Britain at the Argentine Government's interpretation of the duties of a neutral in regard to the effective internment of the officers and crew of the former German battleship Graf Spee. Mr. Eden said that steps have already been taken to inform the Argentine Government of the view taken in Britain of their action, and the British Ambassador in Buenos Ayres was in constant touch with m regarding this matter. (*Belfast Telegraph,* 29 July 1942)

The *Ottowa Journal* reported the same day.

Will Probe Escapes By Graf Spee Crew. BUENOS AIRES, July 27.-(AP)-The Chamber of Deputies investigating anti-Argentine activities announced today it would study the internment of officers and crew of the scuttled German pocket battleship Admiral Graf Spee to determine if official laxity has been the cause of so many escapes.
Four members of the crew were arrested Saturday on the Spanish ship Alborade. Of 1,055 officers and men who were interned when the ship was scuttled in December 1939, 128 are known to have escaped, according to official information.
It was announced tonight that three ministries, - The Navy, Interior and Foreign Affairs – are preparing a complete report on the status of the German vessel's crew at the request of the British Embassy. It was emphasised that the British request did not constitute a protest. (*Ottowa Journal,* 28 July 1942)

McCall was replaced as Naval Attaché at the British Embassy in Buenos Aires at the end of July by Captain Herbert Forster. Lloyd Hirst would have brought him up-to-date with the details of the Graf Spee story and he probably read with interest the following newspaper article published in Mendoza and sent to the Admiralty.

TRANSLATION

"Critica" – 12th August, 1942

"GRAF SPEE" SAILORS FO SHOOTING IN THE ANDES WITH RIFLES OF UNKNOWN ORIGIN.

Mendoza, 12th (From our own correspondent).

The very special and benevolent treatment accorded to nazis from the "Graf Spee", 100 in number, here interned by decree of the national Executive Power, has been the subject of lively comment.

It would appear that all manner of privileges and facilities have been accorded to them by the authorities, forgetful of the true position of these prisoners of war, so to speak, in a neutral country.

It has become known that the Reich recently promoted 17 under-officers, the occasion being uproariously celebrated in a beer-salon in the capital of this province. What were they promoted for? Is the question asked by those who know what the German Government reward.

Perhaps it has been to honour these promotions that special permission was granted to some nazis of the "Graf Spee" to go after guanacos [animal like a llama] in the region of the Cordillera, up to Punta de Vacas. The shoot was naturally carried out with firearms. Who provided them with the Mausers and bullets? Here is another disquieting question. On the other hand, how ere the nazis permitted to go on a shooting trip which is prohibited to others?

For a week the happy internees of the "Graf Spee" were allowed to absent themselves 140 kilometres from the place of their internment, come close to the Chilean frontier, study the countryside, take notes, surely, and do other things which Nazism will not fail to put to use.

Amongst others, Jareslso Kletschk, the under-officer Federico Clement and the marine Rodolfo Matzke, took part in this excursion. As it was in this zone that the escape of over 200 nazis (of the 1000 interned in this country) began, everyone is asking himself if measures will, or will not, be taken to avoid the repetition of such acts as those above denounced. (TNA ADM 116/5475, 12 August 1942)

A couple of days later, Johnston informed NID, BAD Washington, DNI and the SO(I) in Jamaica that,

A signal was intercepted on the 7th August from the Master of the Swedish ship "COLUMBIA", which left Bahia Blanca [port city about 700 km southwest of Buenos Aires] on the 4th August for

Lisbon, stating that he had loaded three stowaways at the Recalada Light Vessel and believed they were escaped "Graf Spee" sailors.

On checking up this information it was discovered that a further two German stowaways had been landed from the Spanish ship "MONTE SAJA" which left Buenos Aires on the 2nd August for Las Palmas via Montevideo.

The details of these men are as follows: -

Erich Emil Hauer Weingraber German, of Austrian birth, born 16th December, 1903, Stowaway on Spanish "Monte Saja".

Federico Meier German, aged 23, no papers, merchant navy seaman, stowaway on Spanish "Monte Saja".

Friedrich Heyn German aged 28, steward, no papers, stowaway on Swedish "Columbia".

Kurt Glaesmer German, born 20th April, 1916, Internment Identity Card No. 479 issued by the Police of the Federal Capital. Ex member of the crew of the "Graf Spee". Stowaway on Swedish "Columbia".

Dieter George German, aged 23, bachelor, ex member of the crew of the "Graf Spee", no papers. Stowaway on Swedish "Columbia". (Ibid, 14 August 1942)

The following day, the Foreign Office sent Buenos Aires telegram 641.

> Your telegram No. 638 0of July 18th: escape of "Graf Spee" internees.
> Unless you have received satisfactory indications of improvement we are considering following procedure. We should instruct you to address enquiries to Argentine Government.
> If they reply that measures of control have been improved, you should ask that your Naval Attaché or some other member of your staff should be allowed to visit the district where the men are interned to report to us on the position. If this is refused or report is unsatisfactory, or if Argentine reply to your enquiries is evasive, we should consider with other Government Departments whether there is any way beyond mere words in which we can indicate our dissatisfaction. Simultaneously we should examine possibility of taking local action to ensure that internees do not leave Argentina i.e. by "influencing" local police and unobtrusively organising British subjects in district to help and keep you informed.
> 2. Please telegraph your observations. (Ibid, 15 August 1942)

The next document was a translation of a letter dated 15 August sent in Spanish by Hadow to Doctor Roberto Gache, Argentina's Under-Secretary of State for Foreign Affairs.

<u>VERY URGENT</u>
My dear friend,

If I return to trouble you once more with regard to the vexed and to us most important question of the "GRAF SPEE" sailors, it is because I am frankly in despair at the information contained in the attached article from "Critica", which will, I think, naturally be interpreted in my country in a manner extremely prejudicial to the joint interests of Great Britain and Argentina. Might I ask, therefore, that a careful report be called for and if possible supplied to me without delay; as it is essential to answer the charges that: -

a) the local authorities are, as the newspaper says, "in the zone (very close to the frontier) where the escape of 200 nazis began", showing a lack of vigilance which is very disturbing;

b) if under-officers and men are allowed to absent themselves 140 kilometres from the place of their internment, what guarantee is there that their escape from a sparsely populated mountain district can be prevented or even reported in time to recapture them?

In short, this report lends most unfortunate support to an analysis of the facts and figures hitherto given to us (for which I should like, at the same time, to express my gratitude) of which the following are the main points: -

a) of 36 officers originally interned, 14 escaped from <u>Naval Barracks</u> in Buenos Aires in March, 1940, and a further 16 who were sent to the Island of Martin Garcia did likewise on the 31st August, 1940. Not one, so far as is known, was re-arrested and it is now established that all got safely out of the country;

b) as a result the only officers left are the Second in Command – who has been allotted a special task in this country; the band-master; two young lieutenants and one paymaster.

The report of the Senate of the 26th November 1941 did not give the name of Teodoro Mohr, although the latter escaped from Cordoba in May 1941. It did, however, contain 14 names of escaped men who did not figure on the list recently supplied. Have these14 been recapture?

c) the fact that only 7 new names – MOHR, DOIL, GAYSER, STEINHOFF, BETZ, SWACZYNA, AUMULLER - appear as having escaped since September 1941 indicates, it is hoped, that increased vigilance is rendering escapes more difficult. Unfortunately, the good effect produced will, I fear, be counteracted by the Mendoza report quoted at the beginning of this letter. May I, therefore, hope for a definite assurance that this list is complete and that, from the Mendoza area in particular – no more men are either missing or have escaped.

d) How serious are these escapes is best shown perhaps by the fact that 80% of the 90 or more men who have escaped are skilled engine-room ratings, now forming the badly needed U-boat crews who are my country's most serious menace; and 95% of the escaped men are under-officers.

e) In a port such as Buenos Aires the continued presence of 148 men – despite the clear statement in the internment decree that the entire ship's company was to be sent to the provinces – is a menace we naturally find is difficult to ignore. Moreover, most of the wireless operators of the ship are here and are reliably reported to be actively employed in the German Embassy. Is it, therefore, too much to ask that the decree is implemented and a list of all these "GRAF SPEE" men employed in Buenos Aires - with the place of their employment – be furnished to me? I think I can justify this request if you will kindly remember the potential danger these men represent from the point of view of sabotage, both to Argentine and British interests.

I have written to you with a frankness that is warranted only by our friendship; but I know you will understand me when I add my most friendly warning that you and I have now exhausted our ability to prevent this question of having serious repercussions, unless the whole question of internment can be dealt with on the basis of providing absolute assurance that: -

a) no more will any officer or man of the "Graf Spee" be able to leave Argentina;

b) the activities, employment and places of internment of the remainder of the crew will be circumscribed as to render them no more a danger, both to Argentina and to Great Britain.

Hoping, therefore, therefore that we may even at this last moment avoid the above, I remain, etc. (Ibid.)

Gache's response, dated 18 August, was translated and forwarded to the Admiralty on 21 August.

My dear friend,

I received your letter of the 15th with the cutting from "Critica" which gave rise thereto. We await information requested from Mendoza in order to take a suitable decision in regard to the situation of which you inform us. I have fully apprised the Minister of this matter, and he, in the same friendly spirit as ourselves, will give it his consideration in accordance with the principles governing the case. These principles – as you will not be unaware – are difficult of application in a country with open frontiers and so extensive and sparsely populated as ours. It is true that no abuse whatever should be permitted, but it is nevertheless interesting to note that since 1941 the escapes have been reduced to the minimum which you yourself acknowledge.

Please believe that I am continuing to attend to this matter in a spirit of the most friendly interest, and accept my best regards. (Ibid, 18 August 1942)

A couple of days later, 20 August, Johnston sent the following message to NID, BAD Washington, DNI and the SO(I) in Jamaica.

Reference my 1301/15/42 of 18th August 1942, I am now informed that KURT GLAESNER is reported to have escaped on 30 July and that GEORGE DIETER, who had no documents, has now been identified as having Internment Identity Card No. 1036. Both these men are reported to have boarded the Swedish "Columbia" in Bahia Blanca on 4th August.

I am also informed that both these men as well as those from the Spanish "MONTE SAJA", made sworn statements to the local authorities declaring that they got on board without anybody seeing them and without receiving assistance from any member of crew. (Ibid, 20 August 1942)

On the same day, Kelly sent the Foreign Office telegram 714.

Your telegram No. 641.

I have addressed frequent enquiries to the Argentine Government who have now allowed us confidentially to copy photographs of ship's crew and have informed me that only seven escapes have taken place since September 1941. Although this figure may not be exact we have no reasons to believe recent leakage has been on scale to justify serious complaint, especially considering the sparse population and general administrative inefficiency. (Recent leakage appears smaller proportion than amongst our own interned soldiers in Switzerland). It is clear that mass escapes and escape of officers and most skilled ratings took place during 1940. It appears also that majority of these took place after quarrel with Argentine Government when owing to Minister of the Interior having been directly approached, the Minister for Foreign Affairs raised national honour complex, which whenever raised in this country makes all practical results impossible.

This must be borne in mind when considering asking that Naval Attaché should visit the districts (there are six) where men are interned. It is at least possible that request would provoke a rebuff and I feel that it would be better that the consideration of possible further action referred to in your telegram should take place before rather than after making request and particularly the consideration of whether practical dangers of the situation now justify any drastic action such as suggested and which might have been justified in 1940. It looks as if our grievance which was very serious against previous President's Administration in 1940 may be largely retrospective.

As regards local action British residents in co-operation with Consular Officer have organised efficient supervision of interned [grp. omitted] in main provincial areas, and there are regular reports from railway companies regarding districts concerned. I think this could be further improved if we could arrange with local port authorities for last minute search of outgoing neutral ships. The Minister of the Interior is being as helpful as he can but I will continue constant pressure on the Minister of Foreign Affairs. It has been suggested that we should ask for 148 internees in the federal capitol, some of whom are technicians said to be working for the German Embassy, to be removed into the interior but opinion is divided as to whether supervision is more easy in provinces than in the capitol, and I am enquiring into this question. (Ibid.)

On 24 August, Johnston provided NID, BAD Washington, DNI and the SO(I) in Jamaica with more information about 'Stowaways'.

Reference my 1301/15/42 of 14th August and 1301/16/42 of 20th August 1942, the following additional information about these stowaways has now been received: -

George Dieter: Internment identity Card No. 1036. He was interned in the Federal Capital and worked for various German firms. On the 4th August he boarded the Swedish vessel "Columbia", at the port of Bahia Blanca, and after the vessel left port was discovered by the Captain who went alongside the Recalada pilot vessel and handed him over to the Maritime authorities.

Kurt Glaesmer: Internment Identity card No. 749. No further information concerning this man has been discovered.

Friedrich Hefn: This man deserted from the S.S. "Monte Pascoal" in the port of Buenos Aires. He made his way to Cordoba in order to hide, and remained there until two months ago. Later, in Buenos Aires, he became acquainted with the two men mentioned above and they planned to fly from the country. He embarked on the Swedish "Columbia" with the other Germans, and was handed over to the Maritime authorities at Recalada.

Erich Haver Weingraber: He was in business in Uruguay. His wife left in April in the "Cabo de Buena Esperanza" for Spain, and thence to Germany. He and Meyer, whom he knew in Buenos Aires, planned to get away to their country: they, therefore, stowed away on the "Monte Saja", and after spending eight days in the storeroom and thought that they had been on the high seas for two days, they came on deck and were surprised to find that the vessel had only just left Montevideo. The Captain made for Recalada and there handed the two men over to the Maritime authorities.

Federico Meyer: This man deserted from the S.S. "Frankfurt" in a Chilean port. From there he made his way to the Argentine, and finally became acquainted with Weingraber and planned to stowaway on the "Monte Saja". In company with Weingraber he was disembarked at Recalada. (Ibid. 24 August 1942)

Two days later, Forster informed DNI, Johnston and BAD Washington, OIC, DSD, M, FO, DOP, DEWD and DAST that,

Ship's Agent for Spanish Steamer ALBAREDA have informed Embassy that Maritime Police of Buenos Aires found and removed 4 Graf interned sailors just before ship sailed yesterday. Report independently confirmed Grade B.1.(One). (Ibid, 26 August 1942)

During this time, two Uruguayan ships were sunk in the Atlantic by German U-boats. Research by Jose Maria Ferrari Goudschaal revealed that,

Uruguay remained neutral until January 25, 1942, when it broke diplomatic relations with the Axis powers. But the lack of merchant ships to transport products to and from our ports forces our government to seize four merchant ships, belonging to the Italian and German navies that had sought refuge at the beginning of the hostilities. The Adamello and the Fausto, with the Italian flag, which were named, with the names of Montevideo and Maldonado respectively and the Danish flag ships, Isaura and Cristian Sass, which took the names of Rocha and Colony. We clarify that for that year Denmark was already a country occupied by Germany.

The seizure of the Italian steamers gave rise to a strong diplomatic incident with the Italian government, surpassed by our diplomacy as well as the US claim that these seized merchants should be administered by the Moore Mc Comark shipping company, from New Orleans, as had happened in 1917, with the merchant ships, seized in our port by our government that constituted the founding nucleus of our Overseas Merchant Navy, which were managed by a North American shipping company, Emergency Fleet, until the conclusion of hostilities between the great European powers.

The first of the ships to be enlisted was the Montevideo, former Adamello, with a crew belonging to our National Navy for their training and experience. which left for the port of New York with an important load of national products, having to bring materials for the national industry on the way back. Trip that could not complete because it was sunk by a submarine, on March 9, 1942, north of the Virgin Islands, with the loss of 14 brave men from our navy.

Said sinking without prior notice, and consequent loss of valuable lives of fellow nationals, caused an explosion of pain and illegitimate indignation in public opinion, which was translated into diplomatic protests and popular demonstrations, especially against German firms and citizens of that nation, as attributed in the first news to a German submarine. Years later it was clarified that the cause of the aggression was the Italian submarine, Tazzoli, as was clarified by the historian Omar Medina Soca, in a publication of the magazine Barlovento, of the Naval School. [...]

At the end of June 1942, the next one was ready, called Maldonado, which set sail from the port of Montevideo on July 8, 1942, under the command of Frigate Captain (CG) Mario Giambruno and operated by the National Port Administration. [...] El Maldonado, in its slow and risky journey to the distant port of New York, transported 5,800 tons of general cargo in its warehouses, consisting of canned meat (corned beef), 1,000 tons of leather and wool and other products.

The Maldonado, after almost a month of slow sailing along the east and northeast coast of Brazil, entered the submarine-infested Caribbean Sea, bound for the port of New York, its destination for its cargo. Which is why Captain Giambruno had taken due precautions and rehearsed the corresponding procedures for the rapid evacuation of his crew to the rescue boats. The crowbar lookout warned that a submarine was following them for 5 hours when nightfall, full of uncertainty, the

Captain ordered to sail at maximum speed of the Maldonado, (10 knots) and only with the Uruguayan flag well lit.

Everything in complete calm and telegraphic silence. The night was clear, with the moon and good visibility, calm sea, gentle east wind, no ships in sight.

At 23 hours, 45 minutes GMT, the submarine emerged and fired 2 warning cannon shots ahead of the bow, forcing it to stop and proceed to abandon ship. Captain Giambruno, orders to stop the machines and orders the evacuation of the 49 men of the crew, which is carried out with total order and safety towards the four boats, as had been previously rehearsed. The commander of the submarine orders our Captain to move to the submarine, taken prisoner. Then the sub quickly dived and headed north. [...]

In addition to the strong emotional impact that it produced on national public opinion, already sensitized and inflamed by the painful and unjust death of the 14 sailors from Montevideo, for example, it is worth transcribing the articles that appeared in different press organs in Montevideo and the Interior.

The Morning of the capital and El Telégrafo de Paysandú dated August 8, 1942, and the newspaper El Pueblo de Santa Lucía, August 12, 1942, which headlines: "The Nazi assault on Maldonado. There is fear for the fate of the boat in which our compatriot Ángel Azcoitía embarked". - And another enthusiastic article dated August 19, 1942 with a great headline: SAVED! Which for its brevity I transcribe:

"... On Sunday at 7:30 p.m., the ether gave us the pleasant news of the arrival on the east coast of the United States, of the boat from the Uruguayan ship Maldonado, in which our compatriot Captain Ángel Azcoitía was going. Fifteen days after the treacherous attack perpetrated by a Nazi submarine, the missing boat happily appeared, of the four in which our sailors had embarked, the sunken ship ... ". (A photograph of Captain Azcoitía is shown). "... The news caused deep joy in our city and its vast area, where the Azcoitía family enjoys wide sympathies and everyone accompanied them in their days and hours of so much uncertainty. The home of her sisters in the traditional house on Brasil and Artigas Street, has celebrated such a happy new with joy and we adhere to it." (Goudschaal, Jose Maria, 'The Sinking of the Maldonado', Cycle of Conferences, 2013; https://www.histarmar.com.ar/AcademiaUruguaya MyFl/2013/HundimientoMaldonado.htm #_ftn1)

There was no mention of these attacks in the Graf Spee files examined, nor of what action was taken by the British and Americans.

Also during August 1942, the SOE's South American Section submitted a report to the on the Axis threat to South America.

ARGENTINA

The self-styled leader of the South American republics, with the highest wealth and literacy per capita among her 13 million population Argentina has a navy that equals Brazil's; an army of 100,000 first line troops and 300,000 reserves; and an air force of between 250 and 300 planes.

The German organisation in Buenos Aires issues orders for the whole of South America. In the area between the Parana and Uruguay Rivers, the German population is between one and two millions. They have air fields suitable for light planes, and it is reported they have motorised courier service to call enough fighting men to make up five lightly armed divisions so strategically located Stutspunkte [?credit points].

The four million Italians around Buenos Aires and on the coast of Bahia Blnca are less well organised and more apathetic. The Japanese are negligible. There is a large native Fifth Column of wealthy landowners in control of Argentine's governing party. Two native Fascist parties, Aliansa de la Juventud, with 30,000 members, and the Union Nacional Argentine, with 10,000 members, work closely with the N.S.D.A.P. [German Nazi Party].

Control of Rio Plata, Argentine's most vulnerable spot, could paralyse the country's trade.

URUGUAY

Little and weak, but strongly pro-Ally. With its two million population of which three-quarters live in Montevideo, Uruguay has 200,000 Italians. One a few of the very rich ones, however, are Fascist-minded.

The Nazi plan to use Uruguay as a bridgehead for a lightning coup since it dominated the Plata River was discovered in 1940. Success in this move would have put the Germans in control of half the continent. But the plans counted on Fifth Column operation, and Uruguayan authorities hope to make its operation impossible by the defeat of the pro-Nazi Herrerista party in the November elections. Greater security will be ensured if the pro-Ally Batllista party is put in power. [...]

CONCLUSION

At present, the Fifth Column in South America is basically a negative passive force. But in case of invasion or a large-scale raid, it could become active and destructive.

The German plan to penetrate ever deeper into South America, with its undeveloped riches of agriculture and minerals, will not be relinquished easily. The arrival of German airplanes on the South American continent could herald, and set off, an uprising among the enemy minorities.

To destroy what the Germans, Italians and Japanese have systematically built up, the Allies must consider themselves on the offensive, and put the enemy on the defensive, south of Panama. This must be done at once. It is a tactical position of great immediate advantage to us.

Axis agents can be exposed, and their usefulness destroyed. Some can even be controlled, without their knowledge – and that would give our side some measure of control over German headquarters.

These are twin objectives which we ourselves must reach in conjunction with our American colleagues, collaborating wherever possible with the local authorities. Where such collaboration is not possible, we should be able in some cases to take the law into our own hands.

It is not too late, yt, to win the Battle of South America – but it is almost too late. We have neglected that continent too long because we have felt it was too far removed from any possible theatre of war.

If Hitler decides to act on it, South America can become a Second Front – and not one of our choosing! (TNA HS8/113, 6 August 1942)

Over the following months, consular security officers and representatives of the British and American companies operating in South America were sent to Camp X, a joint SOE/OSS school in Whitby, Ontario, for a fortnight's course in industrial security – anti-sabotage measures. On their return they were expected to ensure colleagues were aware of how best to protect their buildings and machinery.

On 1 September, Marshall made a note,

> Foreign Office telegram No. 641 to Buenos Aires and Sir D. Kelly's reply are enclosed. There can be no denying that while a very small number of escapes has taken place since the Autumn of 1941, the position does appear to be very much more satisfactory in the last few months. In addition much stronger representations have been made to the Argentine Government since Sir D. Kelly became Ambassador.
>
> 2. While there is some substance in "X" [Possibly the Admiralty file containing Graf Spee correspondence] of the Ambassador's telegram it must not be overlooked that our primary concern is to prevent recurrence of the status quo

through decrease in vigilance, especially in view of the increase in Axis Submarines operating off the American coasts.
    Subject to remarks of D. of P. it is suggested that we should write to Foreign Office in the terms of the enclosed draft letter. (TNA ADM 116/5475, 1 September 1942)

The following day, *El* Mundo, a Buenos Aires newspaper published the following article. Translated it read:

GRAF SPEE OFFICER REFUSES TO TESTIFY.
BUENOS AIRES: AN OFFICER OF THE LATE GERMAN BATTLESHIP GRAF SPEE IS UNDER DETENTION IN ONE OF THE BUILDINGS OF THE CHAMBER OF DEPUTIES, FOLLOWING HIS REFUSAL TO TESTIFY BEFORE THE PARLIAMENTARY COMMITTEE INVESTIGATING ANTI-ARGENTINE ACTIVITIES. THE ATTITUDE OF THIS GERMAN OFFICER WILL BE CONSIDERED IN TOMORROW'S SESSION OF THE CHAMBER. (Ibid, 2 September 1942)

The following day, Marshall wrote to the Foreign Office.

Dear Gallop,
    Will you please refer to Sir D. Kelly's telegram No. 714 of 20th August on the subject of "Graf Spee" internees in Argentina.
2. While there may be some substance in the suggestion that our grievance is largely retrospective, it is essential that everything possible should be done to ensure that there is no slacking of Argentine vigilance which might encourage further attempts to escape.
3. We fully concur with Sir D. Kelly's suggestion that an endeavour should be made to arrange local port authorities for last minute searches of outgoing neutral ships, and we shall be glad to hear that he intends to initiate action in this respect.
4. With regard to the suggestion that a request should be made for permission for the Naval Attaché to visit the internment districts, while it is possible that an official request at this stage might meet with a rebuff, we feel that if an informal suggestion were made, instead of an official request this might be successful. It could be suggested that while serving to satisfy use as to the adequacy of internment measures now being adopted, the Naval Attaché might, as a result of his visit, be in a position to make suggestions for facilitating the Argentine task, thereby obviating the disagreeable business of making continual diplomatic representations. (Ibid, 3 September 1942)

As there had been concern about the activities of some Germans in Argentina, President Ortiz ordered the Chamber of Deputies to set up a Special Commission of Inquiry into Anti-Argentine Activities. The Chairman was Juan Antonio Solari and as his investigation included anti-Semitism, the United States Holocaust Memorial Museum has a record of the proceedings which includes reports, testimonies, financial records, publications, pamphlets, and photographs relating to National-Socialist activities by the German secret services, local German-Argentine organizations, German-Argentine schools, and the German embassy and others. https://collections.ushmm.org/search/catalog/irn105654)

On 5 September, the *Dundee Evening Telegraph* reported the arrest of an escaped Graf Spee man.

GRAF SPEE OFFICER ARRESTED Rio de Janeiro, Saturday. The former chief engine-room officer of the Graf Spee, Werner Hanne, is among the Germans recently arrested in Brazil. Hanne escaped just a year ago from the concentration camp at Cardoba [sic] in Argentina, where some of the Graf Spee officers were interned after their ship had been scuttled. (*Dundee Evening Telegraph,* 5 Saturday 1942)

The next document in the Graf Spee crew file was a copy of an unnamed American newspaper article with an underlined note 'Please pass a copy to A.D.N.I.'

> Argentine – Escape of Graf Spee Internees
> Our New York representative reports: -
> We now learn that the following four escapees from the GRAF SPEE were found as stowaways aboard the S.S. "ALBAREDA" prior to her departure from Buenos Aires early in August.
> > Bernhard VISSER
> > Alfred TETZNER
> > Paul BERGNER
> > Guillerme KOPMANN
> Visser had been interned in Buenos Aires in order to work as an electrician in the Condor Syndicate in Quilmes and the other three escaped from the island of Martin Garcia.
> All four men were found in the bunkers of the ship and it is understood that local police are searching for the intermediary with whose connivance such escapes are made possible. It is reported that each captain receives $500 in Argentine currency from this unknown intermediary for each man who makes a successful getaway but this is said to be only a small proportion of the amount received by him from the German Embassy.

It appears probable that all four men will be transferred to Martin Garcia. (TNA ADM 116/5475, 7 September 1942)

The following day, the Foreign Office sent telegram 689 to Buenos Aires.

> Your telegram No. 714 [of August 20th: escape of Graf Spee internees].
> While there is considerable substance in your view that our grievance is largely retrospective we regard it as essential to leave nothing undone to ensure that there is no slackening of Argentine vigilance. We hope that you will be able to arrange for local port authorities to make last minute searches of outgoing neutral ships as suggested in third paragraph of your telegram, and we await the results of enquiries mentioned in your last sentence.
> It occurs to us that while official request for facilities for Naval Attaché to visit internment districts might meet with rebuff informal suggestion by Naval Attaché himself might be less likely to do so. Do you agree, and would such a rebuff by involving the national honour complex risk undoing such good results as have so far been achieved? (Ibid, 8 September 1942)

On the same day, the Argentine Government issued a new decree to concentrate the Graf Spee sailors in one place. Details did not arrive in Britain until a week later.

Two days later, 10 September, the *St Louis Post-Despatch,* reported,

> ARGENTINA ACTS TO STOP ESCAPES OF GRAF SPEE MEN. BUENOS AIRES, Sept. 10 (AP). -The Argentine Government yesterday ordered all interned members of the crew of the scuttled German pocket battleship Graf Spee placed in a single internment camp in order to avoid further "escapes from Argentine territory."
> Juan Antonio Solari, chairman of the Chamber of Deputies committee investigating anti-Argentine activities, said last month that more than 100 of 1000 interned Nazis had fled the country and at least six were fighting against the United Nations. (*St Louis Post-Despatch,* 10 September 1942)

On the same day Kelly updated the Foreign Office on developments in Buenos Aires in telegram 765.

> Your telegram No. 689.

Semi-official newspaper Nacion today publishes inspired statement as follows:

(a) Ministry of Foreign Affairs took the initiative in demanding the adopting of effective measures for interning Graf Spee crew; latter having failed, by attempting to escape, to respond to humanitarian internment regulations based on international law.

(b) As a result the Minister of the Interior is empowered under a decree signed by the President, to "concentrate" them under appropriate custody in an appropriate place to be determined".

2. Friendly Minister of the Interior has already been supplied privately with suitable suggestions for internment of the entire crew in a distant place in the interior and is considering the plan.

3. At the risk of being proved over optimistic, I feel this is promising result of pressure exerted unceasingly by us and that there is a possibility of the majority if not all of those still in Buenos Aires being removed shortly to a relatively safe internment camp.

4. You will no doubt agree in these circumstances that the action suggested in the last paragraph of your telegram is at least for the time being unsuitable.

My adviser agrees that it would be likely to raise national honour complex unless at any rate we could say that the procedure was customary but I can hardly believe the German Military Attaché would be allowed to parade [sic] British internees in Sweden or Switzerland. (TNA ADM 116/5475, 12 September 1942)

The Californian *Los Gatos Times* reported on a statement made in the anti-Argentine investigation about the Graf Spee escapes in an article dated 11 September.

ESCAPE: Of the more than 1000 officers and men interned when the German pocket battleship Graf Spee was scuttled in Montevideo more than 100 have escaped internment in Argentina Juan Antonio Solari chairman of a senate committee investigating anti-Argentine activities said. (*Los Gatos Times*, 11 September 1942)

The following day. Kelly provided additional detail in telegram 775.

My telegram 765.
Press has misread decree which quotes international law empowering incarceration in fortress as justification for the Argentine Government's intention, now that humane measure have been answered by escapes, to concentrate the crew inland.

2. CONFIDENTIAL. I learn that internment camp under consideration is in Sierra de la Ventana about 100 miles inland from Bahia Blanca. (TNA ADM 116/5475, 12 September 1942)

One of the SOE files on South America contains the following report:

UNITED STATES
   LONDON REPORT SO/964
SOURCE: G140 from G426
   September 11th, 1942
Following for GM:

APPEASEMENT IN THE ARGENTINE

President Roosevelt's suggestion of a meatless day has caused some concern in Argentine government circles. They fear that it will set a precedent which will injure them economically. In the opinion of this source, the British Government has only to diminish or even threaten to diminish its purchases of meat from the Argentine in order to bring the Castillo administration to heel. Or even overthrow it. He may be over-optimistic but it is quite clear that this is the best weapon we have, and it is deplorable that we do not make use of it.

The present situation is that so far from putting economic pressure upon the Argentine ruling class, we are pursuing a policy which is giving the estancieros [cattle ranch owners] the benefit of the greatest boom that they have known for years. Not only are we buying the entire Argentine meat surplus at inflated prices, but we are letting it be understood in the Argentine that we shall continue to do so both during and after the war, however unsatisfactory its political conduct may be. A terrifying illustration of this was given by the Brazilian YP [symbol for Ambassador] in London to G.100. The exigencies of the war have allowed us to take an increased quantity of Brazilian meat, and the Brazilian YP had expressed the hope that some proportion of this increased trade would be continued after the war. He was told that this was impossible in view of our understanding with the Argentine. This was extremely disillusioning to him in view of te difference in the behaviour of the Brazilian and Argentine Governments, and made him doubt, with some reason, how far we wholeheartedly engaged in prosecuting the war. No doubt we have great capital interests in the Argentine which would stand to lose by the application of any economic sanctions, but it is intolerable that they should be allowed to impede our war effort in this way.

Politically also our present foreign policy in relation to the Argentine is one of appeasement; and it has become quite clear that it is not serving our interests. It may not in fact be true that there is any disagreement between the British and the U.S. Governments about the standpoint that should be adopted in the face of Argentine neutrality; but we have good evidence that the Argentine Government is making capital out of this possibility. Indeed, G6,000 reported reported that RUIZ GUINAZU [pro-Axis Argentine Foreign Minister] actually said in his speech in the secret session of the Argentine Chamber on July 17th, that his policy of neutrality had the secret support of the British Government which did not approve of the economic pressure which the U.S. was trying to put upon the Argentine. This was immediately and hotly denied by our YP in the Argentine; but subsequent evidence from both S.O. and S.I.S. sources makes it reasonably certain that even if RUIZ GUINAZU did not actually make this allegation, he contrived to give the Deputies the impression that it was true. The theory is that Great Britain is jealous and apprehensive of the extension of U.S. influence in South America, and is opposed to the Argentine breaking relations with the Axis for fear that this step would bring her more closely within the U.S. orbit. Whether this is true or not is not the decisive factor. The point is that it is believed to be true in the Argentine, and the fact that it is so believed very greatly strengthens the Government's position. Our friends have been doing their best to discredit the rumour. For example, a denial of it was published by DAMONTE TABOADA [one of Argentina's leading anti-Fascists] in "Argentine Libre" and resulted in the suspension of the paper. But their denials cannot carry the necessary conviction as long as the actions of the British Government continue to suggest that the rumour is true. The Americans would undoubtedly support us in any strong action that we proposed to take. Only the Foreign office tradition and private economic interest are holding us back. If the right people are approached in London, surely something can be done. (TNA HS8/113, 11 September 1942)

A copy of the translation of the Argentine Government's decree was sent to London by bag.

Enclosure in Buenos Aires despatch No. 210 of September 14th 1942.
ARGENTINE REPUBLIC
MINISTRY OF THE INTERIOR
(Dossier No. 269/1942) Buenos Aires, September 8th 1942.
Having regard to the present proceedings by which the Ministry of Foreign Affairs and Public Worship formulate various

considerations about the general situation of the ex-seamen of the German ex-battleship "GRAF SPEE"; and

WHEREAS:

By reason of the arrival in the country of the crew of the German battleship "GRAF SPEE", sunk in River Plate waters, the Executive Power in fulfilment of the duties which international law imposes on neutral countries, ordained the internment of the said crew by Decree No. 50.826 of December 19th, 1939; and

WHEREAS:

These obligations are governed by dispositions consonant with the international conventions on the rights and duties of neutral powers in the event of land and sea warfare, the general principle of which is stated in the following disposition: - "The neutral power which receives in its territory troops belonging to belligerent armies will intern them if possible far from the theatre of war". "That power will be entitled to detain them in encampments or imprison them in fortresses or places suitable for that purpose". "That power will decide whether officers may remain at liberty under parole that they will not leave the neutral territory without authorisation". (Article 57, Regulation regarding the laws of land warfare. 1889 text); and

WHEREAS:

Up to the present the Argentine authorities have endeavoured, within the limits of the obligations imposed on the Argentine republic as a neutral nation, to see that the internment was carried out in the best form possible for those comprised under it, the latter not having responded to these humanitarian intentions in the required measure, since in the time which has elapsed since the Decree of 1939 various escapes from Argentine territory have taken place; and

WHEREAS:

In consequence measures assuring the efficacy of the internment prescribed at that time must be adopted.

THE PRESIDENT OF THE ARGENTINE NATION
DECREES:

Article 1. The relevant instructions to the effect that the ex-crew of the ex-battleship "GRAF SPEE" should be concentrated under proper vigilance in a place to be duly fixed shall be issued by the Ministry of the Interior.

Article 2. The Governors of Provinces in which there are internees to be informed.

Article 3. To be communicated, published, given to the National Registry and filed.

CASTILLO

Miguel J. Culaciati
Decree No. 129.358 (TNA ADM 116/5475)

On 17 September, Marshall wrote the following note.

> Our continued pressure on the Foreign Office insisting that the strongest representations should be made by our Ambassador at Buenos Aires over the slackness of Argentine internment measures for Graf Spee internees, has now borne fruit. Arrangements have been made that the Embassy will be supplied with photographs of the crew of the Graf Spee [Leandro Bustamento published *Los Rostros del Graf Spee*, a book which includes photographs and details of all the officers and crew found in documents released by the Uruguayan Ministry of Foreign Affairs] and an effort is being made to have last minute searches of outgoing neutral vessels.
> In addition we had suggested that the N.A. Rio might, on an informal basis, suggest to the Argentines that he should be permitted to visit the internment areas as a result of which he might be able to make friendly suggestions for improvements which would minimise the number of escapes thereby obviating the necessity of continued diplomatic protests by us! However, in view of the terms of the enclosed telegrams nos. 765 and 775 from Sir D. Kelly, empowering the Minister of Interior to place the crew in an inland concentration camp, Foreign Office have been informed that we agree that any suggestion that the N.A. should make a visit to the internment areas is, at least for the time being, unsuitable. (TNA ADM 116/5474, 17 September 1942)

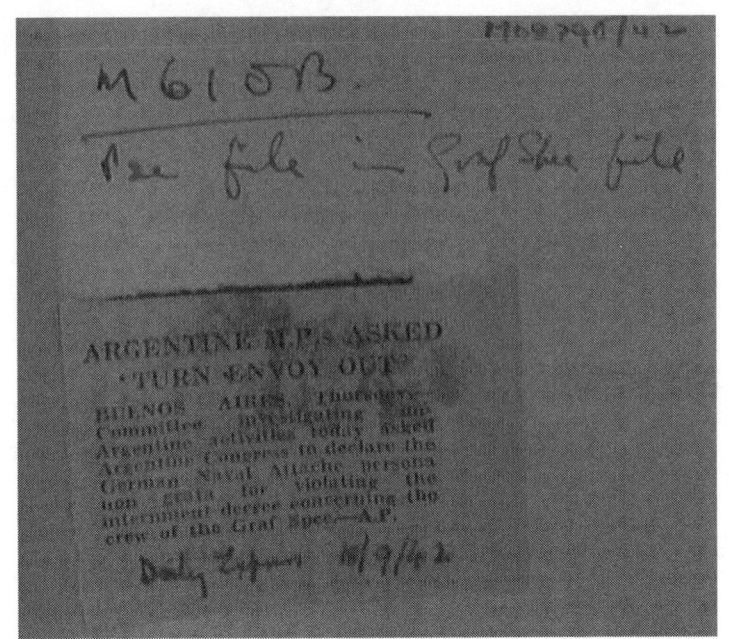

Request to expel Niebuhr 18 September 1942 (TNA ADM 116/5475)

On 18 September, Forster sent a note to the Admiralty and S.B.N.O. [Senior British Naval Officer Western Atlantic with copies to OIC, DSD, N.L. and M.

> For Lt. Izard B.N.A. Washington from B.N.A. Buenos Aires Congress Committee studying anti-Argentine activities published today long report on escapes of GRAF SPEE crew accused German Naval Attaché Niebuhr of having ordered arranged and facilitated escapes by provision of false passports etc., and asks Government to declare that he is persona non grata.
> Any evidence that you could spot supporting charges would be exceptionally useful. (Ibid.)

On 18 September, the *Halifax Evening Courier* reported on Chamber of Deputies' decision.

GRAF SPEE CREW
German Naval Attache and Escapes Buenos Aires, Friday.— The German Naval Attache in Buenos Aires is declared persona non grata in a Bill introduced in the Chamber of Deputies by the committee investigating anti-Argentine activities.

The measure follows the publication of a lengthy report, drawn up by the committee, on the escape of a number of the interned crew of the Graf Spee, in which the Naval Attache is held responsible for the escapes. It is declared that he even established an office known as the Graf Spee Bureau.

A second Bill introduced by the committee provides that the criminal court shall determine what responsibility should be attributed to the members of the staff of the Graf Spee Bureau.— Reuter.

Montevideo, Friday. Representatives of Uruguay Argentina. Brazil. Paraguay and Bolivia will discuss the attitude of their Governments to aliens—particularly those belonging to the Axis countries—at a conference to meet next Monday at Rivera.— Reuter. (*Halifax Evening Courier*, 18 September 1942)

The *Windsor Star* reported,

Inquiry Shows Niehbur [sic] Aided Escape of Graf Spee Sailors.
BUENOS AIRES, Sept. 18.-Asserting that the German naval attache at Buenos Aires, Capt. Dietrich Niehbur, had aided interned crewmen of the scuttled Nazi pocket battleship Admiral Graf Spee to escape from Argentina, a congressional committee sought today to have him expelled.

In a report submitted to the lower House the committee, which has been investigating anti-Argentine activities, recommended that the government be asked to declare Niehbur persona no grata.
 EARLIER DENOUNCED ENVOY.

The action came just a year after the Chamber had requested similar action against former German Ambassador Edmund von Thermann, whom the same committee had denounced for propaganda activities. Von Thermann left Argentina last March, although the government never acted on the request for his expulsion.

In recommending that Niehbur be expelled, the committee also accused the Argentine Government of "deficient vigilance" over the German internees, declaring that despite repeated escapes they had been granted all sorts of privileges.
 NOW IN U-BOATS

"The position of neutrality of the Argentine Government has been compromised," the report said, "by the fact that some of the fugitives now are in active service in German submarines operating in American waters."

Altogether, the report said, more than 130 of the 1055 interned Admiral Graf Spee officers and men had fled the country. (*The Windsor Star,* 18 September 1942)

The *Belfast News Letter* reported the same event the following day.

GRAF SPEE MEN BACK AT SEA
Officers Command U-Boats BUENOS AIRES, Five ex-officers of the Admiral Graf Spee are commanding German submarines operating American waters, and another has been taken prisoner, according to report published last night by the Argentine Deputies' Committee, appointed to investigate anti-Argentine activities. The report, covering the internment and escapes of officers and crew of the Admiral Graf Spee, accuses the Argentine authorities of negligence. It says that the person who was primarily responsible for these was the German naval attache, Captain Dietrich Niebuhr, who supplied the fugitives with false passports. The committee recommend that Niebuhr should be declared persona non grata by the Argentine Government. Times telegram (copyright), per Press Association. A Reuter message from Buenos Aires says that the German Charge d'Affaires [] called on Senor Gace, Under Secretary for Foreign Affairs, to ask him to make it clear that none of the Graf Spee officers had broken his parole by escaping from Argentina, since no parole had been given. Senor Gace agreed that no parole had been given by any of the escapers. (*Belfast News-Letter*, 19 September 1942)

The same day, the Australian newspaper, *The Mirror*, reported the same story.

GRAF SPEE ECHO
BUENOS AIRES, Today: Inglorious end of the German battleship Graf Spee, scuttled by her crew after she had been battered mercilessly by British fight cruisers, was recalled here today when expulsion of German naval attaché, Captain Dietrich Niebuhr, was recommended to the Government.

Committee investigating anti-Argentina activities made this recommendation on the grounds that Niebuhr had arranged the escape of the Graf Spee crew who had been interned in Argentina. The German charge d'affaires, Dr. Meynen, asked the Argentine Government to deny publicly Argentine newspaper reports that 130 Graf Spee internees violated a pledge when they escaped from the internment camp. (*The Mirror*, Perth, Saturday 19 September 1942, p.14)

The *Irish Independent* reported on the same day.

Argentine Revelations ESCAPE OF GRAF SPEE OFFICERS Five ex-officers of the Admiral Graf Spee are commanding German submarines in American waters and another has been taken prisoner, according to a report published by the Argentine Deputies Committee appointed to investigate anti-Argentine activities.

The report, covering the internment and escapes of officers and crew of the Admiral Graf Spee, accuses the Argentine authorities of negligence. It says that the person who was primarily responsible for these escapes was the German Naval Attaché, Capt. Dietrich Neibuhr [sic], who supplied the fugitives with false passports. The Committee recommend that Capt. Niebuhr should be declared persona non grata [unwelcome person] by the Argentine Government. – Times (Copyright) for Press Association. (*Irish Independent,* 19 September 1942)

Kelly sent telegram 788 to the Foreign Office, Washington, Montevideo, Santiago, Rio de Janeiro and Asuncion on 19 September.

Various incidents and trends indicate a certain degree of effervescence in the Argentine Republic.

2. The Foreign Affairs Committee of Congress has reported on private members' motions for rupture of relations with the Axis and for ratifications of the Rio de Janeiro agreements, radicals and socialists being in favour, others against both measures. The opposition of the latter is based on the argument that the Rio de Janeiro agreements do not constitute a ratifiable treaty but are "a collection of norms" [accepted patterns of behaviour] on which the Argentine Government should base their decree and laws.

3. Congress Committee investigating anti-Argentine activities issued a report on September 17th on the Graf Spee internees, of which satisfactory features are that it indicates that the Minister of the Interior has released to the Committee information provided by this Embassy especially in regard to the escape of officers now actively engaged in submarine warfare and contains severe criticism of the German Naval Attaché and a request for his removal.

4. A series of apologetics between pro-totalitarians and democratic students at the Law School Buenos Aires has resulted in indefinite closure thereof by the university authorities: similar disturbances followed in the School of Economics. All these disturbances started with a demonstration against Justo [General Augustin P. Justo, the former President of Argentina,

was flown to Brazil on 6 September by their President Getulio Vargas "to defend liberty against tyranny"] but the demonstrators' vociferous support of Castillo probably causes the Government more embarrassment than pleasure. Justo's visit to Brazil has had a good press though the Radical Party organisation has taken the opportunity to show their dislike of Justo's methods thus hinting at their determination not to be drawn into any combination with him for the next election. Justo stated privately to a member of my staff that he would not, as currently rumoured, go to the United States "until the Argentine Government authorises me to take decisions in their name".

5. The mass meeting to express [grp.undec: ?solidarity] with Brazil is scheduled for this afternoon and is to be addressed by one or more ex-Ministers for Foreign Affairs.

6. Proprietors and employees of private bus companies on strike for 10 days against absorption into the Transport Corporation are again at work pending further negotiations: but there is still talk of possible general strike which the police actually feared a week ago. Owing to the identification of Buenos Aires Tramway Company with the Corporation this strike has been accompanied by some anti-British talk.

7. The Government proposals for increased control and taxation of private enterprise of all kinds has united the chief Agricultural and Industrial organisations into launching a joint campaign of propaganda against these measures; and there has been general and continuous attack in the press against the steady increase in the number of Government employees and Government expenditure.

8. It is too early to assess the general effect of all this on the Government's foreign policy but suppression of the German organisation in my telegram No. 782 is at least a hopeful sign as is the publicity to Graf Spee question. (TNA ADM 116/5475, 19 September 1942)

The *Sunday Times* of Perth, Australia, reported the following day that 'A committee investigating anti-Argentine activities has recommended the Government to expel the German naval attaché, Captain Dietrich Niebuhr.' (*Sunday Times,* Sunday 20 September 1942, p.1)

Richard McGaha described Niebuhr's role in the escapes in his PhD thesis on 'The Politics of Espionage: Nazi Diplomats and Spies in Argentina, 1933 – 1945'. He stated that following Langsdorff's suicide,

The German embassy in Buenos Aires asked the Argentine government to accept the internees. The Ortiz government vacillated and claimed it did not have facilities to house the men. While the embassy awaited an answer Niebuhr arranged with his friend Rudolf Hepe to hire Delfino company vessels to bring the surviving one thousand crew members to Argentina. The arrival of the crew members presented the Argentine government with a fait accompli and caused a storm of protest in Argentina. Niebuhr managed to calm the situation by suggesting that the officers and men be housed in German structures such as rest homes and schools. The Argentine government rejected Niebuhr's suggestion and placed the crew in internment camps controlled by the Argentine military. It helped that Niebuhr was generous in handing out bribes to prevent the crewmembers being returned to Uruguay. ("Memorandum, re. Dietrich Niebuhr," RG 65, 64-20041, Box 9, p. 8, Rout and Bratzel, The Shadow War, p. 332)

After ensconcing the crew in their internment camps, Niebuhr set about arranging their escape back to Europe. He and his assistants, Lieutenant Franz Mammen and Lieutenant Martin Müller, visited the camps several times and ascertained that the Argentine guards would do little to stop a determined escape effort. Mammen was a merchant marine officer whose ship was interned in Uruguay in November 1939. When the ship was sold to Argentina in March 1940 he moved to Buenos Aires and obtained a job on Niebuhr's staff. Mammen's duties were limited to being a cipher clerk and performing general duties. Müller was a timber merchant from Hamburg who was caught in South America when war broke out. He was subsequently attached to Niebuhr's office where he acted as Niebuhr's assistant. Müller also functioned as Niebuhr's contact with the various agents employed by the attaché's office. ("Full Report on Brandt et. al.," February 28, 1946, NARA, RG 65, 65-56876-1, Box: Targets, pp. 2-3) Under Niebuhr's orders he directed missions, made payments to agents and contacted informants. Both men were also commissioned reserve naval officers. ("Interrogation of Brandt et. al.," NARA, RG 59, 862.20235/10-1646, Box 6742, p. 2.) They stated to their post-war interrogators that their knowledge of intelligence operations was limited. Both men claimed Niebuhr was extremely secretive and the only person he appeared to confide in was Chargé d' Affairs Meynen. (Ibid, p. 11) In January 1940 two other men, Eugen Langer (code name: "Eugen") and Wilhelm von Seidlitz (code name: "Dicker") helped arrange for some Graf Spee crewmembers to be smuggled back to Germany on Spanish and Portuguese ships leaving various ports in Argentina. Other men were taken to Chile where another member of Niebuhr's network, Friedrich von Schulz-Hausmann, director of North German Lloyd's Valparaiso affiliate, arranged for their passage back to Germany via Vladivostok on Japanese flagged ships. (For more information on Schulz-Hausmann's background see NARA, RG 319, GELA, p. 101)

Like the escape of the merchant ships, the repatriation of the Graf Spee crew was considered a success. Nearly two hundred crewmembers were returned to the Third Reich. Most were officers and technicians who returned to the war in the Atlantic. The cost of the operation was at least seventy thousand dollars. ("Final Interrogation Report of Kapitan zur See Dietrich Niebuhr," NARA, RG 65, 64-20041, Box 9, p. 6 and "Sworn Statement of Esteban J. Amorin," 8 May 1947, NARA, RG 65, 64-20041, Box 9, p. 1) In some ways, it was a bargain for the German Navy since it got back trained, battle-tested crewmen. In his post-war interrogation Niebuhr expressed surprise that the Argentine parliament and press had attacked him for aiding the escape of the Graf Spee crew. He stated that no crew member had broken his word of honor or taken advantage of any furlough to escape. Niebuhr emphasized that the sailors were duty-bound to do everything possible to escape. Nevertheless, Niebuhr explained that the sailors had only promised not to escape when on leave and it was only valid for the duration of the leave. Besides, Niebuhr innocently explained, he had not taken part in the escape of the crew members. How could he, when he was sitting at his desk in the embassy? ("Memorandum, re. Dietrich Niebuhr," NARA, RG 65, 64-20041, Box 9, p. 9 and "Interrogation of Captain Dietrich Niebuhr," NARA, RG 59/M679/3, p. 11) Thermann and Niebuhr decided in November 1940 to halt the escape of the Graf Spee crew. ("Thermann to Berlin," 30 November 1940, Handakten Clodius, NARA, RG 242/T-120/178/86484, also "The Embassy in Argentina to the Foreign Ministry," 30 November 1940, Doc. 429, DGFP, D, XI, p. 754) The operations were causing diplomatic problems with other Latin American nations. (McGaha, Richard, 'The Politics of Espionage: Nazi Diplomats and Spies in Argentina, 1933 – 1945', Ohio University, 2009, p.176)

The Admiralty and Foreign Office files examined made no mention of Niebuhr's involvement in the escapes. His expulsion from the Argentine was the result of the activities of American Federal Bureau of Investigation (FBI)'s Special Intelligence Service. According to the FBI website, Argentina, unlike other South American countries during the Second World War,

...as a result of its policies—distanced itself from the U.S. and drew itself closer, diplomatically, to Germany. This meant that Argentina was a hotbed of intrigue, and it proved to be a tougher environment for members of the FBI's Special Intelligence Service (SIS), the U.S. intelligence component whose mission was to identify and counter Nazi operatives in South America.

Although it obtained little official cooperation from Buenos Aires, the SIS was able to work with local officials, funneling them evidence that would result in the arrest of German operatives. To do this, the Bureau had assigned its first non-official cover agent to Buenos Aires in September 1940, and by mid-1942, agents had been assigned in an official liaison capacity to the U.S. Embassy and two consulates. By late 1943, at the height of SIS operations, the FBI had several agents operating as official liaisons as well as 37 agents working against the Nazis in undercover positions.

These agents had their work cut out for them. Although Buenos Aires was ostensibly neutral, U.S. Undersecretary of State Summer Welles had identified it—in 1942—as being a base for Axis espionage operations. The Nazis were using Argentina's ambivalence to funnel their own intelligence agents into the Western Hemisphere, to enhance radio communications across South and Central America for its agents, and to smuggle strategic minerals back to Germany. The FBI needed to put a stop to all of these actions.

SIS personnel faced many dangers as they were surveilled, harassed, and—in one instance—arrested.

Through one investigation, our agents discovered that an official in one of the American firms that provided cover jobs in Argentina for SIS members was strongly pro-Nazi and used the company to the detriment of the U.S. The FBI was successful in bringing this derogatory information to the attention of the firm's New York headquarters, which fired the employee before he "succeeded in doing either the SIS program or his company any particular harm."

Smugglers were an even bigger concern. The Bureau wanted to ensure that the Nazi war machine did not have access to valuable commodities that would allow them to build higher-tech weapons. In one of our biggest successes, SIS agents learned that the German naval attaché in Argentina, Dietrich Niebuhr, was orchestrating the smuggling of strategic war materials through the British naval blockade. He and his operatives would buy mica, platinum, and industrial diamonds on the black market and use seamen aboard Portuguese and Spanish freighters to courier it back to German industries.

FBI SIS agents surveilled these operations and collected a wealth of intelligence against Niebuhr's smugglers that could be shared with local law enforcement willing to work with us. The intelligence also helped the U.S. to develop an extensive "List of Certain Blocked Nationals" (a predecessor to today's U.S. Department of Commerce's Entity List) that U.S. and British customs officials could use to disrupt Niebuhr's smugglers in the Caribbean. And Niebuhr was eventually expelled from Argentina. (https://www.fbi.gov/news/stories/special-intelligence-service-in-argentina-during-wwii)

What the SIS did not investigate was Niebuhr's role in the escape of the Graf Spee internees. Further details about this will be examined later.

Also on 20 September, Marshall commented, that

> After consulting the D. of P., who agreed, a copy of SO(I) Montevideo's R/S [Radio Signal] 1301/15/42 of 14th August has been sent to Foreign Office with a request that Sir D. Kelly should make strong representations for the return to internment of the Graf Spee stowaways.
>
> With regard to S.O.N.D West Atlantic's telegram No. 1222P/22 Sept to B.N.A. Washington, M. Branch will appreciate if DNI will ascertain what information, if any, is available for Anthony Patric [?], as any such information might be of great use in reinforcing further representations to the Argentine Government. (TNA ADM 116/5475, 20 September 1942)

The Examiner of Launceston, Tasmania, reported on the Graf Spee in late October that the Uruguayan Government has authorised a private firm to raise the hull of the scuttled Nazi battleship Graf Spee from the bottom of the River Plate to reclaim the ship's steel. 'The Graf Spee has been gradually sinking in the mud since salvagers removed her superstructure a year ago.' (*The Examiner,* 21 October 1942, p.1)

On the same day, 21 October, Forster updated the Admiralty with details about the escapees. Copies were also sent to DNI, OIC, DSD, M.34, DOP and the Foreign Office.

> (i) After deducting 8 medical personnel excluded: Officer 36 Warrant Officer 47 P.O's 197 seamen 751 civilians 19 total 1046.
> (ii) Escapes acknowledged by Argentine Government Officers 30 Warrant Officers 7 P.O's 37 seamen 79. Statistics probably only up to May 30th 1941. With reference to my 2152Z Aug. 29th if you have confirmation of that escapes have been made in Spanish

vessels I recommend action against S/S Lines [? Spanish Shipping Company].
(iii) Lengthy detailed Government statement was translated and posted you by HIGHLAND MONARCH Oct. 6th. In view of (i) delicate political situation (ii) excellent personal relations between Naval Attaché and Ministry of Marine, Ambassador assumes no action will be taken as to a protest without further reference to him. (TNA ADM 116/5475, 21 October 1942)

HMS *Highland Monarch* took Graf Spee sailors back to Germany in 1946
(http://shippingandshipbuilding.uk/files/201710161814260.HIGHLANDMONARCH.jpg)

https://www.britisharmedforces.org/pages/nat_troopships.htm

There was a pencilled sum underneath 37 + 37 + 79 = 153. Two days later, SBNO Western Atlantic sent BNA Washington, DNI and Forster the following message. Copies were also sent to OIC, DSD, EH, M34 and NL.

British Naval Attaché Buenos Aires 1520 18th Censorship report indicates that cables Editor Chicago Tribune could give address of Anthony Patric who may have information about escape of Graf Spee crew. (Ibid, 23 September 1942)

Johnston informed the Admiralty the next day that the men referred to in their note of 22 September were still being detained awaiting a legal decision as to their disposal. Admiralty then queried whether they had been returned to internment. (Ibid, 24 September 1942)

At the end of September a copy of a letter from Robert Meynell and Company, Reconquista 314, Buenos Aires, wrote to Leng Robert and Company, 1 Royal Exchange Street, London, dated 11 September. Given its relevance copies were sent to ADM, DNI, NID, MEW, PET, INF, FOOD, FO and DRW.

WEEKLY NEWS BULLETIN nos. 377 and 378
Ref. NEVY/WLM.613.
Cover encloses WEEKLY NEWS BULLETINS issued by writers. […]
"GRAF SPEE" SAILORS, Para. Dated 10 Sept. 42. States as follows:
"According to a decree issued by the Government yesterday, the "Graf Spee" sailors are to be concentrated in a place to be determined later. The decree states that the Argentine Authorities had tried to supervise the interned sailors, within the obligations of Argentina as a neutral country, in the best possible manner, but that the sailors had not reacted in a way appropriate to these humanitarian considerations, as evidenced by the fact that since 1939 a number of them had left Argentine territory (see News Bulletin 329)" .(Ibid, 29 September 1942)

The following day, Marshall wrote another letter to the Foreign Office.

Dear Gallop,
I enclose a copy of a reference Sheet from our Intelligence Officer at Montevideo concerning some Graf Spee escapees who have been landed by the masters of a Swedish and a Spanish ship. You will note that it is stated these stowaways were landed at

Lecalada Light Vessel. I understand, however, that this should probably be Recalada Light House, in the Argentine.

Following this report, we sent a telegram to the Naval Attaché Montevideo enquiring whether these men were returned to internment. In reply we were informed that these men are still detained pending a decision as to their disposal. Since the men have escaped from Argentina and they have been returned to Argentina, it is not easy to understand what legal difficulty arises to prevent the return of these men to internment.

Will you please take this matter up with our Ambassador at Buenos Aires requesting him to represent strongly that these men must be returned to internment. (Ibid, 30 September 1942)

The following day, the Acting Director of Naval Intelligence (ADNI) sent NID.2 a minute stamped SECRET in red regarding a copy of a report received from a secret source.

GRAF SPEE INTERNEES

1. A press report published in New York on July 21, suggested that former members of the crew of the German pocket battleship GRAF SPEE, had managed to escape from internment in Argentina and joined the German submarine fleet. It was stated that of the 1,055 officers and men interned after the scuttling of the German ship, at least 128 were reported in an official document dated September 1941, to have escaped. Since that time no further information on the escapees has become available. The newspaper reported that the Buenos Aires paper "Critica" had demanded that the Government reveal how many of the original number were still in the Argentine and what measures were being taken to ensure that they remain there.

2. We referred this report to C.S.O. Buenos Aires, asking for his comments. He states that a full report of the situation is being prepared in Buenos Aires by the British Naval Attaché for forwarding to the Naval Attaché in Washington. He confirms the belief that a number of ex-Graf Spee men are now serving in German submarines, and in particular he expresses grave concern at the fact that 148 of these men are still interned in Buenos Aires with liberty of action, in spite of the fact that the terms of the internment clause demand that those not placed on the Island of Martin Garcia should be interned well inland. It is clear that these men could very easily be organised into a group of expert and dangerous saboteurs.

C.S.O. expressed the hope that the British Embassy in Buenos Aires will make further representations to the Argentine Government to have the men concerned removed to a place of greater safety. In view of the great potential danger to our shipping arising from their relative freedom, we too heartily concur in this hope. (Ibid, 1 October 1942)

The British Naval Attaché in Washington informed Forster and S.B.N.O.W.At., [Senior British Naval officer Western Atlantic} that 'Anthony Patrick [sic]'s address was Rio de Janeiro, Caica. The following day, DNI sent a secret note to Johnston and Forster.

Your 2031. 23 September note to Buenos Aires Presume Dieter and Clasesmer have now been returned to internment. If not please report reason and nature of any representations which have been made to Argentine Government.
What is position regarding remaining stowaway? (Ibid, 14 October 1942)

Two days later, 16 October, Kelly updated Eden personally about the investigation of the anti-Argentine activities committee.

Sir,
With reference to my telegram No. 775 of the 12th September I have the honour to transmit herewith a memorandum prepared by the Naval Attaché of this Embassy summarising the report of the Committee of the Chamber of Deputies which investigated the escape of the interned men of the "Graf Spee."
2. the resolutions referred to therein were published in a Congressional report of the 22nd September of which a copy was sent by sea bag to the Director of Naval Intelligence on the 25th September last. [Sea passage Buenos Aires to Belfast was between 18 and 19 days] They received a certain amount of notice in the press; but had not been approved by the Chamber of Deputies when the latter ended its session on 30th September.
3. As shown in Captain Forster's summary the Committee – which was predominantly anti-Government in character and composition – charged the Government with negligence and maintained that the German Naval Attaché in Buenos Aires was responsible for the systematic organisation of the escapes which take place: mainly via Paraguay and Chile, so long as these routes could be used to connect with Japanese ships in the Pacific, or the German trans-Atlantic airlines.
4. Captain Niebuhr's action in setting up disciplinary courts has further been the subject of condemnation by "La Prensa" and other newspapers as derogatory to Argentine sovereign rights. A demand for his removal was therefore sponsored by part of the press; but seems for the present to have died down.

5. The Committee further suggested that the crew should be concentrated in some safe place and, as reported in my telegram under reference, the Minister of the Interior has considered amongst other places Sierra de la Ventana, about 100 miles inland from Bahia Blanca. This proposal, when put privately to a member of this Embassy for approval, had to be answered guardedly because the area in question is believed to have a considerable German population. Since then Senor Culaciati has toyed with the idea of Corrientes as a suitable and not too pleasant internment area. Unfortunately it would be dangerous to take up his jocular suggestion that the Naval Attaché should himself inspect the proposed place of internment; since so to do would be to assume at least a moral responsibility for any subsequent escapes.

6. Meanwhile the enclosed report from the British "watcher" in Mendoza gives satisfactory proof of increased police vigilance in the town in question, as a result it may fairly be surmised of the pressure exercised upon the Argentine Government by this Embassy.

7. The question of concentration and internment of the remaining members of the crew is kept constantly before the Argentine authorities; who are further disposed to take action since various members of the crew who desire to marry Argentine citizens have apparently complained of the German Embassy's attempts to send them back to Germany. There is however some disinclination on the part of the authorities to declare Captain Niebuhr persona non grata; on the ground that in engineering escapes he was doing no more than is the duty of any Naval Attaché in war time.

I have, etc. (Ibid, 16 October 1942)

Enclosure in Buenos Aires Despatch No. 234 of 16-10-1942
INTERNED CREW OF "ADMIRAL GRAF SPEE"

The following are comments on the Report of the Committee of the Chamber of Deputies which investigated the escapes of the interned men.

The first resolution (p.2044) is that the German Naval Attaché shall be declared "persona non grate" on account of his intervention in violations of the decrees governing the internment and of his collaboration in escapes of the same.

The second resolution asks that the police should close the "Administration office of the "GRAF SPEE" for similar reasons.

These resolutions have not yet been approved by the Chamber.

Pages 2038-2044: Decrees governing internment.

Pages 2045-2052: German Government protest against internment and Argentine Government's reply.

Pages 2052-2055: Recommendations by the Interamerican Neutrality Committee (Rio de Janeiro 26/1/40) for control of interned men.

(The above have been fully covered in Embassy despatches)/

Page 2056: ESCAPES OF OFFICERS AND MEN:

"The Committee considered that these have only been possible owing to the negligence of the authorities charged with watching them and because an organisation had been created with the object of arranging escapes."

"An excessive tolerance was shown in the granting of transfers and permission to journey which helped plans to escape.

"It is noteworthy that the majority of the fugitives were either officers or ratings with special technical qualifications. Amongst the latter were 5 warrant officers, 3 telegraphists, 26 mechanics, 5 electricians and 28 other specialists."

"This warrants the supposition that escapes were not made spontaneously or singly but in selected groups.

"Moreover, the proverbial discipline and obedience to superior authority which characterises the German sailor, the strict vigilance which the "Office of Administration of the GRAF SPEE" crew" and also the German Naval Attaché exercised over the crew would prevent individuals deciding on their own responsibility to commit acts which transgresses their situation as interned."

HOW ESCAPES WERE MADE:

"Two indispensable elements were necessary: personal documents and means of transport to where they wanted to go/

The Committee denounce:

That the personal documents, that is the passport, would have to be false and was prepared by order of the German Naval Attaché, Captain Niebuhr, as will be established elsewhere in the report.

That amongst other methods of travel employed by fugitives were the Condor and Lati air service and Japanese and Spanish shipping lines.

As regards the last named, attention is drawn to the capture of 4 ratings in the hold of the Spanish S.S. "ALBOREDA" by the Maritime Police on 24th July 1942.

THAT THE FOLLOWING ROUTES WERE USED FOR LEAVING THE COUNTRYTHAT THE FOLLOWING ROUTES WERE USED FOR LEAVING THE COUNTRY:

a) To Paraguay by river steamer and then Asuncion – Pernambuco – Caniries [sic – Canary Islands] by aeroplane.

b) Buenos Aires – Mendoza – San Rafael – Talca (Chile – Antofagasta and embarked on Japanese ship.

c) Buenos Aires – San Juan – Calingasta – Ovalle (Chile) – Antofagasta.

INSTRUCTIONS TO THE INTERNED CREW:

The fact that the crew were under strict control and that disobedience led to severe disciplinary measures is proved by the reproduction of letters from the Naval Attaché summoning members to the Embassy and by statements by members of the crew before the police.

Pages 2060-2069: Give the names of fugitives and the dates of their escape.

Pages 2070-2083: Give photographs of the majority of the above.

Pages 2084-2099: Give photographs and details of 38 men who tried to escape but were captured and of 6 who have also been sent to Martin Garcia for bad conduct.

Pages 2100-2105: Give photographs and details of a further 13 under trial for disorderly conduct.

Pages 2106-2117: Reproduce letters from the crew abusing Argentina and details of insults to the Argentine flag etc.

Pages 2118-2119: Give photos and details of escaped officers known to have returned to active service (based on Admiralty telegram 1251.B of 18 June 1942)

Pages 2120-2125: Accuse the German Naval Attaché of having organised the escapes, proof having been obtained when papers were seized in the house of Alfonso HAUN in Rosario in November 1940.
HAUN's statements fully prove that Niebuhr arranged escapes and provided false passports.

Pages 2126-2127: Describes the "Office of Administration" and allege that it maintained an improper disciplinary control over the crew.
It is mentioned that the Minister of the Interior gave Captain Kay permission to visit the interned men in February, 1940, at the inland settlements in order to study their living conditions.
This tour was followed by a further 51 escapes.

Pages 2127-2127: Criticise the authorities for their slackness in not preventing escapes, especially from supposedly well-guarded naval establishments, also for allowing 5 men to be employed by the Condor (German) air line. A further 6 are employed at the German Embassy on unknown duties.

Pages 2130-2133: Reports by the Ministry of Marine on how escapes had taken place from Martin Garcia. They invariably state that they have been unable to prove complicity or negligence of the naval guard and that how escape took place was an impenetrable mystery.

Pages 2134-2139: In order to find out the real activities of the "Office of Administration", the Committee summoned before them the Paymaster Lieutenant in charge (Herbert Drewe). He appeared but refused to declare without written permission from the Argentine Minister of Marine in whose charge he was declared to be.
He was therefore place under arrest for contempt of court but was subsequently released.

Pages 2140-2142: Government Decree of 8th September, 1942 deciding that the interned men should be incarcerated as by frequent escapes they had failed to respond to the liberal treatment the Argentine Government was prepared to give them.

Pages 2143-2146: CONCLUSIONS: The original internment arrangements did not comply with international law, nor were the necessary steps taken to prevent the interned becoming a disturbing element.
2. The German Embassy sustained their objection to the internment by facilitating escapes.
3. Escapes were due to the tolerance of the authorities in allowing the second in command [Kay] to tour the camps to organise escapes.
3. [sic] The method of escapes betray a standard of organisation which prevented tracing complicity.
5. The intervention of the "Office" and of the German Naval Attaché is proved without doubt.
5. [sic] The German Naval Attaché exercised an absolute control and at times threatened and punished the crew to the detriment of Argentine authority.
7. Argentine neutrality has been compromised by some of the fugitives now being again on active service in American waters.
8. it must be pointed out that the interned responded to the generous and humane treatment of the Argentine authorities by wounding Argentine sentiments and by acts which showed that they forgot or despised the hospitality shown them.
The Committee therefore asked that the crew are incarcerated in a safe place and that the German Naval Attaché should be declared "persona no grata" and that the Courts should investigate the illegal activities of the "Office of Administration". (Ibid.)

On the same day, 16 October, Johnston informed DNI. NID 18, BAD Washington and SO(I) Jamaica that the two captured Graf Spee escapees had been returned to internment in Martin Garcia.

On 21 October, Thomas sent the Admiralty an American report on the Graf Spee.

U.S. CONFIDENTIAL – BRITISH SECRET
GRAF SPEE

Internment

1055 crew members and officers of GRAF SPEE arrived in Buenos Aires December 18, 1939, and were housed in the "Arsenal Naval de Darsena Norte" and the "Direccion General de Immigracion". On December 19, 1939, an Argentine Government decree was issued (No.50826) whereby the officers of GRAF SPEE were to be interned in Buenos Aires and required to give their word of honour not to leave the city without written permission from the police authorities.

The German Embassy made an attempt to have GRAF SPEE survivors declared as "shipwrecked". Had this thesis been accepted they would not have been interned. However, the Argentine Government refused to adopt this point of view, specifically, because arrangements for vessels to pick up survivors had been made by the Germans before GRAF SPEE sailed for the last time.

Escapes

By March 16, 1940, 31 officers and man had escaped, and by the end of July, 1942, this number had risen to 120. Eight internees were arrested while attempting to stow away on the Spanish ALBOREDA on July 26, 1942.

Passports were provided for escapees by Kapt. NIEBUHR, German Naval Attaché. Planes of the "Condor" (German) and "Lati" (Italian) air-lines were sometimes used, as well as Japanese and Spanish vessels. The following routes were used:

(1.) Argentina – Paraguay (by river boat).

(2) Pernumuco – Canary Islands (by air).

(3) Buenos Aires – Mendoza – San Rafeal – Talca (Chile) – Antafagasta.

(4) Buenos Aires – San Juan – Calingasta – Ovalle (Chile) – Antafagasta.

Escapes left Antafagasta on Japanese vessels.

Of the 31 escaped officers, the following are stated by Argentine authorities to have joined the U-boat arm: K.K. WARRENBERG, Klt. Gunther SCHIEBUSCH, Klt. Friedrich MUMM, Klt. Dietrich BLUDAU, Heinrich KUMMER (Klt.)

OP 16-Z-P/W Comment

Of the above, only K.K. WATTENBERG (now P/W) has been identified with U-Boats (U-162). It should be noted that Argentine authorities were in error in stating that Georg BATSCH (now a P/W in Canada) commanded U-38. BATSCH commanded the Motor Torpedo Boat, S-38.

Forged passports were provided by the German Embassy and other false documents were procured by a German resident of Buenos Aires named Alfonso HAUN, who later confessed his participation to the Argentine police.

Escape Routes:

(I) From Buenos to Rosario, to Cordoba, to Villa Dolores, to San Luis, to Mendoza by bus. At Mendoza escapees stayed at the Hotel Maxim (owned by 2 Germans: Eckhardt and Suess). From Mendoza to San Juan, by train. Here they stayed at the home of an optician, Albert ZIMMERMANN, Calle Rivadivia 910. From there to Calingasta, where they stayed at the home of a German manufacturer, Wilhelm HANCKE, who also supplied the horses for the crossing of the Andes to Ovalle (Chile). Here the escapees reported to the German Consul at Coquimbo, Karl THARGER, who arranged for their transportation to Antofagasta, where they stayed at the home of Robert KULENKAMPF until their sailing on a Japanese vessel. This route was used by Kapt. Sur See KAY and NARKOERTER, Olt. DREW, and P.O.'s HENKEL and LAMMER, who were accompanied by HAUN up to Coquimbo (Chile).

(II) One officer, with HAUN's assistance, escaped to Paraguay. He was driven to Santa Fe in the car of Robert DIERS (manager of Siemens – Schuckert in Buenos Aires, offices at 977 Calle San Martin) and turned over to Karl WALTER at Santa Fe, Calle Belgrano 856. This officer had a forged passport in the name of Carlos ROPESKI, born at Warsaw, January 8, 1910. The officer's name is not known, but he escaped from the island of martin Garcia, where the more unruly elements were interned.

(III) Two tickets (No.'s 84,085 and 34,083) were issued by the "Agencia de Navagacion Mihanovitch Ltda." On September 25, 1940 to two escapees under the names "Maximo SCHNARCHENSTORF" and Herto FIKANTSCHERT. These were for passage on the S.S. GENERAL ARTIGAS from Rosario to Asuncion (Paraguay).

(IV) Several frustrated escape attempts from the island of Martin Garcia showed internees equipped with rubber boats, lifejackets, compasses, charts and a lantern with a white and blue lens. Information from Argentine Congressional Record, Orden del dia No. 166, September 16, 1942.

About a week later the Admiralty was sent the following telegram from 'El Mundo' in Buenos Aires.

GRAF SPEE: TWO OF CREW TRANSFERRED TO ISLAND
BUENOS AIRES: THE GOVERNMENT HAS DECREED THE TRANSFER TO MARTIN GARCIA ISLAND OF TWO FORMER MEMBERS OF THE 'GRAF SPEE' CREW, WHO HAVE BEEN LIVING IN THE PROVINCE OF CORDOBA. (Ibid, 22 October 1942)

Johnston reported on 28 October to DNI, and Forster that the remaining three stowaways were still being detained in the Central Police Department.

On the same day, Kelly wrote to Eden with information that the Argentinian authorities had imposed stricter controls on the internees.

Sir,
I have the honour, with reference to my despatch No, 234 of October 16th, to inform you that the press has recently given considerable publicity to the visit to Buenos Aires, with police permission, of 5 sailors from the "Graf Spee", interned in the Province of Cordoba, in order to have conversations with the Minister of the Interior in regard to their personal situations. The five sailors in question are: - Carlos Baldamus, Herberto Kleis, Erico Munsch, Walter Gehrke and Enrique Pursche; and it is understood that three of them are already married to women of Argentine nationality and the other two are engaged to Argentines.
2. Dr. Culaciati [Minister of the Interior] received these men on October 26th, one by one, and listened to what they had to say, promising to communicate further with them yesterday, after he had had time to study their position. No official statement has been issued by the Ministry, but the press has been given to understand that the chief reason for the visit was that the men wanted to know what their situation would be after the war and what action would be taken in regard to them when the time came for repatriation of the crew of this German warship. While the men themselves seem to have been cautious in their statement to the press, they have let it be understood that they have informed Dr. Culaciati of the various ways in which they have been subjected to pressure on the part of the German authorities owing to their "desertion" and their desire to settle in Argentina. They are said to have complained that they are the objects of hostility on the part of the officers and non-

commissioned officers of the ship, and of the embers of the German community in this country who are cooperating with the ship's officers in maintaining discipline among the sailors. The "Prensa" further states that they informed the Minister that many of their comrades would like to be able to escape from the severe "Gestapo control" to which all are subjected.

3. It may be presumed that the Ministry of the Interior is now studying whether, if the German Government were to demand the extradition of these members of the "Graf Spee" crew after the war, the Argentine Government would have to accept this demand; and whether it is possible, under International law, for these 5 men to be separated, now or in the future, from their fellow-inmates.

4. Commenting on the legal aspects of the case, the "Prensa" writes, in a leading article, that there is no foundation for the theory that interned belligerents are subject to extradition from a neutral country when hostilities cease. Such internees could not be held to have military status and their rights and obligations arose only from the sovereign laws of the country under whose jurisdiction they found themselves, not through their own free will but owing to an act of war. Traditional doctrine did not impose upon the interning country the obligation to order the departure of such belligerents when the state of war had passed. Thus, Argentina's only problem was, in the opinion of "La Prensa" to decide, in regard to these men, whether it would be of value to the country to admit them to become part of its population; or whether those laws were applicable in their case, which permitted expulsion of people who entered the country without fulfilling all the requirements of the immigration laws. Their custody as belligerents would end with the end of the war; they could not be considered as criminals; and as the military law of their own country would not be applicable to them, they could not be extradited even if in their own military law, they were held to be offenders. (TNA ADM 116/5474, 28 October 1942)

Perowne commented to Waldock that 'Prima facie [on first sight] it seems unlikely that Germany will claim extradition, but it is idle to speculate'. (Ibid.)

On 14 November, Kelly sent telegram 955 to the Foreign Office.

Your telegram No. 811.

Police surveillance undoubtedly stricter and no further escapes known.

2. Minister of the Interior states that the German Naval Attaché is under police surveillance.

3. Enclosure is being sent by air bag. (TNA ADM 116/5475, 14 November 1942)

The enclosure was a document sent from the British Security Co-ordination's Security Division in New York to the Security Executive in London. It was forwarded 'as information' to Sub. Lt. Wood ADNI, and Capt. Christie of SIS, the Admiralty and the Foreign Office.

THE CREW OF THE GRAF SPEE

1. On December 18. 1939. 1055 crew members of the sunken German cruiser 'GRAF SPEE' landed at Buenos Aires and were temporarily quartered in the Naval Arsenal at Darsena Norte and in the Immigration offices. On the following day a decree ordered their internment, "under word of honour not to absent themselves without official written authority". Commander Hans LANGSDORFF committed suicide on December 18, and three officers and five men were allotted the special work of liquidating [finalising] the ships affairs. The remaining 1046 were interned.

2. In May 1940, 31 men were found to have escaped from the Naval Arsenal and the remainder were allotted to different districts as follows:

Buenos Aires	177	Mendozo [sic] Province	100
Cordoba Province	252	Santa Fe Province	200
San Juan Province	50	Martin Garcia Island`	<u>236</u>

               1015

By the end of July 1942, 120 more had escaped and three had died, while eight were being specially held after being caught while stowing away.

3. Four days after the original internment the German Embassy registered a protest, claiming that the 'Graf Spee' crew, having been "brought ashore in a neutral country on a neutral ship", should be regarded as shipwrecked mariners, and left at liberty. The Argentine Government refused to agree that a ship intentionally scuttled could be regarded as a wreck. The latter decision was confirmed by the Inter-American neutrality Committee in Rio on January 26, 1940.

Analysis of Escapes

4. The subsequent escapes are attributed by the Investigation Committee on Anti-Argentine Activities as solely due to official negligence. Guarding was inefficient, and frequent permits for trips and transfers were granted, encouraging evasion. It is particularly notes that the great majority of the escapees were officers and technicians:

| Navigating Officers | 6 | Engineers | 26 |

Lieutenants	21	Electricians	5
Sublieutenants	3	Various Technicians	28
Petty Officers	5	Crew	23
Radio-operators	3		

This clearly suggested that the escapes were planned in groups, and might well have ulterior motives, such as sabotage or re-enlistment. Very strict discipline also appeared to have been maintained among the men by the officers and by the German naval Attaché, Dietrich NIEBUHR.

5. The main routes of escape are given officially as:
   (a) Argentine – Paraguay (by river), then Pernambuco – Canaries (by Condor and Lati plane).
   (b) Buenos Aires – Mendoza – San Rafael – Talca (Chile) – Antofagasta.
   (c) Buenos Aires – San Juan - Calingasta – Ovalle (Chile) – Antofagasta.

From Antofagasta, the escapees left on Japanese boats. Exact instructions as to transport were given by the German naval Attaché, and infringements severely punished. The men received individual summons to the Embassy, at definite times, and some were punished for having married locally.

Return to German Service

6. The report of the Investigation Committee provides evidence that a number of the escapees have succeeded in rejoining the German armed forces. Armed with false passports provided by the German Naval Attaché, 14 officers escaped from the Naval Arsenal on April 8, 1940, and 16 from Martin Garcia on August 31, 1940, not one of whom was recaptured. Of these, one Georg RATSCH was later taken prisoner on the sinking of the German submarine U38, while five others, Captain Jurgen WATTENBERG and Lieutenants Gunther SCHIEBUSCH, Frederick Mumm, Heinrich Kummer and Dietrich BLUDAU were also understood to be in command of submarines. Watterberg broadcast on the German radio, June 20, 1942, a description of his sinking of the Brazilian 'PARANAHYBA'.

Work of German Naval Attaché

7. The whole system of escapes seems to have been engineered by the German Naval Attaché with the assistance of a network of German agents., particularly in the frontier zones, who facilitated the escapees' passage over the Andes in Chile. On November 15, 1940, for example, the authorities at Rosario received news of a possible attempt organised by the local German resident, Alfonso HAUN. Haun had been teaching the internees Spanish, and on September 24 received a telephone call from Niebuhr at the German Embassy to meet a certain train from Buenos Aires.

Here he was introduced to two officers from the 'Graf Spee' and instructed to get them aboard the S.S. 'GENERAL ARTIGAS'. These were Lieutenants RECKOFF and LANG, both members of the Nazi Party, carrying false passports in the name of Maximo SCHNARCHENDORFF (Polish) and Herbert FIKANTSCHER (Czech). Later the tickets issued to these two by the shipping company, Mihanovic Ltda., were produced.

8. Later HAUN had to prepare seamen's papers for other escapees. These were passed back to NIEBUHR who counterfeited suitable passports, enabling the Vice-Commander of the 'Graf Spee;, and four other officers in charge of the 'Graf Spee' Administration and Rolls Office at Buenos Aires, to travel by bus, train and horseback across the Andes and into Chile, staying each night at prearranged German inns.

8. Haun also gave evidence of meeting another train when a messenger gave him an order to convey to a certain Karl WALTER, resident locally, who was to assist the escape into Paraguay by the City Police when about to heave Alta Cordoba for Santa Fe by bus, declared that "they planned to escape in accordance with orders received from their superiors". These superiors could only be 'The Graf Spee Administration and Rolls Office' and the Naval Attaché.

The Graf Spee Administration Office'

11. As has already been suggested, a 'Graf Spee Administration and Rolls Office' was opened at the Banco Germanico building at 25 de Mayo, 145, Buenos Aires, on the day of the original internments. This was directed by Captains Walter Kay, Robert HOEPENER, Wilhelm NAHKOTTER, Lieutenant Herbert DREWS and Petty Officer A. JERICHA, who should by law have been interned.

12. Drews, for example, lived freely in Buenos Aires for a year and a half with a permit, renewed monthly by the Ministry of the Marine. At his office, fifteen sailors a day would call for orders. On two occasions, on February 3, 1940, for five days and on February 11 for 30 days, the Ministry of the Interior granted Captain Kay permission to visit Cordoba, San Juan, Santa Fe and Mendoza "to acquaint himself with the situation of the interned sailors and to maintain discipline among them." After his visit 51 sailors escaped from these places. Not until June 19, 1942, was Drews detained for interrogation on the activities of his office. When questioned by the Investigation Committee, he steadily refused to answer, claiming the he recognised no authority but the Ministry of Marine.

Laxity of Guarding

13. The general ineffectiveness of the guard system is demonstrated particularly by the case of Walther BONISCH and Gerhard KADEL, who escaped and were recaptured twice (once in Brazil) before getting away. Despite such cases the authorities continued to permit trips, exchange visits, etc., often simply on the word of honour of the individuals concerned. in some cases, internees were permitted to travel within 50 kilometres of Mendoza, limits which they immediately broke. Others took part in a feast at the Rosario German association for the benefit of German Social Aid. Groups of ten and twenty Buenos Aires internees were even employed by local chemical and metallurgical firms under German control, while four others, Johann HANS, Oswald GERTLER, Ekhardt FRITZ and Gerhard HAVERNICK joined the Condor Air Lines until their suppression. Still others, Jose WAGNER, Heinrich WISSSEN, Waldemar PIEPER, Ernest August Parbst, Helmuth HIRTH and Johannes FRITZLEN were engaged on unspecified work for the German Embassy.

14. Particularly well organised were the escapes from Martin Garcia Island. On several unsuccessful attempts, rubber-boats, life-belts, oars, lanterns, charts and stores were confiscated by the authorities. Most of the official reports of such attempts state that the seized goods were 'of unknown origin' and that 'guards were reinforced', while the successful escapes are habitually noted, 'methods not established' and 'no negligence proved'.

Stowaways on the 'Alboreda'

15. From Consular Security Officer Buenos Aires came confirmatory details concerning some of the apprehensions of escapees in July and August. On July 23, an official of the Prefecture went aboard the ;Alboreda' and told her Captain that he would not be allowed to proceed until a paper packet (or packet of papers), denounced by the British Embassy, was delivered to the authorities. A guard was placed on board, and the Chief Officer showed every sign of agitation, but with the Captain denied all knowledge of the package. Representations were made by the ship's agents, Maura & Coll, that the authorities had no right to search for or seize a packet of papers.

16. on the following afternoon a message was received on board that the ship could proceed. However, at 7 p.m. one of the firemen reported to the Chief Officer that there were four strange men aboard. The four were very weak, asked for food and water, and were handed over to the Prefecture. It was felt that the Chief Officer knew of their presence, but handed them over to clear himself. The four were Bernhard VISSER, Alfred TETZNER, Paul

BERGNER and Wilhelm KORMANN, the latter three all escaped from Martin Garcia.

Arrangements for Stowaways

17. there was however, no confirmation that these men had in fact been assisted by members of the crew, though it was rumoured that a Master receives $500 Argentine for each man. A subsequent report indicated that the chief enemy agents for the smuggling of 'Graf Spee' men in Buenos Aires were Diego and Fidel Jarregui of Ybarra & Company, and in Rosario, Justiniano Escudero, working on commission for Barclay & Company. It was also learned that on one occasion in June 1941, the Master of the S.S. 'JUPITER' was approached by Senores ESCANO, QUINTANA and SATILLO (one of the President's sons), and in an apartment in the 3000 block of Calle Cordoba, on the 4th floor of a private office devoted entirely to shipping information, was pressed to take 'Graf Spee' officers to Europe. U refused, as a loyal Basque.

18. A similar instance came to light early in August, when it was learned that the Swedish S.S. 'COLUMBIA' had put into Recalada Light Vessel (pilot station at the entrance to Plate River) to land some stowaways discovered after sailing from Bahia Blanca. Two of these proved to be 'Graf Spee' men. About the same time the Spanish 'MONTE SAJA', en route from Montevideo to Las Palmas, also dropped two German stowaways at Recalada, though these were civilians.

Recent developments

19. Finally, on August 8, 1942, after two years and eight months internment, a Governmental order authorised the concentration of all the internees in a single spot. Some weeks later, on September 22, the report of the Investigation Committee, from which most of the above information is taken, clearly revealed the highly efficient system of escapes, illegally organised by the German Naval Attaché, and made possible by the extreme negligence of the responsible Argentine authorities. This was followed by a supplementary report, complete with documents, corroborating NIEBUHR's absolute jurisdiction over the internees, his threats of punitive action against relatives in Germany for disobedience, and his assumption, on Argentine soil, of powers of court-martial.

20. It was hoped that these revelations would eventually lead to effective action to curb this dangerous body of German subjects who, as long as they remain in partial freedom, for a potential group of highly skilled and disciplined saboteurs. (Ibid.)

Commander Lloyd Hirst, paymaster at the British Consulate in Buenos Aires and Assistant Naval Attaché.(Millington-Drake, op.cit.)

In early December, the Chancery, the office attached to the British Embassy in Buenos Aires, was sent the following note from its consulate in Rosario:

> With reference to your letter dated the 14th November relative to Graf Spee sailors in this Consular district, we have received the following report from Santa Fe i.e.:
> "From private sources I have heard that 89 men from the Graf Spee are actually in Santa Fe and are living in a house in Boulvard Calvez. Nothing has happened so far but if any events or any developments take place I shall not fail to inform you."
> As regards Rosario see enclosed copy of a report from a local contact which would appear to indicate that the local police are keeping a check on the Graf Spee men in this city. We understand that the Graf Spee men are still living in a big house in Alberdi as reported in our letter to Lloyd Hirst of October 17th, 1941. [Commander Lloyd Hirst of Royal Navy was paymaster at the Consulate and Assistant Naval Attaché.]
>
> 288 British Consulate, ROSARIO, October 17th 1942
> Dear Lloyd Hirst,

With reference to my letter of September 13th last, I am informed that about eighty-six "GRAF SPEE" sailors are now living in a big house at No. 2, Calle J.C. Paz, in Alberdi, Rosario.

This house, which has about sixteen rooms, was formerly the property of a British subject named Mr. McGarrell, who died some ten years ago and now belongs to an Argentine. As you are aware, there are quite a number of British subjects living in this district and the fact that these eighty-six "GRAF SPEE" sailors have suddenly descended in their midst has caused a great commotion.

A lot of the men in question are employed by various German firms in Rosario but, I believe, they still continue to draw their ninety pesos a month [probably from the German Embassy as payment to interned sailors] through the Post Office here.

I am told that a new aerial has been put up on the roof of this house. These men appear to be under no supervision whatsoever and seem to be at liberty to do exactly as they please.

I have asked various people to keep an eye on this house and if anything unusual occurs I will let you know. I am sending a copy of this letter to Fowler [?].

Yours sincerely,
Frank S. Gibbs

No. 41 16/11/42.

Apparently local police are keeping some check on Graf Spee men. An employee of the Camara Arbitral de Cereales, Rios by name, appears to have been employing one of them and later had meetings at his house attended by these sailors, with the result that he had a visit from a Buenos Aires detective and was asked to explain his connexion with the sailors.

Rice, who was reported to have nazi tendencies, was also "got at" privately and asked to explain his attitude.

Rice has several hobbies and one of them is fish and he says a friend of his sent him one of the sailors who was supposed to be a bit of an expert on fish breeding, and that in consequence he employed him for some time, and that regarding the other sailors he had at his house, it was to satisfy a natural curiosity about the war. While his explanations are not satisfactory it is possible that Mr. Rios will keep well out of the way of German sailors in the future. (TNA ADM 116/5474, 7 December 1942)

The Argus of Melbourne, Australia, included an article on 16 December about the Graf Spee. 'According to shortwave department of the ABC, Saigon Radio quotes a message from Montevideo that the German pocket battleship Graf Spee has been refloated. Graf Spee was scuttled off Montevideo on December 17, 1939, after having been defeated in action 4 days earlier by HMS Ajax, Achilles, and Exeter.' (*The Argus*, Melbourne, 16 December 1942)

As there were no further reports from Rosario related to the Germans in Alberdi, one has to imagine that there were no incidents. Before returning to the internees, it is important to understand other events that had occurred in Argentina which the Admiralty documents omitted to mention – the existence of a Nazi spy ring which had assisted the escape of Graf Spee seamen. The Argentinian newspaper, *El Ciudadano*, shed light on their activities in South America in a 2019 article. After detailing the sinking of the Graf Spee, their translated article continued,

Edmund von Thormann, German Ambassador to Argentina
(https://www.ciudadanodiario.com.ar/nota/2019-12-19-19-50-57-el-hundimiento-del-graf-spee-y-la-actuacion-de-los-agentes-nazis-en-nuestra-provincia)

Nazis in the land of the sun and good wine
Before the European conflict began in 1939, and then the Second World War, our province was not exempt from what the crossing of Nazi spies and agents implied.
Since the mid-30s, sympathizers of Nazism began to appear. Many activists were of German origin, but Argentines attracted by the propaganda of the Third Reich also joined.

At the beginning of the war, a group of Germans began to work with precise instructions from the then German ambassador Edmund von Thormann.

His role had to do with the activation of the Deutscher Verein Mendoza Social and Cultural Center and other institutions, inserting "the new order" and a defined political formula: "totalitarianism".

In 1937, the institution was chaired by Carlos W. Beier and some of its members were affiliated with the party.

In 1940, very few people from Mendoza imagined that in the heart of the city there was a place where Gestapo agents concentrated to carry out espionage operations.

The meeting place was a prestigious hotel and restaurant located at 32 Lavalle Street: Maxim. This was built in 1937 and its owner was Pablo Eckardt, a prominent member of the Nazi Party in Mendoza and vice president of the Deutscher Verein.

Mendoza was a strategically important place for espionage, both German and Allied. That is why orders were received from Berlin to execute a plan.

The objective of these orders was to extradite most of the former Graf Spee crew members who were under surveillance in different ranches or farms in Buenos Aires, Rosario, Córdoba, Mendoza and San Juan.

Escape plans

The escape route of the German sailors was supported from Buenos Aires and at the Maxim hotel Eckardt and his partner Suesse were waiting for them, who had prepared clothes, money, forged documentation and a train ticket to San Juan.

Ex-Graf Spee sailors arriving at Mendoza railway station (https://www.ciudadanodiario.com.ar/nota/2019-12-19-19-50-57-

el-hundimiento-del-graf-spee-y-la-actuacion-de-los-agentes-nazis-en-nuestra-provincia)

Another member of the Nazi party, surnamed Zimmermann, attended them and notified them by radio that they were ready to travel to Calingasta.

Agent Zimmermann would take them by car to that San Juan town, where another member of this network, called Hancke, was hosting them in a house that pretended to be a mechanical workshop.

From there they left to cross the Andes by mule, and already in Chile they marched in the direction of the towns of Ovalle and Coquimbo.

There, the German consul gave them new instructions and they were sent by car to the city of Antofagasta, more precisely to the house of a certain Kulenkampf, to embark from that port on a Japanese-flagged ship bound for Germany.

In this way the escape was closed and 151 crew members of the Graf Spee escaped from our territory to fight in the war again.

The network is down

In early 1941, the Federal Coordination investigated various members of the embassy and members of the Graf Spee. In particular, one of the brains of this organization, Alfonso Haun, who was arrested in Rosario, Santa Fe province, was investigated.

By confessing, he denounced the flight operations of these sailors and implicated several comrades and Nazi agents from Buenos Aires, Santa Fe, Córdoba, Mendoza and San Juan, who had close ties to this network.

Gerardo Winkler's Internment card (Ibid.)

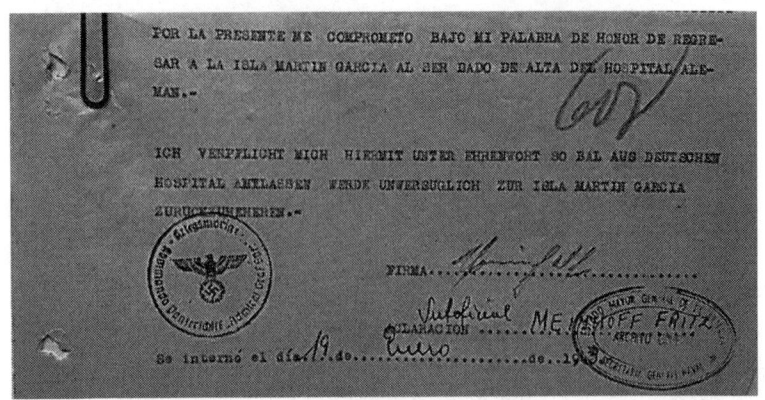

(https://forum.axishistory.com/viewtopic.php?f=13&t=242942&p=2211048&hilit=graf+spee+escape#p2211048)

In our province, these Nazi agents were interrogated and prosecuted by federal authorities, and received sentences of more than two years. Members in Mendoza were released in late 1945.

As a result of these events, the crew of the Graf Spee remained in a kind of concentration camp on Martín García Island until the end of the world war. (The sinking of the Graf Spee and the action of the Nazi agents in Mendoza, *El Ciudadano*, Mendoza, 19 December 2019)

Friedrich Wolf, German Military, Naval and Air Attaché in Argentina after expulsion of Niebuhr. Photograph taken during 1945 interrogation by British Intelligence (TNA KV2/1489)

The article failed to mention the mastermind of the escape operation, Dietrich Niebuhr.

On Christmas Eve, 1942, the Chancery at the British Embassy in Buenos Aires sent the South American Department at the Foreign Office the following note.

> Dear Department,
> The following passage occurs in a United States postal censorship slip which has been communicated to us_ -
> Argentine detective maintaining check on German internees".
> The writer describes a new way of checking on internees used by Argentina. The pertinent passage reads as follows: 'Here everything has changed somewhat because now comes twice a day a detective namely at a set time, a roll call of all us is taken (to see) whether all of us are still here. Otherwise nothing further has changed and we may otherwise do as we please.'
> This seems to us of some interest as showing the results of our recent representations on this subject to the Argentine Government. (Ibid, 24 December 1942)

For several months in the latter half of 1942, there were messages sent between Montevideo, London and Washington regarding a Greek company's efforts to salvage the metal from wreck of the Graf Spee. The concern was expressed that knowledge of important equipment that lay below water and had not been examined might be lost. The Admiralty's Military Branch were unable to send one of their experts over to Argentine to supervise the process and the American Navy did not want one of their staff released from other important work.

To be continued in Volume Two

Bernard O'Connor's publications on SOE and the Intelligence Services during the Second World War:

RAF Tempsford: Churchill's MOST SECRET Airfield, Amberley Publishing, (2010)
The Women of RAF Tempsford: Heroines of Wartime Resistance, Amberley Publishing, (2011)
Churchill and Stalin's Secret Agents: Operation Pickaxe at RAF Tempsford, Fonthill Media, (2011)
The Tempsford Academy: Churchill and Roosevelt's Secret Airfield, Fonthill Media, (2012)
Agent Rose: The true Story of Eileen Nearne, Britain's Forgotten Wartime Heroine, Amberley Publishing, (2013)
Churchill's Angels: How Britain's Women Secret Agents Changed the Course of the Second World War, Amberley Publishing, (2014)
The Courier: Reminiscences of a Female Secret Agent in Wartime France, (Historical faction) www.lulu.com (2010)
Nobby Clarke: Churchill's Backroom Boy, www.lulu.com (2011)
Sir Frank Nelson, www.lulu.com (2011)
Designer: The True Story of Jacqueline Nearne, www.lulu.com, (2012)
Return to Belgium, www.lulu.com (2012)
Return to Holland, www.lulu.com, (2012)
Bedford Spy School, www.lulu.com (2012)
Old Bedfordians' Secret Operations during World War Two, www.lulu.com (2012)
Henri Dericourt: Triple Agent (edited), www.lulu.com (2012)
Churchill's School for Saboteurs: Brickendonbury, STS 17, Amberley Publishing, (2013)
Churchill's Most Secret Airfield, Amberley Publishing, (2013)
Sabotage in Norway, www.lulu.com (2013)
Sabotage in Denmark, www.lulu.com (2013)
Sabotage in Belgium, www.lulu.com (2013)
Sabotage in Holland, www.lulu.com (2013)
Sabotage in France, www.lulu.com (2013)
Blackmail Sabotage, www.lulu.com (2014)
Sabotage in Greece, www.lulu.com (2014)
'Mike' Andrews: Pilot, Manager of Liverpool Airport and Secret Agent, www.lulu.com (2014)
SOE GROUP B SABOTAGE TRAINING HANDBOOK, www.lulu.com (2014)
Agent Fifi and the Honeytrap Spies, Amberley Publishing, (2015)
Agents Françaises, www.lulu.com (2016)
The Spies who returned to the Cold: Iceland's wartime spies,

www.lulu.com (2016)
Operation LENA and Hitler's Plans to blow up Britain, Amberley Publishing (2017)
Bletchley Park and the Pigeon Spies, www.lulu.com (2018)
Bletchley Park and the Belgian Pigeon Service, www.lulu.com, (2018)
The BBC and the Pigeon Spies, www.lulu.com (2018)
SOE Heroines: French Section and Free French women agents, Amberley Publishing, (2018)
Operation EBENSBURG: SOE's Austrian 'Bonzos' and the saving of Europe's cultural heritage, www.lulu.com (2018)
Blowing up Iberia: British, German and Italian sabotage against military and economic targets in Spain and Portugal, www.lulu.com (2019)
Blowing up the Rock: German, Italian and Spanish sabotage against Allied targets in Gibraltar, www.lulu.com (2019)
The SOE and NKVD in Afghanistan: Anglo-Soviet Relations during the Second World War, www.lulu.com (2020)
Operation MAMBA: SOE, NKVD and the deterioration in Anglo-Soviet relations during the Second World War, www.lulu.com (2020)
Kurt Konig: German Spy or British Agent, www.lulu.com (2020)
The Belgian Spies at Little Berkhamsted, www.lulu.com (2020)
Operation DOWNEND: Anti-Nazi Jupp Kappius's subversion and sabotage mission in the Ruhr towards the end of the Second World War, www.lulu.com (2021)
Operations VIVACIOUS and BRANSTON: Anti-Nazi German Jew Robert Baker-Byrne's subversion and sabotage missions in Berlin and Lubeck towards the end of the Second World War, www.lulu.com (2021)

Bernard O'Connor's website

www.bernardoconnor.org

Bernard O'Connor's publications

www.lulu.com/spotlight/coprolite